The Alpine Enlightenment

the
LIFE
OF
IDEAS

SERIES EDITOR
Darrin McMahon, *Dartmouth College*

After a period of some eclipse, the study of intellectual history has enjoyed a broad resurgence in recent years. *The Life of Ideas* contributes to this revitalization through the study of ideas as they are produced, disseminated, received, and practiced in different historical contexts. The series aims to embed ideas—those that endured, and those once persuasive but now forgotten—in rich and readable cultural histories. Books in this series draw on the latest methods and theories of intellectual history while being written with elegance and élan for a broad audience of readers.

The Alpine Enlightenment

HORACE-BÉNÉDICT DE SAUSSURE
AND NATURE'S SENSORIUM

Kathleen Kete

The University of Chicago Press   CHICAGO AND LONDON

The University of Chicago Press, Chicago 60637
The University of Chicago Press, Ltd., London
© 2024 by The University of Chicago
All rights reserved. No part of this book may be used or reproduced in any manner whatsoever without written permission, except in the case of brief quotations in critical articles and reviews. For more information, contact the University of Chicago Press, 1427 E. 60th St., Chicago, IL 60637.
Published 2024
Printed in the United States of America

33 32 31 30 29 28 27 26 25 24   1 2 3 4 5

ISBN-13: 978-0-226-83546-4 (cloth)
ISBN-13: 978-0-226-83548-8 (paper)
ISBN-13: 978-0-226-83547-1 (e-book)
DOI: https://doi.org/10.7208/chicago/9780226835471.001.0001

Library of Congress Cataloging-in-Publication Data

Names: Kete, Kathleen, author.
Title: The Alpine Enlightenment : Horace-Bénédict de Saussure and nature's sensorium / Kathleen Kete.
Other titles: Life of ideas.
Description: Chicago ; London : The University of Chicago Press, 2024. | Series: The life of ideas | Includes bibliographical references and index.
Identifiers: LCCN 2024013177 | ISBN 9780226835464 (cloth) | ISBN 9780226835488 (paperback) | ISBN 9780226835471 (ebook)
Subjects: LCSH: Saussure, Horace Bénédict de, 1740–1799. | Scientists—Switzerland—Geneva—Biography. | Earth scientists—Switzerland—Geneva—Biography. | Mountaineers—Switzerland—Geneva—Biography. | Scientific expeditions—Alps—History—18th century. | Enlightenment—Switzerland—Geneva. | Geneva (Switzerland)—Intellectual life—18th century. | LCGFT: Biographies.
Classification: LCC Q143.S25 K47 2024 | DDC 509.2 [B]—dc23/eng/20240412
LC record available at https://lccn.loc.gov/2024013177

♾ This paper meets the requirements of ANSI/NISO Z39.48-1992 (Permanence of Paper).

For Dan and Julia

Contents

INTRODUCTION. *Saussure and the Alps* * 1

ONE. Geneva: The Walled City * 21

TWO. The Jura Mountains * 53

THREE. The Arve Valley * 79

FOUR. Bodies of Desire * 105

FIVE. High Peaks: From the Buet to the Slopes of Mont Blanc * 133

SIX. Mont Blanc * 157

SEVEN. The Legacy * 181

Acknowledgments * 195
Notes * 197
Note on Sources * 249
Index * 255

Introduction

SAUSSURE AND THE ALPS

The knife that sliced open the body of Horace-Bénédict de Saussure in January 1799 was wielded by Louis Odier (1748–1817), his doctor and friend. Saussure had been dead for thirty-two hours, and an autopsy was being performed to determine the cause of death.[1] It was a not a death that was suspect in any way, not one that would bring into play the office of the *lieutenant de police*, one that Saussure's father had briefly served in during the 1750s, where investigations of suicides or murders would be undertaken. Saussure had not thrown himself into the Rhône River, as had his father-in-law in 1766, a little over a year after the marriage of Horace-Bénédict and Albertine-Amélie Boissier, the richest heiress in the city. Nor had he shot himself to death four years after his marriage, as had his brother-in-law Jean-Louis Tronchin, the husband of Albertine-Amélie's sister, Anne Caroline (Minette), and the son of Jean-Robert Tronchin, the public prosecutor. His "soul," he said, was "tearing him apart."[2] The elder Tronchin, a friend of Voltaire, was responsible in 1762 for banning and burning Rousseau's *Émile* and *The Social Contract* and entering into a conflict with Rousseau on, among other things, the correct relationship between religion and politics in Geneva and the meaning of a Christian life.[3]

These deaths were part of a flutter of suicides in eighteenth-century Geneva and mark the stress lines of the culture into which Saussure was born.[4] Enormous wealth rested upon a moral base of Puritan values. Voltaire was feted in a state where the theater was banned. Formally a republican city-state, Geneva was run by a patriciate, a tiny ruling class of two thousand people, knitted together in almost incestuous family units, whose power stretched back to the days when Geneva was the Protestant Rome. Jean-Jacques Burlamaqui (1694–1748), the natural-law theorist whose arguments would influence the American Revolution, called it an "aristo-democracy" and defended it as such.[5] How Saussure negotiated these paradoxes, using his patrician privilege to explore more expansive ways of being, is a theme of this book and a key to his life. Extremely wealthy—on a par, if just barely, he notes in a letter to his mother from Paris, with the French high nobility and financial aristocracy—he spent almost every summer tramping through the Alps with peasant guides. After marriage, his yearly income was 60,000 livres. Although the very richest nobles in Paris such as the duc d'Orléans had incomes in the millions of livres, some "hundred noble families" there had "incomes of 50,000– 300,000 livres and three or four hundred more . . . 10,000–50,000 livres."[6] He assumed that with his "moderate" income, living in Paris would be difficult, though it sufficed for visiting.[7]

By 1799, however, he was living in straitened circumstances, the family fortune lost in the French Revolution. His fabled library of works on natural history had been broken up and sold. Offers of teaching positions in Paris and America had slipped away too, or become irrelevant. Still, it was a premature death at fifty-nine compared to expectations based on the longevity of his relatives. His mother—Renée de la Rive—was seventy-four when she died in 1789; his father, Nicholas, was eighty-two at the time of his death in 1791. His sister Judith de Saussure (born in 1745) was alive, though socially dead to Geneva since 1772. That was when Mme. Denis (Marie-Louise Mignot, 1712–1790), Voltaire's niece and mistress, spread the rumor that the twenty-seven-year-old Judith had had sex with the seventy-eight-year-old Voltaire in his bedroom at Ferney. This was an amusing story for fans of Voltaire: he had already joked about seducing the daughters of the clergy while living in Geneva at Les Délices.[8] Though skeptical, Friedrich Melchior Grimm circulated it to the royal courts of Europe in his newsletter for the month of January 1773, with Judith figuring as the "Genevan Messalina."[9] This was a gross insult, suggesting promiscuity, even "nymphomania." While Voltaire was congratulated on his sexual prowess by the duc de Richelieu and Louis XV and Mme. Denis scored points in a complicated game against her neighbors,[10] Judith lost her social standing. She had looked on Voltaire as a mentor. "What should I read next?" she wrote in a letter of 1770 thanking him for a missive. "How good of you to think of me, to actually consider me worthy of the admirable books that you have sent. What happiness to have a colporteur like you." Continuing: "and that you would allow me, Monsieur, to depend upon you for the employment of my mind. I should like to place that entirely in your hands."[11] Mocked throughout Europe, she was decried for a fool at home. "I am convinced that one could travel the entire world without discovering a city where ill will is pushed so far," she would later say about Geneva.[12] We will visit Judith's trials again in this book. In 1799, however, she had been living in Montpellier for over twenty years, independent, single, and seemingly content, and we can happily cheer her on.

Her brother's physical decline was manifest to many witnesses in the 1790s. It was there in the history of his magnum opus, *Voyages dans les Alpes*. Volume 1 had appeared in 1779. Then followed the glory years of the 1780s, which culminated in two shining triumphs: the summiting of Mont Blanc in 1787 and the unprecedented three-week stay in 1788 on the Col du Géant at 3360 meters, where he established the basics of meteorology.[13] In 1789 he circuited Monte Rosa, climbing to some 3000 meters on a spur for a view of the massif. His last great trek was to the Matterhorn in 1792. The second volume of the *Voyages* appeared in 1786, on the eve of the Mont Blanc climbs. The final two volumes however, published in 1796, were drafted only with the help of his older son, Théodore (Nicolas-Théodore de Saussure, 1767–1845), who had assisted in the experiments on the Col du Géant and in Chamonix during the ascent of Mont Blanc.

Saussure's relationships with his three children figure in his life story, of course. While Théodore had embraced the training in science that Saussure offered his progeny, the younger brother, Alphonse Jean-François (1770–1853), opted for a rich social life instead.[14] This would have its own benefits, as Alphonse's son Henri Louis Frédéric (1829–1905) became celebrated for his work on wasps, and his grandson, Ferdinand, (1857–1913) with whom most general readers will associate the name of Saussure, for revolutionizing the field of linguistics. Moreover, the discipline of his homeschooling would seem to have wounded Théodore. Some associates offered its unrelenting nature as an explanation for his misanthropy.[15] His major research on photosynthesis, published in 1804 as *Recherches chimiques sur la végétation* (Chemical research on plant growth) was worked on in seclusion.[16] This way of proceeding was a break from the sociability presumed by the Société de physique et d'histoire naturelle de Genève (Geneva Society of Physics and Natural History), to which both he and his father belonged, and for which—as we will see below—Odier's autopsy was performed.

The oldest child, Albertine-Adrienne (1766–1841), became Albertine Necker de Saussure after her marriage to Jacques Necker (1757–1825), the nephew of the French finance minister and the son of the mathematician Louis Necker (1730–1804). She would go on to write an influential book on the importance of girls' education.[17] She may have had early hopes of becoming a chemist. Genevan histories of botany credit her for working alongside her husband on the so-called Herbier Necker.[18] This was a collection of plants displayed neither through pressing and drying nor through illustration. Rather, the Neckers employed an unusual technique called "nature self-impression" in which prints were made from the plant itself by inking the specimen and rolling it through a press between papers.[19] This project would have mobilized Albertine's talents as a naturalist while demonstrating a comfort with machines and instruments that she would have gained also from her father. The book on education and a valuable first biography of her cousin by marriage, Germaine de Staël—distinct in its age for being an encomium of one important woman by another[20]—earned her a tile in Judy Chicago's *The Dinner Party* (1974–79).[21] An interest in education as social reform connected her to her father. Saussure's own "Projet de réforme pour le Collège de Genève" (Proposal for the reform of the Collège de Genève, 1774), which advocated a modern scientific curriculum for secondary school students and the opening of enrollment to all classes of Genevans, was prompted by thoughts about both how to educate his children and how to prepare citizens of a democratizing state.[22]

All three children may have been at Saussure's bedside in January 1799.[23] Théodore had returned from abroad in 1797.[24] He had run away to Britain in July 1794, during the violent phase of Geneva's democratic revolution, which his father, a deputy to the National Assembly, had sought to moderate. Failing that, Saussure *père* withdrew to the family home outside the city at Conches.[25] Saussure's decline began just before the Genevan Terror. His wife described an attack of vertigo and numbness that seized him while at the Assembly in mid-March and "'deprived him of any sense of touch in his arms and fingers but not of power of movement.'"[26] A more serious attack ensued in 1795 that affected his entire left side, "from his leg to his tongue."[27] This left him seriously impaired, as noted by visitors such as Rosalie Constant, the botanist cousin of Benjamin Constant, who exchanged plants with Saussure.[28] He had trouble walking, especially through doorways. There he would pause, sway, and then practically throw himself forward, as if over a perilous passage in the peaks.[29] Though practiced in walking along narrow paths above dangerous precipices, he could no longer follow the straight line of walnut that ran through the parquet floors of his home.[30] Enfeebled, he would listen with pleasure as his wife read aloud from the novel she was writing, which at times would bring him to tears. "'M. de Saussure takes so much interest in his wife's production that directly the story becomes at all moving it is interrupted by his sobs,'" Rosalie Constant recalled. This was an epistolary novel entitled "Les méprises, ou Mémoires de Mylady D'Ossery" (Errors made: The memoires of Mylady D'Ossery), which was never published but whose themes might be guessed.[31] Like other savants of his generation, Saussure shared a sensibility that allowed the expression of emotion. He wept openly.[32]

These vignettes project an image of Saussure's life as deplorably "feminized" after illness withdrew him from the peaks, when considered—as Saussure's life has all too poorly been—from the vantage point of Victorian-era mountaineering, which celebrated a particular form of virility and masculinity.[33] These qualities are enshrined in the reports of first ascents published by the Alpine Club, which became the model for subsequent climbing culture. Leslie Stephen's retirement from climbing in 1867 to marry and start a family—Virginia Woolf and Vanessa Bell are the offspring of his second marriage in 1878—is a case in point. Home life and mountain climbing are inimical, he announced to the world; to marry is to give up the peaks.[34] So too in reverse is George Mallory's lamented return to Everest in 1924, leaving behind Ruth and their three small children, with his son John (born in 1920) later revealing that he would have rather had a living man than a hero for a father.[35] Genevan norms were more complicated. Early mountaineering offered far richer approaches to nature than just those enshrined in modern climbing's celebration of conquest and submission and exultation of heroic masculinity, as we will see unfold below in the autopsy, so to speak, of Saussure's life.

In the meantime, we find Saussure's futile hopes for a recovery from his debilities in the 1790s resting on assumptions about the therapeutic value of mineral springs. He tried the sulfur springs at Aix-les-Bains on the Lac du Bourget in the summer of 1794, went to Bourbon-l'Archambault in central France in 1795, and then to Plombières-les-Bains in the Vosges in 1797.[36] These were all three important spas in the eighteenth century. Their springs were like in nature to those whose chemical composition and origins he had investigated in the course of his travels.[37] He sought to reestablish the equilibrium of "ses humeurs internes" (his bodily humors) by following the advice in the home health guide "Conseils des Médicins pour moy," which he took along with him, and which dictated the sequence of dousing and dosing to be followed at the spas.[38] He had primed himself by reading more serious medical books, including one that pointed to the efficacy of sulfurous waters in cases of paralysis.[39] Philip Rieder and Vincent Barras are historians of medicine who have written the premier study of Saussure's health from which much of this detail has been extracted. They explain that the absorption of "mineral waters, drunk or 'taken' in the form of showers or baths, was the therapy he manifestly placed his greatest hopes upon" during these last crises of his life.[40]

Saussure's understanding of his body was strongly Galenic. It was one of the two basic views about the body that he carried with him to the mountains. The Galenic viewpoint explains his interest in mineral springs, suggesting evidence of an internal economy of the planet dependent—like the human body—on effusions and the circulation of fluids.[41] Following the Galenic was the empirical, focused on identifying what rocks lay where and how. This was influenced by the new anatomy and physiology, which his great mentor Albrecht von Haller (1708–1777) played a leading part in establishing, and his current doctor, Odier, a role in developing.[42] This view also shaped Saussure's aesthetic response to the Alps, based as that was on verifiable detail rather than a priori emotional needs.

His doctor's approach to Saussure's ailments was eclectic; this made sense given his training at the medical school at Edinburgh, one of the most progressive in the world. A success in Scotland—at "age 20 he was president of its society of medicine"—Odier returned to his native Geneva in 1773, when he was twenty-five years old. His practice grew quickly thanks to his ability to actually remedy patients' ailments.[43] Saussure became one of those patients, perhaps after the death of Haller in 1777.[44] Along with being a proponent of vaccination against smallpox (a commonplace for enlightened physicians at the time, but he was among the most influential),[45] Odier introduced "castor oil for the expulsion of tapeworms and bismuth oxide (Pepto Bismol contains a slightly different form of this) for the treatment of stomach cramps."[46] This last was of great interest to Saussure for various digestive issues, as we will see. Edinburgh trained Odier in anatomy and in understanding disease as a malfunction of the organs. This placed him in a line with Haller and Hermann Boerhaave (1668–1738), one of Haller's teachers, as well as G. B. Morgagni (1682–1772), the star of the University of Padua, who was highly effective at bringing anatomy to the center of medical training. And it made Odier the perfect choice to perform Saussure's autopsy.

First Odier cut into the brain, where he found a large quantity of serum filling the cavities and resting between its membranes. It was especially thick on the right side of the cerebellum. That would explain the symptoms of stroke in his patient, which were concentrated on his left side. Still, Saussure's illness was progressive rather than sudden, Odier noted, and it was the effect of the diffusion of this serum throughout the brain, he explained, "which by compressing its parts had weakened the faculties dependent on it."[47] Nothing untoward was noticed about his lungs and heart, except that the lungs seemed small and were displaced somewhat upward under the collarbone.[48] It was the intestines that caught Odier's attention, and what he described was completely unexpected—in his terms, unparalleled in his experience of medicine (*complèttement* [sic] *inouïe en médecine*).[49] "The conformation of the lower abdomen was extraordinary [*fort extraordinaire*]. . . . Neither the stomach nor the liver nor the colon was visible. Only the small intestine and the cecum were visible. The cecum was of a monstrous size [*une grosseur monstrueuse*]." Its circumference measured 378 millimeters (37.8 centimeters), when a diameter of 9 cm would be considered enlarged. The appendix was long, and the colon—completely hidden by the small intestine—was also very distended, having traveled up to below the left breast. Possibly, Odier surmised, the displacement of the intestines had led to the malfunction of the brain by "compressing the major vessels [of the heart] and thus inhibiting the circulation of blood in the brain."[50]

The immediate cause of Saussure's death was clear.[51] The clinical evidence and the autopsy concur. Something had happened to his brain. As for "long-term causes,"[52] Odier hazarded that the "monstrous" state of the intestines could explain those. We will see how Odier linked their dysfunction to Saussure's trips through the mountains, an explanation that speaks to social norms rather than human physiology. A study of Odier's report in 1970 by Georges de Morsier, a neurologist, and Raymond de Saussure (son of Ferdinand, the linguist, who was Horace-Bénédict's great-grandson) agreed, however, that the two organs described an underlying cause. For Morsier and Saussure, some kind of inflammatory disease may have affected the digestive system and then later the brain.[53] They suggested that an autoimmune disease such as multiple sclerosis, or its rarer relative Schilder-Foix, or even Creutzfeldt-Jakob disease could be at fault.[54]

That an autopsy was performed on Saussure is not in itself historically significant. Then as now, autopsies were useful for establishing or confirming the cause of death.[55] As Odier further noted, knowing this could lay to rest fears that what had happened could have been prevented. An autopsy could lighten the pain of remorse by assuring that the death in question was inevitable. It was a matter of consolation to the living, in that age of sentimentality, and when "God's will" was open to question.[56] What is of interest, as Rieder and Barras emphasize, is its public nature. Saussure's health was "the focus of considerable and sustained scientific attention."[57] Odier's autopsy report was not delivered to his family—his wife, his two sons, his daughter, his sister, and his sisters-in law, Jeanne-Françoise and Minette. It was presented to a gathering of scientists, the elite of Geneva, the Société de physique et d'histoire naturelle (Society of Physics and Natural History) on 1 March 1799, very soon after Saussure's death and possibly at the first meeting of the society since.[58]

Odier dismissed a concern that was much on the minds of this privileged group, in March 1799 citizens no longer of the Republic of Geneva but of the nation of France.[59] Could the events of the French and Genevan

Revolutions have caused Saussure's deterioration and death? "One may," Odier said, "credibly blame the distress brought to bear on our illustrious colleague by these upheavals" for the decline in his health, though he would go on to demur.[60] Saussure's mental turmoil was apparent to his intimates and reasonably an effect of his misfortunes. These included not simply the loss of the family fortune, invested in French bonds, which put an end to Saussure's self-funded research and prompted the sale of his library and the search for an academic post.[61] Thomas Jefferson suggested that he come to Virginia to teach at the university he was founding.[62] The bishop of Derry suggested he move to Ireland and "'travel at [his] cost in a country the most rich in the world in natural history, a virgin country, untouched by naturalists, Ireland.'"[63] Madame de Staël worked her connections and a more likely position at the University of Göttingen seemed briefly possible, if the teaching language could be Latin, not German.[64] What was meant to be a secure solution in a position in Paris at the newly founded École Centrale in 1796 was also a chimera. Would the pay have been enough to cover travel, and housing?[65]

There were also the stresses involved in helping to establish Geneva as a democratic state in the face of disapproval on the right among his own family members and of rejection on the left of his policies. Neither of Saussure's sons, for example, swore the required oath of allegiance to liberty, equality, and fraternity in June 1793,[66] which Saussure supported. The Genevan Terror in July of 1794 resulted in the execution of friends. Eleven colleagues were shot to death along the southern wall of the city, *le Bastion bourgeois*.[67] While his life and his property were spared, the violence was traumatic and led him to drop out of politics. The Terror was the "antithesis" of his politics of "rapprochement,"[68] ending his efforts to establish a liberal consensus. Odier explained to his audience that nonetheless politics was not to blame for Saussure's condition. A fall on the high stone steps of his townhouse in 1793 could account for some of the symptoms. Moreover, according to Théodore, his father had been having difficulty with his speech for some time before that, "confusing one word for another, without noticing," and getting angry when he was not understood.[69]

From his daughter's point of view, Saussure was a "victim of science." The Alps had destroyed him. Albertine made that connection in 1796, when the Saussures were visiting the Neckers for the winter and her father's symptoms were manifest.[70] The mountains had made him who he was; they were cutting him down now, in his prime: "What a sad return for his noble and useful labors," she wrote. "If old age in itself commands respect, what sentiment ought to be excited by this premature decay, this voluntary sacrifice? How much more ought we to reverence the victim of science than the victim of years? .... If he still lives for his own reputation and the progress of science, he no longer lives for happiness. ... The devouring activity which raised him is fated to consume him."[71] As early as the beginning of the 1770s colleagues were concerned that his travels in the Alps were damaging his health. Rieder and Barras cite an anonymous letter written to Haller about this. They wanted that celebrated doctor, Saussure's mentor, to intervene: "Many of his friends were uneasy about the poor state of his health."[72] Saussure's health seemed to be suffering either from the "physical strains of his Alpine excursions or even," they suggested, "a lack of moderation in his relations with his young wife."[73] Either the mountains or his wife was draining him.

This was the point of interest for the Société de physique et d'histoire naturelle listening to Odier's report on the findings of his autopsy. It was Saussure's body and what the mountains had done to it, not the questions that had drawn him to the Alps, that concerned the audience of savants that day. Eulogies written to celebrate Saussure's contributions to natural history had been published already or were forthcoming, and Earth science was not Odier's concern. Augustin-Pyramus de Candolle, who was to become the leading botanist of the next century (having disregarded Saussure's personal advice to study geology instead),[74] had published his "Notice sur la vie et les ouvrages de Saussure" the previous month, in February 1799. Jean Senebier, in attendance at the meeting of the Société de physique, was working on his lengthy *Mémoire historique sur la vie et les écrits de Horace-Bénédict Desaussure* (1801). This would become the most valuable source for later biographers until Douglas Freshfield (1845–1934) of the British Alpine Club and Royal Geographical Society published his *Life of Horace Benedict de Saussure* in 1920. And Saussure and his uncle Charles Bonnet (1720–1793) were chosen by Georges Cuvier, that most powerful scientist in post-revolutionary France, to be the subjects in 1810 of the first *éloge historique* of luminaries deceased during the course of the French Revolution to be presented to the Parisian Academy of Science.[75]

The *Voyages* had made Saussure famous. "Toute Europe" was aware of his importance.[76] The ascent of Mont Blanc turned him into a celebrity. Immanuel Kant invoked Saussure by his surname alone in *The Critique of Judgment* of 1790 — recognition of his achievements being presumed — when the philosopher discussed the role of judgment on the experience of the sublime. Kant contrasted the "soul-stirring sensations" experienced by "Herr von Saussure" and made available by him to his readers with those of the "untutored," who would see in the "ravages of nature" only "misery, peril and distress."[77] Saussure was elected Fellow of the British Royal Society in April 1788 and an associate member of the French Academy of Science in 1790.

Saussure's body in the Alps, not just his body of works on the Alps, was of interest to Odier's audience because Saussure had done what no other member of that learned society had done: he had used his body as a tool of science, consistently, in almost yearly explorations of the Alps. This is what in 1760 he promised himself he would do, when he first arrived in Chamonix and saw the high peaks up close. He would not let a year go by without venturing back into the Alps.[78] Two of his *tours du Mont Blanc*—a circuit he established—were made with friends. Ordinarily he traveled without Genevan companions except servants, and when climbing, with local guides. These excursions lasted several weeks, occasionally five or six.[79] For a mountaineer such as Freshfield, who helped plan the Everest attempts of the 1920s, Saussure's climbing exploits were tame, except for Mont Blanc and the Col du Géant. For an eighteenth-century Genevan, such extended time in the Alps was unique.[80]

How those excursions marked Saussure's body is a question Odier's report addressed. The mystery to be solved was the monstrous condition of the intestines. Their dilation, Odier posited, "may have stemmed from the great appetite that the frequent excursions to the mountains had given Professor De Saussure, since the bulky food he ate in response was exactly that which would produce a great amount of fecal matter. That then would accumulate and harden in the large intestine."[81] The gentleman ate like a peasant, is what was meant. In the Savoy Alps of the Mont Blanc massif, that meant gorging on bread or porridges of oats and barley, combined with some rye, beans, and vetch, or other fodder crops.[82]

That rough, coarse food suits rough, coarse stomachs, not the refined systems of the upper classes, was a contemporary falsehood with roots in medieval and antique Europe.[83] It reflected the fact that bread for the poor was often adulterated with sawdust and the like. The "black bread" of the peasant hid nonfoods, whereas the light wheaten loaves of the rich were proof of their purity. How comforting it was to those whose bread was made of wheat to believe that the lower classes were made of tougher stuff (a view prevalent among slave owners in the Americas, of course.) Here is how it was explained in a medical guide for landowners in northern Italy in the 1780s, and with which Odier would concur: "[peasants] have no choice, and are obliged to eat what they have. It is true that bread made of barley, beans, and sorghum is very hard to digest and may lead to a thickening and slowness in the blood, and dispose the body to obstructions and other ailments, but this rarely happens because the robustness of their bodies, their hard life and continual exercise suffice to overcome the hardness of these foods and convert them into good animal juices.'"[84]

We could easily understand, Odier said, how the bulky material from Saussure's unorthodox diet could fill the intestines, in lieu (it is implied) of being turned into "good animal juices." How to explain why the weight of that material did not push downward through the colon was the puzzle. Why did the intestines instead push upward to the heart? Travels in the Alps could explain this effect also, Odier suggested: "What must be taken into account is the muscularity of Professor de Saussure and the continual exercise to which he was accustomed." It was especially the climbing that was the problem. The forward, upward, repetitive motion affected the abdominal muscles. These became so strong and large and extended that they impeded the work of the intestines. They "forced the intestine upward," "counterbalancing the effect of gravity."[85] The food and exercise typical of an Alpine regime were pernicious in the case of Saussure, the autopsy suggested, and this despite Saussure's own claims for the salutary effects of his travels on his health: "he never felt better than when climbing," he would write to his wife and in the *Voyages*.[86] Saussure's digestive problems were very real, however. They present as acid reflux disease and began in the early 1770s.

The distress he felt and tried to hide from associates was what prompted the complaint to Haller about his excessive activity, discussed above. As Saussure himself explained to Haller, every day around midday, acid would begin to flood his throat. He began to prophylactically vomit after eating to prevent the burning of his esophagus. The symptoms would seem to have begun after having consumed a large quantity of sour fruit while visiting the Borromean Islands, on Lake Maggiore (Italy.) Senebier suggests an earlier onset, in England en route to the tin mines of Cornwall, when a throat condition (perhaps strep throat) began. Haller prescribed "'forty drops of Huile de Tartre par défaillance'" ("a mixture of potash and potassium carbonate rendered liquid by deliquescence") and an early form of milk of magnesia.[87] Odier presumably suggested his "Pepto Bismol."[88]

Saussure's experience of the mountains commands interest today not simply because he explored the Alps at the peak of the Little Ice Age, describing glaciers as they were expanding—grinding up villages in the Arve valley near Chamonix—and we are living in an age of global warming. What was new to him, and his readers, is becoming lost to us. Indeed, the source of the Aveyron, a feeder stream of the Arve River, has long since disappeared, as any visitor to Chamonix in search of this wonder will find. The "Source of the Aveyron" was once an iconic illustration of the beauty of the glaciers, depicted as gushing from under a grotto carved below a tail of the Mer de Glace—now shrunk back—which had extended into the hamlet of Bois.[89] What is endangered or extinct is not simply this or that landmark, however. It is, rather, the ways in which we orient ourselves in space or, in the phrase of the physicist John Edward Huth, how we "find our way in the world."[90] Urban lighting has obscured the night sky such that the constellations are hardly visible. The Milky Way is rarely seen. Star maps, once published in daily newspapers such as the *New York Times*, have been dropped from the weather pages. Both the maps and what they depicted—the night sky—are now for many of us unreadable, victims of light pollution. And Global Positioning Systems have replaced road maps.[91] Internet technology has replaced, rather than, as we will see instruments doing in Saussure's age, extended the senses as we shift our bodies from one place to another. Although all of nature is "mediated" by culture, basic habits of locating ourselves in space—reading a compass or a street sign or even just looking around—are weakened as GPS dependency increases. The navy understands this as a national security issue. "The United States Naval Academy has once again begun training midshipmen how to take their position from the stars with a sextant," they say, in case the satellite system is "disabled" and the navy is literally lost at sea.[92]

So Saussure's bodily engagement with the Alps is intriguing. While the question of what actually killed Saussure is moot (though clearly it was something like a stroke), his autopsy directs us to think about his life, and about his body in its social context—that supposedly indigestible porridge, those muscles presumably not made for walking—in contact with the Alps. Moreover, the environment in which Saussure grew up was also withdrawn in many ways from nature and in that respect not completely unlike our own. The walls of Geneva, newly fortified in the 1740s, set it apart from the surrounding plain. Heavy chains crossed the lake where it fronted the city to protect it from invasion by boat. Though the Alps were visible from the north shore of Lake Geneva, summer estates were built to look inward, away from the peaks. The country houses of Charles Bonnet in Genthod and the Neckers at Coppet are examples of this architecture of aversion. Germaine de Staël in exile at Coppet wrote of how much she hates the Alps: "These high mountains seem to me like the grilles of a convent, separating us from the rest of the world. One lives in infernal peace here. One expires in this nothingness."[93] Their gardens were stylized, following the French fashion. Elsewhere the shores were deployed for processing textiles. The *indiennes* industry—which produced the printed cotton cloth in much demand throughout Europe—needed an abundance of the water offered by the lake and the Rhône, and used it, and wasted it.[94]

Nature was also complicated by ideology. The Savoy Alps were largely Catholic. The Genevan perimeter was established to protect its Protestants from Catholic invasions, especially from the dukes of Savoy. The repulsed invasion of December 1602—the Escalade—was vivid in the Genevan memory in the 1740s. Reports of murders by Catholics of Protestants continued into the 1770s. Thomas Blaikie, the Scottish botanist, walking back to Geneva from the Aiguilles Rouges in 1775, was threatened by villagers who believed he was German. They set fire to a shed where they thought he was sleeping. His friend later explained "how they had killed two people at that village under pretext of Religion and it was the greatest miracle how I had escaped from hence."[95] Moreover, the Catholic Alps retained the magical spaces that the Reformation had erased, had aggressively rejected, in the belief that if God is everywhere, no one space is more holy than another.[96] Nature itself was a barrier to approaching the Alps. In the middle of the century, cold winters even brought wolves to the outskirts of the city.[97] Chamonix peasants would occasionally come to Geneva to sell honey and crystals.[98] (Why honey from the Chamonix valley was so flavorful was discussed by Saussure in the *Voyages*. It was white and lightly scented and prescribed by doctors for colds and pneumonia. Probably the valley's larches, to which bees are strongly attracted, gave the honey its special qualities, though this would have to be tested, Saussure continued, by comparing the honey with that from other spaces where larches abound.)[99] However, trading was irregular, and paths along the Arve from Geneva to the peaks were dangerous, as they crossed over and along its banks. When Saussure made his first trip to the glaciers, it was on foot. He walked the fifty miles from his home to Chamonix.

In so doing, he moved outward from a mediated universe into something distinctly other. Saussure's decision to explore the peaks brought him to a radically different landscape from that of Geneva. He entered a world of glaciers broken by ice pyramids and lined with plunging crevasses, and of caves slit deep into the sides of mountains, holes that could be explored only by slithering around face first like a snake. It was a place of intense cold and white heat, of deep-toned skies where massive storm clouds could form in a blink. His was the disorienting space of the inner ranges of the Alps, where the shape of things changes with one's vantage point, where a mountain such as Le Môle, triangular when viewed from Geneva, becomes a sloping rectangle when approached from the valley carved by the Arve. To read the *Voyages* is to walk into a panorama or a relief map that presents as a vertical plane as it faces Geneva, but is revealed as multidimensional and marked by gargantuan shifting shapes, as one pushes past the first early curves of the Arve River, and enters the valley of Chamonix.

The exploration of the high peaks of the Alps on the part of Saussure, and by proxy, his readers, has been poured into a more general discovery of the Alps, credited to Jean-Jacques Rousseau and before him, Haller. Haller's 1732 poem *Die Alpen* (The Alps; something of a contemporary *Georgics*, adopting Virgil's themes about the agricultural world) brought the uncorrupted Alpine peasant to the attention of cosmopolitan Europe: "Here all live well, by simple nature led; / Alone the heart directs and not the toiling head."[100] Rousseau's novel, *La Nouvelle Héloïse* (*Julie, or The New Eloise* [1761]), one of the century's bestsellers, widened the appeal. The key passages of *La Nouvelle Héloïse* (part 1, chapter 22, and part 4, chapter 17) in which contemporaries were introduced to the seductions of Alpine scenery are set, however, in the middle or *moyenne montagne*, that is, the Alps of waterfalls, high meadows, and cliffs. These are precipitous spaces but not ones of scrambles above 2000 to 2400 meters. As Saint Preux explained to Edward in his letter about his return with Julie to Meillerie, "We reached the place after an hour's walk *over winding and cool paths which, ascending imperceptibly between the trees and the rocks, were not otherwise inconvenient except in their length*" (emphasis added).[101]

Haller himself on his celebrated walk through the Alps with Johann Gesner (1709–1790) in July and August of 1728 crossed the Gemmi Pass in the Bernese Alps and the Joch Pass in the Uri. This is the journey that inspired his *The Alps* (with its powerful cultural ramifications) and that began his work on Swiss botany.[102] He would have climbed no higher than the Gemmi, however, at 2270 meters. Possibly the highest space Rousseau himself traversed was the Mont Cenis Pass at 2083 meters, which he crossed when he was sixteen years old and being sent to Turin from Annecy by Mme. de Warens. It was a positive experience for Rousseau— "This memory has left me the strongest taste for everything associated with it, for mountains especially and for traveling on foot"—but the *Confessions* are vague on the details. It was a walking tour of Italy that he proposed to Denis Diderot and Grimm, not the Alps per se.[103] Les Charmettes, which lay in its wooded valley of the Rhone-Alps, was Rousseau's idyll. This country house and gardens "remain[ed] his ideal," as Sainte-Beuve (1804– 1869) and others have noticed.[104] As Rousseau says in the "Septième promenade," a countryside is never more dispiriting (*triste*) than when it has only "stones, clay and sand" to offer to the walker. It is "brooks" and "singing birds" that speak to the soul.[105] Even Le Chasseron, a peak he climbed while in exile in Môtiers, between Neuchâtel and the border with France, to collect flowers and other plants, is less than 2000 meters.[106] These romantic heights are of a far different order from the 4807 meters of Mont Blanc summited by Saussure in 1787, or the 3215 meters reached on his *tour du Monte Rosa* in 1789, or the 3360 meters of the icy Col du Géant, where, during an absolutely unprecedented seventeen-day stay in the summer of 1788, he camped in order to measure the blueness of the sky, the humidity of the air, and the velocity of the wind,[107] and where he recorded some of his own most exhilarating experiences.

The cultural pathways—our opportunities for thinking and doing—opened up by Saussure's *Voyages* are distinct from those available as romanticism, as we see when comparing Saussure to Rousseau, and are important because of what they can offer alongside them. They take us beyond the weathered generalizations about the Alps that have dominated most cultural histories of this space, dependent as they are on one set of charismatic experiences. Rousseau's Alps are a setting for the exploration of his self and thus, by extension, ourselves. Saint Preux, Julie, and Clare were facets or projections of Rousseau's own self, as he reveals in the *Confessions* and implies in the *Les Rêveries du promeneur solitaire*.[108] The canvas of the Alps facilitates this projection, as we see Rousseau imagining Saint-Preux imagining Julie with him in the heights above Meillerie: "While I was delightedly traveling in these places, so little known and so worthy of admiration, what were you doing in the meantime, my Julie? Did your friend forget you? Julie forgotten? Should I not rather forget myself? . . . I led you everywhere with me. I did not take a step without you. I did not admire a view without hurrying to show it to you. . . . Sometimes, seated at your side, I gazed with you at the scene before us. . . . Did I come to a difficult pass? I saw you leap over it with the agility of a fawn bounding after its mother." And so on.[109]

Nature reflects the self and reflects it back to us, just as the backdrop of autumn in the outskirts of Paris (the fields and vineyards between Ménilmontant and Charonne) described in the "Second promenade" of *Les rêveries* allowed him clarity about his approaching old age. "The countryside, though still green and cheerful," promised the lonely winter to come. The leaves on the trees had begun to fall; the paths on which he walked seemed already deserted. The impression forced on him was too obvious to be missed, "too analogous to my age and sort for me not to have made the connection."[110] So, too, does the lapping of waves against the shore of the Île de Saint-Pierre on the Lac de Bienne in the Jura allow him access to his deepest self, beyond thought: "The ebb and flow of this water, its sound constant though magnified from time to time, striking without respite my ears and my eyes, substituted for the currents inside me [*suppléaient aux mouvements internes*] that reverie had extinguished and was enough to make me pleasurably sensible of my existence, without taking the trouble to think."[111]

Saussure's *Voyages*, by contrast, are directed toward the physical reality of nature. What this rock looks like, tastes like, feels like—what this sound presages, and that—how clear is this air, what color is that cloud—what do height and cold do to one's appetite, to one's head. One finds an engagement of the animate self—the narrator's, the reader's own—with an inanimate but knowable nature. The *Voyages* describe a sensual, even occasionally eroticized relationship to the Alps, a geophilia, that differs from romanticism's relationship to nature, with its focus on knowledge of the self, and that is distinct too from that implied by geology, understood—it was Saussure's own understanding—as a knowledge of the Earth, geologia, and its causal operations.[112] The term recalls "topophilia"—love of place[113] but the term "geophilia" underlines the difference between a connection to a culturally infused space or place—Protestant Geneva, say—and a generalized embrace of the physical Earth that operates in the *Voyages*.

This is an engagement of the entire body. All his senses are involved, not just sight, the sense privileged in the Age of Enlightenment.[114] As Claude Reichler, a historian of the literature and images of Alpine travel, explains so well, sound helps us determine distances. Touch, as is obvious if one is a hiker or climber, is vital for walking. Is the ground stable; is the snow hard? Which way is the wind blowing? Is the air hot; is it cold?[115] Smell can help identify types of snow cover and warn of fallen rocks.[116] Saussure will use this sense on granite. If it smells like earth, for instance, it is formed of hornblende.[117] "Above all," Reichler continues, our directional signals, the senses that orient us in space, are in play in this multidimensional landscape,[118] or *sensorium*, where nature so forcefully sends the messages that create sensations in us. This is what is meant here by describing the mountains as encountered by Saussure as nature's sensorium. The Alps were where Saussure's full-body, sensual experience of the nonhuman world was realized.

For some two hundred years the full account of Saussure's explorations, the four-volume *Voyages dans les Alpes* (Travels in the Alps), has gathered dust on library shelves. Though eagerly read at the time of its publication, nineteenth-century publishers recognized that the *Voyages* had its *longueurs*, especially for readers looking for adventure.[119] Volume 1, for instance, includes three chapters running well over one hundred pages detailing and comparing all the rocks to be found in the environs of Geneva.

Thirteen types are presented in the book's chapter 4 as "a listing and description" of rocks to be found in the neighborhood. More in chapter 5, a "continuation of the same subject," with a focus on composite rocks, and yet more in chapter 6, on the Alpine origin of small rounded stones and giant boulders. (Erratics, we would call these last, though Saussure posits the action of water, not ice, in transporting them from the peaks.)[120] Moreover, Saussure's contributions to the new discipline of geology, a term he helped define, were superseded by those of Charles Lyell, whose *Principles of Geology* (1830–33) became the standard work in the field.[121] And it was Louis Agassiz and James Forbes who showed how glaciers work.[122] From 1834, the *Voyages dans les Alpes* appeared only in editions of its *Partie pittoresque*, a collection of the works "picturesque sections" with much of its scientific description excised.[123]

After Cuvier's éloge in 1810, Saussure was mostly of interest regionally, as an important member of an illustrious family, or to climbers such as Stephen and other members of the Alpine Club who hailed Saussure as the first Alpinist, and who read the *Partie pittoresque* or Saussure's *Relation abrégée d'un voyage à la cime du Mont-Blanc en août 1787*, initially published by Saussure within weeks of his ascent. John Ruskin was the exception. Having read the *Voyages*, he urged Freshfield as early as 1878 to write a life of Saussure, though he then demurred.[124] Freshfield's own point of entry into *Saussure's* life was that of a mountaineer, though the biography, written with the collaboration of Henry Fairbanks Montagnier, is comprehensive and indispensable for scholars as well as enthusiasts of mountain literature. The 1920 *Life of Horace Benedict de Saussure* was based on family papers—letters and journals—then in private hands, now in the Archives de la famille de Saussure at the Bibliothèque de Genève, which Montagnier was able to review (as an American of French descent in Switzerland during the First World War).[125] In *Into the Silence: The Great War, Mallory, and the Conquest of Everest*, Wade Davis describes Freshfield as an "iconic figure of British mountaineering," one of the "leading figures in the Everest adventure."[126] He served as president of the Alpine Club and the Royal Geographical Society. He explored the Caucasus, making a number of first ascents of peaks above 5000 meters, including the lower peak of Mt. Elbrus. He also climbed in the Himalayas.[127] When Éditions Slatkine, Geneva's premier publishing house, reissued the *Voyages* in 1978, Saussure the Alpinist was also evoked. Yves Ballu (b. 1943), climber, writer, and scientist, wrote the preface, in which he described the *Voyages* as "immortal." "His extraordinary campaign of exploration in the Alps and the precious account of it that he has left will rest as determining elements in the birth of alpinism ... he is without doubt one of the founders of alpinism."[128]

The bicentennial of the summiting of Mont Blanc renewed interest in Saussure. Though the first ascent was in 1786, a year before Saussure's, that and the second—Saussure's was the third, following the second within the month—were largely in response to the publicity generated by the *Voyages*, and the prize offered by Saussure since 1760 for the first person to summit, or even to indicate a path to the top.[129] Conferences and colloquia associated with the bicentennial have built a deep reserve of material on Saussure, ranging from the architecture of his homes, the instruments he invented or improved—on display at the Musée d'histoire des sciences de la Ville de Genève (History of Science Museum in Geneva), along with his climbing clothes—to the details of his investments in French bonds and the catalog of his library.[130]

Historians of geology have made new claims for Saussure's importance. Martin Rudwick, in *Bursting the Limits of Time: The Reconstruction of Geohistory in the Age of Revolution* (2005), places Saussure at the center of a revisionist account of the history of geology that emphasizes developments on the Continent rather than in Britain. He takes Saussure's oeuvre as the "historian's golden spike, a symbolic baseline from which the gradual spread of a newly geohistorical outlook could be traced in the practices of the sciences of the Earth."[131] Albert Carozzi (1925–2014) credited the *Voyages* with offering an argument that anticipates plate tectonics: "Without suggesting the collision of plates, Saussure's observations of the primary and secondary arrangement of rocks in mountains—that is, massifs with a central granite base with limestone crashing in, suggested a moving up, from an originally horizontal plane. Saussure was the first to signal the implications of FOLDS of rocks—especially the folding back upon themselves of 'horizontal antagonistic thrusts' [*les refoulements horizontaux en sens contraires*]."[132]

While Peter H. Hansen's *The Summits of Modern Man: Mountaineering after the Enlightenment* (2013) offers an argument about the political significance of the Mont Blanc ascents, most work on the *Voyages* is split between addressing Saussure the scientist and Saussure the bold climber. As described by Cuvier in the language of adventure, Saussure was both. "Making long treks in those high valleys unreachable by carriage . . . having as a path only the rocky bed of a torrent, clinging with one's hands and feet to the sharp edges of crags, leaping from one point to another above a precipice, remaining for days and nights on the glaciers—those fields of ice where the outer limits of life are reached, and to which only a love of science could draw a living being—such was the existence to which the historian of the Alps was condemned."[133] By reading the *Voyages* in the tangled way in which it first appeared—part travelogue, part natural history, part adventure tale—this book recenters the question of his life—why explore the Alps?—on the person, in all his physicality. It addresses a new set of questions, of significance to our understanding of changing attitudes toward nature in the eighteenth century. Rather than focusing on the problem of ideas—what people thought or believed about the natural world—it asks about the experience of nature. How was the natural world *experienced* in the eighteenth century?[134]

The emphasis in the *Voyages* on Saussure's physical engagement with the Earth makes it an ideal source for exploring this question. It also invites historians to borrow from the field of environmental psychology, which measures the human body's engagement with its surroundings and argues for the importance of sensory ecologies or systems in understanding how we make sense of the world.[135] That work on how we experience the natural world opens a field of contact between our views of the environment and Saussure's, which were formed both by his Enlightenment background and in direct contact with a new physical reality. Following in his eighteenth-century footsteps, this book is organized spatially, tracing ever-widening arcs from the constricted city of Geneva outward and upward to the Mont Blanc massif. There, on the summit and on the Col du Géant, with both his body and his imagination pushed to their limits, the spatial and biographical protagonists of this project—Saussure and the Alps—come together in intimate encounters, with implications for the human understanding of the planet.

Noticing the somatic in the *Voyages* helps us make sense of its Lucretian frame. An often-quoted passage from the "Discours préliminaire," the preface to volume 1, presents Saussure's musings about the fragility of civilizations from the top of Mount Etna on an Italian journey in 1772–73[136]—a rather typical eighteenth-century glance at the ruins of time. (The philosopher looks down at the remnants of once-powerful kingdoms and ruminates about the puerile nature of ambition.)[137] Typically overlooked, however, is the earlier section of that passage, about the place of humans in the natural world: "However, if in the midst of these meditations, one thinks of those little beings who creep across the surface of the globe, and if one contrasts their life span to the great epochs of nature, how not to be astonished that those who occupy such a minor place in time and space have been able to consider themselves the unique goal of the creation of the entire universe."[138] To underscore his point, Saussure ends with a specific reference to Lucretius's *De rerum natura* (*On the Nature of Things*), nods to which will return on his ascent of Mont Blanc in 1787.[139] Humans believe they are the special creations of God, or the gods; but we are all part of the same natural order.[140] This Lucretian theme is Saussure's boldest point.

Saussure was witness to an expanded universe, one that had its own life, distinct from his own, as this book will detail. From a shelter at the base of the Aiguille du Goûter in 1785 high up along the route to Mont Blanc, as evening turned to night, he imagined that he could see the "cadaver" of the universe below, with only the "phosphorescent snows" of Mont Blanc "sparkling above, still suggestive of motion and life."[141] This is a sense of our relationship to the universe akin to that described in the photographs of Earthrise in 1968.[142] We are part of something bigger but not lost in that hugeness. We have some perspective on the universe but are not dominant over it. The high peaks allowed for a heightened consciousness of that relationship as Saussure's understanding of mountain formation grew. On the Col du Géant the night before their departure from the prolonged camp in July 1788, and with the weather clearing, moonlight flowed over the "vast enceinte of snow and rock slopes," softening the brightness of the whites. A "majestic silence" ensued. It was one of those moments to live for, compensation for all the sacrifices made to enable them. Deep in that quiet, he seemed to be able to "hear the voice of Nature" and "to become the confidant of its most secret operations."[143]

The *Voyages* open up the Genevan Enlightenment to an analysis far more interesting than that which would box up Saussure with determined, if progressive, Calvinists, such as Charles Bonnet, and the search for God in the works of nature. It was the voice of nature that Saussure would listen for, not that of God. At the same time, the Alps remained a physical other, not as "nature" will sometimes seem in the materialist thought of the eighteenth century, or the *Cosmos* of Alexander von Humboldt, as something we are merged into. Still less was nature solipsistic, that is, a way of reflecting back to us aspects of ourselves. That the natural world has intrinsic value—independent of us and of its value to human life and well-being—is the message that runs through the *Voyages* and has resurfaced today in the world of environmentalist thought. It offers one way out of the climate crisis. Readers themselves will have to decide whether the notoriously baggy *Voyages* fit this streamlined explanation of their meaning. In the meantime, this new life history of Saussure introduces them to the author, and to one of the most dynamic spaces in Enlightenment Europe—Geneva, in engagement with the Alps.

❋ 1 ❋
Geneva

THE WALLED CITY

Geneva was walled in the eighteenth century, and its gates had both real and metaphorical value. They enter the modern imagination through the *Confessions* of Jean-Jacques Rousseau. Fifteen years old, abandoned to a miserable life as an apprentice by wealthy relatives and a delinquent father, Jean-Jacques took flight at the Porte de Cornavin, which connected the workshops of Saint Gervais with the roads to France and Switzerland.[1] He and two companions had been wandering the countryside outside the city in the Sunday afternoon freedom of an early spring day in 1728. Although the *Confessions* are silent about where they roamed, geography suggests forays to the north toward the Jura, and to the east along the lake.

The gates of Geneva closed just after dusk and opened at dawn at regularly established times throughout the year, though gatekeepers of early modern cities were known to shave off their working day by opening late or closing early.[2] In winter the city would close at around 4:30 or 5:00 p.m., so even on 14 March, the date of his escapade, this would not make for a very long half-holiday from the engraver's workshop to which Rousseau was apprenticed. Sunday services would have filled the morning, with no one allowed on the streets during that time and the gates of the city closed.[3] Nonetheless, Rousseau claims, they were in advance of their time when, hearing the drumbeat announcing the imminent disaster, he ran with all his might toward the outpost. In sight of the soldiers on duty, panting and out of breath, he cried for them to wait, but was too late, he says. Twenty feet away the first drawbridge was rising: "I trembled as I watched its dreadful horns rising in the air, a sinister and fatal augury of the inevitable fate which from that moment awaited me."[4]

The *Confessions* pretend here that Geneva was a paradise lost. It was a world Rousseau would have been better off remaining in, and would have remained in, he claims, had he not had such a hard master, and had his unloving guardians not encouraged his departure, slipping him funds to lubricate his flight. He would have been neither celebrated nor reviled: "I should have been a good Christian, a good citizen, a good friend, a good workman, a good man in every way. I should have been happy in my condition, and should perhaps have been respected. Then, after a life—simple and obscure, but also mild and uneventful—I should have died peacefully in the bosom of my family. Soon, no doubt, I should have been forgotten, but at least I should have been mourned for as long as I was remembered."[5] Perhaps. In any case, in the first flush of freedom, in the dawn decision for flight after a night in the rough outside the walls, those terrible horns of the drawbridge would seem to represent a sort of birth canal that had released him, jubilant, into the "vaste espace du monde": "The only thought in my mind was the independence I believed I had won. Now that I was free and my own master, I supposed I could do anything, achieve anything. I had only to take one leap, and I could rise and fly through the air. I marched confidently out into the world's wide spaces."[6]

The Genevan enceinte shaped Saussure's life as well, though more discreetly. Bankrolled by privilege and wealth, the *Voyages* served to flatten the walls of Geneva, to integrate the closed-in, circumscribed space of the city with the gigantic natural environment beyond. Figure 1.1, from the first volume of the *Voyages*, shows how the course of Saussure's mountain traveling dwarfed the space confined within the city's walls. Saussure's explorations involved an expansion of the physical self—a touching

FIGURE 1.1 "Carte du lac de Genève et des montagnes adjacentes et Carte particulière des glaciers du Faucigny et des environs du Mont Blanc." Saussure, *Voyages*, vol. 1. Fold-out map, *hors-texte* at beginning of volume. Watkinson Library, Trinity College, CT: DQ823.S246. Photo credit: Amanda M. Matava.

not of the deep stillness of mind before thought, as we saw in Rousseau's reverie on the Lac de Bienne, but the deep caves and high peaks of previously unknown mountain spaces. This was travel that entailed a successive opening of wider and wider vistas. Though, like the great Victorian climbers who would follow in his wake—the Leslie Stephenses, the Edward Whympers, the Douglas Freshfields—what was left behind is as important to understand as what was found. In Saussure's case this was a tightly strung, coiled, and nervous city-state, a tense ecology that the history of its walls will describe.

Geneva entered the eighteenth century as anomalously small, almost precariously so. It would have appeared to contemporaries as dominating a space unto itself.[7] One of the oldest cities in Europe, it had entered written history as a fortified city under the Romans.[8] Until the eleventh century, its basic footprint was that of the Roman *castrum* within its Burgundian perimeter.[9] Expansion followed in the High Middle Ages. By the end of the fifteenth century a substantial enceinte had been constructed incorporating eight major gates and an interior port that closed off the city to invasion from the lake.

No further broadening of the enclosed space of the city would be undertaken.[10] To the contrary, an unprecedented shrinking of the city as an urban space would ensue in the sixteenth century.[11] Unlike other modernizing cities, whose suburbs would grow and be absorbed within the city proper, beginning in the 1530s Geneva set out to destroy the neighborhoods that had grown up outside its walls. Threatened by predatory Catholic powers, especially the dukes of Savoy but also the kingdom of France, Reformation Geneva established a glacis around itself, a clear open space that would thwart or discourage an invading army. The city seemed to surge up out of nowhere, looming over its emptied landscape—"une zone pratiquement désertique"—closed off to the world, except for its few gates.[12] Renovation had reduced these to three. The Porte de Cornavin faced France and the Swiss territories; the Porte Neuve and the Porte de Rive looked toward Savoy.[13]

By the 1550s, when the Republic of Geneva stood as the Protestant Rome with Calvin at its helm, the walls had a dual purpose: protecting the city from attack and welcoming through its gates refugees from Italy and the French wars of religion. The "eyes of the city" had become ideological.[14] This first wave of religious refugees was followed by a larger one in the aftermath of the St. Bartholomew's Day Massacre in 1572, and a steady stream continued throughout the seventeenth century, with families arriving from intermediate points of safety. The Saussures entered the city via Lausanne, for instance. Antoine de Saussure (1514–1569), a Grand

Falconer to the Duke of Lorraine, was exiled in 1552 for supporting the Reformation first in Metz and then in Strasbourg. After stays in Neuchâtel and Geneva, he moved to Lausanne in 1556. His grandson Jean Baptiste (1576–1647) "settled at Geneva, where he married into another family of exiles, the Diodati" from Lucca in Tuscany, thus establishing the oligarchic credentials of our Saussure.[15] The revocation of the Edict of Nantes in 1685, which outlawed Protestantism in France, brought more refugees, and these were poorer, more numerous, and less enthusiastically absorbed.[16] Their needs strained the city's charity.

The early refugees included families whose descendants would constitute the elites of the seventeenth and eighteenth centuries. This patriciate monopolized seats on the small or restricted councils that included along with the four syndics, the Petit Council—otherwise known as the Council of Twenty-five—the Council of Sixty, and the Council of Two Hundred. These directed the government of Geneva at the expense of the General Council of Citizens and Bourgeois, which had been understood as sovereign since the late fourteenth century.[17] The extent to which these families had entwined themselves in a powerful bloc by the eighteenth century was revealed to Cardinal de Fleury, Louis XV's chief minister, by France's special envoy to Geneva in 1738. As the plenipotentiary reported, shortly after the death of Calvin in 1564 the Council of Two Hundred included representatives from 176 families, at least as he judged from the list of their names. No more than 94 family names appeared on the roster in 1734, however. Moreover, ten families made up one-third of this council: the Lullins, the Trembleys, the Rilliets, the Pictets, the Gallatins, the Buissons, the Mallets, the de la Rives, the Cramers, and the Favres. And as Lautrec would have noticed, counting family names alone would not reveal how closely these councillors were related. Jean Lullin (1675–1750), a former first syndic, had ninety-seven close relatives on the Council of Two Hundred and thirteen on the Council of Twenty-five in 1738. Jean Trembley (1674–1745) sat on the Two Hundred with 108 of his relatives.[18]

The restricted councils were in addition "*emboîté*, that is, nested together such that members of the restricted (or, small) councils were at the same time part of each and every larger council."[19] This meant that if one was a syndic, one was also a member of the Council of Twenty-five, the Council of Sixty, and the Council of Two Hundred. If one was a member of the Council of Twenty-five, one also sat on the Councils of Sixty and Two Hundred. The knots that tied these families together were tightly drawn, and Saussure, as we will see, was bundled closely within this system, with a mother who was a de la Rive and a future wife who was a Lullin.

What poured into the city through its Reformation gates was not simply a set of desperate people but agents of its transformation into a center of early modern capitalism. From antiquity an entrepôt, funneling products from the Mediterranean to northern Europe via the Rhône and the western passes of the Alps, Geneva became a center of printing, silk production, banking, watchmaking, enameling, and the finishing of highly desirable *indiennes*. These printed cotton fabrics were sold in France and elsewhere (subject to the vicissitudes of the economy and to the more or less successful attempts of states to limit their import and protect their own nascent industries).[20] Avatars of this new type of Genevan were the Lullins, merchant-manufacturers who had become bankers in the seventeenth century and "based on the tax rolls of 1690 had hold of the largest family fortune in Geneva":[21] in 1690 their taxable income was one-seventh more than that of the next richest family, and by 1716 it was double that of the Gallatins, the second-richest family ("4.284.000 versus 2.183.000 fl.").[22] These fortunes were given material expression in impressive townhouses: "Léonard Buisson (1643–1719), delegate to Louis XIV at Versailles in 1696, built the first townhouse sited between courtyard and garden 'to a plan imported from Parys,'" that is, in the style of the *hôtels particuliers* of the Parisian nobility rising up in the faubourg St. Germain. Joseph Abeille (1673–1756) was commissioned by Jean-Antoine Lullin-Camp (1666–1709) to design the "opulent building of La Tertasse," the Hôtel Lullin, in 1705.[23] This was the mansion—"the finest in Geneva"[24]—that Saussure lived in after his marriage to Albertine-Amélie Boissier, heiress to the vast wealth of the Lullins.

In the meantime, the Calvinist texture of the walls thickened alongside laws that regulated behavior according to the dictates of the Old and New Testaments. This was an interpretation of biblical teachings that demanded austerity in dress and other ornamentation and saw the Republic's survival as dependent upon following the word of God.[25] The critical test was met in 1602, when the city repulsed a nighttime invasion by Catholic Savoy. Charles-Emmanuel I, Duke of Savoy, whose territories then looped around Geneva, longed to capture the city-state. The prize for Savoy would be a capital city for a kingdom of Savoy, with Charles-Emmanuel as monarch of a coherent set of territories. On the night of the winter solstice (11–12 December, that is, 21–22 December by our Gregorian calendar), three hundred elite troops, using extendable ladders and grappling hooks, scaled the outer walls of the city. Finding the inner gates unguarded and unlocked, all they needed to do was wait for first light, when the 2000–3000 troops massed outside of a Savoy-facing gate could enter to ravage the city. The advance guard was detected and the "humble

Isaac Mercier," the only one of the thirteen soldiers guarding the Porte Neuve who had not run away or hidden in fear, scrambled up the gate and cut the cord attached to the portcullis so that down it fell. As one patriotic historian explains, "Without his courage and presence of mind more than 2000 fanatics would have wreaked carnage on the enemies of their faith. . . . But the grating fell, and no one could pass!"[26]

A street in the city is named after the brave Mercier. Annual celebrations of the Escalade today—a civic holiday—honor another hero of the night, "la mère Royaume" and the full cauldron of soup that she supposedly threw at one of the Savoyard soldiers, cracking his skull. René Guerdon points out that at 3 a.m., it was unlikely that soup was being prepared. Probably some other missile—maybe a tankard—was launched from her kitchen window. Still, who could begrudge the joy of crushing a *marmite* of chocolate or releasing a spray of marzipan vegetables, all the while declaiming, "Ainsi périrent les ennemis de la République!" (Thus perished the enemies of the Republic!), if only once a year, on the shortest day of the year.[27]

The logic of centralization was on the side of Savoy, God on that of Geneva, as figure 1.2, portraying the deliverance of the city from its Catholic enemy, shows. The city walls of Geneva, tempered into legend by the Escalade, became a point of contention between the people-—in the restricted sense of the General Council of Citizens and Bourgeois—and patricians in the early eighteenth century. The resolution of a set of crises on the eve of Saussure's birth in 1740 ensured the security of patrician rule until the tremors of the 1760s and 1780s, presaging the Revolution of 1792. This early turmoil established the dividing lines, "the great split in Genevan politics in the eighteenth century," as Richard Whatmore argues, between Francophiles and Franco-skeptics, the latter fearful of both absolutism and Catholicism.[28] Like the ancient Israelites with respect to their people, many contemporaries believed Geneva owed its "miraculous deliverance" to God. A new "literature of the Escalade" was centered around this notion, linking "the city of Calvin to the people of Israel."[29] On the other hand, an alliance with the kingdom of France—Catholic, aristocratic, and hostile (on account of *raison d'état*) to assaults on Genevan independence—was also desirable. This alliance seemed to the patrician leaders good supplementary insurance to God's, and also a mark of excellent taste.

The first of these crises broke out in 1707, in part over taxation. "No taxation without the consent of the General Council!" became the rallying cry of a protest against the small councils, led by the patrician and patriot Pierre Fatio. "Il faut simplement ne pas souffrir que l'on fasse des lois

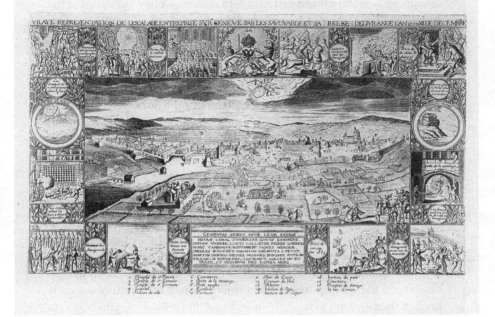

FIGURE 1.2 *Vraye représentation de L'Escalade entreprise sur Genève par les Savoyards et sa belle délivrance*, print after François Diodati (1647–1690). Bibliothèque de Genève, phot 46P 1602 25. Photo credit: Bibliothèque de Genève.

sans consulter le peuple" (One simply must not permit laws to be made without consulting the people), Fatio concluded.[30] The people, as manifest in the General Council, were sovereign. These claims would seem to herald the democratic revolutions of the eighteenth century and are one of the reasons historians of modern life have been interested in the history of this small commercial city.[31] Geneva was precocious, in highly surprising ways. The patrician Fatio cast his rebellion in classical republican terms and was hailed as a Gracchus, ready to die on behalf of the people. His conservative brother, Whatmore explains in *Against War and Empire*, from which most of this account of Fatio is taken, was thus cast as the "absent 'second Gracchi.'"[32] His sacrifice *à l'antique* was achieved by firing squad in September 1707.[33] He was also deeply Protestant, though. The objection to oligarchy—patrician control of the councils—was that it was eroding the "clerical culture" of the state. Fatio stands as "the first citizen who demanded more popular government as the sole means to the continued independence of the state and its Protestantism."[34] This is a sensibility—sectarian and patriotic—that Linda Colley has placed at the center of British identity as well, and that "complicated," in Whatmore's words, "any civic humanist or classical republican heritage."[35]

Fatio's claims were for a strengthened Protestant republic, resting on a sovereign General Council. When protests broke out again over the issue of taxation, the role of the city walls in defining this state became central to these protests. In 1715 a decision was made by the restricted councils to rebuild the fortifications. The work would be paid for through borrowing, at the low interest rates that Geneva's place at the center of European banking would ensure. New taxes on consumer goods were levied to secure the loans. Protests ensued. From the point of view of the General Council, there were two problems. First, it was the small councils, not the General Council, that had levied the taxes; and second, taxes on "wine, meat, and wheat" hurt ordinary citizens—artisans such as themselves—more than the rich.[36] Delays and cost overruns forced a review of the project in 1727. A report by Jacques-Barthélemy Micheli du Crest (1690–1766), a patrician like Fatio, and like Fatio, destined to be executed—though in effigy[37]—challenged the assumptions of the project. Would the refurbished walls protect the city from invasion? No, claimed this military engineer, an expert on fortifications. Would Geneva's most powerful neighbor even have to attempt a siege? Or would not the city open itself to a French army if they came knocking on its gates—or, in Micheli's words, "'on receipt of just a simple letter from his Majesty'"?[38] (In April 1798 this is almost exactly what did happen, though on the part of Revolutionary, not monarchical, France: "At 12:30 on the afternoon of the 15th, detachments of grenadiers, hussars, and artillery poured through the gates of the city, disarmed the guards, and to the beat of their drums debouched in front of the Hôtel de Ville [City Hall],"[39] ending Genevan independence.)

Micheli's report offered an alternate vision of Geneva. Why not expand the city walls to include the hinterlands, thus doubling its fortified size? Geneva would become the Carthage of the Alps, not simply the Protestant Rome. Safe from invasion, able to feed its population with its own fields, and able to mobilize "eight thousand soldiers in arms at short notice," it would make of Geneva "a refuge for Protestants, devotees of liberty and tradesmen."[40] It would become an "international power."[41] For Micheli, the walls were to be a physical representation of the Genevan state, strong and independent. The state would rest on the people, ramparts of liberty. The "sovereign populace" would "check... aristocracy" by "making executive power, the small councils, wholly dependent on the will of the citizen body."[42] His "Mémoire pour le Magnifique Conseil des Deux Cents" (Report for the Magnificent Council of Two Hundred of Geneva), which circulated privately in 1728, was published in 1735.[43] This is the document that a regretful Rousseau claimed to have found among the papers of his uncle and that he shared with an agent of Savoy: "Fortunately, of all future contingencies one of the least probable is that the King of Sardinia will lay siege to Geneva. But, since this is not absolutely impossible, I shall always reproach myself for my foolish vanity in revealing the city's chief weaknesses to its oldest enemy."[44]

After several years of instability and uprisings, the French did step in to force an agreement between the parties, working with the two lessor guaranteeing powers, Zurich and Berne. The Règlement de l'Illustre Médiation pour la pacification de la République de Genève (Ruling of the Illustrious Mediators for the pacification of the Republic of Geneva) of 1738 established a compromise.[45] Taxes to support the walls would not be allowed to continue without the consent of the General Counsel after 1750, nor would new taxes for this purpose be allowed without that consent. Patrician rule through the restricted councils was maintained, though nepotism was reined in. No longer were the brothers or nephews of sitting members of the Small Council admitted. The size of the Council of Two Hundred was increased to 250, and the minimum age of its members raised from twenty-five to thirty, this last in a gesture toward competence.[46] The General Council was understood as a sovereign body with the power "to validate all new laws of the state,"[47] but it could no longer "debate proposals"—"it could simply reply 'aye or no, approve or reject.'"[48] Geneva remained, as the government had intended, an "'aristo-démocratie,'"[49] in the approving words of Jean-Jacques Burlamaqui, the political theorist of checks and balances and adviser to the Small Council in 1734,[50] that is, under patrician control.

French influence on Geneva was also clarified. Supporters of the General Council were brought to heel by French threats to ban commercial relations with Geneva and to expel Genevan residents in France.[51] They would ruin the economy. Moreover, the comte de Lautrec (Daniel François de Gélas de Voisins d'Ambres, 1682–1757), the mediator sent by Versailles to work his diplomatic magic, brought to Geneva its French charm. Affable, attentive in negotiations, used to being at home abroad, Lautrec's charisma was subversive. (Rousseau met him at the home of Mme. Warens. Rousseau felt he had charmed Lautrec, though that seemed an illusion: "he seemed to view me with great interest, and made me several promises, which he did not remember till the last year of his life, when I no longer needed him.")[52] Genevans crowded into the makeshift theater ("a simple wooden structure") he had built for him as a condition of his residence.[53] Theater had been banned in Geneva since 1617, though wealthy patricians were known to have "staged private performances in their own homes."[54] These scofflaws were meant to be checked by the Sumptuary Laws of 1732, which renewed the ban on the theater and other sources of moral and especially French contagion.[55] The French theater built on the Place Neuve (near the gate) and supported by a French troupe of actors and actresses was dismantled when Lautrec's mission was complete. The ban was renewed, but its soft power remained to circle around the culture like drifts of warm and fragrant if somewhat decadent air. As historians of the Enlightenment know well, the theater in Geneva became a polemical battleground between Rousseau and Voltaire in the 1750s and '60s (with Rousseau against it and Voltaire in favor.)[56] For Genevans it was a source of destabilization and contention throughout the century.[57]

To understand Saussure's niche, it is enough to know now how that wooden stage stood for a cosmopolitan culture outside the walls of the city, which was alluring but also alarming. Rousseau had succumbed to its charms after his rough departure from Geneva, in the incident described in the beginning of this chapter. He became a Catholic for a time and entered into mainstream Enlightenment culture. In 1749—and in Paris on his famous walk to Vincennes to visit the imprisoned Diderot—he was redirected toward his life's themes in considering the prompt posed by the Academy of Dijon for its essay competition: "Si le progrès des sciences et des arts a contribué à corrompre ou à épurer les mœurs" (Has the progress of the arts and sciences contributed more to the corruption or purification of morals?). To the corruption of morals, he thought: "The moment I read this I beheld another universe and became another man."[58]

Austere, moral, plain, transparent, and Spartan ideals grated against pleasure-seeking, playful, and *mondaine* ways of being. The stress of these competing sensibilities was felt throughout Geneva in the eighteenth century. Haller had already announced its themes in *The Alps* ("Praise high Heaven, that to your land denied / Riches, true source of every vice and ill. . . . True Reason is your guide, by Nature led / that seeks the needful, counts all else for harm . . . O artless happy land!").[59] It was manifest in opposing political camps, but also within patrician lives, sensitive to debates on the moral costs of luxury.[60] These were played out in Saussure's family life, helping to sanction decisions he made to range far and wide, distanced from these and other conundrums of aristo-democracy.

Saussure was born in 1740 on a family estate called Les Conches, which is now a close suburb of Geneva, south of the city. It lay nested in the penultimate loop of the Arve River as it makes it way from the Chamonix valley to Geneva, below the Rhône's exit from the lake. That is where the turbulent, gray-green waters of the Arve slide next to the blue of the Rhône, until, as an invigorated river, it makes its way to Lyons and then south to the Mediterranean Sea.[61] The house at Conches no longer exists, though a hundred years ago Saussure's biographer Douglas Freshfield (of the Royal Geographical Society and the Alpine Club and otherwise absorbed in decisions about the Everest expeditions) looked for its site.[62] He found a modern villa "standing among meadows close to a picturesque weir. Near at hand an ancient barn and stable and some old garden walls indicate[d] an earlier residence."[63] The grounds hugged the Arve, with the opposite bank, at least in Freshfield's day, "high, abrupt, and wooded." It would have seemed a world apart from the town, though Geneva lay only some two miles away. "There [was] little distant view;"[64] instead, as contemporary documents suggest, it was a palette of rural delights. Almost one hundred acres of land was divided into "gardens, orchards, vineyards, hutins (or hautains—where the grapevines are trained to run up trees), fields of wheat or other grains, meadows, woods and scrub."[65]

This was a pastoral, rather pretty and domesticated landscape, such as that viewed by Saussure from the Dôle in the Jura Mountains. After a disorienting experience of feeling stranded on a rock in the middle of a wild ocean, with the high peaks of the Alps beyond appearing as a ragged, rocky shoreline, the fog lifted above his head to reveal "the superb vista of the lake below with its cultivated and charming shores dotted with small towns and beautiful villages."[66] Saussure's vision on the summit of the Dôle (one of several visions he has on the summits of peaks) is described in volume 1 of the *Voyages* (1779) and stands as a centering image of his experience of the mountains, whereby the Jura, the high peaks of the Alps, and Geneva itself are brought into communion.[67] We will join him there later on in this book. Here we rest at Les Conches in its picturesque calm in order to stress its importance.

Saussure's father, Nicolas de Saussure (1709–1791), appears fleetingly in these sources. We find him in lease agreements for Les Conches that assured his rights to honey and fruit. He kept for himself its hives and some of the white walnuts, to be used for their piquant oil.[68] From the small orchards, he claimed apples—the little *pommes d'Apic* or lady apples, pippins, and aromatic winter queens—and pears, both winter pears for picking in autumn and storing for the winter and sweet, creamy butter pears for eating right away.[69] His historians speak of "un propriétaire gourmand" (a gourmand of a landlord).[70] The leases speak also of decorative plants, and of Nicolas's right "when on his walks to pick whatever fruits and flowers he wants for his own pleasure."[71]

Nicolas's influence on his son is easily missed. His mother was more powerfully present in his life, as we shall see below. Prominent themes of the *Voyages* are connected to Les Conches, however. The sensuality of Saussure's experience of nature—the attraction for an immediate experience of the natural world beyond the city's gates—seems to be due to his father. The landscape itself—the diversity of Les Conches, with its woodlands and flower gardens, vineyards and fields—models the integrated body of the environment that the *Voyages* will present on a grand scale. Moreover, Les Conches offered Nicolas a space for his research. One of the signal marks of Saussure's *Voyages* is this same use of nature as a laboratory. For Horace-Bénédict, the goal will be to discover the secrets of the Earth: what is the function of a mountain? For Nicolas, it was merely the productivity of a blade of grain that was at stake.

How to increase yields was his primary research question. Why only one seed out of twelve would grow to fruition was the great puzzle: "one must understand exactly what causes the twelfth grain to flourish and what explains the demise of the eleven others."[72] The question of yields would seem to have been answered already by the 1740s. The Dutch and the English, in the combination of practices that constituted the "second agricultural revolution,"[73] had brought yield ratios up from 3:1 or 5:1 to the modern ratio of 10:1 (meaning that for every seed sown, ten are reaped). The key innovation was the adoption of new crops—clover, alfalfa, and turnips—and the folding of them into the agricultural cycle. These crops would be sown on ordinarily fallow fields. Until then, one-half to one-third of arable land would lie fallow each year. Described another way, common practice would have it that a field would be planted with spring wheat one year and with oats a second year, and would be allowed to rest the third year. The resting year would ensure the fertility of the soil by not depleting it. It was known that planting the same crop year after year in the same ground resulted in poorer yields.

The new crops offered a cascade of benefits, one extraordinary result leading to another and another. First, the crops themselves increased the fertility of the soil by fixing the nitrogen in the soil. This happens because the bacteria, which grow on the roots, turn nitrogen into a usable form. This process feeds the plants themselves. It can also leak out to the surrounding soil to feed neighboring plants. If the crops are plowed over, the nitrogen will be released throughout the field. Fields grown with clover during that three-year cycle then would be more fertile than if they had been left fallow. Second, the crops could be fed to animals, and thus pigs and cows could be kept alive and healthy over the winter. Without sufficient fodder, most pigs would have to be slaughtered in the fall, and few cows could winter over. Fodder crops led to the greater availability of protein in the form of meat, milk, and cheese, and animal protein was no longer the prerogative of the elite. Finally, the manure collected over the winter from the stabled animals could be spread as fertilizer on all fields, massively increasing their fertility.

Nicolas had traveled to Great Britain in 1740 and was aware and appreciative of "English" methods of sowing "turnips, potatoes, peas, clover etc., which improve the soil better than by leaving fields fallow and which moreover allow for the feeding of livestock without having to maintain such large pastures which consume so much of our fertilizer."[74] In 1740 he had traveled to Britain. However, he was never very interested in turnips or potatoes. Because the science of plant growth was still largely empirical (Nicolas-Théodore de Saussure—Nicolas's grandson, "Théo"—would describe photosynthesis), other methods to increase productivity could be hazarded through trial and error.[75] The vineyards and fields of Les Conches were used for this purpose, and starting in the 1760s Nicolas began to submit reports to agricultural societies. In 1764 his "Lettre sur les avantages des Semailles hâtives et profondes" (Letter on the advantages of sowing seeds early and deeply) appeared in the *Mémoire de la Société Œconomique de Berne*. In his "Essai sur la cause des disettes de bleds" (Essay on the failure of wheat crops), he discussed sowing autumn seeds in August, showing "that the longer the growing season, the larger the harvest."[76] After Geneva had to import grain from the Mediterranean owing to a series of poor harvests in the early 1770s, Nicolas experimented with growing seeds from the types of grain used in Tunisia and Algeria. He also pondered the relative advantages of adding fertilizer or added labor to a field (that is, working the soil more), responding to a question posed by the Société royale d'agriculture d'Auch (Royal Agricultural Society of Auch [in the Pyrenees]): "Can frequent tilling of the soil supplement the use of fertilizers? Up to what point does tillage have an effect on vegetation and will tillage alone suffice for this, (the sprouting of seeds and the growth of the plants)?"

Nicolas's work earned him membership in agricultural societies in the 1770s and thus established his citizenship in the Republic of Letters, which had become enamored with the question of grain.[77] Voltaire quipped that after becoming "sated by verses, tragedies, comedies, operas, novels, histories," and the like, the French began to argue about grain.[78] In 1769 and 1770, Ferdinand Galiani and André Morellet—*philosophes* both—argued in print over the trade in grain and whether it should be governed by market forces. In 1774 Turgot's edict freeing the grain trade from government control triggered bread riots, and a strategic attack by Necker. His "Essai sur la législation et le commerce des grains" (1775), published in opposition to Turgot's policies, helped position Necker's rise in turn to minister of finance.[79]

For France and the French, the harvest was of obvious importance. Nicolas's interventions gained him little prestige at home, however. He was elected to the Société pour l'encouragement des Arts et de l'Agriculture de Genève (Society for the Encouragement of Agriculture and the Arts—arts in the sense of artisanship, techniques to improve watchmaking and other industries) in 1776. However, this was an institution founded by his son that year. Nicolas's work was also to the side of the central questions being asked of the natural world by his celebrated contemporaries Haller and Charles Bonnet (who was married to Nicolas's sister-in-law.) In their correspondence, Haller and Bonnet refer to Nicolas as "Notre Cultivateur" (Our Farmer) and "Triptolemus"—the Greek demigod who spread the art of agriculture.[80] These were affectionate nicknames, though in the context of the immense gap between Nicolas and themselves with respect to prestige in the world of science, they were also patronizing.

In a world where banking and commercial interests were strong, improvements in agriculture were other people's affairs. Geneva drew its grain from a wide local region and if necessary could purchase it from places far abroad, including Spain and North Africa.[81] To ensure its supplies in the case of war or crop failure, it had established a Chambre des Bleds in 1628. This grain warehouse banked it at low cost and released it on the market as needed to keep Genevans supplied with bread.[82] Nicolas's tinkering with improvements on his yields, even if successful, would be of marginal gain to Geneva. Les Conches was a marginal space in the business of Geneva, and Nicolas was marginalized in the family and political dramas that would ensue. (Perhaps, too, the scandals associated with Nicolas's nephew, Théodore Rilliet de Saussure, diminished Nicolas's stature. Rilliet was an atheist, for one thing, and a recidivist divorcé, for another. Moreover, he accused his second wife of incest—publicly, in the courts—in a transparent attempt to influence the divorce settlement in his favor. Obviously, his historians conclude, this Saussure, the son of Nicolas's sister, "refused to conform to ... behaviors ... expected from a member of the ruling elite.")[83]

It was Frontenex, not Les Conches, that mattered to the social standing of the Saussures. They moved to that estate when Horace-Bénédict was ten years old, and Nicolas had inherited it and Les Conches from his father. Though the basic structure was built between 1708 and 1711 and two wings were added in the 1730s,[84] the name suggests the antiquity of the landscape. It lay—as did Les Conches—about two miles from the city gates. It was closer to the lake, however—on its south shore—and one of a network of country homes that lined the shores both north and south and were used as summer retreats. Like these, Frontenex was divorced from the great spectacle of nature that surrounded it—the lake itself, the Jura Mountains, and the Alps. It was inward-looking, and its French-style garden, carefully shaped and maintained in geometrical forms, ground against the natural terrain.[85] As Henri de Saussure—Horace-Bénédict's grandson, the father of the linguist Ferdinand de Saussure—explained at a conference of Alpine Clubs held in Geneva in 1879: "'Fashion at that date preferred the picture formed by an artificial landscape ornamented with a geometrical frog-pond to the magnificent panorama of our Alps and our lake.'"[86] A sense of this cloistering can be gained today by visiting the house of Charles Bonnet at Genthod, the French gardens of which were planted as late as 1756,[87] or the Neckers' Chateau de Coppet, which seemed nestled away from the lake.

An apartment on the rue des Chaudronniers in Geneva linked the two spaces,[88] as country houses and city homes were linked for other families of the elite. Bonnet grew up in two houses, the family's summer house at Thônex and the city house on the Place du Molard, where the family spent the winter.[89] Mobility was a privilege and a mark of high status. We saw what happened to Rousseau in March 1728 when he was caught outside the gates as they closed at dusk. Even for important families such as the Samuel Constants, if they were of moderate or reduced means, the locking up of the city at dusk was a hardship. Rosalie Constant (1758–1834) lived with her grandmother at an estate called Saint Jean (now a neighborhood of Geneva) after the death of her mother, née Charlotte Pictet, in 1766. While Voltaire lived next door at Les Délices (1755–60), Saint Jean was an attractive place. Voltaire adored Charlotte and played Cupid in her engagement with Samuel Constant, dissolute rake that he was.[90] For Rosalie as a teenager, Saint Jean was isolating. With neither a family apartment in the city nor obliging friends (a presumed fault of her upbringing by her father), she was unable to participate in the *sociétés du dimanche* (Sunday circles) where young Genevans socialized. She would have been trapped in the city without a home, even if she had managed to enter before dark.[91] Boswell noted his regrets (Voltaire was less sad) about having to "hasten away after dinner" at Ferney on his visit to the *philosophe* in December 1764 because the gates of Geneva would close at five.[92] The streets of the city would be dangerously dark, in any case, so entering the city at night would be risky. Street lighting only developed slowly from midcentury, beginning with requirements that private houses illuminate their thresholds with lanterns.[93]

Mobility for the Saussure family meant that the father, Nicolas, could more easily fulfill his civic obligations, scattershot as they were. He was briefly a member of the Council of Two Hundred, with a position of *auditeur du droit*, serving under the *lieutenant de police*. This post had him working for the office investigating suspicious deaths, suicides, and the like.[94] He also served once on the Chambre des vins, which set taxes and other regulations, and in 1760 was a member of the Council of Sixty, which by that time was a nugatory position.[95] For Horace-Bénédict, it allowed travel back and forth to the Collège (at six years old) and then to the Academy of Geneva (from age fourteen), at which he first excelled and then taught.

Saussure's inauguration as professor at age twenty-two was an important civic event "on a par with the Escalade."[96] A letter to Haller from Saussure marveled at the event: "I had moreover the pleasure of seeing that the public shared my joy. . . . I do not really know why." Possibly, he surmised, the general enthusiasm in his favor that erupted in excitement at the Cathedral of St. Pierre was due to his youth.[97] For the mother, largely invalid, thus sessile, patrician money allowed her to receive visits from family and friends, and she enjoyed the stimulation offered by her son's activities and triumphs. For Judith de Saussure (1745–1809) it meant only that minimum of social excitement and intellectual options open to the younger sister of a treasured and successful male, whose ways upward and outward were all closed to her by law.

Saussure's childhood is sketched by Jean Senebier (1742–1809), a friend and colleague, in his *Mémoire historique sur la vie et les écrits de Horace Bénédict Desaussure* (Historical memoir on the life and the writings of Horace Bénédict Desaussure). (He is Desaussure, not de Saussure, since particles—"de"—as marks of noble status were suppressed in the Revolutionary era.) The biography was presented to the Société de physique et d'histoire naturelle (Society of Physics and Natural History) in 1800, the year after Saussure's death, and published soon afterward. Although today the memoir is read only by specialists (though it is essential reading for them), its audience of fellow naturalists and relatives at the Société de physique et d'histoire naturelle suggests that the characterization of Saussure's early life might not stray much from the truth, even allowing for the hagiographical structure of such eulogies. The Saussure who emerges from this text is supremely self-disciplined: "he allowed himself to go hunting only one day a week and entirely renounced the reading of novels, which had otherwise captivated him." "He would recall with pleasure [it is Senebier who seems self-satisfied] how every evening he would bring home to his mother books of this genre which he was tempted to devour himself, and how he would always give them to her unopened."[98] His mother, Renée, was Saussure's "best friend," Senebier claimed, who instilled the discipline in her son that would shape his work in the Alps. It was she who "hardened him against the pains of fatigue and the onslaughts of the weather," who "taught him to support without complaint the discomforts one cannot avoid, and to happily sacrifice pleasure for duty."[99] It was a masculine discipline that she encouraged, according to Senebier, in the belief that "effeminate upbringings weaken the moral forces needed to achieve great things" and produce instead "self-centered individuals [*des égoïstes*]" "who never outgrow the nursery [*qui désirent toujours des jouets d'enfants*]."[100]

Renée de la Rive (1715–1789), daughter of Horace-Bénédict de la Rive and Jeanne-Marie Franconis, was a Spartan mother, rewarding strength in her son while despising cowardice or softness. Life might be comfortable at Frontenex, but that comfort was an illusion of wealth. De la Rive wanted "to accustom Saussure at an early age to the privations that are a part of human life."[101] Beyond the clichés of the age—classical republican and Protestant—and the hyperbole, the passage suggests the strong pressure to achieve that was placed upon Saussure and his audience's approval of this approach. He was meant to do great things, and his mother meant for him to do great things.

Parental pressure was familiar to Senebier's audience at the Société de physique et d'histoire naturelle. High expectations were set within the terms of duty and delayed gratifications. These shaped the lives of several of the families represented. The Gosse family was one of them. Henri-Albert Gosse (1753–1816), pharmacist, botanist, and, along with Jacob Schweppe, a local inventor of "artificial" mineral water, relentlessly pushed his son Louis-André Gosse (1791–1873) to succeed.[102] René Sigrist, historian of the Société de physique et d'histoire naturelle, references four cartons of letters held by the University of Geneva Library between the father and the son, as Louis-André was encouraged, cajoled, and admonished to persevere in his studies of medicine in Paris. Nonetheless, he never became "a great scientist" (*un grand savant*).[103] (*Savant* has broadly the meaning of "scientist," a word that would not come into use until the nineteenth century.) Louis Jurine (1751–1819), another member, similarly leaned on his son André, who killed himself.[104] Nicolas-Théodore de Saussure (1767–1845), Horace-Bénédict's oldest son and assistant on later travels, accompanying him to the Col du Géant, would also have been present. A successful scientist (as we have noted), he was also known as a misanthrope. "We master early on the art of being tired of life," he is known for saying.[105] His funeral eulogy blamed his unhappiness on his upbringing: the "severity of his education probably explains his temperament, which was taciturn and even a bit misanthropic."[106] Théodore and his siblings were taught by their father when traveling together in France and Italy, and he oversaw their education at home. How stressful this could be for the entire family is suggested in the father's notebooks. While in the Auvergne in 1776, investigating the nature and origin of basalt, he complained that reading his children's daily journals—a task he set for himself—was liable to scramble his own observations. Here he is near Clermont-Ferrand, at the foot of extinct volcanoes, unnerved by his nine-year-old son's writing. "I have written this in a state of disorder," he noted in his journal, "because of Théo, who is finding grammar so hard to master." At Avignon, he was relieved at some progress.[107]

Not unique to the world of science, of course, this type of upbringing was something of a Genevan, or Swiss or Calvinist, specialty. Théodore Tronchin, Genevan physician to the Parisian elite, diagnosed the too-intense tutelage of her mother as the cause of the young Louise-Germaine Necker's mental breakdown in 1778, when she was twelve years old. A vacation from learning was prescribed. Her mother sighed with dismay at this failure. When later complimented on her daughter's success—Germaine de Staël became a leading intellectual of her age—Suzanne Necker could only say, "It is nothing, absolutely nothing next to what I wished to make of her."[108] When Haller was readying his son Rudolf Emanuel for an apprenticeship in Geneva with a firm of cloth merchants (a position secured for him by the Saussures), the father was happy not to be spoiling him. The son's wardrobe was reduced to the essentials and included only necessities: "Even if he were rich, he would want it so, for love of the child. The passions in general only grow as they are satisfied."[109]

That Saussure was the child of a demanding parent is thus not the presenting point of his upbringing, though its undercurrent is sensed. What one sees is the rhythm of escape and return that begins for Saussure in his youth, with his weekly climbs in the Jura, on the Salève, and in the Prealps. This yo-yo movement between home and away would structure his life. From the 1760s, his time away from Geneva in the peaks would be stretched from hours to days to weeks and even months every year. The mountains lured him away from the family home at Frontenex and the apartment on the rue des Chaudronniers, behind the cathedral. After his marriage they took him from the mansion on the rue de la Cité and the country estate at Genthod—from first his mother and her circle, and then, much more complicatedly, from his wife.

In the meantime, Saussure's involvement in his mother's body—noting, recording, monitoring and reporting fluids, temperature, and various pains—is a way to see the displacement of Nicolas in the family dynamic.

It was the son, not the father, whose responsibility this became. It was also the means by which Saussure came under the tutelage of Haller and the general mentorship of Bonnet. These two formidable men shepherded Saussure as he began his climb into the ranks of Genevan science, and not the least of the tensions that ensued was his need to please them.

The mother's health problems began after the birth of Horace-Bénédict, her first child. "My mother, previously very robust, has been in uncertain health since she gave birth to me."[110] She became "delicate" and would succumb to serious colds every winter.[111] By 1758 she was under the care of Dr. Tronchin and not improving much.[112] Meanwhile, in 1756, Charles Bonnet had married Saussure's aunt Jeanne-Marie de la Rive (1728–1796). Bonnet was already a well-known savant. His work on parthenogenesis in 1740 when he was only twenty years old had stunned Europe. (He had closely watched a single female aphid for more than a month, observing four successive generations of aphids being born without a father.")[113] Almost blind as a result of an illness in 1745, and partly deaf since birth, Bonnet continued to publish on the regeneration of animals and the reproduction of plants. His work on perception and how the mind-body organized its understanding of the world (he claimed a place for the "soul"), which he then began, would help Saussure formulate his experience of the Alps, if only by pushing back on some of the points.

Haller was then director of the salt works of the republic of Berne (from 1758 to 1764, at Roche) and among other things a physician of great importance as a practitioner, teacher, and researcher. He was one of Bonnet's most important correspondents from 1754 until Haller's death in 1777.[114] As one reads their close to one thousand letters, we see how intimate they became through this exchange, with only one or two major rifts (on the subjects of Buffon and of religion). In 1760 Haller could ask Bonnet to find out if the charity hospital of Geneva would take care of a pregnancy and subsequent illegitimate child from outside the city and how much that would cost. It was on behalf of "a friend," otherwise very respectable except for this one fault.[115] The editor of their correspondence suggests that the "friend" was Haller himself.[116] Bonnet's response hints at this also. He hastened to carry out this charge for Haller's friend, who was "already forgiven" by Bonnet "for his mistake."[117] The Saussure family was one of the minor themes of their correspondence. Bonnet arranged for the mother and son to meet with Haller at the other end of Lake Geneva near the salt works in Roche and hear his recommendations on her health. This was in 1758. The mother would then be taking the spa waters there in Bex.

Renée's progress was detailed in a series of letters from Saussure to Haller between October 1762 and May 1763. Twenty-five letters crossed between Geneva and Haller's chateau at Roche in those eight months that addressed Renée's symptoms and Haller's prescriptions in response. One of those letters, dated 7 April, was a comprehensive 4500-word medical history of Renée (a substantial twelve pages in manuscript) that included an explanation of the son's anxiety to secure Haller's aid:[118] "Such a balm it would be for me, if having with my birth been the cause of the loss of her health, I could also credit myself with having returned it to her, by engaging you to give her your advice."[119] He had caused the problems by being born, so he would fix them in return. Saussure's involvement in his mother's health had begun even before the initial engagement with Haller in 1758. It was Saussure, he said, who had visited Tronchin on his mother's behalf: "it was I who always did so."[120] This would have been begun in 1756, when Saussure was only fifteen years old (and Tronchin was honorary professor of medicine at the Academy of Geneva, which Saussure was attending).[121] "And she is sicker now than ever," he complained.[122] What was at stake for Saussure in his mother's recovery was relief from the guilt that her illness had placed upon him, and the responsibility he had taken—or was asked to assume—for its management. It was only her son Horace-Bénédict, as he explained to Haller, who was fully in her confidence with respect to her symptoms and its attendant anxieties.

Saussure insisted on this point in the medical history he presented. Only he knew that she spat blood from time to time while coughing. Tronchin was informed, but only he—no one else in the family, "not even my Uncle Bonnet"—knew anything about it.[123] Nicolas is not mentioned, and even if he is presumed to be in his wife's confidence—and not just one of the relatives such as her sister, Bonnet's wife, and others in their family circle who were excluded—it seems an odd omission. Saussure was asking that Haller not mention to anyone—including his friend Bonnet—that Renée was spitting blood (as inconsequentially as it will present to both her doctors, by the way) because of the danger an assumption of pulmonary disease (tuberculosis) in the family would hold for the prospects of his sister and himself.[124] Prospective spouses would hesitate; their families would be alarmed. It was for this reason—the fear that word would go around Geneva that Renée had something wrong with her lungs—that Saussure had written the medical history and that they had not had it prepared by a doctor, and that Saussure could stand as proxy.

Consulting by letter was not uncommon in the eighteenth century.[125] Some 1300 letters from patients to Samuel-Auguste Tissot (1728–1797) were sent to him in Lausanne from 1760 until he died.[126] Along with Tronchin, Tissot was one of the most fashionable and celebrated of doctors, advocating inoculation against smallpox (as would Odier of a later generation) and heathy diets and good exercise as the basis of health. He wrote a guide to the health of philosophes—*La Santé des gens de lettres*—and one for families.[127] His *L'Avis au peuple sur sa santé* (first ed. 1761) went through forty editions and many translations by the end of the century.[128] It was a medical self-help bestseller.[129] A contemporary British translation has the title *Advice to People in general, with respect to their health*.[130] We might call it *The People's Guide to Health* today. The *L'Avis au peuple* presumed the importance of consultation (1799 ed.) and included a set of instructions for so doing.[131] The formula required that information on family members be offered as context. The sick person was to be understood as one element in a collective, a family body that extended from the past through the present and into the future in a "temporal chain" of which the patient was only one link.[132]

What was offered about Renée's medical history follows suit and indicates some of the concerns of the family that reached beyond the crisis of the mother's health alone, so it is relevant here. Saussure began his account: "My mother had the misfortune to inherit from her parents, who had it from theirs, a rough and dry skin, which prevented transpiration [the release of waste products through the pores of the skin]. Consequently, my mother, her parents, and her brothers almost never perspire, and are subject to those maladies that one attributes to the *acreté du sang*, and to the lack of transpiration, for example, *dartres*."[133] The basic Galenic template for understanding bodily health can be seen in Saussure's presentation. Bodily fluids needed to be in balance. In the absence of perspiration, a toxic concentration of these fluids might ensue. Skin ailments were often associated with acidosis and its effects. Beyond these generalities was the fear of *dartres*.

Dartres is a type of eczema. Its appearance was especially alarming for women, though it was a concern for young males in the eighteenth century also. Marriage prospects would be weakened, and "social death" could ensue. "No surprise then to see the place *dartres* hold in the consultations," as reviewed in Tissot's archive.[134] "To save someone's looks and thus save them from reclusion and social death was the real reason for writing."[135] *Dartres* was an indication of bad health. Above all, it was disfiguring. A female disfigured—as was Mme. de Merteuil in *Les Liaisons dangereuses* by smallpox—was placed out of bounds. "'An ugly woman has no place in nature nor any position in the world,'" explained a novelist of the 1760s.[136] Even those of the highest rank could be "ruined," in contemporary terms, by their skin. One of the daughters of the Empress Maria Theresa caught smallpox in 1767: "she was left disfigured and unmarriageable."[137]

Money and position could mitigate some of the effects of *dartres*, but not always. Renée's sister had health issues, including possibly *dartres*,[138] and married at the age of twenty-eight; her husband, Charles Bonnet, was nearly blind and deaf. Gossipers would quip that Bonnet's interest in asexual reproduction was aligned with their infertility. However, from the correspondence with Haller we know of at least one miscarriage.[139] Saussure's sister, Judith, would be subject to *dartres* in her late twenties and early thirties and would fare quite differently. Haller was consulted in 1773 and 1774 on her condition and was asked not to speak of it to anyone, "since just hearing the word *dartres* seems to frighten some people."[140] Though Haller's prescriptions had some effect, that the attack on her face followed on the heels of a social disaster seemed to defeat her. She left Geneva—"that cold horrible gossipy place, as she would later describe it"[141]—for Montpellier, not to return except for the briefest of family visits until the French Revolution. Geneva had shut her out, closed its gates—first of all on account of the effect her pretty face had had at Voltaire's Ferney, and second on account of the social death that the *dartres* would confirm.

Asthma also ran in the family. Renée's grandfather and two of her brothers were afflicted. She was free from it until sometime after that first pregnancy, when she began to suffer attacks. These would occur especially, and most ferociously, with the "change of air" when moving back and forth between the country house and the city home.[142] It was for this reason that she now remained in the country, Saussure explained, resting there all year round, immobile, as it were. Most of Saussure's account of his mother's health reflected an intense observation of her bodily dysfunctions. This maneuver also followed the script for a consultation by letter. A table would be included detailing the atypical manifestations of the body with respect to temperature, color, pulse, and the like, and reporting on the quantity, appearance, and nature of her bodily expulsions such as stool, urine, sputum, and perspiration.[143]

Just how detailed these could be is revealed by documents in the Lullin archive in Geneva. Ami Lullin (1695–1756) was the grandfather of Saussure's wife, the heiress Albertine-Amélie Boissier (1745–1817). Ami was worried about the health of his oldest son, Jean-Antoine. His concerns were only too realistic: Jean-Antoine would die in 1745 at the age of nineteen. Tronchin, then in Amsterdam, and Tissot in Lausanne were both consulted as Jean-Antoine's health deteriorated.[144] Understanding—as one of the givens of the age—that a sign of consumption was the bitter taste of the diseased sputum, and wanting to avoid that diagnosis, the letter to Tronchin explained: "'The patient does not cough excessively. Occasionally, a little string of blood is present in the sputum. Never does the patient detect a bad taste in his mouth.'"[145] All the senses were placed on alert in the effort to grasp the nature of the malady. The color, smell, and consistency of his son's various excretions were recorded in a "Tableau de santé d'Antoine-Louis Lullin" (Table of health of Antoine-Louis Lullin). How many stools and what they looked like, the amount of urine and the degree of its clarity, the type of sputum, the frequency of coughs, the timing of fevers, the type of sweating, whether he was pale and to what degree—all these details were recorded daily in a table that was meant to reveal the nature of the illness—pernicious or passing—and the efficacy or lack thereof of the treatment. Each day the *remèdes*—his treatments and medicines—were also recorded, in the last of the table's eight columns.[146]

That Mme. de Saussure's menstrual bleeding, her perspiration, her sputum, and her urine were described, noted, and reported to Haller makes sense in this context. Saussure's letter to Haller of 15 October 1762 notes that "her last period arrived eight days early and was very heavy. That was six weeks ago. Since then, it has not come, and thus it is fifteen days late." He also reported a cold and a "fever that comes every day around three or four o'clock."[147] The letter of 19 March 1763 reported that his mother's period was again two weeks late, and that as soon as it was over with, "she spat blood, although only a little bit." She had anticipated this, Saussure continued, "since for a long time the same thing has happened under the same circumstances." Then, something revealing about her treatment, "she does not dare to take her 'emulsions,' however, while she has her period."[148] Each of Saussure's fifteen or so letters to Haller describes his mother's periods. Many mention the characteristics of her sputum, and some address her urine. A good many note the purgatives and *lavements* (enemas) she took to evacuate her bowels. The medical history letter of 7 April noted all of these, along with the quality of her perspiration.

So many and varied were the potions applied and consumed by Mme. de Saussure that it would be difficult to sort out what the initial complaint was and what might have been caused by the substances (metals, herbs, other flowers and plants, salts and waters and milks—donkey's and goat's) ingested by the patient. Tronchin himself blamed "des incisifs & des émollients" (the irritants and counter-irritants) she was taking for the blood that she spat in September 1760.[149] Tronchin's prescriptions seem relatively harmless. As Roger L. Williams has noted, "many vegetal remedies were merely harmless," and that was a boon. "The testimony of such physician-botanists as Villars, Candolle, Biria, and Roques argued convincingly that medicine at its best by the end of the eighteenth century was served by a highly imprecise knowledge of the virtues of plants."[150] Moreover, Tronchin appears to have been skeptical about her complaints. Exercise, moderate eating, and donkey's milk were suggested in response to her general malaise, these being Tronchin's typical recommendations to society women.[151] Saussure told Haller that he believed Tronchin's prescriptions were simply palliative, as the following potion ordered in January might imply: "Cachou 1 drachme, Fleur de pavot rouge 2 poignées; faites en une infusion de 10 onces & ajoutés y Syrop [sic] de Pavot rouge 1 once, Syrop de Guimauve 1½ once" (one dram of an extract from the wood of the catechu tree [Senegalia catechu] and two handfuls of red poppy flowers made into an infusion of ten ounces, to which are to be added one ounce of poppy syrup and one and a half ounces of syrup of marsh mallow).[152] This was a typical prescription of Tronchin's for Mme. Saussure, and a typical mixture of exotic and local plants. Quinine from the bark of the cinchona tree from the Andes was often offered for fever; rhubarb, star anise, and comfrey for other complaints.

Irregular periods, fleeting and intense fevers, premenstrual insomnia, and some leg cramps—all symptoms reported by Saussure on behalf of his mother—suggest the possibility that Mme. de Saussure was experiencing menopause. The consultations with Haller took place when she was between forty-three and forty-eight years old. Whatever else was wrong reached its peak in May 1763. So intense was Renée's distress that the family abandoned a plan to take her to Roche to be examined by Haller in person, and they once again called in Tronchin. Tronchin said she was suffering from gallstones, a diagnosis that Haller dismissed. He knew only too well the signs of gallstones, he said. Since she was seeing another doctor, he would no longer be involved in Mme. de Saussure's health—"release me," he demanded—though he would describe for Saussure the symptoms of that ailment and he could compare them himself with those of his mother. Of course they would not fit; she did not have those symptoms (Haller's voice here). Sufferers are more constipated, for one thing, and their excrements are lighter. Their stomach pains and headaches are more intense, and these acute attacks would come and go: "Fever is not associated with this disorder, nor is the spitting of blood, nor the other symptoms you describe and which are affecting the chest of Mad. de S." Moreover, her pain is not where the gallbladder lies, this last point seeming definitive, as it would be to us.[153]

The letters to Haller about Renée's health end in May 1763, and not much more is known about her health. Neither the existing set of letters between Saussure and his family during the Grand Tour of 1768–69 with his wife nor the few letters we have from Judith to home in the 1770s and '80s have the mother's health in view. Nor do the letters from Saussure to his wife from the Alps indicate any concern. Renée would live for another twenty-six years after the supposed gallstones, dying in 1789. The timing of her health crises in 1762–63 suggests something else was at play. Of course, panic about consumption—the little stream of blood in her sputum that would typically appear to Renée at end of her menstruation—seems very real. So is the desperation we hear in Saussure's pleas to Haller for help: by 20 April 1763 Saussure was evoking Haller as "nôtre unique refuge" (our only hope).[154] He was their last resort.[155] On 25 April he wrote to ask if Haller might evaluate his mother in person. She would go to him as soon as possible, "aware as she was that from one day to the next, her forces might diminish to the point of making it impossible for her ever to travel again."[156]

What unfolds along with this correspondence is the tension between Saussure's anxieties about his mother's health and his developing adult interests. One of Haller's last letters to Saussure on the subject of his mother's health—prescribing "plant juices" and "seltzered mineral water"—includes a postscript: "Have you forgotten entirely your good friends the plants?"[157] These were precisely the years when Saussure was moving away from his mother and into other circles. As Charles Victor de Bonstetten (1745–1832) would recollect (living in Geneva in 1763–66, later moving within the Coppet Circle of Germaine de Staël and Saussure's daughter), "At twenty-four de Saussure came out, so to speak, from the maternal lap to enter into the world."[158] In 1762 he received his professorship at the Academy. His first trip to Chamonix and the high peaks was undertaken in 1760, ostensibly to collect plants for Haller, a practice he had begun in 1758 in the Jura, the Salève, and the Prealps. By 1763 he was falling in love with Albertine, and by 1764 he was engaged, though secretly.

In the meantime, the observation of his mother's ailments offered a template for his study of the Earth and its atmosphere as a complex system of checks and balances. Tronchin's course in physiology, which he followed at the Academy of Geneva, would have provided the modified Galenic interpretation of bodily functions then in fashion, with Tronchin's focus on diet and exercise as the fundamentals of good health.[159] Inoculation against smallpox worked, and electricity—irritability—somehow might explain how organs such as the heart did their work. Basically, however, the body functioned as a system of humors, whose stability maintained good health and whose dysfunctions when measured carefully would provide clues to how the body—any body, the planet included—did its work.

Saussure was already thinking of the Alps as a system when he explained to Haller in the winter of 1764 why simply botanizing was not enough for him.[160] By 1767, on the eve of his first *tour* of the Mont Blanc massif—that is, the circling over and around the peaks and passes that encircle Mont Blanc, from the Chamonix Valley to Les Contamines to the Col du Bonhomme through the Lée Blanche to Courmayeur, then the Val Ferret and over to Martigny and back—he had prepared "a comprehensive program of observations to make in the fields of lithology, physics, and natural history."[161] The great project was to understand the history of the planet, and mountains, not plants, would open this up to him. His advice to Augustin-Pyramus de Candolle (1778–1841) in the mid-1790s to forsake botany for a more serious science fortunately fell on deaf ears, as his understanding of competition among plants helped pave the way for the theory of evolution.[162] As Candolle complained in his memoirs, "He seemed to place a value on drawing me into the sciences he loved, and turning me away from botany. Every time we met, he would assure me that the study of botany led to nothing [*ne promettait aucun succès*] and was not worth pursuing except as a form of recreation."[163] And admirers of Alexander von Humboldt, another independently wealthy scientist-explorer, would explain that Humboldt's observation of which types of plants grew at what elevations led to our understanding of ecosystems on a planetwide scale.[164] So the study of plants could have implications for understanding the Earth overall, though in ways that Saussure was not prepared to see.

Haller's project for which Saussure had been recruited was grand enough for its time but was mainly a matter of collecting and identifying. When Bonnet introduced Saussure to Haller in 1758 (when Saussure was eighteen and his mother so sick), Haller had begun the second of his two major works on Swiss plants. The first, the *Enumeratio Methodica stirpium Helvetiae indigenarum*, appeared in 1742 (and was used by Thomas Blaikie "with pleasure" in 1775 when collecting in the Alps for British patrons), and the second, the *Historia stirpium indigenarum Helvetiae inchoata*, in 1768. This was to be a description and identification of every distinct plant to be found in the Swiss region. Their collection would define the Swiss region in a way that we have seen articulated in his poem *The Alps*. Something Swiss there was about plants that were so healing—that were used so effectively as medicines—and that grew so tenaciously on mountain slopes. *Les citoyennes*, Haller coyly called them.[165] The *Historia stirpium* was an expression of nascent nationalism or patriotism, enclosing within the covers of the book a botanical expression of the Swiss state.[166]

Saussure was one of over a hundred contributors to the *Historia stirpium*:[167] "'most of the naturalists of Switzerland [were employed by Haller] to scour the various nooks and crannies of the Alps to find new plants,'"[168] and it was obviously an honor for the young Saussure to be counted among them. Suggested to Haller in 1758 by Bonnet, who was encouraging his interest in natural history, Haller asked Saussure to search for unusual plants. A catalog of desired specimens was eventually supplied. Despite the optimism of these mentors, reports to Haller are a litany of disappointments. Saussure's first letter to Haller in July 1760 sets the tone: "On Wednesday evening I botanized along the banks of the Arve rather far upriver. I saw nothing there that appeared at all uncommon to me."[169] He adds in a footnote, "On Sunday I went to the Voirons [a set of peaks in the Chablais Alps], but I did not find much of anything there."[170] Two weeks or so later, he claims not to be discouraged, "hoping that under the auspices of the Immortal Monsieur de Haller the desire to succeed will fill in for my lack of ability."[171] Though ashamed of his lack of success, he says, he does believe that he has been doing everything possible to find the desired plants.[172] Hum, Haller seems to say in reply. He has had some very good news from some other collectors—a team from Mendrisio (in southern, Italian-speaking Switzerland) "has found several new citizens [*plusieurs citoyennes nouvelles*]"—but he also says that others sent to the St. Bernard Pass "have returned—incomprehensibly—without finding anything except one Italian plant, the *hesperis siliquis strictissimis*" (a garden variety of which is dame's rocket).[173]

Was Saussure really trying? Was he focused on plants? Bonnet tried to reassure Haller: "No mountain will be too high nor any cliffs too steep to limit the passion that my nephew has for being useful to you and for contributing to your works on botany."[174] Bonnet spoke after some further dashed expectations of that summer of 1760. Saussure was to go to Chamonix, his first visit to the high peaks. Haller was newly hopeful: "I am convinced that you will find some very beautiful plants there."[175] Apologetic again, Saussure wrote to report: "I am in despair over having acquitted myself so poorly with respect to the commissions you have honored me with. I have had the misfortune, Monsieur, of having not been able to find any of the plants that you want."[176] The same letter offered Haller a flower from the family's garden at Frontenex, an Erythronium (presumably *Erythronium dens-canis*, or dogtooth violet) that Saussure had transplanted from a wooded spot near the confluence of the Arve and the Rhône. Perhaps Haller would like that one, next spring, when it bloomed again?[177]

As Haller wrote in reply, "It is very unfortunate that, given your keenness [*le Zele et l'ardeur*] for botany, nature compensates you so poorly. I understand nothing of this."[178] Pondering further, Haller wrote to Saussure with advice on how to notice the plants that would be growing along his way: "I fear that, enthusiastic as you are, you are walking a little too quickly on your excursions. You need to go as slowly as possible, and above all, when on the alps [the mountain meadows], you need to sit down from time to time, even lie down, to be able to distinguish one small plant from another.... A league covered thus, slowly, is worth more than two at some speed."[179]

Slow down, sit down, lie down, and look down. This was exactly not how Saussure was proceeding in the Jura, the Voirins, on the Salève, and finally—in 1760—at Chamonix. He was looking up at the high peaks, scrambling up the Dôle, the Môle, and the Brévent, trying to seize the shape and fundamentals of the mountain chain. He was imagining what being at the summit of the highest peak, Mont Blanc, would allow him to see about the organization—the layering, the leaning, the clustering, thus the historical sequencing—of mountain chains in general. Nevertheless, he continued to botanize for Haller and slowly improved, despite continuing gaffes. Here he is in 1761, hopeful about a nasturtium: "I have not seen anything rare except for that [a different plant] and one or two *Nasturtium*." They did not look precisely the way they should, if they were the rare ones desired by Haller, but except that they were different, they were exactly the same.[180] Haller was brusque, made irritable by gout: "The nasturtium is rather common."[181]

Botany had many enthusiasts in the eighteenth century. States were involved, as the practice of identifying and collecting plants went along with European expansion.[182] Private individuals joined the hunt in ways that could have offered models for Saussure's ambition. Michel Adanson (1727–1806) accompanied the French Compagnie des Indes in 1748 to West Africa, collecting and identifying plants throughout Senegal for the next five years. As he noted in 1763: "'Very few botanists have traveled at their own expense, prompted by zeal alone.'"[183] On his return he published a first volume of a *Histoire naturelle du Sénégal*, prefaced by an account of his travels, *Voyage au Sénégal* (1757). (In Saussure's library when cataloged in the 1790s.)[184] He was made a member of the Academy of Sciences and the Royal Society. His career ran aground after 1769 (mostly on account of his own eccentricities).[185] Joseph Banks, for another instance, used funds from his own immense fortune to outfit himself as the *Endeavour*'s official botanist. Accounts of his adventures and the collections acquired while accompanying James Cook on his first voyage to the South Pacific (1768–1771) secured Banks's' reputation. As president of the Royal Society from 1778 to 1820, he became one of the most influential savants of the long eighteenth century.[186] Plant collection remained important throughout Banks's tenure. London's Kew Gardens, which he directed, and the Jardin du Roi (from 1793, the Jardin des Plantes at the Muséum d'Histoire Naturelle) in Paris were the institutions via which a great many plants from around the world were assimilated. These included flowers such as chrysanthemums from China and hydrangea from

Japan. The hydrangea one sees in Paris today are related to those planted by Banks at Kew in 1789 and imported by André Thouin (1727–1806), gardener of the Jardin des Plantes, just as today's dahlias are relatives of the ones Thouin brought from Spain in 1789.[187] (The first female ginkgo tree in Europe was planted in a garden park just outside Geneva in Bourdigny, a specimen Blaikie and presumably Saussure as well would have seen and smelled.)[188]

The botanical gardens of Europe, one recalls, originated as places where simples—plant-based remedies—could be harbored, and this mission was still vital in the eighteenth century.[189] The instructions given to the savants accompanying La Pérouse on the doomed exploration of the Pacific (1785) included a typical recommendation to look for new medicinal plants, such as those deployed by Mme. de Saussure's doctors to treat her illnesses: "Take care to collect those remedies, whether internal or external, that are claimed to be specifics for diseases by different peoples. Describe the nature of such specifics, the way they are prepared, the way they are used, the doses, their effects, and at what point in the illness they are employed. This is the way the Peruvians taught us to understand the properties of quinine."[190]

How to classify plants stimulated debate that at its root was about how the natural world should be understood in relation to the human. Was the simple though "artificial" system of Linnaeus based on sexual characteristics—the number and position of stamens and pistils—really superior to other systems that allowed indigenous and folkloric names, or that placed the plant in the context of its environment, swamp or desert, to offer a set of extremes? Should not the whole plant be observed, its fruits and seeds (as Adanson attempted to do in his *Familles des plantes* of 1763, and Haller did more successfully in his *Historia Stirpium* of 1768).[191] These were questions of potential interest to Saussure and some of the most richly interesting of modern questions, as environmentalists today reconceive agriculture to fit within local sources of water and fertilizers, and native plants are valued over exotics, at least in private gardens.[192]

Moreover, botany engaged a large number of amateurs, male and female, Saussure's mother included, who collected plants in her garden. Rousseau's *Lettres élémentaires sur la botanique, à Madame de L**** were directed toward this audience. These were written in 1771–74 to Madeleine-Catherine Delessert, née Boy de la Tour, as instructions for teaching botany to her children ("convinced as I am that at any age the study of nature dulls the taste for frivolous amusements [and] forestalls the tumult of the passions").[193] Rosalie Constant was inspired by Rousseau, and though some collectors argued for the importance of dried plants, began her *her-*

bier peint in the 1790s. This is a beautiful collection of highly detailed illustrations of plants collected by her and for her over the course of forty years.[194] The illustrations of flowers from the Jura Mountains in the following chapter are drawn from this valuable source. Mary Delany's (1700–1788) decoupage plants are equally stunning.[195] Botany was scientific, aesthetic, and, with the publication of *Les Rêveries du promeneur solitaire*, romantic. The "Septième promenade" argued against the practice of collecting plants for medicine. Botanizing for a purpose beyond the contemplation of beauty and the experience of the sublime was an act of alienation. It brought the country into the city, nature into culture, and it corrupted. It was a "denaturing," an alteration, akin to that sustained by plants "transplanted from their native surroundings into the gardens of collectors." They "degenerated."[196]

In order to develop the field of geology, Saussure had to evade his mentors' pressure and his culture's inclinations—romantic, scientific, and aesthetic—to become a botanist. Haller and Bonnet enabled his appointment as professor of philosophy at the Academy in 1762. Encouraged by Bonnet, Saussure had written a paper based on a microscopic analysis of the leaves and petals of plants, *Observations sur l'écorce des feuilles et des pétales de plantes* (Observations on the epidermis of leaves and petals). Haller was responsible for its publication and allowed Saussure to have printed a letter of approbation from him to Saussure about the essay as a preface (in the form of a reply to Saussure's note accompanying the envoy of the manuscript to Haller). It was engineered by Saussure with the backing of "important people who wish me well." If you would only write this letter, my appointment would be assured, wrote Saussure in so many words, soliciting Haller's support. The essay alone might be too slight to convince or too easily ignored by the judges who would determine the appointment in philosophy. And his competitors—his two "Antagonists"—were both ministers, and more senior. Only one thing could spare Saussure a defeat: "That, Monsieur, is a word of praise from you. You are held in such high esteem and are so honored here, and the Ministers [of the Church], my judges, respect you so much as a great *philosophe* and as a Christian *philosophe*, that my little work would be assured of its success if it has the good fortune to appear under your protection."[197]

Saussure had to say one thing—that he wanted to study plants—and do another as he began his work on the study of the Earth in those years in which his career at the Academy was being launched and his mother's health demanded Haller's care. Bonnet's interest in the physiology of plants and Haller's in collecting and taxonomy weighed in favor of botany,[198] as would the drift in European culture toward Romanticism, with

the Swiss Alps as a focus. A gentleman-savant—a patrician with Francophile ties—could have easily combined leadership of the Genevan city-state with the study of plants, as had Saussure's father, to a degree. Finding a way under and beyond the "the adornment and clothing of the Earth" (*la parure et le vêtement de la terre*), which is how Rousseau described "the trees, shrubs and plants" that covered the globe,[199] meant slipping through unseen gates in the walls of Geneva, to the high peaks beyond. This was a less dramatic escape than Rousseau's through the gate of Cornavin in the spring of 1728, though one with equally important implications for the modern experience of nature.

To the mountains then, to the Jura and the Salève, out and over the tight walls and flattened enceinte of patrician Geneva, where the boldness of Saussure's embrace of a sensual, living Earth—a sensorium—comes into view.

✹ 2 ✹
The Jura Mountains

The Jura Mountains stretch for more than two hundred miles along Switzerland's border with France, rising northeast like a bent fly line cast above Lake Geneva and dropping north of Neuchâtel. Limestone based and heavily forested, the Jura are a softer version of the Prealps, the Alps, and the sentinel high peaks that successively rise from the opposite banks of the lake in increasingly indistinct waves. The Jura and the limestone-layered Mont-Salève, which crops up almost at the southern outskirts of Geneva, were where Saussure first began to feel out a relationship to nature that would shape both geology and alpinism *avant la lettre*.[1] They were where he would first become intimate with the Earth, as one body to another, the human being exploring the living Earth, in a novel and unprecedented fashion.

His passion for the mountains may have begun with hunting. Jean Senebier, the eulogist and friend we have already met, suggested as much in his comments on Saussure's self-discipline. (As a student he went hunting only once a week, a sacrifice he made in order to leave time for his studies.)[2] Hunting must have been simply an excuse for wandering beyond the bounds of the city, however. Firearms formed a part of his training as a citizen-gentleman, and the Jura would have offered *chevreuil* (roe deer) on the wooded slopes and chamois on its peaks. Nonetheless, nowhere in the *Voyages* do we read of Saussure shooting these animals for sport, though he did once shoot birds to stuff and mount for his *cabinet* near the Chartreuse du Reposoir in the vicinity of the Arve, frightening the monks, who feared bandits.[3] Even on the Salève in July 1761 in the aftermath of a double murder, his servants, not he, carried the arms.[4]

What the Jura had in abundance was flowers. The sensual appeal of the plants to be found in those mountains are delectably evoked in the *Voyages*. We read of the cottony white of the edelweiss, the golden rays of the ragwort, the lilylike scent of the *œillet des Alpes* (which is a type of dianthus or pink), and the delicious vanilla fragrance of a black orchid, "le *Satyrium nigrum*," or black gymnadenia.[5] A "pretty *Androsace villosa*," a species of rock jasmine, could be found on the Dôle, a peak of 1677 meters lying north and east of the city often climbed by Saussure and central to his first intimations about the structure of the Alps. This hardy little plant had "milky white flowers" with starlike centers "which are first green, then yellow, and finally a rosy pink." The Dôle "well merits its reputation among the botanists," noted Saussure, or, in the words of the Scottish plant collector Thomas Blaikie, with some unconventional spelling, "is reconed one of the richest in plants in this country."[6] It harbored also the *Buplevrum longifolium*—an orchid of "polished bronze"—and the *Aster alpinus*, presumably with the pink and purple flowers one finds today. Other plants could be found nearby, including a blue-sow-thistle and two varieties of *Dentaria* (or *Cardamine*): the *Dentaria pentaphyllos*, or showy toothwort, and a *Dentaria heptaphyllos*. These, says Saussure, could be rooted in home gardens, where they would blossom forth in early spring.[7]

Another dozen or so noteworthies nested along the even higher slopes of Le Reculet (1718 meters), situated about ten miles north and west of Geneva. These included the *Ranunculous thora*, a type of buttercup, and its "supposed antidote, the *Aconitum anthora*" or healing wolfsbane, meant for cows who had unwittingly indulged in the attractive yellow flowers of the former.[8] Figures 2.1 and 2.2, which show the *Ranunculous thora* and the *Aconitum anthora*, are by Rosalie Constant, a family friend of the Saussure's, as we have seen. She collected these rare plants from the same slopes in the Jura as did Saussure, as her accompanying notes detail.

Saussure would gather plants such as these for Haller's catalog of Swiss flora, sending them to him in Bern or to La Roche by courier or coach, dried and pressed or packed in moss. He would also plant them in the family's gardens at Frontenex and, after his marriage, on the grounds of the townhouse on the rue de la Cité and the country estate at Genthod. Flower gardens such as these flourished in the second half of the eighteenth century, with rare and "exotic" plants in demand.[9] The exotics could be camellias from Asia, or African geraniums, or aloes, which Haller counseled Saussure to maintain at 10 degrees Réaumur (12.5 degrees C; 54.5 degrees F) in a greenhouse over the winter.[10] Or they could be captures from outside one's region—"noncitizens," to use Haller's terminology. (A newly discovered plant by one of Haller's collectors was hailed always as a "nouvelle citoyenne."[11]) An arnica, a plant in the sunflower family, that Saussure had collected and planted in his garden was identified by Haller as a *Senecio* (maybe a ragwort), from the daisy family—in any case, a rare plant, no. 957, in Haller's *Enumeratio stirpium quae in Helvetia*

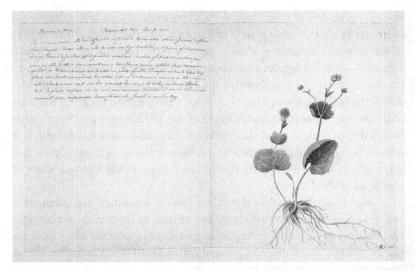

FIGURE 2.1 *Ranunculos thora*, by Rosalie de Constant. Plate 31 of *L'Herbier peint de Rosalie de Constant* (Muséum cantonal des sciences naturelles, Lausanne). Photo and permission: Muséum cantonal des sciences naturelles, Lausanne.

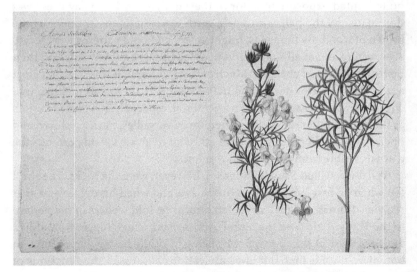

FIGURE 2.2 *Aconit salutifère* (*Aconitum anthora*) by Rosalie de Constant. Plate 41 of *L'Herbier peint de Rosalie de Constant* (Muséum cantonal des sciences naturelles, Lausanne). Photo and permission: Muséum cantonal des sciences naturelles, Lausanne.

rariores proveniunt of 1760.[12] Speaking of his mother's garden at Frontenex in a letter to an Italian botanist in spring 1761, we catch the slight arrogance of the youthful Saussure—already certain of the superiority of the Earth sciences—making light of an occupation to which the head of the Botanical Gardens at Turin was devoting his life: "I enjoy cultivating a small garden filled with the very rarest plants that I have myself found in the Alps and other mountains, and with a collection, already very pretty, of exotic plants drawn from various other places."[13] We also sense his delight. It is easy to imagine the color, scents, and even textures of these alpine and other plants after reading descriptions of flowers in the *Voyages*, some of which we offered above.

These tapestries of colors in gardens like the Saussures' complemented the newly floral and colorful interiors of well-to-do homes in the eighteenth century. Joan DeJean speaks in terms of a revolution when describing the effect that printed and painted cotton cloth—the *indiennes* whose importance for Geneva we have already seen—had not only on dress but also on interior decoration: "It was one of the biggest revolutions in color and pattern of all time. . . . In the 1660s and 1670s, both dress and décor were overwhelmingly monochromatic, and even elite consumers had a quite limited exposure to color in their daily lives. Everyday dress was dominated by the beiges and pale earth tones of linen; interiors by the brown of wood. By the 1770s, bright colors and bold patterns were found everywhere and at all times—on people's backs, on their beds and their tables, and on their chairs."[14] Much of this was floral; it was "the first great age of floral interior decoration in the West."[15] Curtains were floral, wall coverings were floral, and chairs were floral, especially in bedrooms, such as the bedchamber of Madame Victoire at Versailles, newly restored and open to the public since 2013. There the riot of flowers inside extends the gardens visible from the chateau windows.[16]

What electrified Saussure's senses, however, were the rocks. The thrill felt when he first laid hands on the Salève, and when his eyes swept over the view from its heights, never left him, as he told readers in the preface to the *Voyages*. He used the term *le saisissement*, which suggests a sudden, violent, physical shock to his very being.[17] While he would continue to botanize, and his first and last publications addressed the functions of plants—the first was a study of their epidermis, the last of the movement of their sap—it was the mountains that moved him, from his young adulthood on.[18]

This chapter follows Saussure into the Jura Mountains on walks that began in his youth. The contrast with how his Genevan peers—as well-educated, privileged, and scientifically minded as himself—engaged with the natural world demonstrates how those climbs took him not just to the Dôle and the Reculet and other high points overlooking the lake, but to unprecedented intellectual terrain. These were paths for which the Genevan Academy had left him unprepared—unsurprisingly, since so very little was known about the Earth sciences even in the late 1750s, as something else this chapter makes clear. Buffon, imagining the birth of the Earth, and Haller, forwarding the study of anatomy—implacable foes though they were—inspired Saussure as he pledged from the top of the Dôle to correct this ignorance. He would understand the structure of the Earth and its development. The future of his life was set. He would write the history of the Alps—in his words, he would become the "historian of the Alps."

How unusual it was that Saussure found his vocation in what would become the Earth sciences can be seen by comparing his interest in nature with the absorptions of his friends, especially François Jallabert (1740–1798; his name also appears as "Jalabert")[19] and Jean-Louis Pictet (1739–1781). These were his two walking companions in the Jura. They were schoolmates—intimates, he calls them in the *Voyages*—with whom he had been close since childhood, and who would join him in 1767 on the first *tour du Mont Blanc*.[20] This is that circuit of the massif which has become Europe's best-known *grande randonnée*, with more than ten thousand hikers each year "following in the footsteps of Saussure."[21] François was the son of Jean Jallabert, whose unique success in using electricity to bring paralyzed muscle back to life in 1747 brought him acclaim in Paris and London,[22] and a nod to immortality in Shelley's *Frankenstein*. Jean's "therapeutic" healing" of a M. Nogues "consisted in drawing sparks from [his] paralyzed arm for 2 hours in the morning and 2–3 hours in the afternoon, for a month and a half," and in "subject[ing him] to electric shocks at least four or five times a day."[23] François himself was "electrified" along with Pictet and Saussure as they climbed the Brévent in 1767, a drama that stimulated Saussure's interest in lightning rods and in meeting Benjamin Franklin, which he would in London two years later. Touched by an electrified cloud, sparks flew from the bits of metal on Jallabert's hat and Saussure's walking stick, and even from the tips of their fingers, they surmised, from the shocks felt, and the crackling sound that they heard as they each waved their digits in the air.[24] As Bonnet noted to Haller: "Our great *Alpinier* . . . was almost *beatified*: you divine that I refer to his *electrification* from storm-clouds" (Bonnet's emphasis).[25]

What Jallabert preferred was to draw the world around him, transcribing what he saw in the mountains with pen and paper. This was an exercise similar to what Rousseau was doing in *La Nouvelle Héloïse* (1761), drafting his novel of the Alps in the same years—1756–58—when Saussure,

Jallabert, and Pictet were roaming the Jura,[26] and mountains were entering into "the sensibility and culture of the age."[27] Jallabert's illustrations from that first *tour du Mont Blanc* in 1767 "sweep the valley" of Chamonix. They show the glaciers almost touching the town, and the high peaks, the sky.[28] These capture the romantic themes of depth, and breadth, and individual awe, in the familiar medium of art. Though effective, they coast along known cultural currents, unlike the one's that Saussure will catch.

Pictet was already looking up to the stars—above the Earth and its plants and peaks and other "ornaments" (*la parure*) in Rousseau's image of earthly beauty, which were the focus of Romantic attention.[29] In 1768 this friend of Saussure would travel from Geneva to Russia with Jacques-André Mallet (1740–1790) to observe the transit of Venus. They were two of some 150 observers funded by European states to time the transit in June 1769 from scattered locations throughout the globe. The goal was to determine the distance of the Earth from Venus, and thus to establish the distance of the Earth from the sun. Mallet was another school friend of Pictet, Jallabert, and Saussure. He graduated from the Academy in 1755, just one year later than did they. Mallet would go on to establish Geneva's first observatory—mostly with his own funds—on the bastion Saint-Antoine, near the cathedral and the highest, most central part of the city, building upon, as it were, the renown of the Russian adventure. He had come under the patronage of Joseph-Jérome (Lefrançois de) Lalande (1732–1807), the eminent French astronomer, on a learning tour of Europe that had brought him to Paris in 1765. He was also attached to the celebrated Daniel Bernoulli (1700–1782)—like Haller, an influential polymath—through his nephew Johann III Bernouilli (1744–1807), the precocious director of the Berlin Observatory, being only twenty-three years old at the time.[30] Lalande and the senior Bernouilli recommended Mallet to the Russian Academy of Science, and Mallet in turn brought along Pictet.[31]

Theirs was a quest initiated by Copernicus in the sixteenth century. The planets revolved around the sun, and in orbits that placed them at distances from and in relation to one another. Kepler's third law of planetary motion later described these proportions with precision. However, still to be figured was the distance between the Earth and the sun. Astronomers such as Jean-Dominique Cassini (1625–1712), the first director of the Paris Observatory, knew that if "the true width of a single interplanetary gap" could be determined,[32] then all the gaps could be measured, and the astronomical unit, the distance from the Earth to the sun, could be known. Cassini tried to work out the distance of Mars from the Earth. Edmond Halley (1656–1742) then proposed Venus. Venus would transit the sun on two occasions in the eighteenth century, in 1761 and 1769. If viewers from two faraway—but known—locations could time the transit at four established moments, then its parallax could be established. With the parallax established, trigonometry would yield the distance from the Earth to Venus, and extrapolation would give the sought-after unit. The size of the solar system could be known.

As was the case with Cook's first voyage to the Pacific, with Joseph Banks in tow to observe Venus from Tahiti, the adventure itself—the European encounter with the far reaches of the planet—was more satisfying than the results from the telescopes. Pictet's vantage point was marred by rain, Mallet's by clouds, while the observations from Tahiti were imperfectly timed. Pictet may have been considering publishing his journal, as other savant-explorers would, including Banks.[33] It certainly was discussed at home. The manuscript shows revisions, with notes offering comments on Russian mores and on the uniforms, training, and discipline of the Russian army.[34] The Kola Peninsula in Murmansk, above the Arctic Circle, where Pictet and Mallet found their stations, was "very little known" even to Russians themselves,[35] and there was general interest in the "unknown." Saussure welcomed specimens of birds sent back by Pictet, and Haller received plants.[36] The Arctic in general was "mysterious" and exotic,[37] as were the islands of the Pacific and the coasts of Australia, the regions explored not just by Cook in his three voyages, but also by Louis-Antoine de Bougainville (1729–1811) on his voyage around the world between 1766 and 1769, and by Jean-François de Galaup, comte de La Pérouse (1741–1788?) on his ill-fated, incomplete circumnavigation, launched in 1785. After writing to Paris in February 1788 describing their intended itinerary home, the ships of La Pérouse—*La Boussole* and *L'Astrolabe*—left Botany Bay, and "were never seen [by Europeans] again."[38] They had dropped off the face of the Earth, the vessels wrecked on reefs off the island of Vanikoro (Santa Cruz Islands) and the crew missing.[39]

Impressive as they appear, Pictet's adventures—like Jallabert's paintings and the exploits of other explorer-savants—followed convention. Unlike Saussure's exploration of the Alps, the trek from Geneva to Berlin to St. Petersburg, and northward to the Barents Sea, was state-funded. Catherine the Great paid the bills, and the expedition was supported by the Russian Academy of Science. The project formed part of a large collective endeavor. It was a signature of European science to launch these expeditions in the eighteenth century: they were the "'big science'" of their age, as Kapil Raj has explained.[40] The French Academy of Science already had sent Pierre Louis Moreau de Maupertuis (1698–1759) to Lapland, and Charles-Marie de La Condamine (1701–1774), his friend, as a member of another team, to the equator in Peru.[41] Each was to measure an arc of the meridian. The objective was to determine the truth of Newton's proposition that the Earth was oblate, that is, flattened at the poles. Maupertuis, sent in 1736, returned promptly, to fame. La Condamine, after heroics measuring at the equator in Quito, Ecuador (then Peru), spent ten years wandering home via the Amazon and establishing the exploration of that river system as one of the lunatic tropes of European exploration. (Werner Herzog played to this theme in his 1972 film, *Aguirre, the Wrath of God*.)[42] Like Alexander von Humboldt (1769–1859) after him, wandering the Orinoco on his Latin American travels, La Condamine returned with observations, measurements, and discoveries—about rubber and quinine, for example—that remain the practical achievements of these far-flung adventures.

Saussure's mostly solo, and always self-funded, expeditions were something else entirely. They offered a model for Humboldt, whose immense inherited wealth funded his travels to the Americas and who wanted to follow in his tracks. In 1795 he did so directly, visiting Chamonix and the peaks with a copy of Saussure "in hand." This could have been Saussure's brief account of his summiting of Mont Blanc in 1787, which was published in the *Journal de Genève* almost immediately, and in later separate editions.[43] Humboldt could also have been referencing the first two volumes of the *Voyages*, since they contain descriptions of Chamonix, the glaciers, and the peaks in a long section entitled "Tour Mont Blanc/*Voyage autour du Mont-Blanc*." The first volume was published in 1779 and the second in 1786. These hefty books would have been difficult to carry along, even metaphorically. In any case, "the masterpiece of M. de S. in hand," he reported to Marc-Auguste Pictet (1752–1825) in Geneva, "we have traversed these classic lands" unable to judge, he claimed, what was the more marvelous, the nature they passed through or the "genius of the great man" who described its wonders with "an exactness above all praise.'"[44] Tamping down a bit on that florid style so much at odds with the prose of the *Voyages*, Humboldt again wrote to his correspondent, a close friend of Saussure, in 1798, on the eve of Humboldt's own great adventures: "'Tell the venerable Saussure that I have reread this winter, word for word, *all* his works, and that I have made a note of all the experiments that he wants to have done. Such a pleasure to follow in the footsteps of a great man [*J'aime à marcher sur les traces d'un grand homme*]" (Humboldt's emphasis).[45]

By 1798, when Humboldt was sharing his plans with Pictet, Saussure's works included the final two volumes of the *Voyages* and notably the *Agenda ou tableau général des observations et des recherches dont les résultats doivent servir de base à la théorie de la terre* (Agenda or general table of observations and research necessary for establishing a theory of the Earth). Contemporary "theories of the Earth" sought to establish general principles for understanding the history and systems of the planet, on a par with Newton's achievement in explaining celestial mechanics.[46] That was the great prize. Saussure's *Agenda* included his recommendation to observe at what elevation plants cease to grow. Humboldt took that advice along with him to South America; the result was his *Essai sur la géographie des plantes* (Essay on the geography of plants), the Chimborazo Map, and credit for establishing the field of biogeography.[47]

Humboldt's exploration of Latin America was state sponsored, however, in the usual way. It was authorized by the Spanish monarchy, and moreover he was accompanied by another savant. This was the long-suffering French botanist Aimé Bonpland, who, in the accounts of their travels, appears bewildered and bullied. An indictment of charisma, perhaps, or of the romantic hero, Humboldt's exploits differ in this way too from Saussure's, whose work with Genevan artisans and alpine peasants would lead him to support the democratic revolution of 1792 in Geneva. These themes unfold later on in this story of Saussure. They are noted here, in passing, simply as a de rigueur corrective for Humboldt's dazzle, and perhaps as a transparent demonstration of the author's partiality for the more humble Saussure. (Maren Meinhardt offers a beguiling portrait of Humboldt in *A Longing for Wide and Unknown Things: The Life of Alexander von Humboldt*, and this reader is warming to him. Meinhardt says that Humboldt "seems to have been incapable of discerning the point of deep water if he wasn't, sooner or later, going to step right into it."[48] Readers of this life of Saussure will see that Saussure seems to have been unable to see deep water without taking its temperature, several times, with various thermometers. Still, though Saussure's courage was quiet, it was very real, as I hope readers will see.)

The project of Pictet and Mallet, a scientific measuring of the solar system, drew on centuries of human views of the sky, and the mathematics used to measure the transit of Venus was based on a geometric understanding of the universe well established by 1769. As a part of natural history, and understood as such in the eighteenth century,[49] describing, classifying, and *mapping* the stars is nonetheless one of the oldest of human endeavors. Mapping the mountains tells a different story.[50] No map was on hand for becoming a "naturalist of the mountains," which is how Saussure would describe himself.[51] In the late 1750s, when he was roaming the Jura with friends, even topographical and geographical maps had yet to appear. Cassini maps, the only reliable maps for the territory of France, and a model for the mapping of Europe, would not begin to appear for the Jura region until the 1760s.[52] Later, in 1779, in the first volume of the *Voyages*, Saussure could recommend to his readers that they review the Giovanni Maraldi and Jacques Cassini maps numbered 117, 148, 147, 146, and 145, which covered the Jura, and note how the range was oriented from south-southwest to north-northeast.[53] These gave a bird's-eye view of the region, a perspective lost to Saussure and his friends as he and they found their way to the Dôle and up its slopes. From Geneva, the Jura mountains overall appeared as "a long bluish wall, its monotony only broken by a few gaps and some not very impressive heights."[54] In no way was the region mysterious or a patchwork of villages and trails along and above a river valley, as were the Alps on both the French- and Italian-speaking sides of the Mont Blanc massif. Local knowledge of the Jura was widely shared and known administratively and economically to the French state and other dominions. However, Saussure had to cobble together exact directions from Geneva to the Dôle from experience. Until the guidebooks of the nineteenth century—cribbed from Saussure, almost word for word—there was nothing to hold in one's hand.[55]

To climb the Dôle, Saussure explained, one had three options. The most challenging route was the shortest. One goes via Beaumont (Bonmont, site of a former Cistercian abbey from the twelfth century), not far from Nyon, which lies directly below the peak. "From there," encouragingly, "one can get to the summit in three short hours by a good path," preferably on foot, it being "too steep and narrow to comfortably do on horseback." Or one could take an easier way via St. Cergue, which lay on the road to Burgundy. From there, one would go by horse or cart (*chariot*) to below the summit, then walk the rest of the way. From Geneva, one would need two days for this jaunt, but if departing from one of the lake towns Nyons or Prangins, which lie in a direct line with the peak, "one could easily get to the Dôle and back in one single day."[56] As the *Manuel du voyageur en Suisse* detailed in the 1840s, "As it is primarily in the morning or evening when the view from the summit presents in all its magnificence, one must set aside two days for this little journey."[57]

By the 1780s tourists were climbing the Dôle and other peaks in the Jura for the views. At sunrise, it was said, on a perfectly clear day, the summit of the Dôle offered views of seven lakes: Geneva, Annecy, Rousses, Bourget, Joux, Morat, and Neuchâtel. This was a promise Saussure doubted. Despite climbing to the summit before dawn on several occasions—and waiting in the frigid air for the sun to rise—he was never able to see more than the first three lakes. Some puffs of vapor in the right places may have indicated the others, but that was all.[58] Sunset viewing had other drawbacks. On a trip in 1775, Thomas Blaikie climbed the Dôle several times in search of plants for botanical gardens in London. In August he dawdled there in the afternoon "in purpose to see the sun sett from the top of this high Mountain," though the difficulties of finding his way back in the dark "made me regrate my curiossity."[59] (Blaikie spells phonetically.)

The summit of the Chaumont, a hill of some 1160 meters above Neuchâtel, brought other delights. Jean André de Luc, resident savant and reader to Queen Charlotte, climbed there in 1775 with "a lady of the court of George III," a "Mlle. S." This was Juliane Elisabeth von Schwellenberg (1728–1797), Queen Charlotte's intimate and Fanny Burney's nemesis when they later shared the position of the queen's Keeper of the Robe in the late 1780s.[60] In his published letters to the queen, de Luc reported on that little trek. "They climbed along delightful paths until, without even noticing, they had arrived at the summit," he explained in a section he called "The Soul in the Mountains." Then came the real surprise. With one "sweep of the eyes" they saw to the east the lakes of Neuchâtel, Morat, and Bienne; to the west, "some charming valleys"; and ranging north and south, the Jura Mountains, "so pleasantly interspersed with cliffs and green meadows." "In a word [would that it were, for the garrulous de Luc], it was *à la lettre* a profusion of superb views that covered the horizon." For Mlle. S., the experience was transformative. The sudden expansiveness of the landscape drove her deeply and abruptly back into her past. She fell into a reverie of memories of her childhood, living again that childhood self. She awoke in tears, returned whole, healed, and happy in herself.[61]

Perhaps she or de Luc was remembering their John Locke, who argued that the integrity of the self was dependent upon its memories. The self was formed by sensory perceptions, and the continual change of our environments would naturally destabilize that self but for our memories, which fix our identities. It was Rousseau who was foremost in their minds, however. Claude Reichler explains in his work on alpine landscapes, *La Découverte des Alpes et la question du paysage*, that "in returning to the simple happiness and naturalness of the tears of her childhood," she rediscovered something about herself; "Her soul revealed itself to her, through its harmony with nature."[62] De Luc called this experience the *phénomène des montagnes*. De Luc himself had often felt this in the mountains, he claimed, on "isolated summits," and when the air was "calm and serene." Indeed, de Luc boasted, "M. Rousseau has had the very same experience. I even had the happiness once of our enjoying it together."[63]

For Saussure, the view from the Dôle forced a different set of recognitions—not about how he was related to his past, but how the world was related to itself. The Jura and the Alps and Lake Geneva were all connected, and no one knew exactly how. Perhaps the Jura were a subsidiary of the Alps. "Two reasons persuade me of this," he writes. First, because the highest part of the Jura lies closest to the Alps, and second, because of its converse. The lowest part of the Jura was the farthest away.[64] This visual integration of the two mountain ranges eventually led to a number of questions that would guide his explorations, including the examination of the types of rocks and minerals found on the slopes of the Jura, the Prealps, and the Alps, and along the shores of the lake. It may also have had—we can speculate on the basis of his reading of the *Voyages* and the accompanying agenda for subsequent research—an influence on Humboldt's later insight into the connection between the coasts of Africa and South America, which suggests that they may once have been connected. The Jura manifested the same phenomena internally: "Several of its valleys lie between two chains of mountains that have the same form." The shape of their peaks match, the layers of the rocks on each side seem the same. And "one would say that they must have been formerly attached, and that the middle sections had been destroyed . . . leaving the valleys in their place."[65]

Still, no one knew how these spaces were united, or even *if* they were, and what had torn them asunder. And the part mountains played in the history of the planet overall was also a mystery. Were they, as some had claimed, the skeleton or scaffolding of the planet upon which the flesh of the Earth was set? Or perhaps they held the Earth together, like a zipper? Maybe the mountains one saw in Europe did continue in a line across the globe; but how would one know? One idea was that the Alps might begin with the Pyrenees. Those mountains then dipped under the Mediterranean to reappear as the Maritime Alps, where they continued their march across Europe to China, to the true giants of the Himalaya that Europeans would begin to map in the nineteenth century.[66] (That little was known about the Earth is the theme of Alain Corbin's recent synthesis, *Terra Incognita: A History of Ignorance in the Eighteenth and Nineteenth Centuries*.)[67]

From the summit of the Dôle, Saussure could see the line of the Alps. He wondered about their shape, and about how the curvature of the Earth would distort one's view. He could see how Mont Blanc, "appearing astonishingly high, even at that distance," was flanked by mountains that appeared to diminish in size the farther they were from that center: "One sees the high peaks of the Alps drop appreciably to the right and the left of Mont Blanc, the farther they are from their majestic sovereign."[68] At the end of his life, Saussure reviewed the questions that he had asked himself about the mountains that he had encountered in his decades of exploration. These would form that "Agenda" for work in the field that he would offer as an appendix to volume 4 of the *Voyages* (and that Humboldt promised to take to heart on his own explorations).[69] They echo the thoughts he had about the Jura and the Alps in the late 1750s. Douglas Freshfield called it a "'pathetic document" in that it "outlin[ed] . . . a task which he did not live to accomplish.'"[70] George Sarton, who pioneered the history of science in his journal *Isis*, viewed *The Life of Saussure* enthusiastically, parting ways with the alpinist simply on this point, after quoting Freshfield: "the [essence] of [Saussure's] work was probably done. He had conceived it before he was thirty and devoted more than 25 years to its execution" (rather more nearly forty years on, as we shall see in this chapter).[71]

Did a mountain stand alone, or was it part of an assemblage of mountains? If it was part of an assemblage, what were the form and dimensions of that group? How did the separate parts align with each other? With respect to a mountain range, what was its orientation?[72] The Jura, Saussure had noted, ran from south-southwest to north-northeast.[73] Of the Alps from the Dôle, he could see a line from the Dauphiné in southeastern France to the St. Gotthard Pass, thus a north-northeast curve. This was only a slice of the approximately 1200 kilometers of the Alpine range we recognize today, which begins on the Côte d'Azur, rises above the Mediterranean, and ends less definitively in central Europe.[74] What was its span? Saussure wondered.

If a range was a composite of smaller chains—as the Jura seemed to be—what was "the nature and disposition of the partial chains which enter into its composition?" In considering an individual mountain or massif, what was its shape and its height? Where was its summit, and what was its height, relative to sea level, to the valleys below, and to the nearby peaks? What types of rocks made up those mountains, and were they of the same nature throughout? At what elevation did trees, bushes, and flowers cease to grow?[75]

That so little was known and understood about the body of our planet in the mid-eighteenth century, even those parts—the lake and the mountains—that form the landscape of Geneva, seems surprising given that Geneva was one of the most important centers of scientific learning in Enlightenment Europe.[76] It was already a city of science, surpassing any other town of its size in the number of accomplished savants. Between 1700 and 1790 thirteen Genevans entered the Academy of Sciences in Paris as either associate members or corresponding members, and twelve were received into the Royal Society of London. Saussure himself was made a member of both the Royal Society (1788) and the Parisian Academy of Sciences (1790).[77] Despite Geneva's eminence in science, Saussure's education had provided few tools for understanding the mountains. This was already clear to Saussure while wandering the Jura with his friends. The school system was set up to train pastors for the Church and administrators for the state. The Academy of Geneva, the state's body of higher education (not quite a university), "consisted of ten chairs . . . four in theology, two in law, two in philosophy, one in math, and one in letters."[78] Mathematics, physics, and philosophy were covered in a two-year course of "philosophy," which Saussure himself from 1762 would teach.[79]

So much remained unknown about the basic workings of the human body, however, that ignorance in the 1750s about how the planet was organized seems more understandable.[80] Saussure's mother, for example, was treated by Théodore Tronchin—that most fashionable physician of Enlightenment Europe—for gallstones, even though, as we have seen, the source of Renée's distress was not the gallbladder ("Le siege de sa douleur n'est pas la place de la Vesicule").[81] His aunt Bonnet, for another example, sustained a miscarriage in the late summer of 1757 that left her in pain.[82] The following April a part of her left fallopian tube seems to have been expelled during her period, according to the doctors in charge. No, explained Haller, whom Bonnet consulted, what was being described was not that needle-thin part of a woman's body, but rather a fragment of the chorion, a bit of the placenta, left over from the earlier miscarriage.[83] Lacking was not only a clear sense of what each part of the body was and how it functioned, but also an accurate understanding of reproduction, that is, the generation of new individuals in the animal world. Were individuals "preformed" in the egg—or maybe in the sperm? If in the egg, how could characteristics of the male become imposed on the new individual?

Even less was certain about the Earth. Of course, and as Saussure will underline for the students in his lectures at the Academy on *géographie physique* (physical geography) in 1775, humans had recognized for millennia that the world was not flat. Saussure offered four proofs, three of which, he explained, were known in antiquity. First, lunar eclipses show the shadow of a spherical body. Second, at sea, only the tips of a ship's sails might be seen on the horizon. As that ship approaches, one gradually sees more of it. So the Earth must be convex, a sphere. Third, at night, a star observed at its zenith will no longer appear so when one moves away from the initial vantage point, which would not be the case "if the surfaces of the Earth and sky were flat and parallel." Definitive proof comes from circumnavigation—"a fourth and final argument superior to any other proof, though it is modern and was unknown to the ancients": "Explorers . . . have circumnavigated the globe in different directions and yet returned to the point from which they set out."[84] This was "real evidence," as defined by Saussure in connection to his point about the Earth being oblate that Maupertuis and La Condamine, who measured the Earth, the one at the Arctic Circle and the other at the equator, had established directly. We have the course notes of a student and Saussure's rough outline of his lectures, so we can see how his teaching emphasized the importance of tactile, bodily experience in answering basic questions about the planet.[85] This sensualist approach was the basic lesson of the *Voyages*.

How the Earth was formed in the first place—its birth—was a matter of contemporary debate, and the question of the origin and function of mountains was central to the discussion. Buffon reviewed the most recent speculations in his "theory of the Earth" to dismiss them in favor of his own hypothesis. Buffon suggested that all the planets were formed at once, as a result of a comet slicing into the sun and cutting off a chunk of material that then became the six known planets (Uranus was not discovered until 1781, by William Herschel.) The force of gravity, as revealed by Newton, kept them in line. Unlike the theories of Thomas Burnet, William Whiston, and John Woodward, Buffon's argument did not begin with Genesis or focus on the deluge; rather, like Burnet especially, he was concerned with explaining how the Earth came to take the shape it has today, with much of its surface being covered with seas, and the mountains a prominent baffling jumble. Burnet had argued that the Earth had been formed by God as a smooth, round globe, a perfect and beautiful shape. God's anger about human perfidy triggered the Flood. Water covered the globe, and as it dissipated—in response to God's forgiveness—the ugly, irregular contours of the planet appeared, most perfectly manifest in all the mountains scattered around the globe. Mountains, then, misshapen and ugly, were a reflection of the fall of mankind—famously and evocatively, "the ruins of a broken world."[86]

Buffon had a different view of mountains. Although apparently a sign of disorder—they present as a jumble and are hard to understand, as is the rest of the planet—they must have an underlying order to them. In his "Histoire et théorie de la terre" (History and theory of the Earth, 1749) he offered a beautiful description of our planet and an evocation of its unity (like in shape and perhaps inspired by Ecclesiasticus [Sirach] 43:11– 26, which the omnivorous reader Buffon would have been familiar with): "What we see on the surface of this immense globe are great heights and profound depths, vast plains, seas, swamps, rivers, caves, chasms and volcanoes." If we could break below this shell and penetrate into the interior, "we would discover metals, minerals, rocks, salts, sands, earths [in the understanding of the time, elements], and water scattered haphazardly and following no obvious rule." As in time-lapse photography, a speeding vision of the Earth appears in Buffon's imagining of this: "we see mountains collapsing, great rocks cloven in two or shattered, land engulfed or islands newly appearing, and caverns filled with rubble. We find heavy substances pressed against light ones. Hard against soft; dry, wet, hot, cold, solid, and friable, all materials are mixed together in a species of confusion that cannot suggest anything but a mass of debris and a world in ruin."[87] Yet, Buffon continues, "we inhabit these ruins in absolute security. Generations of [humans], animals, and plants follow without interruption. The land supports them, the sea is contained within its bounds, its tides are regulated, and the winds subject to rules. Air is organized in currents that shape their course around the globe. The seasons turn. Springtime green follows the frost of winter. All is in order and all is ordered." Thus, "a world of chaos is revealed as a delightful abode where calm and harmony reign, animated and directed by a power whose intelligence fills us with admiration and lifts us up to the Creator."[88]

According to Gabriel Gohau's account of the origins of geology—*Les Sciences de la terre aux XVIIème et XVIIIème siècles: Naissance de la géologie*—Burnet's shift away from cosmology to a focus on the Earth itself (despite the goofiness of his model of the mundane egg) was vital to the establishment of the Earth sciences.[89] For Buffon, more realistically than for Burnet, the unit of study was the Earth. Chaos might present, but order and regularity exist. The apparent chaos is not the disorder of a postlapsarian world, nor even the simple manifestation of God's desire to present human eyes with a diversity of views, with a picturesque landscape, as it were, which was another contemporary view. The world is *lisible*, readable. It operates according to "natural laws," the search for which was the basic Enlightenment project. Said Buffon, "In paying closer attention we will find there perhaps an order we did not suspect, and the basic connections [*des rapports généraux*] that we did not see at first glance."[90] The Earth was both knowable and beautiful to know.

One can almost grasp in one's hands the globe as described by this eighteenth-century giant. Despite the contrast of seas and mountains, of storms and calm, somehow it holds together, the wild wind flowing in measurable currents around the Earth, the seasons following one by one. It is this same recognition of cohesion that explains the appeal of Saussure's vision from the summit of the Dôle in the 1750s, described in the *Voyages* as well as in the *Partie pittoresque* versions. Here he is alone, at dawn:

> A thick cloud covered the lake, the surrounding hills and even the lower mountains. The summit of the Dôle and the high Alps were the only peaks whose heads were raised above that immense veil. Brilliant sunshine illu-

minated the entire surface of this cloud. And the Alps, lit up by the direct rays of the sun and by the light reflected back on them by the cloud, appeared vividly and though from extraordinarily far away.[91]

"But there was something strange and terrible too about this," too. Anticipating Caspar David Friedrich's iconic painting *Der Wanderer über dem Nebelmeer* (The Wanderer above a Sea of Mist, c. 1817/18),[92] a kind of social alienation was emphasized in Saussure's evocation: "I seemed to be alone on a rock in the midst of a rough sea, far away from a continent lined by a reef of unassailable rocks." As the fog lifted however, "rising above my head," a vision of integration was articulated:[93] "All of a sudden, the superb vista of the lake and its pretty shorelines, cultivated, charming, dotted with small towns and beautiful villages" was revealed as having been there all along, its picturesque promise of human industry forming part of the landscape of the Alps.[94]

Just as Buffon's word painting of the planet shifts our focus from chaos to harmony, so too does Saussure's. Saussure's vison was reduced, however, to what could be seen, rather than what was imagined from Paris or Montbard, Buffon's country estate in Burgundy, where Buffon lived for most of the year and where his description of the natural world—the *Histoire naturelle*—was composed in an incredible thirty-six volumes.[95] The Genevan lake surrounded by its towns and villages, its vineyards and fields, the Prealps—that is, the mountains between Geneva and the peaks—and the great Alps themselves were captured by Saussure in one encompassing view. This was the first major contribution of Saussure to the Earth sciences. It shrank the scope of the project to understand the Earth to knowable proportions—the Alpine region—that could be investigated directly. How the lake, the rivers that ran into and through it, the hot springs that bubbled above its shores, the caverns and crags, the meadows, the waterfalls, and finally the glaciers, along with the storms of the Mont Blanc massif—how these elements might connect in a whole was Saussure's research question. It defined Saussure's work for the next forty years and prompted his first walk to Chamonix in 1760.

It also opened up Geneva to the high peaks. A Geneva understood as part of a natural world that extended into the Alps—a region—is radically different from a Geneva locked behind its walls. This spoke to a different sensibility, even from that expressed by "early travelers in the Alps" such as Conrad Gesner (1516–1565),[96] whose explanation for walking in the mountains, given in a letter to a friend in 1541, would be echoed almost word for word by Haller, and then by Saussure: "Henceforth, every year for as long as God allows me to live, I will climb several mountains or at least one during the season when the plants are in full bloom to examine these, and to procure for my body a noble exercise while delighting my intellect [*mon esprit*]."[97] Other humanists described the special equipment one needed to adopt when traveling in the mountains, along with their classical education. Crampons—though for rocks, not ice—and dark glasses were recommended by Guillaume Grataroli in a medical treatise written in Latin and published successively in Basel, Strasbourg, and Cologne in 1561, 1563, and 1571, and later.[98] Josias Simler described snowshoes in his *Memoire sur les Alpes* (*De Alpibus Commentarius* [Treatise on the Alps], published in 1574) in a section titled "Difficultés et dangers des passages à travers les Alpes" (Difficulties and dangers of Alpine passes).[99]

Gesner, Grataroli, and Simler—avatars of the patrician-savant that was Saussure—described an urban elite going into a mountain wilderness and returning, without much effect on any city of origin beyond the generalized germ of the romantic view of Haller and Rousseau. While Saussure's *Voyages* invite proxy travel—most of us will not summit Mont Blanc—his viewpoint, as glimpsed here from the Dôle but pronounced throughout the *Voyages*, is that of a Genevan. It is as proxy Genevans that our worldview is expanded, that our vistas are opened up, and that we are changed, as Geneva was changed. As Rosalie Constant quipped, "It might seem that the great immovable mountains had only become noticeable since the observations and travels of Monsieur de Saussure."[100]

That Buffon influenced Saussure, if only as a point of departure, is indisputable. He was an unavoidable presence in the salons—the "chat rooms"—of eighteenth-century thought. Buffon's *Histoire naturelle* was one of the most popular works of the century, even more so perhaps than Rousseau's *La Nouvelle Héloïse* or the *Encyclopédie*. It certainly appeared in more libraries.[101] Buffon's first three volumes, with the "Theory of the Earth" forming a part of these, were published in 1749 and initiated that success.[102] Buffon was already a very influential figure, having become the intendant (i.e., director) of the Jardin du Roi, the Royal Botanical Garden in 1739: "Given his prominent position in the Republic of Letters, as the director of one of the leading institutions in the world center of the sciences, the profound impact of his ideas is hardly surprising."[103] Buffon's volumes appear in the catalog of Saussure's library, prepared in 1797, when, in desperate financial straits, he was attempting to sell his books.[104] Though Saussure only began to build his collection in 1760, his father, with his Enlightenment interest in the natural world (and who possibly contributed essays on agronomy to the *Encyclopédie*) would already have had Buffon's volumes on hand in the family home.[105]

Saussure's mentors, Bonnet and Haller, read the "Theory of the Earth" upon its publication or soon after. Haller reviewed it for the *Bibliothèque raisonnée des savans de l'Europe*, which offered extracts and reviews of important books.[106] Bonnet reread it in the late 1760s, his admiration of it prompting a quarrel with Haller. Bonnet reported that he was deeply impressed: "I am rereading Mr. de Buffon's *Theory of the Earth*," he wrote to Haller in the summer of 1769. "I see things there that I like a lot, and that demonstrate an expansive genius. I do not refer to his visions on the formation of the planet. I am speaking about his ideas about the formation of rock strata, and that of mountains, etc."[107] Haller dismissed Buffon, on principle and, as usual, as a *philosophe* suspected of materialism, and the "Theory of the Earth" on the basis of evidence: "Distrust, my illustrious friend, everything these philosophers say." It is all of a piece.[108] Haller, said he, was concerned with what nature really was like. Faced—indeed, barraged—with its embarrassment of riches, "I scarcely give thought to the conjectures of M. de Buffon, who, for that matter, knows very little about mountains and their structure."[109]

Buffon claimed that shells could be found on the summits of the Alps. Haller said, no, not above 1829 meters. Buffon described the corresponding angles of mountains facing each other across valleys, which Saussure would begin to notice in the Jura. (Imagine it as "*one* mountain cut into two by a valley and not two mountains facing each other," as the historian of geology Gabriel Gohau has explained.)[110] Haller called that "a fable."[111] Bonnet countered by saying that it was the research of Louis Bourguet (1678–1742), who was well-known to Haller, that Buffon had drawn upon and credited. Haller could not accuse Bourguet of being suspect "in matters of religion." And Haller must know that Bourguet "was a very good observer." Maybe, Bonnet suggested, Haller did not have Buffon's "Theory of the Earth" as fresh in his mind as did Bonnet: his memory was fooling him.[112] No, said Haller, it was not. And as for Bourguet, Haller had traveled so often through the Alps, the Jura, the Herz, and the Vosges that if what Bourguet claimed to be true about valleys was true, Haller would have noticed it. Well, said Bonnet, Bourguet reports having "passed through the Alps thirty times in fourteen different places, and having twice traveled through the Apennines, and again in the Jura. It is scarcely possible that he could be mistaken about so salient a fact, and impossible to believe that he would want to insinuate this."[113] And so on. Haller, as usual, had the last word over Bonnet, wrong as he was, though, about Bourguet.[114] "Beware, my illustrious friend, every man with a system," he said, dismissing Bonnet's arguments as irrelevant. "That is the case of M. Bourguet. I know the mountains too well to be mistaken. He has taken as a general law what is only a particular case."[115]

It is no wonder that Saussure, caught between two powerful points of view, would spend years verifying the basic facts that he discovered about the Alps before even beginning to sketch out—as he does in the appendix to the last volume of the *Voyages*—a general theory about the Earth. This reluctance would come to irritate Buffon, and the irritation itself would serve as a means to distinguish for Georges Cuvier—the most powerful of scientists in the post-Revolutionary years—the superiority of careful observation, Saussure's trademark, over Buffon's speculations.[116] Saussure himself was impressed by Buffon, however, when they met in Paris in 1768. "He was open and friendly in conversation," very welcoming, he explained to Haller.[117] The least one can say is that a reading of Buffon's "Theory of the Earth" was an invitation to look with open eyes at what a view from the Dôle might describe.

Being stimulating is one thing; having one's facts straight is another. Buffon was wrong about shells having been found on the high peaks of the Alps. (He would correct that error in his "Epoques de la nature" of 1778, which formed a supplement to the *Histoire naturelle*.) He was wrong, as well, to point to the St. Gotthard massif as the "highest point in Europe."[118] It was even difficult to say what a rock was in the 1750s. Mineralogy was a cabinet science, with samples displayed for observation. Linnaeus and others were trying to establish means of distinguishing one type of mineral from the other on the basis of visible characteristics, as was being established for plants. Even what basalt was, though, was a matter of debate until the second half of the century.[119] Saussure worked on this question in 1776. Not until 1774 did Abraham Gottlib Werner (1749–1817) publish his *External Characters of Minerals*. This "was essentially a guide useful for fieldwork, as Werner enumerated those properties allowing for accurate identification of minerals and rocks."[120] And it was only toward the end of the century that methods for identifying and classifying minerals on the basis of crystal structures were clearly established, and later still on the basis of chemical composition.

Much of what was known about what lay beneath the surface of the Earth in the 1750s was known from mining. Miners needed to know where lay veins of sought-after minerals—iron, silver, lead, tin, coal, and so on—and this led to a three-dimensional mapping of rock masses, of the *Gebirge*, as the German leaders in this occupation called it, meaning in this sense not the topographical feature, the mountain, but what might lie below.[121] Miners worked in a "three dimensional world of rock *structures*" (emphasis in original), as Martin Rudwick has explained,[122] and these were depicted on maps that represented "what it was thought would be visible if it were possible to slice the ground open along a specific vertical plane:

they were in effect 'virtual' cliffs or quarry faces."[123] Some of these were available in the 1750s, but the great mining schools only opened in the 1760s and beyond. ("Although important academies were established in Ekaterinburg in Siberia, St. Petersburg, and Paris [the prestigious École Royale des Mines (in 1783)] between 1763 and 1783, the new academies tended to cluster in central Europe."[124]) The Freiberg Mining Academy in Saxony, where Werner would later teach and develop his Neptunist theories of the Earth, was established in 1765.[125] Though the work of these institutions helped Werner and other savants close to the mining industry develop theories of rock formation and encouraged a three-dimensional view of the landscape, their mapping closely described only discrete areas of the Earth.

Still, the basic notion of strata may have been known to Saussure in the late 1750s. Nicolas Sténon in the 1660s had already established the principles of stratigraphy after visiting mines in the Tyrol and in Hungary.[126] What he discovered was not simply that the Earth was shaped by layers of different rocks, but that "the ordering of the strata indicates the sequence of its formation." The deepest layers are the oldest.[127] As Gohau comments, "Every student of geology will recognize here the principle of superposition.... What is harder to see is how it took until 1669 for that to be established, so self-evident does it appear today."[128] That there were "primary" levels of rocks that were older and that underlay the "secondaries" was becoming a given in the eighteenth century. The primaries were understood as the hard rocks—"gneiss, schist, and marble"—and the secondaries—the soft rocks—"sandstone, shale, limestone, and 'puddingstone' (conglomerate)."[129] Giovanni Arduino's (1714–1795) work, which established these categories, was based on observations of mines in northern Italy. It was circulated in manuscript from 1758 and may have been known to Bonnet and Haller and thus to Saussure by 1760. It was not until 1776, however, that a report in German on Arduino's classifications was translated into French and English.[130] Werner's influential theory about the laying down of these strata through the crystallization of minerals in the soup of a primitive ocean—the Neptunism that would engage Saussure as he drafted the volumes of the *Voyages* twenty years after his first forays into the Jura—lay in the future.

Though facts about the Earth were few, methods for discovering them had opened up. Buffon's *Histoire naturelle* marked a shift from an approach to understanding the world through mathematics, or abstractions, to that of direct experience of the phenomenon to be understood: "Natural philosophers realized that it was necessary to experiment, to examine things as they truly were, to describe them carefully first, and then to reason afterward. To use the language of the time, it was necessary to find the 'history' of nature before building a 'physics,' to describe phenomena before seeking the causes. Certainly, mathematicians continued to practice mathematics. But there were now other things to do."[131] Buffon himself had followed this path. His early research was in mathematics: it was what brought him to the attention of the Parisian Academy of Sciences and earned him a place there in 1734 for his work on probability theory and calculus.[132] His focus moved quickly to natural history. In early 1739 the Academy shifted him, "probably at his own request, to the Botany section."[133] The appointment to the Jardin du Roi followed. As Diderot would explain to Voltaire in 1758, just as Saussure was exploring the Jura, "The reign of mathematics is over. Tastes have changed. Natural history and 'letters' rule now."[134] (This was by way of criticizing d'Alembert, who remained committed to mathematics, and who had recently removed himself from the direction of the *Encyclopédie*.)[135]

Observation represented a sea change from a Cartesian commitment to understanding the world as resting on a set of principles that could be described mathematically or understood through the same deductive methods: "human reason could understand nature," human reasoning "could attain [the] truth."[136] Francis Bacon had argued for the centrality of observation in understanding the natural world, and, Roger explains, "after the whirlwind of Cartesian science," the practice of "putting experience first" would come back into favor with scholars in London as well as in Paris."[137] Locke's *An Essay Concerning Human Understanding* (1690), historians agree, "would influence ... all thought in the eighteenth century. Locke explained that our ideas derive only from a combination of sensations and that the human mind has no other power than that of bringing about that combination."[138] The Academy of Geneva, responsible for training the city's elites, embraced this approach, which privileged observation and experiments. Studies of the Enlightenment in Switzerland emphasize how the adoption first of the Cartesian and then the sensualist practices of the Scientific Revolution were made compatible with Calvinist theology.[139] Knowing the world of creation was a way of knowing God; the Creator could be known through his creation. This is a view that is shot through the correspondence of Bonnet and Haller, where God, written as *DIEU*, in capitals and in other guises such as *cet Être Adorable* (that Adorable Being), appear frequently as exhortations against materialism and on behalf of Protestantism.[140] (And this is in contrast to the almost total absence of references to God in Saussure's letters and lectures, as well as the *Voyages*.[141])

Haller explained his methodology to Bonnet in 1760. In matters of physiology, he was always guided by observations—both those reported to him and those he had made himself (including through vivisections). He collected these facts, and then their agreement, or not, shaped his conclusions.[142] Buffon made similar claims about his methodology in the *Théorie de la terre* of 1758: "However, one must remember that an historian is meant to describe and not to invent." Suppositions are not permissible, and the imagination, Buffon would have his readers know, was to be used only to generalize from the facts. "Natural history depends on experience," he insisted.[143] Saussure would say much the same thing to his students at the Academy in the 1770s: "'It is by the senses that we learn about bodies, and by the senses alone. Observations and experiments are therefore the primary sources for all our understanding of physics. But as all these are only particularities, we have to generalize with the aid of our reason.'" Clearly, Saussure had adopted this "sensualist philosophy" in his approach to understanding the physical world.[144]

Saussure knew one practical application of this approach very well from his shepherding of his mother's health in the 1750s. It was Saussure, we recall, who was responsible for discussing her symptoms with Tronchin and describing them to Haller by letter. "Medical consultation by letter" or other proxy "was unproblematic in the eighteenth century" because of the way in which a diagnosis was understood to be formed. The practitioner would work with a "collection of perceptions" that could be offered by the patient herself, a relative, or the family physician. It was the expert's role "to recognize the essence of a disease, visible by the eye of the mind after having been extracted from" these observations. That is, the signs of a disease were "directly accessible through the senses of anyone" who could note the pattern of fevers, the color of effusions, the textures of the stools, and so on. The disease itself, however—what the signs added up to—were "only visible to the eye of the mind of expert physicians" who could read them in context, who could move from the particular or idiosyncratic to the general, to the type, to the diagnosis of disease.[145] This is the basic formula of the sensualist methodology, as we saw from Buffon and Haller and as articulated by Saussure in his classes.

Looking out over the lake from his vantage point in the Jura, Saussure formulated a plan to reach the high peaks. Logistically, that meant walking to Chamonix in the summer of 1760. Conceptually, it meant thinking about the mountains as a corpus of information, with a first point of reference being the human body. The association of the human with the Earth was a commonplace in the Renaissance—one sees it in Leonardo da Vinci—and had its roots in antiquity. (For Plato in the *Timaeus*, the "world is a living creature.") It led to analogies such as that the waters of the Earth were like the blood running through the veins of a body and that mountains formed the skeleton of the Earth. A correspondence was assumed between the microcosm (the human) and the macrocosm (the cosmos). Gohau has suggested that the connection between the human and the Earth weakened in the Middle Ages with Christianity's "accent on direct rapports between man and God." He also suggests that the revival of the analogy in the Renaissance occurred because, "paradoxically," the age was on the cusp of a new paradigm—the Scientific Revolution—that would offer a way forward to understanding the material world in entirely new terms: we are not made in the image of God. "Before committing to new ways of thinking," he says, "the history of ideas suggests that older models be thoroughly interrogated before being discarded." Thus the return to earlier modalities of thought.[146]

By analogy, some readers might explain Saussure's vision on the Cramont and his arguments about the feelings of plants as a regression. From the summit of that peak of 2737 meters, lying south of Mont Blanc, climbed in 1774 (as its first ascent) and again in 1778, for a view of the massif, he saw the mountains around Mont Blanc as in some way alive, as "living beings" [*les êtres animés*].[147] In a late essay he exclaimed, "How sweet it is to think of the many pleasures that rain or a summer dew gives to the great quantity of plants that it waters!"[148] (New work on eighteenth-century views about plant sensibilities is appearing in France along these lines. Jan Synowiecki, a student of Antoine Lilti, has published an article titled "Ces plantes qui sentent et qui pensent: Une autre histoire de la nature au XVIIIe siècle" in the *Revue historique*, another measure of the interest Saussure holds for a revived environmental history of the era.)[149] If we were to follow Gohau, however, we might say that before the turn toward the laboratory sciences of the nineteenth century—chemistry, physics, and biology—there is a turn backward to almost animistic views about the world and intuitions about the connections between humans and the Earth. Its beings are *not* us, but they are *like* us. A more intriguing way—a better way—to understand Saussure's employment of these terms, however, is to see how they look forward to views today of a "living Earth," at least as a premise, and to see the nineteenth-century developments as instead obscuring these lines of thought, so vital to us today. The National Aeronautics and Space Administration (NASA), for instance, presents our globe this way on its website, depicting "vegetation wak[ing] up in the spring" and the blooming of algae in the ocean; their "satellite data lets scientists watch Earth breathe and improves our understanding of our home planet."[150] Exploring this theme in the *Voyages* is one of the goals of the book as we probe how much the Earth was—heuristically, at least for Saussure—something alive.

In the meantime, we are on solid ground, so to speak, with Saussure as he precedes off the Jura to Chamonix with a set of goals not unlike those he would have learned from consulting with Haller about his mother's health. Before diagnosing a condition, know where the gallbladder is, know what the fallopian tubes look like. See where the high peaks are, know what a glacier is. Discover the rock upon which the mountains are built.

* 3 *
The Arve Valley

It all begins with the Arve. It rushes into the Rhône on the outskirts of Geneva, swirling like a top, full of color and indiscriminate force, infused with the minerals that it churns up from the rocks over which it surges and which it carries along. Many of these rocks have tumbled down from the Mont Blanc massif as bits of the peaks themselves. The Rhône too has its source in the high peaks. It bubbles out of a glacier near the Furka Pass, at the upper end of the Valais in Switzerland. After swelling with a dozen mountain streams while pushing southwest to Martigny, it then shifts north to enter Lake Geneva. There it washes up and west toward Lausanne, relaxing out and down to form the crescent expanse of the lake. After dipping south, it exits through the city. The larger river by then is pacified, tranquil, and sky-toned until its encounter with the Arve. The Arve, however, is turbulent throughout its course from the glaciers of the upper Chamonix valley to Geneva, where, when swollen with rain and snowmelt, it will occasionally push back against the confluence of the two rivers, crushing back the Rhône and flooding the lake. Always the Arve is a marble-gray-green, a consistent milkiness distinguishing its palette from the moodiness of Atlantic waves. It exudes an ice-cold charm.

Already, as Saussure was collecting dog-toothed violets (*Erythium*) for Haller and for his mother at its wooded borders along the junction with the Rhône, the Arve was whispering adventure. Twenty years old when he left Geneva in August for his first walk up the Arve valley to Chamonix to botanize for Haller, Saussure, as we know from his climbs in the Jura, had a larger plan in mind. It was a noticeably bold decision to go to Chamonix that summer of 1760, not only on Saussure's part, but also on that of his parents. They would have had to fund the trip, though the expenditure was not very high. Mostly, they would have had to agree to the risk. Bandits could kill, and so could the Arve. In the first half of the century, "Savoy was saturated with arms and men who knew how to use them," explains Michael Kwass in his book about the celebrated bandit Louis Mandrin.[1] Two "German" botanists were murdered on the Salève itself in the summer of 1761, with deserters from the Seven Years' War (1756–63) suspected.[2] There were wolves. And even in 1787, after paths had been widened and the route to Chamonix improved, a misstep on a bridge could be fatal. Joseph-Antoine Paccard, the notary and *curial* (secretary) of Chamonix and the father of the Dr. Paccard (Michel-Gabriel Paccard [1757–1827]) who made the first ascent of Mont Blanc, was drowned that way near Les Houches in a rainstorm in July 1787.[3] Rushing to inform the intendant of Faucigny (thus, the state of Savoy) of the arrival of Saussure and his entourage in Chamonix and the expected summiting, Paccard slipped off the plank bridge covering the Nant Nailliant. This was a torrent rushing down into the Arve from Mont Lachat, a peak of 2115 meters on the way from Bellevue to the Nid d'Aigle, now on the summit path to Mont Blanc.[4]

The way along the Arve in the Chamonix valley was barred by many such torrents that were crossable only by fording or by walking carefully on boards placed between their banks. Swollen with rains or melting snow, they could be death traps. In August of 1776, Saussure himself came close to the same end when his horse slipped on the path rising above a flooded Arve, a mile or so out of Sallanches. The Arve had overflowed its banks and forced Saussure to climb, leading his horse, onto a narrow shelf above and following the river. The horse fell with its four feet sliding toward Saussure, pushing him toward the edge of the precipice with the roaring river below. Fortunately, Saussure explains and we can agree, he had the presence of mind and just enough time to jump forward out of the way, and he and the horse were saved.[5] In a letter to Haller in July 1760, Saussure expressed his good fortune in having "parents who understood the value of natural beauty, and that of botany, above all, and despite the inconveniences of these types of excursions were delighted to anticipate the pleasure that it would give you for me to return with a plant or two for you." They were very much in favor of this, he explained, "so long it does not draw me away too much from my other studies."[6]

Saussure had finished his education at the Academy the year before, in 1759, offering a thesis on heat titled "A Physical Discourse on Fire." As Freshfield points out, "Amongst other details [Saussure] showed that dark objects are more quickly heated."[7] This is a process at work today in the melting of the Arctic and of glaciers in the Alps and in all the world's high peaks. The more that the ice melts and the white snow fades, the more rapidly the region returns to water or rock. Saussure will see this heating action at work in the Chamonix valley. He is at first bewildered at seeing women at Le Tour (a small high hamlet upstream from Argentière) sprinkling dirt on the snow in the spring until he realizes that they have pragmatically come to the same conclusions as had he. Fields prepared in this way will be ready earlier in the spring for the sowing of grain, something of vital importance where the growing season is so short and uncertain.[8] The problem of "heat," that is, what it does and where it comes from, was a question of Earth science. Was the core of the Earth hot? Could the sun's warmth be mapped? These questions were of broad interest. Voltaire and Émilie du Châtelet, for instance, competed in 1738 in a contest for the best essay on "the nature and propagation of fire" (encompassing the problem of what light was as well as what heat was, and how they might relate), set by the French Academy of Sciences.[9] Neither Voltaire nor Châtelet won, though that the Academy made special note of their contributions added to the charisma of this science.[10]

Saussure's success at the Academy was satisfying. Still, he was at loose ends. What path he should take to secure a name for himself in Geneva and how to become an important adult were still open questions. This is the problem his parents tried to solve by encouraging the connection with Haller. Tied to Haller, as a protégé, at least, he would have a way to advance a career in science. Thus his uncle Bonnet's assurances to Haller about Saussure's interest in botany. These begin in June 1760, when Bonnet describes Saussure as so taken up by botany, that he "is more in need of a bridle than a spur."[11] The next month, Haller is told that Saussure considers it "his crowning glory to contribute to your works on botany."[12] In July of the next year Bonnet's crescendo of commendations reached its peak with the claim that "If he could, my nephew would create new plants in order to please you."[13] A professorship at the Academy was the immediate goal, one only realistic with an independent or ancillary income, since compensation was slight. Was a wealthy marriage already to be understood? With that decision taken, Saussure could avoid, at least for a time, being tied to the law and administration, unlike his friend and walking companion Jean-Louis Pictet, whose interests in astronomy and natural history were part-time. Pictet became a lawyer in 1762. In the 1770s he served successively as a member of the Council of Two Hundred, an *auditeur du droit* (like Saussure's father, with responsibilities for assuring public order), a member of the Small Council, and finally, in 1778, a syndic.[14]

However, walking the Arve in 1760 was taking him decisively away from a concentration on botany—either by way of plant collection and identification, which was Haller's way, or via Bonnet's way. Bonnet would have wanted him to expand Bonnet's own work on the functions of a plant, that is, its physiology. Saussure would do so. It is what the leaf study (*Obser-*

vations sur l'écorce des feuilles et des pétales [Observations on the epidermis of leaves and petals]), which opened up the professorship to him, accomplished in 1762, but it was a side project of his larger interest in the natural world. Saussure left for Chamonix in August 1760 with the weight of parental expectations on him, but also with the weight of immediate responsibility lifted. He was free for a time. Saussure could follow the course of the Arve upward along its dangerous valley, that "dark, deep Ravine . . . many colour'd, many-voiced," as Percy Bysshe Shelley would later declaim.[15] In the process of these travels, this chapter argues, Saussure would become something more than the cherished scion of the Genevan Enlightenment, robotically applying to "rocks" the techniques of the botanists. His embrace of geology—knowledge of the Earth—involved detaching himself from Genevan certainties about place and space and reorienting himself to the sensory demands of a spectacular landscape—its sensorium—and becoming at home there. He "finds himself in his element," he explains after reaching the spot where the river swerves east into the Chamonix valley and the alpine terrain begins. By the time he wrote these words in 1779, he had become less typical of his milieu, more instinctive, more aware of the complexities of natural life—its poetry—than the mentors he left behind. There was no turning back.

Saussure first set off with a servant and a powerful dog.[16] The next year he took some friends. In 1767 he and his walking companions in the Jura—François Jallabert and Jean-Louis Pictet—undertook the first *tour du Mont Blanc*, or wide circling around the massif with Chamonix and Courmayeur as today's compass points. By the time he published the first volume of the *Voyages*, where the account of these excursions begin as the "Voyage autour du Mont-Blanc," he had traveled up the Arve valley a good nine times. This count includes his second *tour du Mont Blanc* of 1774, when he broke off from the Arve at St. Gervais to begin the walk south, up and around the massif, an option today for the *tour*. Saussure's depiction of the Arve valley in the *Voyages* is an amalgam or synthesis of this set of excursions. The narration is from the standpoint of the *tour* of 1778, though it is easy to pick up the threads of his youthful visits in the author's deliberate asides and as he lays out their common themes.[17]

The most immediate of these is the looming importance of Mont Blanc as a kind of magnet drawing one into the valley. Another is the reconceptualization of space as a region defined by terrain rather than politics or religion, as the Mediterranean world will come to be in the works of Fernand Braudel and his successors, and as the multinational Alpine Convention of the 1990s would later articulate for the mountain range. More interesting, considering his milieu, was the problem of perception as it developed in Saussure's exploration along the Arve. How to know what a thing is—a mountain, say—if the shape of it keeps changing? How to trust sight, that cornerstone of the Enlightenment, and that basic human sense that guides our orientation? For us today it is Saussure's solution to this problem that seems revolutionary. It is not simply that he deploys all his senses in his understanding of what he "sees"—his senses of smell, touch, and taste—though he does do this. Rather, he effects a full-body experience of the mountains. Saussure comes close to saying that it is the body as well as the mind, or the body-mind, that "knows" or understands or makes sense of what the Earth is. This was pushing him way beyond his contemporaries and his mentors in exploring how it is that one knows.

Only by proxy, however, could most of Saussure's contemporaries take the same paths as he, though he writes in the *Voyages* as if readers would be following him to Chamonix, covering the eighteen short leagues (the *lieue* [league] *de Berne* in standard use in Geneva then was equal to 5 km) in a day,[18] or, optimally, he recommends, with an overnight pause in Sallanches. Knowing that it is vicarious, and across the gulf of time—another pretense—we will adopt those posed directions as our own as this chapter unfolds. Our guide recommends organizing the trip in our mind's eye as he has done, as a series of links based on the shape of the valley: Geneva to Bonneville, Bonneville to Cluses, Cluses to Sallanches, Sallanches to Servoz, and then on to Chamonix.[19] We head first for Bonneville, following the close-up image (fig. 3.1) sectioned from the map of Geneva and the Alps reproduced in chapter 1.

Mont Blanc appears even before the first step is taken. This giant peak is the "mother mountain": "That enormous block of granite, situated at the center of the Alps, appears to be the key to a great system." If it could be understood, mountains in general could be decoded: "At the very least, the groundwork would be laid for solving the problem of their formation."[20] Stepping out from Geneva, then, along the Arve, "one heads straight for Mont Blanc [*on se dirige droit au Mont-Blanc*] . . . southeast of that city."[21] It is the lodestar, as "one climbs a road that slopes up by easy degrees and leads to a great plateau, about 18–24 meters above Lake Geneva." One notices debris from the peaks scattered along the path. The stones lining the route are alpine rocks.[22] Underneath one's feet is a base of sand and clay, mixed with *galets*, or the rounded stones that Saussure posited were shaped by water as they were forced from the Alps.[23] The peaks are there already to be seen and felt, in the distance above and underfoot.

This rock base extends for several leagues until one reaches Contamine-sur-Arve. One would have already moved beyond the territory of the Genevan republic. The traveler enters Savoy a mile or so from the city, directly

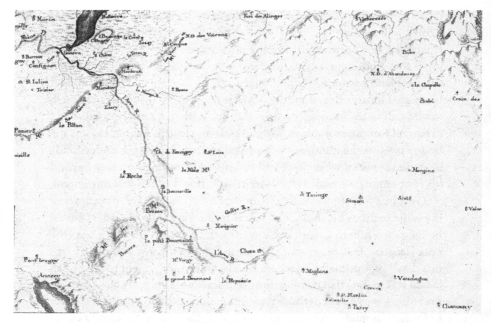

FIGURE 3.1 Detail of figure 1.1, "Carte du lac de Genève et des montagnes adjacentes." Photo credit: Amanda M. Matava.

after crossing the village of Chesne. However, no further mention is made of being in the territory of Geneva's traditional enemy. It is the geological imagination that Saussure puts into play. It is the sand and the clay that we see, the rock base that extends Geneva along the Arve valley up to Contamine as the erratics bring the peaks down to the lake. And the geometric, as we look alongside him. "The aspect of the mountains shifts with each footstep," he says.[24] The Salève we hear about first—understandably, as it dominates the view south from the city: "Almost facing us as we leave Geneva, after about a league and a half from the city it presents in profile, and foreshortened, as trapezoidal. This produces extraordinary effects, especially when its sharply edged layers are lit by the sun. Further on, we see it from the rear, its slopes now gentle and covered with trees."[25] The Voirons, too (1480 m), "farther away and more to the left" when viewed from Geneva, presents in similar ways.[26]

The Môle (1863 m), however, is the main focus on the route to Bonneville, whose distance—five leagues, he says—Saussure covers in three hours and forty-five minutes.[27] He travels a path that rises almost imperceptibly toward that sugar-loaf peak. Once past Contamine, the way squeezes itself between the Arve and the outskirts of the mountain. Soon one is below a mass of rock, an appendage really of the Môle, where the chateau of Faucigny, a twelfth-century ruin, rests on a Roman base. As long as one is directly below this rock body, its structure is impossible to discern. Once past, however, and employing a telescope, one can see that it is made up of layers. These layers lie perpendicular to the horizon, with an orientation of northeast to southwest. Shift your sight below and to the southeast, however, and you will discover some other strata that cut the first at right angles.[28] Then, as one moves farther along, you will find thin vertical layers broken up by long, thick horizontals. From Bonneville, this right angling shifts to reveal some curves. A hole then appears in the midst of the layers of rock where the face must have collapsed. Lines of rock, "rising from below both to the right and the left, point toward emptiness."[29] Angles again, in the shape of Bonneville itself. "Situated on a pretty plain on the banks of the Arve, there is nothing remarkable about it, except its triangular form."[30]

The shape-shifting of the Môle had already been flagged by Saussure in his "Essai sur l'histoire naturelle des environs de Genève," which begins the *Voyages* and through which we followed Saussure in the Jura: "From Geneva, the Môle presents as a pyramid rising in the east-southeast in the space between the Salève and the Voirons." It looks darkly somber against the snowy Alps beyond. Its conical shape and deep color, Saussure explains, "has led people who have only seen the Môle from a distance to conclude that it is a former volcano." However, the Môle is green with vegetation, not black, and no evidence suggests that the mountain ever was a volcano. Moreover, Saussure continues, it is not really even in the shape of a cone. It is more of a parallelogram, stretching toward the east-southeast, from the west-northwest. "But since from Geneva one sees it foreshortened, its length disappears entirely," and a cone appears. These tricks of perspective fool a number of people. Arriving at Bonneville, with the Môle *en face*, they fail to recognize it, "mistaking for the Môle a different mountain [presumably the Brezon], which lies on the other side of the Arve."[31]

Saussure's geometrical vision—expressed in the line segments, angles, and curves, which he sees and describes for his readers—runs in parallel to contemporary efforts to construct accurate maps of the Savoy Alps. This accuracy was not simply a matter of establishing heights for peaks and the correct alignment between mountains and valleys. Marc-Auguste Pictet (1752–1825), who accompanied Saussure in 1778, came along partly for the purpose of taking these measurements and casting them onto a map. His "Carte de la partie des Alpes qui avoisine le Mont Blanc," a map of the Mont Blanc region of the Alps published in volume 2 of the *Voyages* in 1786 (fig. 3.2), aligns correctly the two valleys that define the massif, the Chamonix valley and the Aosta valley (harboring Courmayeur), having used trigonometry to determine the positions of the summits. However, one can see on the map below how Mont Blanc and the aiguilles appear as islands in a massive frozen sea, and how the aiguilles look like shaggy larch trees. The technical challenges had hardly been met.

Topographical maps showing elevation through hatching and later contour lines would be innovations of the French and the British and were not at all perfected on contemporary representations of the massif.[32] The first relief maps of the Mont Blanc massif were constructed in wood in 1787 by Charles-François Exchaquet (1746–1792), a director of mines in Servoz. Saussure purchased one of these three-dimensional models right

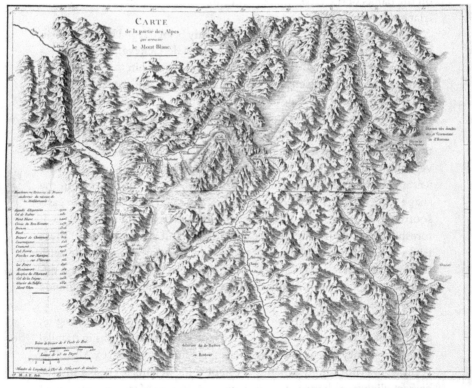

FIGURE 3.2 "Carte de la partie des Alpes qui avoisine le Mont Blanc." Drawn by Marc-Auguste Pictet. Saussure, *Voyages*, vol. 2. Fold-out map, *hors-texte* at end of volume. Watkinson Library, Trinity College, CT: DQ823.S246. Photo credit: Amanda M. Matava.

away, with his path to the summit painted in red. This is the model one sees in Geneva at the Museum of the History of Science,[33] its late execution another indication of the difficulties facing Enlightenment Europe in "fixing" the high peaks in some sort of "knowable" order.

The immediate context for Saussure's descriptions of the Arve valley was not the challenge of mapmaking, but rather the question of how the senses help us make sense, as it were, of the world. This was a problem of some debate among his mentors and his friends. For Bonnet, if, as Locke suggested and Condillac and others were arguing, we are what we experience, then what room for the soul, what role for God in the universe? At the same time, Bonnet's scientific accomplishments were based on observation (whether of aphids, or plants). His *Essai de psychologie* (Essay on psychology, 1754) and *Essai analytique sur les facultés de l'âme* (Analytical essay on the faculties of the soul, 1760) were attempts to answer this question of how we know, with an emphasis on the active engagement of the "soul," or the mind, in the processing of sensory information.[34] It was critical, therefore, to establish how and what it means to observe. Was observation a passive absorption or an active set of processes? These were the questions behind an essay contest set by the Académie de Haarlem in 1769: "Qu'est-ce qui est requis dans l'Art d'observer? Et jusques où cet Art contribue-t-il à l'Entendement?" (What is necessary to the art of observing and how much does it contribute to our general understanding?).[35] Bonnet, since 1765 a foreign associate of the Haarlem Academy, had proposed the competition, and Jean Senebier, Saussure's friend and first biographer, entered with an essay that won silver and that was later reworked into his *Essaie sur l'art d'observer et de faire des expériences* (1802).[36]

In the meantime, the essay had been published in the *Memoirs* of the Society of Haarlem and in Geneva in the 1770s as *L'Art d'observer*.[37] The basic distinction between observation as "the attention of the soul turned toward objects proposed by nature" and experimentation as the "same attention, but directed toward artificially produced phenomena" offered by Senebier had already been established by the *Encyclopédie* in 1765, as had the emphasis on attention.[38] Attention here had the meaning of a learned or prepared way of looking, where the mind was readied to select the important details of its object so as to grasp the meaning of its whole. The mind or "soul" and its workings are the critical foci of Senebier's meanderings around and about the scientific method. Sensory experience was a mere "point of departure," one of Senebier's most recent historians has noted, a "mediocre, if necessary point of departure" for the "soul's activity."[39]

Poor Jean Trembley (1749–1811), though, who would go along with

Saussure and Marc-Auguste Pictet on that *tour du Mont Blanc* of 1778, when Pictet would draw his map of the massif.[40] A former student of Saussure's at the Academy of Geneva, he was drawn into Bonnet's circle. His father, Abraham Trembley (1710–1784), like Bonnet, was known for his work on animals who could reproduce asexually, in his case the hydra, in Bonnet's, as we have seen, aphids. In the mid-1760s, while Saussure is adventuring in the Alps, Trembley will "stud[y] privately with Bonnet."[41] And while Senebier will be rallying Bonnet's psychology into a coherent account of the analytic method in natural history, Trembley will be dissecting Bonnet's *Analytical Essay on the Faculties of the Soul*—almost literally. Trembley will spend his time indoors parsing the work by answering the 2045 questions set for him by Bonnet as a means to understand it.[42]

Saussure's exploration of the Arve valley at first sight can be mistaken for a working out—by walking out—of the method proposed by Bonnet and his disciples for understanding the natural world. Indeed, his relationship to Bonnet, as well as to Senebier and Trembley, was so close that historians of Bonnet's circle—Virginia Dawson and others—can be somewhat excused for overlooking Saussure's originality.[43] Certainly our reading of the *Voyages* confirms the importance of having a mind prepared for what one sees in nature. Saussure's observations from the Jura as well as his reading of Buffon organized for him questions about the valley and its mountains that he had in mind before he set out on foot, on horseback, or in a cabriolet. He was *attentive* in this way to his surroundings. He had an agenda.

However, for Bonnet and his circle, the project of understanding the natural world was clearly teleological, and overdetermined. Not only would natural history lead to proof of the existence of God (a truism of the Swiss or Protestant Enlightenment), it would reveal the "teleological character of the world."[44] Everything for a purpose, God's purpose. Moreover, Bonnet worried over the place in the body where the soul rests. This was understood as the eternal soul, not simply an animation of the mind where thoughts might be processed. That question had been addressed in Christian theology before, with Augustine, Aquinas, and Descartes weighing in. Bonnet, however, asks it in the context of John Locke, and that is the interesting part. Taking it as a given, following Locke, that memory is the key to the stability of the self and "is based in the brain," how, after death, does one's personality remain? How does the self remain stable after death if the soul is cut off from the brain, where memory works? Perhaps "our present brain contains a miniature brain that will develop in the afterlife and give us back our personal identity, body and mind together."[45]

For Locke and his followers, memory was key to the stable personality.

Since experience shapes us, without the thread of memory we would be different people as we moved through the environment and as we traveled through life. (And for Bonnet, strikingly and a little weirdly, after death.) For David Hume, the primacy of experience suggested that "a person is 'nothing but a bundle or collection of different perceptions, which succeed each other with an inconceivable rapidity, and are in a perpetual flux and movement.'"[46] Saussure's problem was not the stability of the self, however, but the apparent instability of what his stable self was seeing. What was the key to understanding an environment that seemed to be constantly shifting, but, being a mountain, was demonstrably not? One tactic was to deploy the other senses. Here he is at the Nant d'Arpenaz, on the way from Cluses to Sallanches, using touch to push back against a possible optical illusion. Behind the waterfall are the famous manifestly folded curves of rock that Martin Rudwick and Albert Carozzi suggest led Saussure to begin to imagine plate tectonics, and that figure 3.3, from the *Voyages*, depicts. The great arcs seemed to the viewer far below to be unbroken rock, layered curves of connected rock, though it was hard to

FIGURE 3.3 "Vue de la montagne du Nant d'Arpenaz entre Maglan et Salanche en Faucigny." Drawn by Marc-Théodore Bourrit, engraved by Christian Gottlieb Geissler. Saussure, *Voyages*, vol. 1, plate IV, *hors-texte* at p. 396. Watkinson Library, Trinity College, CT: DQ823.S246. Photo credit: Amanda M. Matava.

tell. Maybe, Saussure worried, some were actually fissures, cracks possibly bored through by water, and crumbling rock: "In 1774, to leave no doubt on the subject, I climbed very high up to the foot of these layers. I examined them closely, actually probing them in several places. One may therefore be absolutely certain that they are true rock beds, and not fissures or any other optical illusion [*apparence illusoire*"].[47]

And here he is farther along, outside of Servoz, establishing by scent the composition of some granite that the "torrent de Servoz" (presumably the Diosaz, which one can see in a walk from the train station) was tumbling into the Arve.[48] Were these granite blocs composed of hornblende, along with its feldspar, milky quartz, and mica? One breathes on the rock, and the granite in turn "exhales a strong odor of earth or mud, hornblende's telltale sign."[49] A kind of exchange of breath between human and rock, this is a telling intimacy and a key to understanding the *Voyages*. For not only did Saussure put to work all his senses, successively trying touch, taste, and smell, in reconciling his empiricism with uncertainty about what his eyes were saying, he put his whole body into the effort. He would "think with his body," in the phrase of Nan Shepherd, writing about her experience of the Cairngorms in Scotland in the 1930s and early '40s. The senses in the mountains dominate such that the "body may be said to think," Shepherd explains. Robert Macfarlane has pointed out how "arrestingly similar" these thoughts are to those of Maurice Merleau-Ponty, without in any possible way having been influenced by *The Phenomenology of Perception*.[50] Shepherd's insights were a result of intimacy with the mountain, something that is born from direct experience, from what Shepherd called the "interpenetration" of the "place and the mind."[51]

This intercourse Saussure effects rather literally, and precociously, while exploring a cave on the Salève, despite his abhorrence for tunneling deep into the Earth, away from the surface. "It takes a strong resolve to embark on such a course," he explained about his decision to explore below. The entry was narrow and twisting and daunting. Leaving the cave was even worse. After plunging a thermometer several times into the walls of the cave (he was taking the temperature of the Earth), he had to slither head first downward through its canals to escape. The way out was lower than the cave itself. Leading with the feet was not an option, since the passage out splits at several points, and "one needs to see to thread one's way through."[52] On the Môle one enters just as unpleasantly: "One is obliged to lie flat on one's belly and go in backward, feet first. This is because after penetrating into the mountain to a certain point, one gets to a type of stairway cut into the rock. It is so steep that it would be impossible to descend head first, and the passage by which one gets there is too narrow to allow one to turn around." Without his intense desire to see the inside of the Môle, he would never have done such a thing. He would have "lost his taste" for the entire project once he realized what his body would have to do.[53]

In each of these cases, his body had to subdue its responses. Saussure began to retrain or remake his body.[54] This was a solution unique for savants of his time. Haller had no need of doing so while botanizing. Indeed, once he reached two hundred pounds or so, he gave up even the effort of walking, bending, and reaching over for plants.[55] Occasional forays into the Alps or single savant expeditions to the Arctic or the Amazon, or the Pacific, were strenuous though not body-shifting for those adventurous savants. Joseph Banks never learned to climb a mast while on the *Endeavour* with Captain James Cook, for instance. Above Bonneville, on the Brezon, however, we see Saussure teaching himself to be comfortable with heights, even developing an exercise for doing so and recommending it to his readers. The Brezon, a peak about the same height as the Môle and facing it across the Arve, has steep cliffs overlooking the valley. They form a terrifyingly sharp precipice (*un précipice effroyable*). Climbing up, Saussure lay down on his belly and inched his way forward to the edge of the cliff until he could look outward and below.[56] It was an almost vertical drop.[57] Saussure tells us he did this on two or three separate occasions on his way to Chamonix. The *Voyages* recommend this exercise, not for the particular view of the valley below, but rather "to accustom one to see such profound drops without becom[ing] dizzy [*sans tournement de tête*]" and thus safely.[58] Twenty years later in 1784, perched comfortably high above Chamonix, eating a meal, and thanking "Providence" for saving him and his guide, Pierre Balmat, from a fall into a deep crevasse, he reflected on how his body had adapted to the heights: "Very few people from the plains could have dined with such a good appetite on this ridge, which to us felt absolutely secure. Beneath us dropped an extremely steep slope running uninterruptedly down to the bottom of the Chamonix Valley, 793 toises [1468.7 m] below. The view would certainly have caused vertigo in anyone not used to such spaces."[59] If one wanted to be in the peaks, one's whole body had to conform to its conditions. So, while walking up the Arve, Saussure was moving far away from the claims made by Senebier in the "Art of Observation" about how the world was understood through a synthesis of data brought to the mind through a series of observations that, say, allowed a consulting physician to diagnosis a disease. He was moving instead into a world of direct experience, more like that of an attending physician or an anatomist, with the body knowledge of a Haller. His was one body making sense of another.

The themes inaugurated on the first legs of the journey continue to unfold as Saussure takes his readers from Cluses to Sallanches, and then to Servoz, the hinge that opens us up to Chamonix. The geometry of rocks just outside of Cluses on a path "squeezed between the Arve and the foot of the mountain" was found interesting by the Genevan and seems to us a spatial echo of the mountains themselves.[60] Where, on the way to Cluses, the limestone mountains on each side of the valley were found to be "very varied, very irregular, with layers very rarely lying horizontally," so too were the rocks, "found in the debris accumulated from above," variously shaped.[61] This debris is remarkable for its irregularly shaped rocks, Saussure explained. Some were rhomboidal, that is, shaped as parallelograms with unequal adjacent sides; some were parallelepiped, with six sides formed by parallelograms. All were polyhedrons, or many-sided pieces with clear, sharp edges.[62]

Optical illusions continued. On the route to Sallanches, as elsewhere, "one often sees strata that only appear to be lying horizontally" when seen face on but that are very definitely angled otherwise: "One has to look at them not just from the front, but from the side, in profile."[63] As he explained about the Nant d'Arpenaz, "Large objects have to be seen from far away, and from each side, in order to have a sense of them as a whole. However, they also have to be approached close up, to get hold of their detail."[64] One perspective was never enough and was disorienting. In a rough approximation of the uncertainty principle, the more clearly visible was one aspect of a large mass, the more the other sides would be obfuscated.

Mont Blanc itself could deceive. When only its summit is visible and its mass is covered by clouds, Mont Blanc seems disembodied, unconnected to the Earth. "The summit of this mountain, hidden for most of the route by the surrounding heights, begins to appear again . . . as one approaches St. Martin. One sees it very well from the bridge there, and better still at Sallanches, where it looks astonishingly high," Saussure begins. "But it is never so astonishing as when clouds hide the greater part of its body [*son corps*] and the clouds thus recast the mountain as a kind of void or blankness, its summit alone being visible. It seems then impossible that what one is seeing is something belonging to the Earth." Typically, visitors "insist absolutely that what they are seeing is one of those high white clouds that will form sometimes at great heights above the tops of mountains." Only when the clouds below dissipate and the mountain's mass appears can one believe that that "summit lost in the heavens" has roots in the Earth.[65] Its power there to amaze tourists is suggested by the painting by Pierre-Louis de la Rive (1753–1817), a former student of Saussure's at the Academy, seen in figure 3.4.

FIGURE 3.4 Pierre-Louis De la Rive, *Le Mont Blanc vu de Sallanches au coucher du soleil* (1802). Musée d'art et d'histoire, Ville de Genève, Achat, 1969. Photo: Copyright Musée d'art et d'histoire, Ville de Genève, photographer: Yves Siza.

The high peaks met Saussure in earnest at Sallanches, in terrain, as well as in the looming and ethereal massif. Perils particular to the peaks were soon encountered and described. A landslide that he sees in 1767— "impossible to imagine something more hideous"—only seems to move slowly. In reality, it devastates with tremendous speed, tearing up trees by their roots and lifting up great blocks of rock. All the while the thick black waves of mud make "a muffled, doleful sound."[66] The Pont aux Chèvres, a flimsy wooden bridge that crossed the Arve below the heights of Chedde where the river plunged down and into a very steep ravine, was aptly named, since it seemed made only for goats, "as light footed as they were bold." Having survived this crossing twice in 1764, Saussure explains, he subsequently always took a detour.[67]

At Servoz, the Arve valley dips south-southeast to Les Houches. It is there, along a narrow route bordered by granite boulders, that Saussure found himself at home, "in the midst of the keenest pleasures that Nature can offer."[68] First, the flowers. It is along the path to Les Houches that the first truly alpine plants appear: the *Rhododendron ferrugineum*, whose pinky-purple flowers "exhale a scent as sweet as their color is fine," and the *auricule des Alpes*, a type of primrose. Though they become "more richly colored" in Genevan gardens, the flowers lost there "the delicious fragrance they have in these rocks." They needed to be cherished in the mountain air, leaving unsaid a whisper that Saussure thought he had to be so too. The *Astrantia alpina*, a pretty masterwort; the *Saxifraga cotyledon*, a type of rockfoil; and "etcetera," he added to his list.[69] Another cascade of colors, this time in the landscape that "along with the plants. . . . gives the route its alpine character." "The white foam of the Arve deep in its narrow passage is just glimpsed between the tips of pine trees, themselves set far below the footpath of the traveler." Vibrant white and green predominate below on one side, while iridescent black rock rides upward on the other into terraced steps of giant pines threaded with birch. High up all was a "somber green contrasting with pale white." All these sights—the palette and the angles—mark the approach of the high peaks.[70]

Finally, Chamonix. The "narrow and wild defile" is left behind as the Arve shifts north-northeast at Les Houches into the "infinitely soft and pleasant" Chamonix valley, cradle-shaped and covered with meadows.[71] A startling change, enhanced by the glaciers that appear, one by one. The Taconey (Taconnaz) first, "then soon after that the Buissons [Glacier des Bossons]," each descending from the heights of the massif on one's right. The ice of the Bossons "is dazzlingly white and shaped in the form of tall pyramids," which "makes a stunning effect in the midst of the forests of firs [*sapins*] that these ice pyramids tower over and travel through." Then "from afar one sees the great Glacier des Bois" (Mer de Glace), "its walls of ice" standing out among the yellow-brown peaks of the aiguilles while curving away from and then down into the valley.[72] Color and shapes come with sound: occasionally one is startled by thunderous claps of noise, followed by long, rolling rumblings like thunder: "Frightening when one is ignorant of the cause, when one understands that this is the sound of falling ice, one feels something more profound," that is, respect for the enormous dimensions of the place; "one recognizes how massive those blocks of ice must be to cause such a terrible fracas."[73]

Saussure traveled along the Arve as an empiricist alert to everything new that he saw, heard, touched, or smelled. His perceptions were shaped into word pictures in the *Voyages*, though in likeness to contemporary portrait painting rather than to early landscape paintings of the Alps. Contemporary landscapes—like Jallabert's—focused on eliciting emotional responses in the viewer by offering the picturesque or the sublime. The word pictures in the *Voyages*, on the other hand, offer a sense of the Earth itself, a vision of what the planet means as an "other," in the way a portrait offers a sense of another's self and an opportunity for the viewer to see that self, rather than simply a reflection of one's own self. Saussure's empiricism avoided the solipsism that the Alps seemed to invite among his contemporaries, above all by his insistence on the specificity of what he saw. This allows him to evade being the focal point of his travels, to let the Earth, as it were, be itself in its layers, colors, noises, and smells. He seems to give the Earth "its own life," not see it as an appendage of his own.[74]

Open any book about the Alps and you will find an account of the expedition to the "glaciers of Chamonix" by the British adventurers William Windham (1717–1761) and Richard Pococke (1704–1765), who traveled there from Geneva in 1741, twenty years before Saussure. The story of their expedition is a founding myth of Alpine history, having shaped an enduring narrative of conquest and adventure. It is reviewed here to underline to the reader how radical was the alternative relationship of human and nature offered by Saussure, and how appealing that might be. Their journey too began with the Arve, though while Saussure traveled with all his senses, Windham and Pococke looked with fixed and unwavering eyes. They were sure of their way before they set out. It was prescribed already in their worldview and packed along with their luggage. It was manifest in the well-armed band of men with whom they traveled. And it was confirmed by what they saw. They had "route knowledge," an environmental psychologist would say. Although the landscape was unknown, they stayed on "paths they already knew."[75] The upshot of their travel unfortunately was that the first descriptions of the glaciers of Mont Blanc were associated with imperialism, and the Chamoniards as simple beings baffled by the interest of outsiders. It was an adventure that would engage the romantic imagination for almost three hundred years. Something of Lord Byron there was already in the behavior of Pococke, dressing in "oriental" costume to awe the locals.

For Windham and his tutor Benjamin Stillingfleet (1702–1771), on their Grand Tour of Europe, Geneva was an expected lull from the intensities of Italy and France. Saussure's home was understood as a safe place for the British of a still-impressionable age, a stopping place between Catholic Rome, the basic point of the Grand Tour, with its antique heritage, and Paris, the center of all seductions. Though people spoke French in Geneva, they "thought in English," as Voltaire quipped.[76] They were Protestant. Still, Windham managed to get into trouble. In a side adventure to his famous one in the Alps, he became engaged to marry Elisabeth de Chapeaurouge, then jilted her, a breach of contract with this patrician family of syndics that would cost him 2000 pounds (about half a million dollars today)[77] to wiggle away from—and at what cost to Elisabeth's self-respect? Windham's eventual marriage in 1749 legitimized a son (born a month later), though not his daughter. The son, another William Windham (1750–1810), was Secretary of War in two administrations during the French Revolutionary wars. In the meantime, in Geneva in the spring of 1741, the father's circle included half a dozen other young men like himself, enjoying the prolonged adolescence offered to men—but not women—of the British gentry and aristocracy. They sat in on courses at the Academy of Geneva and put on "plays and pantomimes" in the late afternoons. An Oxbridge reference was explicit. Upon returning to Britain, they spoke of their "Common Room" in Geneva. Though on the Continent, they were always at home.[78]

When Richard Pococke joined the group on his way home from four years of traveling through the Ottoman Empire, it was as if they saw for the first time what kind of bold strokes could mark their way in the world. The imperialist leanings and the self-dramatizing tendencies of Windham in particular were realized in the figure of Pococke, older, imposing, and already memorialized in Oriental costume in a portrait by Jean-Étienne Liotard (1702–1789) painted in Constantinople in 1740 and depicted in figure 3.5.[79] Pococke was in Geneva to collect his portrait from Liotard's brother on Pococke's way home to England. Pococke had been preparing his two-volume travel book, *Description of the East and Some Other Countries* (London,1743–45), whose long sections on Egypt anticipate Napoleon's *Description de l'Égypte*, with its illustrations of the pyramids and the Sphinx, the latter strangely, in Pococke's view, with nose intact.[80] By contrast, Liotard's portraits are known for their luscious, exact attention to detail with the same respect for observation we see in the *Voyages*, though Liotard's specifics are fabrics and ornaments.[81] The portrait of Pococke brings to life the outfit he wore in Constantinople and described to his mother in a letter of 1739. We see his "blew [sic] linen garment . . . and over that such a coarse great coat as the common people here wear," and a turban (not the red cap the letter mentions, which Liotard himself wore as a self-styled Turk in his many self-portraits).[82]

Liotard's portrait of Pococke hangs today in the Genevan Museum of Art and History (not far from de la Rive's *View of Mont Blanc from Sallanches at Dusk* [fig. 3.4]). Pococke stands there as a reminder of a certain imperial arrogance that marks the "Famous Alpine Expedition" of 1741,[83] and in which his Oriental costume played a part. Science was its ostensible objective. When Pococke and Windham, along with several other "gentlemen" and tutors, assembled with servants, horses, and arms in mid-June, they may have had election to the Royal Society of London in mind. The Royal Society had a demonstrated interest in glaciers. The glaciers that then pushed into the town of Grindelwald at the head of the Lütschental,

FIGURE 3.5 Jean-Étienne Liotard, *Portrait de Richard Pococke* (1740). Musée d'art et d'histoire, Ville de Genève. Dépôt de la Fondation Gottfried Keller, 1948. Photo: Copyright Musée d'art et d'histoire, Ville de Genève, photographer: Bettina Jacot-Descombes.

up from Interlaken, had been reported on in their *Transactions* since the end of the seventeenth century.[84] Johann Jacob Scheuchzer (1672–1733), a Fellow of the Royal Society, had described glaciers—and dragons—in the Bernese Alps in his *Itinera Alpina*, published in London in 1708 with a dedication to the Royal Society. William Burnet (1687–1729), another FRS (later colonial governor of New Jersey, New York, New Hampshire, and Massachusetts) wrote up for the Royal Society an excursion he had made, to the glaciers of Grindelwald, at about the same time.[85] These were part of the ice rivers that still dramatically cut the massifs of the Wetterhorn, the Schreckhorn, and the Eiger, and the Finsteraarhorn and Mattenberg in the Bernese Alps.

Why not follow the Arve River to the glaciers in Savoy? This was a path trod already by locals bringing honey and quartz crystals to Geneva, as well as by surveyors, miners (of copper, lead, and silver) and the occasional secret agent slipping into southern Europe from Geneva via hunting paths from Chamonix to Courmayeur. Yet it was still open territory for naturalists. They could thus hope to trade adventure for election to the Royal Society. John Shipley Rowlinson, secretary of the Royal Society in the 1990s, has explained that being elected in the eighteenth century "was little problem for a gentleman of means who had good connections with the London-based Fellows." However, "those at a distance from London, or not confident of their claims, were careful to lay the foundations for their election."[86] In the event, Pococke's success would be assured by his Ottoman travels. He was made a Fellow a few months after his return to London in the fall of 1741, his reputation as an Orientalist preceding the publication of his volumes on the Levant.[87] Windham's reputation delayed his acceptance. Even his good friend Aldworth described him, unflatteringly, as someone who "'had an utter abhorrence of restraint,'"[88] and his practice in London of beating up men—"he became known as 'boxing Windham'"—and jilting women gave the Fellows pause.[89] Nonetheless, he was elected in the spring of 1744 on the basis of his "Account of the Glaciers or Ice Alps in Savoy," a write-up of that June 1741 expedition to Chamonix that misleadingly depicts the local inhabitants as fools and, stunningly, ignores Mont Blanc.[90]

With members taking "'the name of Arab chiefs and officers'" and Pococke's costume tucked away in his luggage,[91] the party rode off from Geneva to Bonneville, where they spent the night in that "very delightful situation" of "beautiful meadows and high mountains," then were off the next day to Cluses.[92] On the way they paused "to enjoy the prospect, which is *delicious*" (emphasis in original), of the view over the Arve, and to note the "singular beauty" of the Nant d'Arpenaz,[93] the waterfall that, by contrast, will draw Saussure's attention to the twisted limestone strata behind and above and take his thoughts to something like plate tectonics. At Cluses, the Arve begins to dip south until, at Sallanches, it will curve over to the east. This is the spot where viewers today, even in steel-clad buses, will exclaim out loud at the first sight of the giants of the massif, which seem to present themselves face on, though the high peaks remain at 45 degrees to the road, and from which Pierre-Louis de la Rive painted his *en plein air* picture of Mont Blanc.

There, Windham reports, they "encamp[ed] in a fine meadow near the bridge" that crosses the Arve from Saint Martin's to Sallanches,[94] and this is when the jokes began. Where one would expect to read about the troop's astonishment at the sight of Mont Blanc, the accounts tell us instead about the villagers' reaction to the company. It was one of "'wonder and astonishment,'" according to Windham,[95] though probably—and this is drawn from the *Voyages*—at the ridiculousness of the charade. The elderly of Chamonix still laugh, Saussure explained in the second volume of the *Voyages* (1786), about how scared those travelers of 1741 were, and how needless were their defenses.[96] Pococke's costume was at its center. The servants having set up a large tent, Pococke slipped away and "dressed [him]self in the Arab dress" painted by Liotard and starring in the Art and History Museum of Geneva today.[97] The "Company" was delighted and acted swiftly to develop their theme, as do later chronicles of the episode, embroidering upon Windham's account. Sentinels "with drawn swords" were posted at the entrance to the tent, and Pococke was accompanied there "'with great pomp.'"[98] Then the men simply waited for the locals to react, so that they might snicker, as some readers of the account—though never the *Voyages*—have done since: "Among the inhabitants the news spread like wildfire that an eastern potentate had arrived, and the various comments on the supposed orientals amused the latter not a little."[99] We "were all exceeding cheerful," explained Pococke.[100]

No one was hurt, yet violence was done. The imprint of one large footprint of meaning remains stamped on Chamonix, given the influence of Windham's "Account." The Orientalist twist placed on the visit of a group of British men to a village in French-speaking Savoy is not imperialist in the same way that Pococke's improvement of Ardbraccan, his episcopal estate in Ireland, will be in 1765. There the exoticism is manifest in the groves of Lebanese cedars that Pococke, as (Protestant) Lord Bishop of Meath, had planted on grounds renowned for its holy well, not quite wiped clean of its magic by the Protestant ascendancy (and where one of the five guardian trees of Ireland once stood).[101] Still, a script was in place that obscured the people encountered in Sallanches, and soon at Chamonix. At Chamonix they found the inhabitants cunning, albeit easily outwitted by the British. Attempts to dissuade them from climbing Montenvers by false claims about its difficulties were shoved aside.[102] The simplicity of their script—adventure into the unknown, return with a report on a natural wonder—shaped the economy of their description as well as of their depiction of the valley's inhabitants. Windham and Pococke had phrases ready at hand for each. The country they passed through was "very delightful," of a "singular beauty." It was *delicious*. These are clichés of their age. When they reach the top of Montenvers and are looking down at the Mer de Glace, this word bank proved inadequate: "I own to you that I am extremely at a loss to give a right idea of it." Still, they tried: "The description which travelers give of the seas of *Greenland* seems to come the nearest to it."[103]

Mary Shelley too will pair the Mer de Glace with the icebound northern seas. Frankenstein and his monster meet their deaths in the Arctic, while earlier in their story the moral death of each is recognized in their encounter on the glacier. Frankenstein will be berated there for creating and then abandoning his creature, the creature rebuked for his murderous revenge.[104] A different morality will be on display in 1741, self-satisfied, imperialist, and racist. Windham and Pococke will extend the metaphor of the seas from the whaling Arctic to the Caribbean in a salute to early success in Britain's war against Spain for control of trade in the Caribbean, including that of humans from Africa, the *asiento de negros* of which Britain wanted a greater share. After a half an hour on the glacier, on the rough surface of the ice, looking about and into its "cracks," some "so deep, that we could not see to the bottom,"[105] they "drank there in ceremony Admiral *Vernon's* health, and success to the *British* arms" (emphases in original) in that endeavor.[106]

Climbers during the golden age of British mountaineering followed the lead of Windham and Pococke. A tension between climbing for science (their description of a glacier for the Royal Society) and the thrill of adventure was resolved in favor of sport. As Leslie Stephen sarcastically declared to the Alpine Club in a speech in 1865 understood as a manifesto for alpinism—that is, climbing for fun—his ascent, the first, of the Zinalrothorn (4221m.) above Zermatt in 1864 was achieved without the help of any scientific instruments (though it was enabled by Melchior and Jakob Anderegg, experienced guides).[107] Albert Frederick Mummery (1855–1895), "the best-known climber of his generation,"[108] echoed Stephen's tone in the preface to *My Climbs in the Alps and the Caucasus* (1895), published just weeks before his reckless assault on Nanga Parbat (8126 m.) in the western Himalaya. (Reckless because he assumed that conditions in the Himalaya were similar to those of the Alps, despite the massive difference in scale. He and two porters, Ragobir Thapa and Goman Singh, rank novices at climbing, were swept away while reconnoitering a way around to the northern face of the massif via a treacherous, nearly impossible ridge.) "To tell the truth, I have only the vaguest ideas about theodolites [used for measuring angles] and as for plane tables, their very name is an abomination." The book was addressed "to those who think with me, who regard mountaineering as unmixed play."[109]

As for the Windham and Pococke expedition, Windham dutifully collected instruments for measuring heights and distances along their way, though he left them behind. In Rowlinson's view, Windham was a "competent mathematician" and "a skilled mechanic,"[110] but, as Windham explained in his account, he "chose not to take the trouble of carrying them."[111] The compass, though, he simply forgot.[112] At the edge of the Montenvers, as Windham looked down upon the Mer de Glace, Windham regretted having "unluckily left at *Chamoigny* a pocket compass, which I had carried with me, so that I could not well tell the bearings as to its situation."[113] An insouciance toward basic orienteering (fixing oneself in space with respect to the four cardinal points) did not hurt their case with the Royal Society, however. Since the Chamonix valley runs below the massif, whose peaks scan east to west, visibly, from Geneva, and as the Mer de Glace cuts into it perpendicularly, he guessed correctly that the glacier ran "pretty nearly from north to south" (though its flow is south to north).[114]

Saussure experienced the mountains differently from the predominantly instrumentalist approach to the Alps of Windham and Pococke (Chamonix as a means to an end) and the mountaineering cultures that followed, his empiricism leading the way. On his first trip to Chamonix, Saussure too will ascend the Montenvers and look down at the glacier, then still known as the Glacier des Bois, as its snout is still called today. "One might never have one's fill of the view": the colors of the glacier below—blue and white—the shapes of the waves; the extension of its streams; the ascending sides of the Aiguille du Dru (3754 m), that grand needle of granite, "polished like a work of art," that lay across the expanse of glacier.[115] However, where Windham will write, "You must imagine your lake put in Agitation by a strong Wind and frozen all at once," Saussure will speak with precision. The glacier, he said, looks like "'a sea which has become suddenly frozen, not in the moment of a tempest, but at the instant when the wind has subsided, and the waves, although very high, have become blunted and rounded,'"[116] as indeed they do. And he will continue, describing the waves formed as swells, running parallel to the length of the glacier, cut transversely by crevasses. Still looking down from Montenvers, he says the crevasses look blue inside, the ice outside white.[117] He sees the shapes and colors of the ice and how these seem to change when down upon the glacier, something neither Windham nor Pococke noticed on their brief walk on to its surface.

Saussure urged venturing "at least three or four hundred steps out from the moraine, to get a good idea of these great valleys of ice; from far away, as from Montenvers, for example, their features are lost. The surface unevenness suggests only rounded waves after a storm. However, once well onto the glacier, those waves present as mountains, and the spaces in between, as valleys."[118] One has to wander onto and over a glacier, Saussure explained, to see its strange formations, its "beautiful accidents" (in the geological sense). "Its deep crevasses, its great caves, its lakes full of pretty water, either captured between transparent walls of ice tinted aquamarine, or running quickly along canals to form waterfalls sinking down into the abyss of ice"—all these are described.[119] This respect for detail closes in on the materiality of the natural world, as a thing-in-itself, or a thing-for-itself. Saussure's focus is the Mer de Glace not himself, and as if that spectacular space could exist without himself. The planet does not care about the crawling creatures that are we, as Saussure had suggested in his Lucretian preface to the *Voyages*.[120] Ours is not the only vantage point.

Saussure's difference from the British adventurers of 1741—to their imperialism and disdain for the people they meet—is manifest throughout the *Voyages*, beginning with Saussure's respectful description of his first guide, Pierre Simon (d. c. 1780).[121] A crystal and chamois hunter, Simon led him onto the Mer de Glace and up the Brévent on Saussure's first, life-changing visit. For the next twenty years Saussure explored the Mont Blanc massif with him, Simon becoming for Saussure a model for how to live in nature, for how to integrate one's body into the environment of the high peaks. They both ran risks, Saussure explained, crossing the Mer de Glace in 1760. It was practically impassable on the side opposite Montenvers, below the Aiguille du Dru. Simon had to run to and fro searching for the least dangerous ways forward. Some of the fissures were narrow enough for Saussure to jump over. Others were deep and wide, and they had to slide down into them and then laboriously climb up and out the other side, on steps Simon's axe broke into the slope. Others still had to be negotiated by crossing over ice ridges, "like a tightrope walker," he says, perilously balanced.[122]

Saussure was taught the art, "for art it is," to walk, climb, and descend on ice, the Chamoniard hunter adapting the Genevan patrician to the glacier. It was a matter of training Saussure's body to think differently on that frozen space. He had to learn how to "position his body correctly," "to place his feet just so," and "to use his *bâton* [a type of alpenstock] to help him negotiate difficult passages."[123] Saussure managed fairly well, although he did receive a few contusions when "sliding down those very steep slopes of ice." Simon did this standing up, leaning backward on his *bâton*, "reaching the bottom without getting hurt." "This exercise is much more difficult than it would seem at first," Saussure explained. Like downhill skiing, which would not be invented for another hundred years, mastery of the glissade offers power and precision, and the learning process entails "quite a few falls" before one's body adapts.[124] The illustration in the *Voyages* of someone doing this—"traversant la Mer de Glace in 1760"—is a portrait of Simon and the first-ever depiction of a mountain guide (fig. 3.6).[125]

Saussure and Simon then climbed to the summit of the Brévent, with its stereoscopic views across the valley to Mont Blanc, and from which today one can trace Saussure's path to the top by following the diagram posted nearby. Saussure's goal on that first climb, the first of any naturalist, he believed,[126] was to capture that view. One sees everything, and almost at the same time: "the six dazzlingly bright glaciers between the inaccessible peaks that gave birth to them; Mont Blanc, above all, which presents as so much larger and so much more majestic from this viewpoint than from higher ground." "Those beautiful glaciers," he exclaimed, at this view like no other, "slipping off and down the peaks like solid rivers flowing between great forests of pines [*sapins*] bending and twisting into the valley of Chamouni."[127]

FIGURE 3.6 Untitled vignette, "[Un homme qui se glisse sur la neige]." Saussure, *Voyages*, vol. 1, top of p. 355. Watkinson Library, Trinity College, CT: DQ823.S246. Photo credit: Amanda M. Matava.

When Saussure walked into Chamonix from the Arve valley, he was armed with an empiricism that was proving already to be a powerful tool for a scientific understanding of the Alps. The rock walls near Cluses enclosing the Arve were set in layers that folded back upon themselves, an observation suggestive of the later theory of plate tectonics. Large blocks of granite strewn along the entrance to the valley—the erratics—were recognized as alpine in origin, the central peaks being of this substance. And though Saussure surmised that they were carried down to Geneva in an inundation—just as the bits of rocks coloring the Arve River were brought down from the high peaks to the river in fast-eroding streams—and did not guess at their glacial origin, their identification was crucial to connecting Geneva and the Alps in one geological region. Out of that detail, however—the colors, the shapes, the scents—comes poetry, beyond what his mentors in Geneva could have imagined describing. What emerges from Saussure's pen—or rather, the wax pencil with which he took his notes—is a sensual portrait of the Earth drawn from his full-body engagement with his surroundings. Scientific, yes, but liable as well to be addressed and questioned, as Shelley will in his encounter with Mont Blanc: "And what were thou, and earth, and stars, and sea, / If to the human mind's imaginings / Silence and solitude were vacancy?"[128] How does one make sense of the Earth?

✳ 4 ✳
Bodies of Desire

The Chamonix that welcomed Saussure in the 1760s was a commune of a few hundred people, not unlike other villages in the old regime. Its built environment consisted of some two dozen houses grouped around the church, the whole with fields backed up against the Brévent (2525 m), a peak in the Aiguilles Rouges, which lie across the valley from Mont Blanc.[1] The ordinary precariousness of rural life in the eighteenth century was exacerbated by the environment. Arable land was scarce, and at 1035 meters above sea level and 45.9 degrees latitude, the growing season is short. The Little Ice Age brought other exceptional challenges. Twelve feet of snow was observed by Saussure in spring in 1764 at Le Tour (granted, "the highest and coldest village in the valley"),[2] with ten feet being reported in 1790.[3] Moreover, expanding glaciers had pushed into valley land. They had captured fields at Les Bois and near Les Houches in recent community memory. A little wheat was grown, but the cereal crops were mostly barley and some oats and rye. To feed the population, grain had to be imported—that is, purchased. An "État des récoltes à Chamonix" (Report on the harvest in Chamonix) for 1782 describes this stress in numbers. (Here "Chamonix" means the villages of the Chamonix valley). Three thousand five hundred and forty-five "bushels" (*coupes de la vallée*) of grain harvested, divided by four of these quantities needed to nourish one person, allowed 887 people to be fed. The population of the valley totaled 1553, counting 901 persons living in Chamonix and Argentière, and 652 at Les Houches and its nearby hamlet Vaudagne. Therefore, 2664 bushels of grain would have to be imported to feed the remaining 666 people.[4]

Grain was scarce, and raising cows for cheesemaking was an option open only to some inhabitants. While the *alpages* (alpine or high mountain meadows)—which give the range its name—were held communally, land in the valley was not. Cows from Chamonix could move successively up the slopes of the massif to the lower and then higher Blatière alps below the Aiguille du Midi for summer grazing, or to the pasturage at Montenvers. Or they could eat at Planpraz, the alp resting 500 meters below the summit of the Brévent, where Saussure imagined collecting flowers and butterflies for his wife. Downstream at Les Houches, they could climb to Bellevue, where their clattering bells still define the moment for those setting off for the Nid d'Aigle and the Goûter route to Mont Blanc. These meadows were few. Created by deforesting level areas on the slopes, these flattish regions were small and rare in the heights above the Chamonix valley.

The milk would be churned into butter and cooked into cheese by the women and children who kept the cows, in an engagingly equitable system. Twice a season, each cow's milk production was measured, so that the profits of butter and cheese could be divided proportionally at summer's end, even though each cow had had equal access on the alp to sweet grass and hay. "From each according to her ability, to each according to her needs," as one might paraphrase Marx, but only while grazing on the mountain. As Saussure realized, the "commons" failed entirely in its purported goal. It gave all to the rich and nothing to the poor. At least, he suggested, those who profited from common land should compensate those left out. (True as well, he added, with respect to forests. Held in common, but what use was wood for a man without the resources for building?)[5] With snow lingering into June, cows needed long winter care in barns.[6] Better-off cows ate a mixture of hay and straw; poorer ones made do with straw, which had to be grown, since it was impossible to gather sufficient forage from the slopes.[7] In order to benefit from the high meadow commons, one needed to own enough land for grain, hay, and pasturage, along with orchards and meadows—that is, land enough to support people and cows—and that was not easily done in a valley bordered by steep slopes with few alps and small, shrinking fields.[8]

Saussure entered a world of sensational beauty, straitened circumstances, and limited possibilities. Mining had a long history in the valley, though it was unproductive and could not solve the valley's employment problem.[9] For the cash needed for taxes and other ineluctables, men would travel to other alpine regions to work in cheesemaking during the summer.[10] The exodus of so many men explains one of the presenting features of the valley: that is, the predominance of women in agriculture that struck Saussure and other elite visitors.[11] Women dominated the working world. The need for income helps explain the other determining feature of social life in the 1760s. The men who stayed behind were climbers. They knew the rocky heights above the alpine meadows and the crossings of the glaciers as they searched for chamois and for deposits of quartz crystal, which brought good prices in Geneva. Crystal was in demand throughout Europe for use on shoes and clothing. It was a substitute for diamonds, made fashionable at Versailles, so its resale was lucrative.[12]

Though discoveries of crystal were rare and extremely hazardous, the risks seemed worth it to its practitioners. Deposits or veins were enclosed in the granite slopes of the high peaks. One climbed to spaces that looked promising, tapping with hammers to detect fissures that might hold the bonanza, and for too many aspirants that was the last event of their young lives. So, too, in the chase for chamois. Since chamois could outrun any human they saw and escape by scrambling up precipitous rocky slopes, hunters had to either try to surprise them from above or set traps to entangle them in high webs.[13] The more they were hunted, the more their population declined, and so the harder hunting them became. Saussure noticed how few remained in the 1780s, an alpine loss he lamented along with that of the marmots, whose whistles once echoed around him and whose antics—they would jump up high and dash among the rocks—had charmed him. In 1786 "he heard their occasional whistles from far off, but he saw not a one."[14]

Two sets of interest met in the 1760s in Chamonix, the longing on the part of Saussure to know the Mont Blanc massif and Chamoniards' need for income to provide the necessities of life and allow them to prosper. These came together almost immediately in the close relationship established between Saussure and his first guide, Pierre Simon. Simon welcomed the infusion of funds that the well-heeled Genevan offered him that summer of 1760 and regularly afterward, just as Saussure welcomed his companionship and expertise. Simon would meet Saussure at Sallanches with mules and news, Saussure explained, to shepherd him on those last tricky leagues (30 km) to Chamonix, or on their tours around the massif beginning at Servoz or Les Houches. They corresponded. The archives contain the first surviving letter written by a Chamonix guide—Simon's to Saussure—and volume 1 of the *Voyages* depicts him on a glacier, the first illustration ever of an alpine guide. There is every reason to accept Saussure's estimation that their relationship was one of respect.

It was on coming down from the Brévent with Simon during Saussure's inaugural climb that Saussure made his famous offer of a substantial prize that would go to the first person who could find a way to the summit of Mont Blanc. He had the announcement posted throughout the valley that summer and again in 1761. It included the promise of recompense for income lost while trying, even if the efforts led to nothing.[15] Simon tried for this soon afterward, exploring an approach from the Glacier du Tacul—south and east of the massif, climbing up into it from the Mer de

Glace—and then again from the Glacier des Bossons.[16] In 1775 four other guides attempted the more promising line of the Montagne de la Côte, including Michel and François Paccard, cousins of Dr. Paccard of the first summiting, and Jean-Nicolas Coutterand, son of the woman who established Chamonix's first hotel. Three others followed in 1783.[17] Finally, in 1786 Jacques Balmat received the award, equivalent, Peter Hansen shows, to "about two weeks' work for a hunter or guide," that is, two guineas or forty-eight livres."[18] (Historians now acknowledge that Dr. Paccard, with whom Balmat climbed, may have discovered the route after having made his own forays and having had an eureka moment on the Brévent, glimpsing from there the way to the top. This conundrum has absorbed old and new accounts of the summiting of Mont Blanc, and will be addressed—unavoidably—in a later chapter.)

Chamoniards were responding to questions about how to experience nature in an era when *nature* was a buzzword, and its appeal was bringing outsiders to their region to feel its raw force, coming to regard the glaciers as "their best neighbours" for doing so, as John Moore (1729–1802) on the Grand Tour noted.[19] What they did was novel, without precedent. They began marketing not nature, but the village and the valley as a place where one could comfortably enter it: climb the Montenvers, walk on the Mer de Glace! To some degree, the Lake District in Britain is a parallel, with places to stay developing along with romantic interest in the region from the 1770s onward. The Chamonix valley is more concentrated, however, as is the timeline of its development. Its population multiplied tenfold between 1770 and 1783: a few hundred villagers became fifteen hundred in 1783 and three thousand in 1830.[20] These are remarkable figures, and the numbers of visitors rose in tandem. The intendant of Faucigny—the local agent of the duke of Savoy/king of Sardinia—gathered data on the number of "notable," that is, wealthy and important, visitors to the valley, identifying "30 in 1772" and "more than 2000 in 1785."[21] A list of these by name drawn up by the intendant in 1788—after the first summits of Mont Blanc—and discovered in the departmental archives may be the earliest such record for any tourist town.[22]

How to house these visitors was the first concrete question answered by Chamoniards. When Saussure arrived in Chamonix in 1760, and for the next several visits he stayed with the curé in the house then attached to the church, now the Maison de la Montagne on the Place de l'Église. Staying with the curé was the usual choice for visitors to remote villages, as Saussure explained, and as his experience elsewhere in the Alps shows. The alternate was a "miserable" cabaret or two, "like those found in any rarely visited place,"[23] which could sleep only a few travelers at a time. These auberges, or inns, were as modest as the houses of the villagers and quite possibly essentially comfortable, just undoubtedly "disdained by persons of distinction" (*délaissées par les gens de distinction*).[24]

The first to respond to the expectations of visitors to Chamonix was Thérèse Garny, the widow of a notary named Coutterand, known to Saussure and alpine history as Mme. Coutterand.[25] She transformed one of these humble auberges into the first comfortable hotel in Chamonix, praised and recommended by Saussure, patronized by Goethe and aristocrats such as the duc de la Rochefoucauld and Lord Palmerston. Marketed as the Hôtel d'Angleterre when taken over by her son Jean-Nicolas, it was situated at the edge of the village,[26] and its imposing red-roofed and multichimneyed presence can be seen in the 1787 colored engraving by Jean-François Albanis-Beaumont (c. 1755–1812), now in the Musée alpin de Chamonix (fig. 4.1).[27]

Other establishments followed. Coutterand's son-on-law, Michel Charlet, opened a spillover auberge. The Tairraz family opened a competing establishment in 1775, on the opposite (left) bank of the Arve, called the Hôtel de Londres. François Paccard followed after 1785 with a smaller inn of his own. By the time Saussure published the second volume of the

FIGURE 4.1 Jean-François Albanis-Beaumont, *Vue de l'extrémité du village de Chamouni* (c. 1787). Collection musée alpin, Chamonix-Mont-Blanc, AG. 104.

Voyages in 1786, visiting Chamonix "had become so fashionable [*si fort à la mode*] that the three large and good auberges that were established one after the other were scarcely able to house all the foreigners [*étrangers*] that arrived in summer from all the countries of the world."[28] (Not literally from all over the world, of course. He was catching in his word net visitors from Russia and the new United States of America along with European elites.) Romantic Europe followed suit ("Toute l'Europe romantique prend le chemin du massif du Mont Blanc").[29] In 1816 the Shelleys were staying in the Hôtel de Londres while Mary imagined Frankenstein on the Mer de Glace and Percy pondered Mont Blanc,[30] and, as his poem begins, "the everlasting universe of things."[31]

Chamonix's dynamism dazzles in contrast to the history of Grindelwald, whose glaciers had first drawn the attention of elite Europe in the seventeenth century and the prestige of which lured Windham and Pococke to Chamonix in 1741. Grindelwald's were the glaciers featured in the *Encyclopédie*'s essay on glaciers in 1757, while the Mer de Glace was slightingly and inaccurately mentioned, being placed south of Mont Blanc rather than north and east.[32] Yet Grindelwald's first hotel appeared only in 1820. Until then, its "trickle of visitors" (such as Saussure) "lodged with the minister in the *Pfarrhaus* in preference to the inn or *Wirtshaus*."[33] At a glance, one sees strong parallels between the two villages, Grindelwald and Chamonix. They lie at similar elevations, Grindelwald at 1034 meters and Chamonix at 1035 meters. Like Chamonix, Grindelwald was connected through glacier river valleys—the Lütchen, then the Aare, via the lakes—to a city of some importance, in its case Bern. Now the de facto capital of the Swiss Confederation, Bern was its own city-state in the eighteenth century and the home for many years of the illustrious Haller. It was one of the "guarantors" of Genevan independence, along with France and Zurich. And Grindelwald, like Chamonix, was a space of sensational effect, with its "two glaciers that flowed down almost to the village, and a beautiful, wide green valley overlooked by the magnificent and seemingly impregnable north wall of the Eiger and the fortress-like cliffs of the Wetterhorn."[34] Their economies differed, however. Alpiculture—defined by "summertime pasturing, the elevation of the pasture areas, and the mode of exploitation—carried out at a distance from settlements, but juridically and economically dependent on them"—worked well in Grindelwald.[35] Its "wide green valley" and abundant alps were sufficient to absorb the energy of its inhabitants, who neither looked for employment outside the valley nor were primed by underemployment to invent new forms of behavior within it. So Grindelwald would become a tourist town—for climbing, hiking, then skiing—only in the wake of Chamonix.

The reader will notice some familiar names: Coutterand, Paccard, Tairraz, Balmat, and so on. Hotels and guiding were tied together. Mme. Coutterand built that first hotel in 1770. It was her son Jean-Nicolas who, with three other guides, plotted out the first stage of the route to the summit of Mont Blanc, via the Montagne de la Côte in 1775. It is he who will first understand the importance of the British to the valley, renaming the establishment the Hôtel d' Angleterre. François Paccard was another of the guides who attempted that route in 1775 (and the cousin of Dr. Paccard). His hotel opened ten years later, in 1785. The Hôtel de Londres, run by the Tairraz family, competed with the Coutterands both for visitors and for the best cook of the village. This was understood to be the wife of Jacques Balmat—not the Jacques Balmat renowned as the "hero of Mont Blanc," who first summited, but a relative of his who was also a guide. This was Jacques Balmat *des dames*, who specialized in guiding women and families. All the Tairraz sons—Jean-Pierre, Michel, and Victor—were guides.

Hotels offered pastoral care (good advice along with beds and food), and guides shepherded visitors to the most charismatic spaces in Europe, along, around, and up the Mont Blanc massif. These innovations of the Coutterands, the Paccards, the Balmats, and the Tairrazes all lead directly into the Chamonix of today. They created a new type of capitalism: environmental capitalism, defined as a selling of access to nature. Histories of mountaineering, with their focus on summiting, have relentlessly leapt past Chamonix and Mont Blanc to the Himalaya, to those highest mountains on Earth, and to imperialist projects. Saussure's Chamonix rests in the heart of Europe, where a natural world, mediatized and commercialized—as romanticism's "mountains of the mind"—was first tested against a nonhuman nature running along its own unstoppable rules. This is the history of interest today as we face the consequences of global warming and the loss of biodiversity, alongside a growing industry of ecotourism.

Saussure and Chamonix grew in importance together. The one's success enabled the other's. Saussure's travels to Chamonix riveted Enlightenment attention on the Mer de Glace and Mont Blanc. And he was followed there by curious tourists from English, French and German-speaking Europe. Saussure himself used the word *tourist*, which helped to inaugurate its modern meaning. So well understood by Chamoniards was Saussure's role in directing attention to the valley that—it was said—the mere mention of his name would prompt the tipping of a hat.[36] As Philippe Joutard has explained with some exaggeration, the difference between Grindelwald, with its traditional economy, and Chamonix was Saussure.[37]

To become such a prominent figure, however, money was needed. The rest of this chapter describes the wide scope of Saussure's project to understand the natural history of the Alps and explains how it was enabled by the private fortune brought to him by his marriage in 1765 to Albertine-Amélie Boissier. Investment of her riches in French funds supported his travels and paid for the costly scientific instruments he took along with him. These were purchased from specialists centered in Geneva, London, and Paris, as were the expensive books he accrued for his library, books ordered from dealers throughout Europe. These were housed in two luxurious properties, inherited by Albertine and renovated by the couple to suit Saussure's alpine interests. The mansion in Geneva lay on the rue de la Tertasse, the walls of the street—*tertasse* means walls—hugging hard the façade of the house, as the walls of the city fortified the town. Yet the rear terrace of the property was open to a view of the Jura Mountains. There Saussure built a laboratory workshop where his collection of stuffed alpine animals was kept, where he attempted to form granite from its component parts and heat (impossible to do), and where prototypes of new instruments, such as the hair hygrometer, were developed. Inside the mansion, his library of more than a thousand volumes was where he composed the *Voyages*, that is, where the account of his travels was shaped from notes taken on site in the peaks and recopied at night in tent, cabin, or inn, his alpine experiences brought alive in the comfort of this study.

The property at Genthod on the right bank of Lake Geneva was built by Albertine's family as a summer escape from the city. Oriented toward the lake, it faced the Alps, with Mont Blanc tantalizingly visible to Saussure when he was home, and distressingly so to Albertine when Saussure was away on the massif. A luxury compound, Genthod contained a main house with galleries open to the gardens. These were redesigned by the Saussures in the English way, with nods to a more natural landscape rather than the stiff, formal, controlled French-style spaces of their neighbors. Still, the main house seemed stifling to Saussure, who would occasionally sleep in a simple outbuilding, more like his resting places in the Alps.[38]

The rich materiality of Saussure's Genevan life opens up to us a view of what the privileges of wealth and gender could offer to a naturalist in the eighteenth century—in the absence of today's research universities—and with the ambition, intelligence, and imagination to make it happen. It is a glimpse into the world of the scientific Enlightenment, in that way a life not unlike that of the chemist Antoine Lavoisier, born in 1743, or Joseph Banks, born the same year, both of whom were almost exactly Saussure's age and, like him, extremely wealthy. And Banks too traveled in the 1760s, though his voyages to Labrador and Newfoundland and then with Cook to the Pacific were not repeated, and the rest of his life was focused on botany and presiding over the Royal Society of London. Saussure's comfortable life on the rue de la Tertasse and at Genthod—as we see it now—offers us something more than we typically find in the life histories of other savants. We find tensions at work in environmentalism today—in efforts to reconcile core urban identities with the claims on ourselves as humans in nature—in Saussure's position as a leading member of the city-state of Geneva, caught by his longing for the Alps.

The project to understand the Alps seemed as immense as the mountains themselves. Their topography had to be drawn, that is, the location, size, and shape of its peaks and valleys had to be pinned down, and penned, and what rocks and minerals they were made of needed to be known. Saussure had to confirm his observations that secondary mountains—the Prealps—were limestone, and the primary high peaks were universally granite, with suppositions made about the origins of this arrangement. Limestone was puzzling: how did sea creatures get there? Granite was a mystery. The glaciers remained be understood. Where did the ice come from, and how did it move? The "envelope" of the mountains had to be mapped and understood. What caused storms? Why did the colors of the sky differ at high altitudes? What was the role of electricity?

Mastering the understanding of the alpine region entailed major excursions, repeated to confirm initial observations, and a mustering of information about the physics, chemistry, and biology of what was becoming visible as an experimental unit, the Alps themselves. Though the objective of his first circuit around Mont Blanc in 1767 was the comparison of the southern side of the massif with the northern—were the valleys parallel? were the faces with their flowing glaciers similar?—Saussure also set out to explore the mountain's flora and fauna.[39] These included animalcules, as he explained to Haller—microscopic freshwater animals whose asexual division he discovered in 1765.[40] He would also probe the atmosphere, or "envelope," as he called it, of the Earth, and the physics of what lies below its surface, performing experiments having to do with understanding electricity, heat and cold, atmospheric pressure (the "weight of the air"), and magnetism.[41]

The walking companions from the Jura were enlisted to help him on the first circling observational *tour du Mont Blanc*. François Jallabert came along to do the drawings and Jean-Louis Pictet, the maps. Even with this team, however, there was much left undone. Pictet had to get back to work, so detours and delays along the route were eschewed.[42] The second circuit of the massif was accomplished in 1774 "alone" (though with his servant and guides, of course) to fill in these lacunae. His "Agenda autour du Mont-Blanc en 1774" (Agenda, circuit of Mont Blanc in 1774) included a "list of observations to make with respect to valleys and primary and secondary mountains" consisting of twenty-nine topics, six of these with subset lists of five or six clarifying items.[43] His intention had been to write up his findings when he returned and publish them, but as he began to work he again "found gaps in what he knew and questions that were unresolved."[44] Thus the 1778 excursion with Marc-Auguste Pictet and Jean Trembley, to check again and confirm, before publishing the first volume of the *Voyages* (1779), where its second part, "Voyage autour du Mont-Blanc," begins.

So, too, were travels to the Oberland repeated. As Saussure reassured his wife in a letter written from the village of Meiringen on the Aare River in 1777, as he waited for horses to hire to carry him over the Grimsel Pass: "I did well to return to the Grindelwald glaciers to take another look. I did not see them well in 1770, so I was left with a very false impression." This time around he was able to observe them clearly, having a "remarkably beautiful" day for it.[45] These trips were necessary also to test whether observations of the Mont Blanc massif held true elsewhere. Or might there be other features of the Alps that one needed to take into account somehow in order to understand their history? Commenting on the Schreckhorn (4078 m), "that *corne de l'épouvante* [peak of terror]" on that same trip to the Bernese Alps, he told her: "It truly deserves its name, not simply on account of its height. It fairly bristles with overhanging rock faces and ice. I was happy to see though that it is constituted exactly like our primitive [in the sense of primary, first-formed] mountains in the Savoy. However, its neighbors present some singularities that it was important for me to have seen."[46]

A circuit of Monte Rosa and a summiting of the Rothorn (3103 m) in 1789 and his last major alpine excursion to the Matterhorn in 1792 were made to check whether observations made in the Savoy Alps were true of high peaks and glaciers elsewhere. Then there was the observation of basalt (volcanic rock) in the Auvergne, to address the question of what basalt was, and whether mountains were of volcanic origins.[47] Why was lava not found in the Alps? The visit to Vesuvius with Sir William Hamilton in Naples and the summiting of Etna were also part of this quest. And the temperature of water in the Mediterranean had to be tested in 1780 to compare it with that of temperatures deep in the Earth, in caves. Little enough was there for him to build upon.

The first major expense was the extended "learning tour" with his wife to Paris, the Netherlands, and England, the last including London, Yorkshire, and Cornwall. They left in February 1768, when their daughter was a toddler and their first son, an infant. Both children remained in the care of Saussure's parents.[48] The months in Paris were well spent visiting Buffon and working with the botanist Bernard de Jussieu (1699–1777) and others. They were also very expensive, for they were living among the aristocracy, participating in salon life, and going to the theater. In July they were in Amsterdam, and Saussure was explaining to his mother that he needed to extend his travels by two months in order to visit England. Would she mind? "Everywhere [w]e went," he reported, he was told that he would see more important versions in England: "the cabinets of natural history, the gardens of exotic plants, the manufactories, the commercial establishments, shipping, all these present themselves on a grander scale and more perfectly to type in England." He would always regret not taking advantage of the opportunity of crossing over to England. It was something he would always be longing to do. The opportunity might never be there again. He would dearly love to return to Geneva with his tasks fully completed, or nearly, and not have to worry about finding another time to go. His wife was not pregnant; maybe she would be another time. It was time to "seize the moment or renounce it forever," he insisted.[49]

In England in September, after stays in London, and in Yorkshire for the coal mines, Saussure requested an extension from his teaching duties at the Academy so that he and his wife could stay in England until early 1769. He had not realized, he said, that the summer season emptied London out. He would go to Cornwall for tin mines and visit Oxford and Cambridge till November: "'Then Parliament would have met, the Royal Society opened its session, and he would be able to encounter the men he most wanted to [meet].'"[50] His budget from the trip to the Auvergne to investigate basalt taken in the autumn of 1776 with the entire family, children and all, suggests the expense of this life. A snippet indicates the cost of four horses for their Berlin carriage on the way home in November—a fraction of the journey and the cost: from Lyon to Dijon (125.12 livres), from Dijon to Semur (92 livres), expenses in Besançon (42 livres), and horses from there to Geneva (70.9 livres). We also see a large expense of 192 livres in Lyon for the hotel for five days and a number of smaller payments.[51] It all adds up.

Still, one could almost imagine Saussure's travels in the Alps as something like summer vacations, as they had to be for Marc-Théodore Bourrit (1739–1819), the cantor and precentor of St. Peter's from 1768, if Saussure's were not so determinedly empirical. Bourrit wrote several influential books about the Savoy Alps and was recruited by Saussure to do some of the illustrations for the *Voyages*. Bourrit was a *natif* (native) of Geneva, and thus in the category of Genevans excluded from politics. "Citizens" such as Deluc (whom we met in the Jura at the summit of the Dôle with the friend of Queen Charlotte) claimed Rousseau as an ally in the 1760s. They fought for the power of that group in the face of patrician encroachment on the rights of the General Council of Citizens. They also fought to keep the natives, such as Bourrit, from full civic and economic life.

The reader has sympathy for Bourrit, which, however, is strained in the face of his habitual snarkiness. The short, breezy book he published in 1773 on the peaks and glaciers of Savoy thanked Saussure for outlining for Bourrit what to see there.[52] However, it drew on anecdotes shared by Saussure, which were to appear in the *Voyages* in 1779, and slyly shaped them to his own advantage. So, on the summit of Brévent to which Saussure had returned in 1767 with Jallabert and Pictet on that first *tour du Mont Blanc*—with Jallabert beginning to sketch the glaciers and Pictet deploying a graphometer (a tool to measure angles) to map the peaks— the three found themselves in an electrical field. It drew sparks from their fingers and made the gold braid of Jallabert's hat hum. They first noticed this when Pictet began to point to peaks to ask their guides what their names might be. He felt a shock on his fingers as he did so, which the others then experienced by waving their hands and seeing sparks fly out.[53] It was an extraordinary experience never before described in the context of science, as Haller and Bonnet scrambled to note to each other in the letters about the incident mentioned in chapter 2 on the Jura.

Bourrit, however, has Saussure scurrying for safety, in a seemingly cowardly manner, not bravely, like himself. Two months after Saussure's climb, Bourrit says, he too went to the summit. Describing for his readers how Saussure "found himself naturally electrified but" also "apprehensive of danger, at seeing the lightening form itself too near him," Bourrit describes Saussure "hasten[ing] quickly under shelter," cowering in alarm. "With respect to ourselves" (a botanist friend and Bourrit), despite the sound of landslides and thunder cracking on the mountain, "without any fear at present of the consequences of so terrible a phenomenon," it was only the cold that drove them away. And that was after a good lunch.[54]

It is Bourrit's bombastic language that alienated some of his later readers, including the geologist and physicist James David Forbes (1809–1868), whose familiarity with the massif, hikers will know, is recognized by the Signal Forbes, the highest point on the Grand Balcon Nord walk from Montenvers to the Plan de l'Aiguille du Midi.[55] It appealed to readers such as Buffon, however, who apparently could digest passages such as this, about descending the Brévent: "we looked at one another in expressive silence; our eyes alone could speak what we had seen, and told what passed in our hearts. They were affected beyond the power of utterance."[56] Or, in what passed for a description of Mont Blanc: "no tongue whatever is capable of describing and conveying to others the successively humiliating, elevated, awful feelings of the soul, upon the sight of such an object."[57] Buffon became Bourrit's patron when the latter moved to Paris in 1779, securing for him a pension of 600 livres a year from Louis XVI and complimenting him on his descriptions.[58] As the first volume of the *Voyages* (1779) clearly established, Saussure's methodology was to carefully observe, then observe again and again; the difference between him and Bourrit was inescapably evident. Buffon himself, who published almost forty volumes of natural history under his own name was frustrated vicariously by the length of time it took for Saussure to publish his work. Saussure's *Voyages* had been expected for a decade. Not everything has to be checked and measured and hedged, and confirmed again. Work quickly, use the imagination. Form a theory and set it out before the world.

Bourrit's poetic license in describing what he saw usually was gently corrected by Saussure, never ad hominin, and always in ways that underlined the importance of facts. In volume 2 of the *Voyages* (1786) Saussure reports on his "Observations of the Aiguilles de Chamonix." These are the "pyramids of granite" that rise up above the valley, flanking Mont Blanc and punctuating the massif from the Aiguille de Tricot and the Aiguille de Bionnassay in the west to the Aiguille d'Argentière and the Aiguille du Tour to the east. From Chamonix below they look like sentinels. Bourrit had claimed to have climbed high onto the Aiguille du Plan (summit, 3673 m) east of the Aiguille du Midi. Wanting to see above the Brévent and the Aiguilles Rouges to the north, though "inexpressibly fatigued," he left his companions behind and "climbed anew from rock to rock." Bourrit moved "with the caution of a lizard," he wrote, "making its way upon some bristly plant, edging along those winding ornamented crypts" (above chasms in the rocks, one presumes) until "astonished at his prodigious height."[59] He was higher than the summit of the Brévent (2525 m), he explained, and he could see all the way to Geneva and the lake. In his words, he "viewed with an affectionate regard which it is impossible for me to express, those parental plains upon which Geneva is seated, its beautiful lake and in short the whole extent of the Jura."[60] Anyone today who has looked out from the viewing platform of the Aiguille du Midi (3842 m; platform at 3778 m) will recognize the embroidery. From 3778 meters, and apparent only from the maps laid out there for viewers, Lake Geneva is a pinprick, a wisp.

With Bourrit's claim in mind, Saussure too climbed up into the Aiguille du Plan as he explored the aiguilles in 1784, spending three days and nights there in late August:[61] "I had hoped to descry Lake Geneva and the plains around it, as M. Bourrit said that he had from the foot of that aiguille." He climbed higher than did Bourrit, the guide, Pierre Balmat (spelled Balme) assured Saussure, by 50 toises (c. 100 m) and still he failed to see the lake or its surroundings. Bourrit must have been fooled by his "imagination," and "it is indeed very easy at such distances to confuse a patch of fog or water vapor for a lake." Moreover, Balmat, a hunter, had earlier climbed higher still, chasing a chamois on a path that no "inhabitant of the plains would have been able to go [on], and to which he would never return for any price," and he had not been able to distinguish the lake.[62]

How far up in the Savoy Alps one needs to be to see Lake Geneva may be an inconsequential question in the great scheme of nature. Accuracy, however, was fundamental to Saussure's project. Just as it was indispensable to medicine to know what each organ of the body looked like and where it was found, so too knowledge about the mountains began with precision. How could one explain a thing without knowing what it was? Observation was the first step. The senses have their limits, however, and their faults. To understand the massif as his agenda detailed—what the mountains were made of, how they were formed; what the glaciers were, how were they formed; what the weather was, how it was created—Saussure needed to amplify his senses. Telescopes, obviously, to see farther, and microscopes to detect what was too small for the eye to see, extended the exercise of sight. Other instruments worked to detect information our human bodies are not attuned to noticing, such as the pull of the magnetic field. Saussure and Jean Trembley experimented with a magnetometer of Saussure's design on their *tour du Mont Blanc* in 1778 to determine whether the pull changed with the elevation.[63] The instrument was designed to allow his body to "read" that force of the Earth as expressed in the mountains. So too did barometers and hygrometers permit the reading of air. The "lightness of air" is perceptible above 2500 meters. To measure its distinctions, however, the barometer is used. Humidity also is felt by our bodies and roughly measured in discomfort. Saussure invented the "hair hygrometer," using a blond hair of his wife to calibrate the change in centigrade units. The tighter that strand of hair went, the less water there was in the air.

Scientific instruments were highly expensive, artisanal, exact, and works of art. Voltaire "spent more than a million modern American dollars" in the 1730s equipping his laboratory at the Chateau de Cirey, where he lived with Mme. du Châtelet. "We are in a century where one cannot be learned without money," he knew.[64] Instruments were a major expense, and Saussure's collection was impressive, to us today and to his contemporaries. The Genevan craftsman Jacques Paul (1733–1796) made the instruments Saussure had invented or improved, including the hair hygrometer, a magnetometer, and an anemometer, which was devised to measure the speed of wind.[65] (Paul's son, Nicolas Paul [1763–1806], would go on to produce artificial mineral waters—"Schweppes"—in partnership with Johan Jacob Schweppe [1740–1821] and Henri-Albert Gosse [1753–1816)], taking a different approach from the Chamoniards to the capitalization of nature, though also very forward-leaning and provocative.)[66]

Other instruments were ordered from prominent makers in Paris and London. His brass graphometer came from "Butterfield à Paris."[67] From London he procured a micrometer from the workshop of Jean-Hyacinthe de Magellan (1723–1790), a descendant of the renowned navigator. This Saussure had placed on the end of a telescope so that he could measure the heights of seracs seen from the Dome du Goûter.[68] The famous James Ramsden, who was able to produce giant lenses for the telescopes being used to scan the skies for planets, made the portable, adjustable telescope Saussure took with him in 1787 on his summiting of Mont Blanc.[69] A navigational compass (*une boussole de déclinaison*), invented by Gowan Knight (c. 1713–1772) for the British Navy and made by George Adams (1704–1778), was purchased and used by Saussure on the Col du Géant.[70] So too was a portable sundial (*un cadran solaire équinoxial*) made by Adams.[71] Saussure also had at least two microscopes from England. While waiting for the birth of his first child (Albertine-Adrienne, b. April 1766) and studying microscopic creatures, he reported to Haller on the receipt of "un beau Microscope d'Angleterre" (an excellent English microscope). He already had one on hand. A second, he found, was desirable for checking the results of the first.[72]

A prerequisite for making sense of the body of the Earth was a body of knowledge. Saussure needed to be up to date with findings in physics, mineralogy, botany, chemistry, astronomy, geology, travel literature, mathematics, medicine, philosophy, and natural history, all the categories his scientific library of twelve hundred books and periodicals eventually held.[73] This was the asset—his books—that he offered for sale in the 1790s, after the loss of his fortune in the French Revolution. A list of the most desirable items for sale was prepared by Saussure around 1795 that included a complete first edition of the *Encyclopédie ou Dictionnaire raisonné des sciences, des arts et des métiers* of 1751–65 and some of "the most beautifully illustrated volumes ever published in zoology, ornithology, entomology, and botany."[74] The collection overall "was probably one of the largest and most diversified of the eighteenth century," a "bibliographic and historic treasure," as Carozzi and Gerda Bouvier title their annotated catalog of his library; their work combing through correspondence, purchase orders to booksellers, and catalogs drawn up by Saussure and others is drawn upon here.[75]

Building up one's own library, although "a huge financial investment," was one's only option in a provincial city such as Geneva or Bern, away from London and Paris: "For a highly versatile, active, and enlightened naturalist of the eighteenth century, [such] as Horace-Bénédict de Saussure, the building of a personal scientific library was obviously an absolute requirement. Indeed, in a relatively small independent city-state such as Geneva, away from the major European centers of learning, this library was necessary as a research tool and reference source that enabled Saussure to become an independent naturalist."[76] Haller explained this to Saussure in 1767: "'I see no other remedy concerning [the need for] books on natural history then to buy them. This remedy is costly, but it is the only one. One may be taken in from time to time.'" He explained that recently he had purchased a *Systema Naturae* by Linnaeus that turned out to be a very bad edition: "How, in this century, could such ignorance be possible, he did not know, and yet the book was expensive, very expensive."[77] Saussure started acquiring books for his library as soon as he began his explorations, and he realized how much he still needed to know. After returning from London in 1769, he began buying systematically. By 1772 he had a "critical mass" of material.[78] He could then be selective, adding new books as they appeared.

As in the case of scientific instruments, Saussure bought from specialists in Paris and London. He ordered books from Nicolas-Martin Tilliard in Paris, and after 1773, from Veuve Tilliard et fils. In London he ordered directly from Thomas Payne bookseller, near St. Martin-in-the-Fields, as well as through his relative, Jack Boissier, who belonged to the London banking branch of his wife's family.[79] During his months in London in 1768–69, he made the rounds of bookstores himself. We know this from letters he wrote to Haller offering to procure books for him: "I will be running around to all the bookshops and it would be easy for me to search for them for you"[80]—which he did, as well as looking through all their catalogs for him.[81] Books were ordered through Leipzig, from Weidmann und Reich, and some also from Bern from the Société typographique. The river of coin spent on books is suggested by a commission made in 1770 to the Genevan booksellers de Tournes. They were told to have their representative in Spain buy 300–400 "French silver pounds'" worth of books for him. He wanted "'the most complete and the most recent books in botany, mineralogy, entomology, ichthyology, ornithology, conchology, and in general, on natural history, if possible illustrated with plates and figures, either written in Spanish or in other languages,'" stipulating only that he wanted books on the natural history of Spain, and not of "'countries adjacent to Spain.'" He did not "want to spend more than 400 French silver pounds for the total purchase." He would, however, he said, "'leave it to your representative to use the amount of 300–400 pounds for the purchase of the most beautiful and interesting books of the kinds mentioned above.'"[82]

The Saussures' easy circumstances illuminate by contrast some of the stresses of living a scientific life without family funds. Haller is a key counterexample. Celebrated throughout Europe for his work on physiology, he often made it clear how dependent he was on employment by the state of Bern. He needed his position as director of the salt works at Roche from 1758 to 1764 to support his growing family. He had already held other administrative posts at Bern, including that of *Rathausammann*, or director of the town hall. "Having eight children to take care of, I cannot give myself up to a life of contemplation," he explained to Saussure in a letter dated September 1763.[83] Saussure replied, "It is truly unfortunate for the sciences that you are not able to devote yourself entirely to them."[84] Bonnet lent Haller books, as did the Saussures. In July 1763, for instance, Haller wrote to Saussure complaining about his gout, which had already lasted ten days. He could not work and had no other distractions: "I had botany: the weight of my body deprives me of that almost entirely." The only resource left for him, he explained, was recreational reading, but this he could do little of: "He was not able to purchase any [such books], and none of his neighbors had any either" (and this despite his impressive library of scientific works).[85] Saussure rushed to reply. Just let him know what books Haller might like to read and whether he owned them or not, and it would be the easiest thing in the world to send them to him: "My father has some books, I have friends with libraries at my service, and as long as the books are well packed, no harm will come to them in the sending or returning." Saussure owed him so much that it would be almost an insult not to ask this of him.[86] Haller replied that he did like to read histories and books about travels, from time to time. He would be interested in David Hume's *History of England*, though not the volumes on the Stuarts, which he has already read.[87] Or maybe Paul-Henri Mallet's *Histoire de Dannemarc*, whose second edition in six volumes had just been published. Or Voltaire's *Additions à l'Essai sur l'histoire générale et sur l'esprit* of 1763.[88]

The very deep resources needed to sustain the life of travel and the mind essential to his project of understanding the Alps were secured by Saussure through his marriage in May 1765 to Albertine-Amélie Boissier. She was the richest of the rich. Albertine and her two younger sisters were the heirs of Jean-Antoine Lullin (1666–1709), the merchant-banker who at his death in 1709 was the wealthiest man in Geneva. The Lullin wealth came first from trading in silk, then in money, capitalizing on Geneva's geographical advantage. Geneva's position at the crossroads of Europe had allowed merchants such as Lullin to make enormous sums by trading in letters of exchange for supplying and paying armies, as well as for the sales of goods traveling west to east, and south to north. Lullin had assets of 12 million florins (c. 6 million French livres) at his death.[89] His "personal fortune" was colossal. Tax rolls show it "in excess of 2,000,000 florins, by far the largest of his time in Geneva."[90] This wealth was bagged by his son Ami Lullin (1695–1756), who became a pastor, and whose surviving child was Marie-Charlotte (1725–1750), the mother of the Boissier sisters. Marie-Charlotte was painted by Liotard in 1746, when she was twenty-one years old and already a mother. The portrait depicts her luscious wealth in blue velvet, creamy silk, and a strand of pearls.[91]

After her death four years later and the death of their grandfather Lullin in 1756, the fortune passed to the Boissier sisters, with prerogatives to the eldest, Albertine. This became Saussure's in 1765. That year was golden, "one of the most prosperous of the century—a summit of capital accumulation."[92] The circumstances of the marriage were splendid. Albertine and Horace-Bénédict were married alongside her sister Jeanne-Françoise Boissier and Jean Alphonse Turrettini, whose family's wealth, though nothing close to the Lullins', was considerable and also stemmed from profits made in the seventeenth century from the commerce in textiles.[93] How extravagantly their marriages were celebrated is not known. However, in 1769, when Anne-Caroline Boissier married Jean-Louis Tronchin, the son of the public prosecutor Jean-Robert Tronchin, who was the sometime foe of Rousseau, it was celebrated at the family mansion with a ball of three hundred invitees who "danced until dawn."[94] Saussure would soon assume responsibility for the family's investments, especially after the sisters' father, Jean-Jacques-André Boissier, drowned himself in the Rhône in October 1766 and Anne Caroline's husband shot himself to death in the basement of the family mansion in 1773. Along with many Genevans, though beginning with a vaster storehouse of money, Saussure would invest in French funds at "9, 10, and even 11%" interest until the crash of 1789.[95] Wealth bred wealth.

With the marriage to Boissier, Saussure entered into "a much more prestigious cadre, that of the cosmopolitan aristocracy," leaving behind the comfortable world of patrician-bureaucrats, with their apartments in the city and pretty country estates.[96] The marriage brought ownership of the grandest townhouse in Geneva, built for Albertine's great-grandfather,

Jean-Antoine Lullin, and an expansive summer house—a great house and smaller residences—on the right bank of Lake Geneva at Genthod, shared by the three sisters. The Lullins' Genevan mansion spread over several high acres of the rue de la Tertasse at its junction with the rue de la Cité. (The address today is 24 rue de la Cité, but it was formerly 15–23 rue de la Tertasse.) It was built on the model of Parisian aristocratic hotels of the St. Germain quarter, consisting of a main building with wings framing on each side a courtyard in front, and with gardens behind. The Hôtel de la Tertasse helped prompt a backlash motion from the Chamber of the Reformation in 1720 to prohibit the "hôtel or mansion type of construction," a move rejected by the patrician syndics as undesirable, and impossible to enforce. It also broke sumptuary laws on the "use of fine materials such as polished marble, walnut, parquets made of woods other than pine, or rich wood paneling."[97]

When it became the Maison de Saussure through Albertine's inheritance, the Saussures continued to embellish the interior, employing woodworkers to carve decorative panels above the doors and marble workers to make new mantelpieces for the fireplaces (which never succeeded in heating the large rooms successfully, so portable heaters were also employed).[98] They lived on the lower floors after the death of Boissier *père*, with the sisters and families and occasional other important tenants above. The mansion was large enough not only for separate grand apartments for an extended family (apartments that had their own ballrooms), but for important state visitors to be housed from time to time.[99] The inventory of belongings drawn up at the suicide of Jean-Louis Tronchin, the unhappy brother-in-law, suggests the luxe of the interior in the 1770s. A music room held "three violins and two upright basses." His library contained 376 titles, only seven of which were religious. The rest were by classical authors, on law, or were works of the Enlightenment.[100] It is not a surprise to find the Habsburg Emperor Joseph II stopping by the Maison de Saussure (in the guise of Count Falkenstein) to visit Saussure's natural history collections on his return from saving his sister's marriage to Louis XVI in 1777.

The Boissier-Lullins were more glitzy, less earnest, and less intellectual than were the Saussures, and the strain from this was apparent from the beginning of the relationship. The engagement dates from 1763, when Albertine was seventeen and a half years old, and Horace-Bénédict, twenty-three. Albertine was almost exactly the same age as Judith de Saussure, Judith having been born in April and Albertine in July 1745. Given the insularity of patrician life, an acquaintance between Albertine and Judith can be assumed. If they participated in the same *cercle*, or weekly meeting of female friends described as boring by Parisian ladies used to the salons of Paris, some intellectual frustration on the part of Judith, the would-be mentee of Voltaire, and Albertine, the sought-after but apparently somewhat dull heiress, can be imagined. (They would never be close. Letters between the two after Judith's "exile" to Montpellier are distinctly lacking in warmth.)

Albertine's self-image, at least when she was fifteen and a half, is of a person with little intellectual ambition. She was "devoted to her studies," of course, when these were not impeded by her love of idleness, "her favorite passion." And she was "not actually stupid," though not really clever, she told herself in her diary.[101] Here is Albertine on the eve of her engagement with Horace-Bénédict, offering a glimpse of her social world: "I have not seen anyone among the suitors brought forward this year who could induce me to change my state. All the same, my marriage has been constantly discussed.... I shall be more cross-examined than ever next Monday, as the subject is a cavalier by whom some of my friends would have been pleased to be accorded the preference he has shown me—which I could do without."[102]

Albertine's family insisted that she delay a formal engagement until she turned twenty.[103] In the advent, she married Horace-Bénédict in May 1765, just short of her twentieth birthday, in a joint ceremony with her next younger sister Jeanne-Françoise, whose Turrettini spouse was a first cousin. One might be able to understand the insistence on waiting until Albertine was twenty in the context of her mother's premature death. The gorgeous Marie-Charlotte Lullin died at the age twenty-five of smallpox after giving birth to three children, Albertine in 1745 when she was twenty, Jeanne-Françoise in 1746, and Anne-Caroline in 1749.[104] The mother died within a year of Anne-Caroline's arrival. Perhaps there was some reluctance to hurry procreation. That would not explain the rush to marriage of Jeanne-Françoise however, who at nineteen was married on the same day—within minutes of her sister—to a man eleven years older than she. Since older sisters conventionally married before younger ones, the roadblock to a wedding for Jeanne-Françoise would be Albertine's. And delay itself would not account for the enforced secrecy of her engagement.

Keeping quiet about the relationship would offer hope for other suitors for Albertine, a condition she may not have completely opposed. Saussure's friend Senebier explains that because Albertine's family was allowing her free choice in the matter, Saussure was extremely anxious.[105] Albertine's diary suggests thoughts along those lines: "Mama [her grandmother] is very strongly in his favor. He is of high character and a savant, and I am surprised he has made so little progress in a heart so easily touched by merit as mine. I am very young, in no hurry, and little influenced by worldly considerations or the glamour of fashion."[106] Saussure may not have been rich enough to suit her father's expectations. Jean-Jacques Boissier (1717–1766) had married into the Lullin wealth, and the Boissiers were very well-to-do themselves, with banking houses in Geneva and London. Maybe they worried about his enthusiasm for the Alps. In any case, Saussure was not allowed free access to their house: he was allowed to see Albertine only once a week or so.[107] Nor was their engagement to be broadcast outside the family circle. In late January or early February 1765, just a few short months before the May wedding, Saussure still was compelled to keep their plans to himself. Her family did not want anyone to know, even Haller, he had to explain.[108]

We know about the secrecy because it triggered a rift between Saussure and Haller. Haller's bristles were raised when gossip about the alliance reached Bern. He, an acknowledged mentor and family friend, had not been told. That seems one issue in his apparent wounded pride. The letter from Haller in early 1765 is missing, though Saussure's reply paraphrases Haller's, so we know something of what was said. And we know it was rudely short. Saussure assumes that Haller's anger has something to do with his engagement: "I do not know what *reasons you suspect for my silence*, Monsieur; however, it is true that I have some, and of many kinds. A spouse for whom I have all the respect and tenderness that I am capable occupies me almost entirely. I am not often with her. Our marriage cannot take place until this coming May. The fact that the family does not want the engagement made known precludes the assiduities that would transform into certitude what the public is suspecting.... So I beg you to not speak of this" (Saussure's emphasis).[109] Then, after describing how wonderful his intended is, he says that "even if this is what you have suspected, Monsieur, how could you believe that even in those circumstances I would have forgotten you?"[110]

Indeed, far from having forgotten Haller, Saussure claimed, he had even planned on visiting him in Bern in early January, before Haller's planned return to the university in Göttingen, where he had once starred. He had received permission from the Academy—and from "Mlle. Boissier"—to do so. However, once he found out from Bonnet and Haller's son (working in Geneva under Saussure's sponsorship) that the move had been canceled, he had decided to put off the journey until autumn, when his wife could accompany him. (She had her own friends in Bern.)[111] He then says that he did not write because he did not want to bother him, having nothing to ask or tell Haller about, and besides, he, Saussure, was busy too.[112] Saussure signs off in a huff: "Pardon, Monsieur, my long letter.

May it cause you less ennui than the pain your short one caused me. I am etc. De Saussure."[113] This abrupt closing is in lieu of his usual formulas of politeness, for instance from several months before: "I am with all respect and devotion possible, Monsieur, your humble and very obedient servant H. B. De Saussure."[114]

This, the longest letter that Saussure ever wrote to Haller, not counting the twelve-page report on his mother's health in April 1763, is a declaration of independence of sorts. He owes Haller everything, yet he is now bound to his wife. Her permission grants him leave to visit Haller. His life—the stuff he was busy with—could distract him from writing to Haller. And, his coming fortune would place Saussure in a world of ease distant from Haller's life of inconveniences and anxiety. The money was an inescapable part of Albertine's appeal, as it appeared to Bonnet and as that old friend expected Haller to see. When Bonnet wrote two days after the wedding to announce the news to his dear friend, he explained that the match was to be applauded. Not only was she distinguished, of excellent character, and cultivated, these qualities were combined with "a very considerable fortune."[115] Of course, says Saussure, he would have wanted to marry her anyway. "Without doubt, Monsieur," he says in that angry letter to Haller, "you respect me enough to believe that even if by virtue of her fortune she was not in the first rank of our city, I would have preferred her to all the world."[116]

The relationship would soon find its footing again, with Saussure asking for advice about plants and discussing his research and travels. Most of the letters after the wedding focus on politics, with Haller asking Saussure about Geneva's turmoil, and Rousseau's and Voltaire's various interventions in the struggle over representation. Gone for the most part are recommendations about Haller's health, though Haller will very occasionally complain about his obesity, no longer being able to botanize: "I am reduced to being dependent on my friends for anything new to learn, being incapable of the least exertion on account of my weight."[117] If Saussure knew about Haller's opium addiction, he never addressed it,[118] but his earlier response to Haller's repeated complaints about gout and depression was to urge exercise, offering Dr. Tronchin as a model for extracting Haller from his morass. Go for a walk or a ride every day.[119] Saussure's own vigor would stand in contrast to Haller's progressive decline.

Saussure walked into new sets of spaces in the 1760s: Chamonix and Mont Blanc, where his passion for the heights was focused; and the two imposing properties of his wife, which enabled his travels and where his love life remained. These established the poles of his adult experience, which he subsequently attempted to integrate by bringing his life in the Alps into the terrain of his homes, and more playfully, extending that home life into the Alps by carrying an Albertine of the imagination along with him.

The mansion in Geneva was the site to which Saussure brought home his bits of alpine life and slices of mountain rock. Along the high terrace in the gardens to the rear, facing the Jura Mountains, was the outbuilding that Saussure made into his laboratory. He housed his instruments there, including the portable ones he took along with him to the Alps, such as the hygrometers, anemometers, and magnetometers. There it was that he performed his experiments during the winter months, for instance, on serpentine, feldspar, and quartz. By subjecting these substances to dry heat, heat along with a steady stream of water, and heat with periodic infusions of water, he was simulating conditions in the mountains, concluding that water—as vapor or liquid—was the active agent in the alteration of rocks.[120] Glass-fronted cabinets were filled with minerals or of pinned butterflies spread out for observation. Mounted birds hung from the ceiling, having been preserved according to the century's new methods:[121] instead of stuffing birds with straw, René Antoine Ferchault de Réaumur, a friend of Bonnet and a preeminent French savant of that generation, had recommended drying them in an oven while pinned and shaped in lifelike positions, or soaked in alcohol, or embalmed.[122] These included arctic birds sent to Saussure by Jean-Louis Pictet from Siberia during his attempted observation of the transit of Venus and others collected by Saussure near Sallanches and other heights along the Arve.[123]

Saussure's collection anticipates the dioramas of museums, including the lifelike displays of alpine fauna at Geneva's Natural History Museum (which celebrated its bicentennial in 2020).[124] The difference lies in the position of the human. Even the best of dioramas, and Geneva's are excellent, activate our imagination visually, as might a painting. A wall, if only of glass, separates us from the artist's representation; we are on the outside and gaze in. Saussure, however, worked in the midst of these elements of the mountains, and with them. All his senses were engaged. The laboratory in Geneva was a small part of the whole of the Alps. It was something of the Alps brought home, and not primarily a simulacrum. It was not meant to pretend. Inside the main house, the *Voyages* took narrative shape in Saussure's organized mind. They were drafted in his library, worked over from sets of notes taken while exploring. These were in two forms. Observations taken in wax pencil en route, "mounted on his mule, looking to the right and to the left, and noting down in his red notebook everything that he sees," as he describes it to Albertine,[125] and transcriptions and elaborations of these raw notes. These were done every night or soon thereafter in black ink, couched in waterproofing, taken home, and brought to life on the rue de la Terasse.[126] Other sights were "engraved deeply in his mind to be enjoyed during the winter." They could be turned to when he was thinking through the meaning of what he had seen, such as the ensemble of peaks seen from high up the Aiguilles de Chamonix in 1784.[127]

How earnest Saussure's efforts were to bring the alpine world home can be gauged by the portrait of 1778, executed by the Danish painter Jens Juel (1745–1802). Juel had been commissioned along with two other artists, Johan Frederik Clemens and Simon Malgo, to illustrate Bonnet's eight-volume *Oeuvres d'histoire naturelle et de philosophie* (Works on natural history and philosophy, 1779–83).[128] While living and working at Bonnet's home at Genthod on a hill above the Lullin estate, he painted Bonnet in his study there poring over a Bible, wondering about life after death: the Bible is open to the First Epistle of St. Paul to the Corinthians, containing the verse "Oh death, where is thy sting."[129] He also composed twin portraits of the Saussures, Albertine and Horace-Bénédict (figs. 4.2 and 4.3). While Bonnet's work at home is emphasized—reflecting and thinking— Saussure appears with the peaks in the background, and his tools of climbing and digging on hand. He holds his bâton for walking and ice climbing, while beside him are his hammer and large chunks of crystals and possibly granite. Just behind him are flowering plants. That the painting was not meant to show him really in the Alps is clear not only from the fictive background, which is an amalgamation of scenery—alpine plants, steep cliffsides, and snow-cone mountains—but from his costume. The traveling coat and cravat are almost like those he wore climbing Brévent and the Môle and scrambling and sliding across the Mer de Glace, but not quite. They are too fresh looking, and his coiffure seems newly curled. The portrait, pendant to his wife's, was painted at home to be hung in their home—his alpine life brought into his home. (After the summiting of Mont Blanc, commercial engravings were made of this, so the painting brought Saussure-in-the-Alps into many people's homes.)

Albertine's portrait depicts her outdoors as well. She is sitting on a terrace, possibly Bonnet's, possibly the Boissier-Saussure's below Bonnet's at Genthod. As Paula Radisich has noted, she appears somewhat cloistered. She rests in a triangular space with a backdrop of trees, one large cypress especially echoing her posture. Her headdress too encloses her. Its silks suggest to Radisich that she has "taken the role of harem woman."[130] However, in a miniature we have that was painted before her marriage, she also appears in a headdress.[131] It is a habit of sexual modesty, more about Genevan domesticity than the exotic. Albertine is wrapped up in her thoughts.

The Boissiers' estate on Lake Geneva was where these thoughts were

Madame Horace-Bénédict de Saussure,
par Jens Juel, peintre danois.

FIGURE 4.2 *Madame Horace-Bénédict de Saussure par Jens Juel, peintre danois* (c. 1780). Photo credit: Bibliothèque de Genève, ICON P 1973-45.

harbored. Another part of the Lullin inheritance, it too was planned with luxury in mind. The main house looked over the lake to the high peaks beyond, with Mont Blanc clearly visible. Oriented north and south, the dining room was on the north and the gallery on the south, with terrace views to the mountains and access to the lake below. The salon on the east led to large formal gardens. Two of its showpiece plantings were modified by the Saussures, introducing the English garden style of simulated, sinuous wildness to the grounds based on their impressions of Castle Howard taken on their Grand Tour.[132] Overall, it was a highly domesticated nature

FIGURE 4.3 Jens Juel, *Horace-Bénédict de Saussure* (1778). Bibliothèque de Genève, 0080. Photo credit: Bibliothèque de Genève.

at Genthod that was juxtaposed against those alpine views to the south, as the historians of the estate have explained.[133] The gallery, full of paintings and sculptures — urbanized culture — was contrasted by Saussure to that of the auberge at Sallanches, whose plain gallery looked out on the high peaks, with Mont Blanc majestic above them all.[134]

On the terrace, from the gallery, and in the gardens, Mont Blanc teased and tormented Saussure even at home: every time he saw it — and Mont Blanc, he says, could be seen from so many places around him — he felt it viscerally. Something like a jolt of lightning would run through him; it was "a type of malady."[135] From her bedroom Mont Blanc would call to Albertine, too, while her husband was in the Alps. She would imagine him there, her thoughts of him anchored by Mont Blanc: "I dream of you all night. Often these dreams disturb my sleep. My remedy then is to open the window and look out upon the moonlit Mont Blanc."[136] From the Planpraz, the meadow below Brévent, Saussure imagined her imagining him at Chamonix. She would have joined her family for cards and supper. Talk would turn to Mont Blanc, and its weather, and all would look out over in its direction, even if the peak were then impossible to see. Then while politics distracted the company, Albertine, "Albertine alone, would rush to her husband and at that same moment, the husband would think of her."[137]

Mont Blanc was the touchstone of their emotional life while Saussure was away, the space where their thoughts rubbed against each other's, and from which their miles away were measured. On leaving Pavia, after visiting Lazzaro Spallanzani (1729–1799) in 1771 to discuss microscopic creatures, Mont Blanc soon appeared on the horizon: "My route was taking me almost directly toward it. You can scarcely imagine, my dear Albertine, what pleasure it was to think that each step that I was taking was bringing me closer to you. I kept looking at my watch, gauging the hour that you would awaken, and when your eyes would fix perhaps on this same Mont Blanc and be thinking of your wanderer of a husband. I told myself that as Mont Blanc is vis-a vis Genthod, in going straight toward it, I was going straight toward you."[138]

In 1774 he was planning for Albertine to go with him to Chamonix. "The route from Cluses to Sallanches is always new and always astonishing to me; it is so pleasurable to think that we will be taking it together next year," he wrote from Sallanches.[139] However, the hesitant Albertine did so for the first time only in 1780,[140] and ceremonially in 1787 for the summiting. In the meantime, in the architecture of Saussure's mind, she was figuratively with him. In a high mountain meadow in 1770, he channeled *La Nouvelle Héloïse*, Rousseau's novel, which they had both read, imagining his "Julie" resting in the shade of a shrubby tree while he brought to her the harvest of alpine plants and new species of butterflies that he was eagerly gathering.[141] After crossing the Grimsel Pass in 1777, he saw her eye in the stone of the cliffs: "Absolutely a true portrait of one of your small eyes. It is green like yours, long and narrow, the only difference being that it is seven to eight thousand times larger."[142] And would that she were a trout, he teased, while considering the Rhône swollen with snowmelt, on an excursion to Furka and its glacier: "Every time I see the Rhône I ask it to say many pretty things to you on my behalf as it passes by Genthod. I wish that you could become a trout and swim upstream to me here. I fear though that you would not want to leave the beautiful waters of the lake to plunge into the turbulent waters of this Rhône."[143]

The emotional fit between Geneva and the Alps was less comfortable than the geological connections Saussure drew between the granite high peaks and the limestone Prealps and the shores of Lake Léman, and less clear than the transactional links between Chamonix and Geneva, built on tourism and an incipient environmental capitalism. Inventing a portable hygrometer that used Albertine's "fine, soft, and blond hair" as its measure was not the same as having her with him.[144] Theirs were parallel worlds that were challenging to join, as represented in the twin portraits of Albertine and Horace-Bénédict discussed above, and by the twinned galleries of the house at Genthod and the inn at Sallanches, pendants also, each reaching out to Mont Blanc for contrary purposes. How much this emotional gap was a factor of Albertine, herself, and how much that of entrenched gendered cultures will be addressed as we approach the summers of 1786 and 1787 and the pageant that the summiting of Mont Blanc becomes. In the meantime, we can look more closely at his travels in the 1770s, when he circles on and around Mont Blanc, expanding our understanding of the planet aesthetically, physically, and morally.

✳ 5 ✳
High Peaks

FROM THE BUET TO THE
SLOPES OF MONT BLANC

Mont Buet (3096 m) sits above the Vallorcine valley, which lies north of Chamonix and runs in the same direction. The two valleys, the Chamonix and the Vallorcine, are linked by the Col des Montets. The *Voyages* as always are clear on directions. Keep traveling up the Arve past Argentière, turn northeast into the gorge, be careful, and when just past its highest point, look across the valley that opens up to your left and you will see the summit of the Buet. It looks, says Saussure, just like the almost flattened snow-covered roof of a house.[1] Two leagues from Chamonix village to the turn-off to the Montets, then two more leagues before you can sleep at the foot of the Buet. You can leave Chamonix at noon and be ready for the climb up the Buet the next morning, as Saussure does with Jean Trembley and Marc-Auguste Pictet on their *tour du Mont Blanc* in 1778, to confirm details of the solo circuit of 1776, and in any case to enjoy.[2]

Scrupulous as always, Saussure credits Jean-André Deluc with being the first to draw the attention of science — "le monde savant" — to this snow-covered peak, the "first high-altitude mountain of the Alps" to be climbed, according to Chamonix's Compagnie des Guides, who will take you there today for 345 euros.[3] Deluc's objective was to conduct experiments toward measuring altitude with the barometer and thermometer. These experiments would help establish a scale that would accurately read heights based on atmospheric pressure — as altitude increases, pressure decreases at a known ratio — and so help to launch the practice of lugging barometers up the summit of high peaks, which Leslie Stephen so pointedly later disdained.[4] Climbing is for pleasure, not science, alpinists have no need to pretend otherwise, as that influential voice declaimed in his speech to the Alpine Club in the 1860s.[5]

Deluc and his brother Guillaume-Antoine reached Mont Buet in 1765 from Geneva through a combination of dead reckoning — its peak can be seen from Geneva between Les Voirons and the Môle — and local knowledge. They went on paths that the Scottish gardener Thomas Blaikie was to find so dangerous in 1775 and that crosses into the GR5 (Grand Randonnée Cinq), a long-distance trek today. In 1770 they summited with help from friendly hunters and a sorting-out of the mountain's name. They and the hunters had first to agree on what they were actually looking for. And this was after finding themselves on precipices with no way forward, and many other colorful adventures that, Saussure suggests, one might read directly about in volume 2 of Deluc's *Recherches sur les modifications de l'atmosphère* (Research on changes in the atmosphere).[6]

Saussure had other goals in mind. He followed the easier route from Chamonix, which Bourrit had found in 1775 (see his *Descriptions des aspects du Mont Blanc* [Descriptions of Mont Blanc]), we are told, and was looking to the Buet to help further understanding of the history and science of the planet. Neither Deluc nor Bourrit, he explains, "have considered the Buet, either in itself or with respect to the view from its summit in terms of the Theory of the Earth. This mountain is entirely new from that point of view and thus will form the principal object of my research."[7] Not that for J.-A. Deluc this was an unimportant subject. After disappointments in politics—a return to a purified Protestant republic was rebuffed in 1768—and after accepting a position in 1774 as reader to Queen Charlotte, he had leisure to write more, which he did—much more. His thoughts culminate in the *Lettres sur l'histoire physique de la terre* (Letters on the physical history of the Earth) of 1798, where he presents his "theory of the Earth," explaining how the ages of the Earth being uncovered by Saussure and others fit neatly within the framework of Genesis, with the world being created by God in six days.[8]

Saussure's project was so radically distinct from Deluc's—the Bible was irrelevant to Saussure's thoughts about the Earth—that pausing over their similarities and differences here suggests again the importance of Saussure to readers today, living in a world of complex needs. He and Deluc shared an interest not just in the Alps, but also in scientific instruments, each improving or inventing means to measure facts about the Earth. A pamphlet war ensued in 1783 over the various merits of the hygrometers each had invented, Deluc's using whalebone and Saussure's using human hair, specifically that of his wife, to measure the moisture in the air.[9] To this extent they worked along parallel lines. Far from beginning with Genesis, however, and moving into the mountains to find more proof of God's plan (in creating the Earth or for the Protestant state), Saussure proceeded empirically: first gather the facts, then hazard an explanation. Be a physicist, but work as a physiologist: explore how the material world works, but in the same way doctors were determining how the body works. Saussure's account of his experience on Mont Buet demonstrates again how much his senses were tools of his science. He began with his body. Traveling along the Arve, he had already been thinking with his eyes, his nose, his ears, and his skin. Climbing the Buet, however, offered something even more intense. As his heart rate and respiration changed with the elevation, so too did his mind, he implied. His consciousness was altered, even intensified, he as much as said, as his body responded to the Alps.

This is the first of the insights Saussure drew from his body's experience of heights over 3000 meters, such as on the Buet and the high slopes of Mont Blanc. Elevation affected the heart and the lungs. It also, he explains, allowed an expansion of thought, experienced in powerful visions about the history of the Earth, and the place of humans in that deep history. As we follow Saussure in this chapter up the Buet and Mont Cramont (at 2737 m not technically a high peak we know), and onto the north and south slopes of Mont Blanc, we find his scientific aspirations again becoming poetic as his empiricism reaches to describe the transcendent experience of these spectacular spaces.

Saussure's description of how the body is affected by elevation was the most detailed, complete, and accurate to date. Pierre Bouguer (1698–1758) had climbed near Quito with La Condamine on their mission for the French government to measure an arc of the meridian at the equator (while Maupertuis was in the Arctic), and he had described some of the effects of elevation in his *La Figure de la terre* in 1749: "Some of us, while climbing, became lethargic, and were subject to vomiting." However, he ascribed these symptoms to fatigue: "But these troubles were much more the effect of being weary than from having difficulty breathing." (And, he says, "one can trust him about this." He "reports nothing that he had not witnessed himself."[10]) Even into the 1920s and the British attempts to summit Mt. Everest, mountaineers were arguing over the balance of exertion and hypoxia in causing these conditions.[11]

It could not be exertion, however, noted Saussure, who had read Bouguer.[12] He has seen guides, Chamoniards, who could otherwise walk for hours without resting "forced to catch their breath every 100–200 steps as soon as they are above 14–15 hundred toises" (2800–3000 m), "and if they stop for even a few minutes, they fall asleep almost immediately."[13] Fatigue is of a different order on the mountains than on the plains. At lower elevations, a tired person can push themselves forward, despite themselves. Up high, a person seized by fatigue cannot will themselves to continue.

They experience palpitations of the heart so strong and so rapid that they would collapse if they tried:[14] "Sometimes one sees otherwise vigorous men overtaken by nausea and vomiting, then collapse into lethargy."[15]

The body changes when climbing high. These effects Saussure ascribes to the thinness of the air, that is, to reduced air pressure in the high peaks, which would have an effect on the lungs.[16] (Saussure was among the first to suggest that air pressure was involved.)[17] And different bodies experience these changes to varying degrees. Marc-Auguste Pictet, for instance, "despite being very agile, very strong, and good at climbing mountains," would suddenly feel sick at about "1400 toises" (2700 m)—and lose his taste for food.[18] Saussure, however, tolerated heights better. The only problem was that when "climbing steep slopes at high elevations" he had to stop to rest frequently. He would have to catch his breath every fifty steps or so.[19] It was his ability to think that was most altered from climbing, not the more obvious bodily functions. He thought more expansively. His mind raced toward otherwise elusive explanations.

Above 3000 meters, on the roof of the Buet, Saussure was able to see the range of the Alps with its peaks and aiguilles lined by snows and glaciers and could, he said, be assured of the perpetuity of the rivers that flowed from that ice. (Would that he were right about the future of the ice and the rivers!) Leaving these thoughts aside, however, if one begins to contemplate how such mountains came to be, "if one reflects on their age, their positions, how such masses of rock could come to be so high above the rest of the globe, if one considers the transformations [*révolutions*] already undergone, and those still to come—what an ocean of thoughts!" Certainly one can ponder the history of the Alps when at home, but "only those who have done so while on a summit of an Alp can know how much more profound, more extensive [*étendues*], more luminous one's thoughts are there, than when sequestered between the walls of one's cabinet."[20]

How the Alps were formed and how they came to rest so massively high up above the plains was a process understood by Saussure—he thought—in the vision he had in 1774 on the Cramont, a mountain near Courmayeur, southwest of Mont Blanc, two years before he climbed the Buet. The *Voyages* report on Saussure's experience of the Buet before he talks about the Cramont because the organization he adopts is spatial, based on the *tour du Mont Blanc* with Trembley and Pictet in 1778, and we follow him in this a little way (discussing the Buet before Cramont, though returning to the Buet). From the Cramont, looking northeast to the Mont Blanc massif, he saw the peaks in between as almost "living beings" (*des êtres animés*) throwing themselves at Mont Blanc. Or, at least, says Saussure, "As when a crowd of people are fixed on the same object, and those behind stand on tiptoe to see above those in front," it is a matter of how they are positioned, "almost," he would venture to say, "their attitude."[21]

What follows is a eureka moment, a vision of the history of the Earth. Realizing, he explains, that the secondary mountains, those leaning toward the massif, are limestone, thus obviously made of rocks that were formed under the sea, so too, he says, must the granite mass of the primary chain, Mont Blanc and its neighbors, have been under the sea. Looking at the massif, he saw not only the mountains as they stand today—he envisioned the succession of historical events that brought them into being. He looked into the past: "Retracing then, in my mind's eye, the succession of great transformations [*révolutions*] that our globe has sustained, I saw the sea, formerly covering the entire surface of the globe, forming via successive deposits and crystallizations, first the primitive mountains, then the secondary ones. I saw these materials arranged horizontally, in concentric circles."[22] Then, an explosion. He saw the crust of the Earth being pushed up from below. The deepest part of the crust jutted up, with the secondary or outer layers remaining attached to the interior layers; this explained the arrangement of limestone mountains leaning into the granite high peaks. He could also finally understand (we know he was wrong here, too, as he was about the formation of granite, which begins as magma, not from deposits in the sea) the origin of the erratics, those huge granite blocks that he found scattered as far away as the shores of Lake Geneva. Saussure imagined that the explosion from below left chasms into which the Earth's waters rushed, "sweeping with them from far away those enormous blocks of rock that have been left scattered on our plains."[23]

Alas, Saussure misread the erratics, a vital clue about Earth's history. Louis Agassiz and others in the 1840s will conclude correctly that the erratics Saussure saw were left by retreating glaciers that once covered much of northern Europe and the alpine region. He was also mistaken about the processes involved in forming the Mont Blanc massif. He corrected his own misunderstanding, however—"after further observations and reflections"—by the time he wrote about his vision on the Cramont in volume 2 of the *Voyages*, which was not published until 1786. In the twelve or thirteen years since he had these thoughts on the Cramont in 1774, he says, he modified his views. He shares these original ones, "historically," as he says, as an example of what thoughts the "grand spectacle of Cramont"—what one sees from its height—can "hatch" in minds open to possibilities. In volume 4, he promises his readers, we will see the full evolution of his thoughts. A spoiler alert for readers of this current book, who may be tempted to open the *Voyages*: these are his observations of the folds of rocks that he makes in regions outside the Mont

Blanc massif and that will lead him to recognize general principles, not local causes, of mountain formation, and will hint toward a recognition of tectonic plates.[24]

Saussure's vision owes something to Shaftesbury's "rhapsodic" response, which he published in 1709, to seeing the Alps as presaging the world's end. Speaking in general terms about those young aristocrats like himself— Anthony Ashley-Cooper (1671–1713) was the third earl of Shaftesbury— whose first sight of the high peaks on their Grand Tour provides a salutary shock, Shaftesbury posited the following revelation. "They see, as in one instant, the revolutions of past ages, the fleeting forms of things, and the decay even of this our globe, whose youth and first formation they consider, whilst the apparent spoil and irreparable breaches of the wasted mountain show them the world itself only as a noble ruin, and make them think of its approaching period."[25] It also anticipates Étienne Geoffroy Saint-Hilaire's vision in the midst of the Siege of Alexandria (17 August–1 September 1801), when the British defeated the French in Egypt. In the extreme stress of the battle, as the cries of the wounded, the explosion of bombs, and the fires wrought by the armies surrounded Geoffroy's redoubt, this zoologist—a member of Napoleon's Institut d'Égypte—had an ecstatic understanding of the unity of the natural world. He escaped the "brouhaha" of war, as he described it, through an intense concentration on the "problems of natural philosophy." He was "taken by a fever of work." Manically, without eating or sleeping, he let "pass through his mind all [his] knowledge of science, 64 times, because of the 64 hypothetical formulas that [he] had to examine and compare." He began with the problem of explaining the electric fish that he had discovered and "the nature of nervous action," and "from these examples of animal nature I passed to all the phenomena of the material world. Knowledge is so sweet when one has arrived at a series of deductions that appear to the mind with perfect lucidity."[26] (Indeed!)

Visions about nature in the long eighteenth century are totalizing, in the sense of trying to grasp the whole of a phenomenon, not just a piece or a fragment, and Saussure's approach to mountains shared in this effort. As Saussure explained in his preface to the *Voyages*, naturalists should not be like those antiquarians one sees in Rome, never glancing at the superb architecture of the Pantheon and the Colosseum, instead assiduously searching in the weeds below for bits of colored glass. It is not that small details do not matter. "To the contrary," he says: when it comes to understanding the mountains, they form the basis of what one knows. However, one should never lose sight of the massiveness of mountains, their sheer physicality, and how these huge bodies are arranged in space, their ensemble. Always remember that "knowledge about these great objects is the reason one studies their little sections."[27]

Saussure's impulse to understand the natural world in a grand sense is why he abandoned botany as a sole pursuit. Collecting plants is not enough. Leave the valleys and the beaten paths. Look up, go up, summit a high peak from which one can command a wide view, he says in that preface.[28] Then one has a hope of discovering what were the agents that caused the Earth (*ce Globe*) to be formed.[29] From above, a range of thoughts like a range of mountains can come to mind. His visions let him see the planet as a whole. Seeing the arrangement of mountains—the architecture of the Earth—provides evidence of the deep history of the planet, the stages and matter of its formation. The recognition of this history is the intellectual revolution Martin Rudwick calls "bursting the limits of time."[30] This is the planetary consciousness that eighteenth-century "theories of the Earth" were shaping. Far from adopting a domineering stance, as he is looking outward and around from the Buet and the Cramont, Saussure assumes the humbling position of humans on the Earth. The term Saussure uses in the preface is *dominant*, which may confuse some readers. "Il semble que dominant au dessus de ce Globe" one can do this work of discovery about the Earth, since only from above can one see the lay of the land. He is using *dominant* not in the sense of "manifesting one's superiority" or "submitting others to one's power"—such as "Napoléon voulait dominer l'Europe"—but in the spatial sense, as being above something else in space, which is Larousse's fourth definition of the verb *dominer*.[31]

If one's interest in Saussure has to do with mountaineering rather than with the experience of nature in the eighteenth century, his ascents of the Buet and the Cramont, not to mention Mont Blanc, have to do with heroic masculinity, asserting dominance whether over competitors or over nature. It is in this register that he appears in the history of mountaineering, exercising "domination" in the more general understanding of the term. Virility is performed in a test against nature; conquest and triumph are keywords. The peaks themselves appear as some kind of phallic—male-gendered—symbol of class or political sovereignty, especially prominent in fascist and British imperialist contests to summit north faces of the Alps and 8000-meter peaks in the Himalaya, but traceable back to the early nationalist era, as Hansen's *Summits of Modern Man* shows so well: "The efforts to climb the mountain [Mont Blanc] in the 1770s and 1780s braided together contemporary definitions of enfranchisement in Savoy, sovereignty in Geneva, and the encounter of competitive masculinities into novel aspirations to reach the summit."[32] Paccard and Saussure share "the heroic masculinity of . . . Alpine naturalist[s]." The "heroic masculinities of hunter and naturalist were not just complementary but also in competition."[33]

It is harder, however, to see climbing an aiguille in the Alps as a struggle for the "summit position" when it is described, as Saussure will do, as an artichoke, a vegetable, really a flower! When describing what can be seen from the top of the Buet, he talks about the Aiguille du Midi in these terms. It, and several mountains like it, "have leaves [*feuillets*, or, in this rocky sense, sheets] that turn around about its center or axis almost like those of an artichoke."[34] He has it drawn that way by Bourrit, as reproduced in figure 5.1.

Obviously, the artichoke is a metaphor allowing readers to see what he sees and to understand its importance. Mostly one sees these rocky sheets lean in the same direction in which the massif runs, from northeast to southwest. Sometimes, however, they are arranged in this artichoke fashion. That is what he is saying: their shape is intriguing. Yet the organic, vegetative aspect of the metaphor matters as well, as Saussure's complete description of his view from the Buet suggests.

Saussure first sketched an illustration of the panoramic view from the Buet in 1776, with an artichoke-looking Aiguille du Midi in the south. He then commissioned Bourrit to complete the drawing, to appear as plate VIII in the *Voyages* accompanying his discussion of the Buet. Bourrit managed to make mistakes with respect to the heights of some peaks—Saussure politely explained that it must have been the fault of his instructions—however, the weirdness of the illustration, its conception, is Saussure's own. It is distinctly nonphallic, more like a Georgia O'Keefe painting of a flower. If sexualized, it is feminized. If mountains are gendered, they are feminine here. And the figures of Saussure and his friends, tiny in the center of Buet's flat top, are hardly dominant, or domineering, as figure 5.2 shows.

The illustration is a proxy for being on the Buet, with the tiny figures in its center plain standing in for Saussure and his friends. Contemporary views of the Alps will typically add a human or animal figure for scale. However, here on the Buet, Saussure explains, the figures are meant to orient the reader to experience the panorama, virtually. We are to be in that center, (like them) and to look around 360 degrees. The illustration, a fold out plate of large dimensions, itself can be turned around, as we look first toward the Jura Mountains to the north, then to the east and the Vallais, cut by the Rhône, then the Mont Blanc, and so on. Every detail is numbered and lettered, and listed in a two-column spread, "for the convenience of the reader."[35] This chart is produced in figure 5.3 and as if for the same helpful reason.

FIGURE 5.1 "Vue de l'Aiguille du Midi située au N.E. du Mont Blanc." Drawn by Marc-Théodore Bourrit, engraved by Christian Gottlieb Geissler. Saussure, *Voyages*, vol. 1, plate VI, *hors-texte* at p. 504. Watkinson Library, Trinity College, CT: DQ823. S246. Photo credit: Amanda M. Matava.

So far, so interesting, since this illustration is the first attempt in alpine history to represent a 360-degree view. It will be the model for circular identification plaques that help tourists know what they are seeing when on belvederes, such as La Flégère on the Grand Balcon Sud section of the *tour du Mont Blanc* where one looks south to the Mont Blanc massif, north to the Aiguilles Rouges and east and west across the Chamonix valley.[36] Yet our narrator wants plate VIII to do more than provide labels for important sights. Saussure's instructions to his illustrator explain this.

FIGURE 5.2 "Vue circulaire des Montagnes qu'en découvre du sommet du Glacier de Buet." Drawn by Marc-Théodore Bourrit. Saussure, *Voyages*, vol. 1, plate VIII, *hors-texte* at p. 512. Watkinson Library, Trinity College, CT: DQ823.S246. Photo credit: Amanda M. Matava.

Imagine a horizon that is coincident to the sight line of someone standing on the flat plain of the summit, and that can be drawn as a large circle. Saussure terms this a *cercle horizontal*. All the objects that the illustrator—Bourrit—can see at eye level are to be placed along the circumference of that circle. That is the first step. Second, outside of the circle are to be placed those objects that appear above this horizon. Next, and more challenging still, all those objects that the observers on the Buet see *below* the horizon are to be placed within the circle, on the near side of them. And more: the position of all these viewable objects had to be computed precisely. Where they appeared in the illustration—*exactly* where within or

(1) Comme les explications de la Planche VIII se trouvent dispersées en différens endroits du texte, je crois devoir, pour la commodité du Lecteur, les réunir dans cette note.

a. Le Mont-Blanc.
b. Montagnes des environs du Lac du Bourget, ou peut-être du Dauphiné.
c. La Tournette.
d. L'Eclufe.
e. Le Mont Jura.
f. La Dole.
g. Aiguille du Midi, au deffus de St. Maurice.
h. Le Mont Gemmi.
i. Le Grimfel.
k. La Fourche.
l. Le St. Gothard.
m. Le St. Plomb.
n. Mont Vélan, au N. E. du Grand St. Bernard.
o. Aiguille & Glacier du Tour.
p. Glacier d'Argentiere.
q. Aiguille d'Argentiere, & à droite au deffous d'elle, l'Aiguille du Dru.
r. Le Mont Mallet, ou le Géant.
s. Les Aiguilles de Chamouni.

N°. 1 --- 2 Les Aiguilles rouges. Le Mont Bréven eft fous le N°. 2.
3. Vallée de Megéve au deffus de Sallenche.
4. Mont d'Anterne. Les dentelures

N°. fymmétriques que l'on voit au pied de cette montagne, font des débris qui s'accumulent au bas des ravines très-inclinées, qui la fillonent.
5. Vallée de l'Arve & Bonne-Ville.
6. Le Môle.
7. Geneve.
8. Les Voirons.
9. Portion du Lac entre Rolle & Morges.
10. Dents d'Oche & montagnes d'Abondance.
11. Vallée du Rhône entre Brieg & Sion.
12. Col de Balme.
13. Mont de Loguia ou de Chefnay.
14. Vallée du Col de Bérard, par laquelle on monte au Buet.
15. Pâturages des Fonds.
16. Vallée du Giffre où eft la ville de Taninge.
17. Le Grenairon.
18. Murs de glace du Buet, qui dominent la Vallée d'Entraigues
19. Portion de la vallée de Valorfine.
20. Champs de glace fufpendus fur Entraigues.

NB. J'ai mis les N°. 18 & 20, fur la foi de Mr. BOURRIT, car je ne me rappelle pas d'avoir vu ces glaces de la cime du Buet.

thode

FIGURE 5.3 Key to figure 5.2. Saussure, *Voyages*, vol. 1, p. 512. Watkinson Library, Trinity College, CT: DQ823.S246. Photo credit: Amanda M. Matava.

without the *cercle horizontal*—was to be dependent on their angle up or down relative to the illustrator's own horizon, and placed on one of ninety concentric circles.[37] Bourrit was to use Saussure's small graphometer for this.[38] The viewer—the reader of the *Voyages*—was meant to have an immersive experience. By turning the illustration around and around, pretending to be looking from the center, they—we, the viewers—could "enlarge in our imagination" the objects drawn and see them "absolutely just as they present themselves to an observer placed on the top of the mountain."[39]

Saussure's was the first alpine panorama, and it remains distinct in how it presents the self's relationship to nature. Subsequently, in the 1780s panoramic cityscapes of Paris and London began to appear as efforts to make sense of these globalizing cities: one could "see" them as a whole. In 1787 the panorama as "a massive curved mural painting" was patented by Robert Barker (1739–1806),[40] who coined the word and presented these representations "in . . . darkened room[s]) to convey the illusion of actually being on the scene with a commanding view of interesting or inspiring locales."[41] Then the French Revolutionary and Napoleonic Wars brought history home to ordinary Europeans, and there was an intensifying demand after the defeat of Napoleon for immersive spectacles of the great battles that defined the era. At the Congress of Vienna, which met from May 1814 to June 1815 to reconstruct the map of Europe, blown open from the wars that began in 1792, popular panoramas showed the burning of Moscow, which helped doom Napoleon's invasion of Russia in 1812, and the entry into Paris of Louis XVIII, restoring the Bourbon monarchy to France.[42] These presentations, apparently worth the price of admission and inspired by opera and stage sets, placed the viewer at the scene of some of the era's most transformative events. They suggested that one was a part of this history, as hundreds of thousands were—that it was a human history, despite its massive scale.

On Mont Buet in the 1770s, however, dwarfed in the center of its summit plane, one was viewing a history other than human—an "other" history—greater in scale, obviously different from, and *indifferent* to human life. One might imagine oneself as Admiral Nelson while watching a panorama of the Battle of the Nile; one could never see oneself as Mont Blanc. The little figures in the *Voyages*' plate VIII, proxy for ourselves, do not feel like a part of the Alps and Prealps; they are not submerged into the scene, in some para–human-alpine experience such as that which the now-controversial John Muir (1838–1914) will later describe his experience in the North American mountains.[43] There is no "grand gesture of connection and flow" that admirers exult in when reading the closing passages of *My First Summer in the Sierra*.[44] Muir's "We are now in the mountains and they are in us" is not what the humans on the Buet are saying.[45] Saussure's figures are articulated, separate, and reasoning. They analyze heights and relationships as they name rocky features. The message is not the consonance of human and Alp. Nor do they dominate what they see. It is not an illustration—or an illusion—about possession. The proxy figures stay small, though erect. They are human in the Lucretian sense addressed by Saussure in the preface to the *Voyages*. We think the Earth was made for us, but it was not. It has its own irreducible existence. It is "life" in other ways, with its own web of meaning. The Earth's power is not reduced to human subjectivity, or its value to our little place within it.

Alpine beauty comes out of the materiality that Saussure celebrated. Nature has an irreducible presence that the senses offer up as poetry, as we find in Saussure's experience of the Miage glacier, a last example before we follow him on to the high slopes of Mont Blanc. After summiting the Cramont in 1774, Saussure set off with his guide to examine the southern base of Mont Blanc.[46] Perhaps a route to the summit could be found from the south, and in any case, it would be interesting to see if the rock of the southern slopes matched the rock of the north. This Saussure found to be so. The rock there is the same as that at the foot of the Aiguille du Midi—"same weight, same gray color, same scent of the earth"—except that this rock, unlike the solid mass of the Midi's, would fall apart into rhomboidal fragments.[47]

Straddling the southern slopes of Mont Blanc—"the most extensive glacier on the south slope of the Mont Blanc massif"[48]—the Miage when mapped looks like a ginger root, with one long main branch and several fat subsidiaries running into it. Saussure's description of his walk from Courmayeur and up this glacier and onto a flank of the mountain has the typical Saussurian emphasis on the senses. The aiguilles and glaciers passed by en route are vividly experienced and presented in detail. The language is specific, and the reader can respond, as does Saussure, in a visceral and emotional way to the material reality of the landscape. It is the heart of the Earth that is opened to us, not Saussure's own. Thus it is a joy to find, at the base of the Broglia Glacier, where a great debris field of granite rocks was scattered and massed, "in the midst of this most desolate region of the world," a small lawn of the prettiest green, lined with larches and watered by a spring. To our further delight, we see "the lustrous flowers of *Caltha palustris*" covering the banks of the stream. These are marsh marigolds, whose shiny yellow flowers and glossy leaves catch the glacial sun. A desert of rocks, and within it, an oasis of green and yellow. The "singularity" of the space was magnified by the "bright white snow" into which it flowed.[49] The granite blocks of the debris, in turn, were a mixture of shiny black and matte white. The black was schorl, a black tourmaline that is beautiful as a gemstone, and the white was a feldspar.[50] Greens, yellow, whites, and black, all solid colors are seen, gemstones and flowers.

Then on to the Miage. On a section swept free of snow, and while one treads on "ice of an extraordinary purity," experience becomes a matter of light. With the sun at his back, his shadow was thrown ahead. This shadow "sank down deep into the translucence," he says, far down into the ice "producing the most extraordinary effect in the world," as if he were both above and below the surface of the Earth. Later "they walked along streams of clear water running in transparent canals that the water itself had formed."[51] The walk was a poem: its beauty in the details, the meaning in its materiality. After climbing up a slope leading off the glacier to the right, one that seemed to Saussure the most accessible to Mont Blanc, they were met by a barrier of rock. Having already reached a height of around 2500 meters on the Miage, about three-fourths up its main branch,[52] and estimating another 2200 meters to go before the summit could be reached, there was little hope for this approach.[53] They turned back, with a bag of geological observations and word pictures of the beauty of the space, drawn from life, *en plein air*.[54]

If the map in fig. 5.4 were three-dimensional with colored lines lit up in succession, you might see some faint yellow lines exploring lines of access to the summit of Mont Blanc in 1762 from the south and the north, then a darker one flowing from Courmayeur to the Miage Glacier—that

FIGURE 5.4 Detail of figure 3.2: "Carte de la partie des Alpes qui avoisine le Mont Blanc." Photo credit: Amanda M. Matava.

FIGURE 5.5 "Vue du Mont-Blanc et de la Route par laquelle on a atteint sa cime." Drawn by Marc-Théodore Bourrit. Saussure, *Voyages*, vol. 4, plate II, *hors-texte*, end of book. Watkinson Library, Trinity College, CT: DQ823.S246. Photo credit: Amanda M. Matava.

is Saussure in 1774. After that would appear a bright orange line from the Montagne de la Côte in between the Bossons and Taconnaz Glaciers in 1775. Then a network of pink and red lines would deepen until the first summits of 1786 and '87. Saussure's in August of 1787 would glow throughout Europe. His line follows the Montagne de la Côte to a path discovered by Paccard and Balmat rising from the Grand Plateau up the very risky ascent—avalanches common—to the northeast ridge of the mountain and the summit. Figure 5.5 shows the map of Saussure's summit path as depicted in the final volume of the *Voyages*.

The attempts to find a path to the top of Mont Blanc in 1762 followed Saussure's first visit to Chamonix in 1760 and the offer he had posted throughout the valley. Saussure's guide, Pierre Simon, took up the challenge, with some other hunters exploring approaches from the Glacier du Tacul, which is the right arm of the Mer de Glace if one follows it south and west, up and behind the Aiguilles de Chamonix. Somewhere below the Aiguille des Grands Charmoz and the Aiguille du Grépon he was turned back by seracs.[55] These tall towers of ice form on glaciers as they shift, or from ice falls from peaks above them. Their name, popularized by the *Voyages*, comes from the term in the local patois for the curds formed when making mountain cheese, which these ice blocks resemble but on a massive scale.[56] Beautiful in shades of blue and white, they are highly dangerous despite their homey name and can topple without warning. Simon also tried to work out a way up from the Glacier des Bossons, reporting to Saussure his pessimism about the project.[57] So intimidating was its prospect that he probably did not do much more than climb up onto the moraine.[58]

The high slopes of Mont Blanc were little-known to Chamoniards for several reasons, none of which had to do with superstitions. Chamoniards had routes to circumvent the massif to reach Courmayeur and places south that avoided the glaciers, so knowledge about climbing up and over was not needed. These paths were difficult but accessible if one needed or wanted to avoid the longer route on roads through Savoy. They would be useful if one were a smuggler, say, or on a politically sensitive mission. The *tour du Mont Blanc* follows those paths today by passing in the west through Bionnassay on the circuit made known to readers of the *Voyages*. It was rumored that a way around Mont Blanc from the glaciers leading off the Mer de Glace existed, or had once been possible, but the first known crossings from Chamonix to Courmayeur through the Col du Géant were achieved only in 1786. The guides Jean-Michel Cachat *dit* le Géant ("called the Giant") and Alexis Tournier *dit* l'Oiseau ("called the Bird") were first, with Charles-François Exchaquet, the engineer who would make the first relief map of the massif, following a few days later with another of Chamonix's guides.[59] Moreover, the desired crystals in white and shades of yellow and violet occasionally found in nearby granite peaks seemed out of reach on snowy Mont Blanc, as any chamois were also.[60] Something close to 2700 meters was as high up the Aiguille du Plan as Pierre Balme (Balmat; 1750–1828) had climbed by 1784, "on a path to which he would never return for any price."[61] And there was a very realistic fear of freezing to death if one spent a night in the snow.[62] His son, also named Pierre Balmat, would die on Mont Blanc, killed in an avalanche during an attempt on the summit in 1820. This was the first fatal accident on the peak itself, prompting the establishment of the Compagnie des Guides de Chamonix in part to provide help to the families of dead guides.[63] It was dangerous work.

The prize money was tempting, though it was not in itself the reason for the efforts by Simon and others Chamoniards to find ways to climb Mont Blanc. Simon was already committed to helping Saussure explore the massif by taking him, as we saw, across the Mer de Glace and up the Brévent and supplying other wants for his travels. Accommodating his request to summit Mont Blanc, as he had the Brévent, would make a lot of sense and be an investment in his new practice—the new profession—of guiding Genevans into the high peaks. This was a matter of selling one's expertise in the mountains. The offering of a reward is interesting in the context of Enlightenment practices also, however (and not only with respect to what was specific to Chamonix), it being somewhat equivalent to the prizes being offered by the various academies of Europe for essays on topics of interest. These contests were announced in the form of questions. Did labor or fertilizer work best to improve crop yields? Saussure's father argued for the importance of labor. Have the arts and sciences improved human life? Rousseau famously answered in the negative. How well does observation contribute to our understanding of the world? This is the question Saussure's mentor Bonnet posited and his friend Senebier answered, and that was addressed above in discussing Saussure's first travels along the Arve. The offer of a reward was also really a question. How could one get to the summit of Mont Blanc, the presumed highest mountain in Europe? The answer, Saussure hoped, would open the way to an understanding of how the Alps were formed by allowing the range to be seen in its entirety. One could understand it as a body, that is, as a whole with integral parts. Simon and others' efforts would be essays, attempts by the human body to understand the body of the massif. Which glaciers were crossable, which slopes climbable, which precipices dead ends? Could one survive its snows overnight?

In 1775 a group of four other Chamoniards tried to find a solution to the problem of climbing Mont Blanc by climbing up beyond the Montagne de la Côte, a ridge that lies in between the Glacier des Bossons and the Taconnaz Glacier. They managed to cross over the Jonction (the junction of these glaciers above the ridge before they divide there), making them the first known humans to do so. The Jonction, as De Beer and Graham Brown have described it, is "very difficult" to "force" and "now very rarely attempted." It entails "the finding of an intricate route through [a] maze of crevasses, narrow ribs of ice, and high ice towers."[64] Then the guides certainly reached the rocks now called the Grands Mulets (3051 m).[65] Evidence suggests that they may have climbed in completely unknown territory, beyond the rocks and up the Dôme du Goûter (4304 m), from which most climbers today then cross the Arête des Bosses to the summit of Mont Blanc. They were stopped by fatigue and concerns about the lateness of the hour.[66] In July 1783 three other Chamoniards, the guides Joseph Carrier, Jean-Marie Couttet, and Jean-Baptiste Lombard, explored the same route, turning back when one of them succumbed to what was then called "mountain sickness."[67] These experiences prompted Saussure's observation—and implied reproach to enthusiasts—about the difficulty of the enterprise and "its impossibility for anyone without the head for heights and the strong legs of a good guide from Chamonix."[68]

These efforts were tied, as were Simon's, to the Chamoniards' interest in guiding, which by this time had become solidly linked to the development of hotels, as noted earlier. In the 1775 effort one of the men was Jean-Nicolas Coutterand, the son of Saussure's friend Mme. Coutterand, who had developed the first hotel in Chamonix and who understood how offering a way up over the glaciers to the seemingly inaccessible peak might stimulate business. Coutterand was joined by Victor Tissay and François and Michel Paccard. François Paccard will open his establishment in 1785, a year before the first summit by the Paccards' cousin, Dr. Michel-Gabriel Paccard. This is the same François Paccard (1734–1818) who guided Louis Mandrin, the celebrated outlaw and smuggler, enemy of the French tax collectors (the Farmers General), to safe places in and through the Alps.[69] Louis Mandrin was broken at the wheel and executed in 1755, and Paccard was for a time banished from Savoy. Guiding tourists and offering them pastoral care in hotels shifted his talents into the center of a modernizing alpine economy with Chamonix at its heart. Even before 1789 this world was prevailing over Old Regime patterns of pushback against a predatory state. The Savoy administration was eagerly improving access to Chamonix by improving the way from Sallanches to the village, widening roads and securing bridges over the Arve, all the while monitoring progress as measured in the number of important visitors.

The guides and Coutterand were acting for what was becoming a tourist industry, which publicists such as Bourrit were stimulating in ways that went beyond Saussure's engagement with empirical descriptions. Bourrit's books drew enthusiastic readers to Chamonix, and he was often on hand in the village to sell his illustrated *Nouvelles descriptions des glacières* as mementos of their visit.[70] He also offered itineraries, such as to the Mer de Glace, making himself a center of tourist information by renting a house in Chamonix (behind the church, below the Brévent) where people could go to consult with him if they had not found him in Geneva.[71] Bourrit was something of a guru, not so much selling access to the peaks, like the guides and hotel owners, as offering initiation into a popularized sublime, where feelings trumped observation, and emotion was echoed and confirmed in the scenery. Bourrit's ability to dramatize the experience of being in the Alps, placing human protagonists front and center, comes across in all of our encounters with him. Here he is with the Bérengers of Geneva and Lausanne as recounted in a letter from Mme. Bérenger (Antoinette) to a friend. Mme. Bérenger describes how thrilled she was to have had a visit from Bourrit. It was a joy to relive in the imagination her visit to the Col de Balme, a pass at the northern end of the Chamonix valley, beyond Le Tour, on the way to Martigny, which is still full of wildflowers and sky today. "You know," says Mme. Bérenger, "how excited he gets. He turns us all—us and the dear children—into heroes. I love talking about that climb." She was happy to forgive him his dramatic pauses and exclamations.[72]

Bourrit's approach to the Alps—impulsive, exuberant, careless, and driven by the imagination—clashed with Saussure's in their combined attempt to climb Mont Blanc in September 1785, a turning point in the history of Saussure and that of Mont Blanc. Accounts from guides had led Saussure to believe that reaching the summit was impossible, "that being the view of everyone in Chamonix with any sense."[73] Two more efforts in 1783 to reach the Dôme du Goûter from the route opened by Coutterand—that is, the Montagne de la Côte through the perilous junction of its two glaciers to the Dôme—had failed. One of these forays included Bourrit and Dr. Paccard.[74] Though Bourrit was rebuffed by the cold and ice of the Jonction, he remained enthusiastic, "his judgment diminishing as the difficulties to be faced were increasing." ("Happily so," in the view of his alpinist commentators.)[75] After hearing that some hunters had possibly found an alternative approach to Mont Blanc, Bourrit hired guides in September 1784 to try a route beginning not in Chamonix via the Montagne de la Côte, but from St. Gervais via Bionnassay, avoiding the tricky and time-consuming crevasses of the Jonction. As usual, cold and fatigue overwhelmed Bourrit, and he had to halt. Famously, however, two of the guides—Jean-Marie Couttet and François Cuidet—climbed the Aiguille du Goûter (3863 m), its first ascent, to the Dôme du Goûter (4304 m), its second ascent, placing them in reach of Mont Blanc, as climbers today know who follow this way.[76]

When Saussure heard that a climb to the summit seemed a possibility, he abandoned his wariness. He could, he thought, as he had hoped to do since he first climbed in the Jura in the 1750s, confirm from there his understanding of mountain organization: how the central range of granite is faced by the secondary mountains of limestone, which lean in toward the center. He would also be able to see, touch, hear, and even taste the atmosphere, that is, the environment above the Earth's surface where weather seemed to be forming. As he had explored the rocks of the Earth with a view toward understanding the relationship of its core to its surface, now, with Mont Blanc within reach, he would immerse himself in the surrounding air to gather facts about storms, clouds, and the colors of the sky. Those could help explain how that envelope of the Earth related to its surface, and how the planet itself, an orb in space, related to the worlds around it.

This was the project for the summer of 1785, to climb Mont Blanc with these objectives in mind. But what summer? asked the Chamoniards. The winter of 1784–85 extended well into the summer months as the Little Ice Age maintained its force. Snow fell heavily in the mountains. It was not until the second week of September that Saussure—back in Geneva, and anxious—was advised by the guides that the weather had improved.[77] Thus began Saussure's experience of the high-altitude slopes leading to the 4808-meter summit of Mont Blanc, a beginning complicated by Bourrit. Because Bourrit had been the first person to alert him to the possibility of an accessible route to the summit, Saussure gave in to his pleas to join forces in that abortive climb in September 1785, despite his aversion to traveling with colleagues. His circuits of the massif with friends had been valuable. François Jallabert and Jean-Louis Pictet had joined him on his first *tour du Mont Blanc* in 1767. Jean Trembley and Marc-Auguste Pictet had come along in 1778 to assist him.[78] However, they were also frustrating. There were times when one had to rush to keep to his companions' work schedules. They had only limited time off, whereas Saussure's only obligations were promises to his wife. Like many seasoned travelers, he preferred to go alone, at his own pace, though in his case, necessarily, with guides. But Bourrit had told him about the route, and Saussure felt morally unable to refuse him. So the two Genevans, along with Bourrit's rude and inexperienced older son, Pierre Marc Isaac, a student of Saussure's at the Academy, about a dozen guides, and Bourrit's dog set off from Bionnassay on the morning of 13 September (with porters to carry wood and blankets and other necessities to their bivouac).

The plan was to spend the night below the Aiguille du Goûter to allow a climb from there to Mont Blanc and back in one long day. A hut was built there in advance for this purpose off the rocky Col des Rognes, on the Désert de Pierre Ronde. This was some 400 meters below the Tête Rousse, where the steep slopes of the Aiguille really begin, and it was where the drama that marked the first ascents of Mont Blanc opened. All forebodings about Bourrit's recklessness or lack of mountain sense were realized. The group should have left the next morning at the first glimmer of dawn, by 4:30 a.m. Saussure was already awake, almost regretting his moments of sleep, so sweet were the sensations of that night.[79] The hut of rocks was around eight feet by seven feet by four feet high.[80] When the umbrella that he and the Bourrits were using as a door shifted, he could see the moon rising above the snows and peaks below them. Bourrit, however, had other ideas. Worried about the early morning cold, he delayed their start until 6:15 a.m. During the night Isaac had been sick from the altitude, and neither Bourrit had slept well. The son started on a diet of brandy and water and remained unsteady throughout the day. The father, having declined Saussure's expert advice to wear ice-gripping wear, was hampered by his fur-lined boots, which lost their heels.[81] Saussure had already advertised the benefits of crampons in volume 1 of the *Voyages*, including a full-page illustration of what they looked like and how they should be worn in his section on the Buet. Saussure was comfortable in his nail-studded shoes, which he will wear on his successful ascent.

The first 390 meters (200 toises) were easy, but then it became steep and the rocks treacherous, breaking off when clutched and with snow filling the gaps between them.[82] The ridge up the Aiguille was narrow. Each Genevan walked between two guides, their alpenstocks forming a railing for their clients to grasp. Other times Bourrit, his son, or Saussure held on to the guide ahead while being steadied from behind. On the descent Saussure was roped under his arms with two guides behind, each in charge of one end. This was the first use of the rope in climbing in the Savoy Alps, which, as Graham Brown and De Beer argue in their book published for the Centenary of the Alpine Club, was the significance of the experience, from their mountaineering point of view.[83] At approximately 3600 meters (1900 toises) the group turned back after Pierre Balmat, climbing ahead, reported that the snow on the top of the Aiguille (3863 meters) 200 meters ahead was too soft and too deep, and it was way too late to reach Mont Blanc.

After a dangerous scramble back down the Aiguille, the Bourrits rushed off to the valley and then home to Geneva. Their adventure was quickly cast in soon-to-be-familiar alpinist terms of virility and athleticism, although the facts were changed to suit the narrative and its tropes. They lied when they dramatized the climb to their friends, with themselves cast as frustrated experts on the mountain. The Bourrits were eager to continue to the summit of the Aiguille du Goûter, they said. It was Saussure, fearful, spent, and unable to handle the rocks, who had made the party return. Implied too were aspersions on the guides. In describing the climb in the *Voyages*, Saussure adds a footnote about their guides' courage, strength, and skill. "It is not at Chamonix, therefore, that people from cities will be able to take credit for outdistancing its guides and reaching places inaccessible to them,"[84] he says, in a reproach. Bourrit *père* suggested that only Saussure, not they, had needed help from the guides. The son openly mocked him: "'Do you not envy me my twenty-one years? Who will wonder if a youth of this age, who had nothing to lose, is bolder than a father of a family, a man of forty-six?'"[85] For Isaac, the climb had been a test of manhood. Saussure may be a father, but youth trumped age. The mediocre student surpassed the brilliant professor. Indeed, the Bourrits topped the guides. That was what the climb was all about for them.

Saussure's empirical aesthetic lay outside the experience of the Bourrits, producing scintillating images of the climb, not the climbers. These verbal offerings began when they reached the Désert de Pierre Ronde, where they would be camped, and when they were met by the racketing sound of icefalls from the Bionnassay Glacier that were crashing down toward the valley they had left below. What was solid became insubstantial as these "enormous masses of ice" broke up into "whirlwinds of powder" that then "rose as clouds to an astonishing height."[86] As evening fell, Saussure set up his observatory on the rocks high above the camp. He was now at approximately 2700 meters above sea level, some 1700 meters above Chamonix.[87] The hygrometer, electrometer, and thermometer were unpacked. The thermometer that had been made to order for Saussure failed to operate: Its attached heat source would not light, despite having worked below. Perhaps its mechanism was rushed in its production, Saussure worried.[88] No matter; what he sees from his viewpoint consoles him and is what will linger in the wake of the *Voyages*[89]—an afterglow.

The evening mist "tempered the blaze of the sun." The "immense expanse" below them was "half-hidden" in its veil. To the west, a band of crimson-purple filled the horizon, while in the east, where the lower slopes of Mont Blanc were drenched in the same red light, the color deepened. As the vapor sank, it condensed and turned blood red. "Just at that moment something truly singular occurred. A few white puffs began rising above the blood-red line, and as they rose, it seemed that brilliant rays of light were rocketing out from these clouds, like shooting stars."[90] When night fell, the dazzling display ended. Saussure returned "in the fullness of night" under a clear sky. The stars too were calm, "stripped of their sparkle." The light they cast on the summits of the peaks was weak and pale, and only shapes and distances could be made out. "The profound silence and repose that reigned over that vast expanse" was magnified in his imagination, and he felt "a sort of terror." Here one of the most oft-quoted of Saussure's "visions" begins. He seemed to be the sole survivor in the universe, whose cadaver was spread out in the great expanse below his feet. "However melancholic were these thoughts," he explained, "they had an attraction that was hard to resist." Watching in the cold, "I turned my eyes more frequently toward that dark solitude than in the direction of Mont Blanc, whose phosphorescent snows, sparkling above, alone suggested motion and life.... But the sharpness of the air on that isolated point soon forced [him] to return to the cabin."[91]

Saussure's vision of the universe, lying as if dead beneath him as he watched at night from high up on the Mont Blanc massif, has been read as one of domination—with him as the master of that universe—yet it forms a pendant to that experienced on the summit of the Dôle thirty years before, and its meaning is entirely different from that usual interpretation. In 1758 on the Dôle, in the cold of the dawning day, looking south from the Jura Mountains over Lake Geneva toward the Alps, he had felt himself alone. He stood "in the midst of rough seas, far away from the shore." A thick cloud covered everything he could see except for the tips of the high Alps, which looked like a "reef of unassailable rocks," hiding the distant shore. Then, as now in 1785, resting on a flank of Mont Blanc, there was something "strange and terrible" about the experience of aloneness in a wild world stripped of human contact. The image from the Dôle however, was soon exposed as the illusion it was. As the summer day warmed and the clouds rose above him, the lake, with its cultivated shoreline, reappeared, and the entire vista, the high Alps and the Genevan hinterland, were brought together in an integrated whole. In the cold September night on Mont Blanc, the vision had shifted, as he had shifted in space. He was now on that distant shore, high up on the massif.

The totalizing vision of that night, that view of the planet or universe overall, was an expansion of his experience at dawn from the Jura, which had wrapped together Geneva and the Alps in a physical whole, and which was Saussure's first great insight about the meaning of nature. Walled as Geneva was, sheltered as the lake appeared, they—the city and the lake—were part of a greater whole that his discoveries about the geology of the region would explore. The nighttime vision on the slopes of Mont Blanc embraced the Earth on the grandest scale. It was a culmination of his long sensory engagement with the Earth as a planet, which had begun on the Jura in the 1750s, and which he understood had its own being, its own life—separate from his—and, as implied now in this vision, its own death. What was once alive would die. In Lucretian terms, as Clarence Glacken has explained, the Earth "would die like any other mortal."[92] So, in the shadow of these melancholic thoughts, he returned to the Bourrits and the Chamoniards—to human sociability—and the shelter below.[93]

✷ 6 ✷
Mont Blanc

The charisma of Mont Blanc was well-known by the 1780s. A magnetic beauty drew visitors to the Chamonix valley in a stream of expectant souls, siphoned—from all over the (European and North American) world—through Geneva, and welcomed by the structures of a novel environmental capitalism. The Alps were newly beautiful, and in the cultural shift that made them so, the same peaks being repugnant not so long before, they were understood as a public good. To a degree, this was the world of the sublime, theorized by Joseph Addison, Edmund Burke, and Immanuel Kant, where horrors such as the individual's effacement in the expanse of space sketched in the line of the Alps or the drop of a chasm into a bottomless nothingness, was agreeable. It brought pleasure. And for Kant, it led to the transcendence of the emotions—fear and pleasure—by the exercise of human reason, and thus had value in defining one's self, as that rational being. This sublimation—the root meaning of the word comes from chemistry, and evokes alchemy—of emotion into reason could happen on the edge of a cliff, or simply through the imagination. One did not have to be there, on a perch above a chasm in the Alps or on a narrow bridge above a gorge with a rushing Arve River below. One could experience the sublime by reading Saussure's *Voyages*, Kant explained in *The Critique of Judgment*. The "reader of his travels had the soul-stirring sensations that that excellent man enjoyed thrown into the bargain."[1] Or one could think oneself into paintings or engravings of alpine scenes such as of the Devil's Bridge, which spans the Schöllenen Gorge above the Reuss River at the St. Gotthard Pass, which even Saussure preferred to avoid. And even if one were precariously there, leaning into a seemingly bottomless chasm, it was what the mind could project about the space that mattered. The sublime was about the self, about what mountains could offer the person, and not about the peaks in their immensity. The sublime meant looking outward to look inward. It called for a meditation.

It was more than the pull of the imagination that drew visitors to Chamonix, however. Real and deadly danger was present then and now and shapes the experience of the space. On Saussure's second trip to Chamonix in 1761, he and Pierre Simon were below the Aiguille du Midi when a rockfall missed them.[2] With Pierre Balmat in 1784, and again exploring the Aiguilles de Chamonix, Saussure and the guide nearly fell into a deep crevasse. (Saussure writes "Balme," perhaps phonetically, following local pronunciation.) Earlier in the day they had encountered several of these cracks in the ice but found it easy to cross in the spaces in between (surely via frozen snow bridges).[3] After exploring the base of the Aiguille du Midi in the hot sun—Saussure had no need for his coat—they found, as climbers would so often after them, that conditions on the glacier had changed. A few minutes into their descent, happy at first that the snow had melted enough so that their footing was more secure—less slippery—the snow gave way beneath their feet. Saussure was left half-sitting on, half-straddling a broken beam of snow, with one foot dangling over the void and the other just barely resting secure on the other side. Balmat being caught in the same dilemma, they effect their escape using their alpenstocks as a bridge. Placing these in a cross in the snow beyond, they launched onto the poles to safety. Since they had just begun to go down the mountain, the feeling of safety was short-lived—though they did of course survive for Saussure to tell the tale, and us to repeat it.[4]

The "first death in the history of alpinism"[5]—that is, climbing in high peaks for pleasure—was a harbinger of the recklessness manifest on the Mont Blanc massif today. This occurred during that same summer of 1784 that Saussure and Balmat were exploring the Aiguilles de Chamonix and crossing its deep crevasses. Bourrit saw it as a matter of mad impulse. As Bourrit explained to friends who reported it to other friends, a twenty-eight-year-old banker, Ami Le Cointe, the son of a pastor and former professor of Oriental languages at the Academy of Geneva (thus deeply Genevan), was visiting Chamonix with his mother and sister. They formed part of a larger party that walked up to Montenvers and then down to the Mer de Glace. Le Cointe, their guide, and an Englishmen, Thomas Ford Hill (1753–1795), thought to climb the Aiguille des Grands Charmoz (3445 m), farther up the left bank of the glacier, on their right. The guide and Hill, recognizing its dangers, refused the attempt. As that mass of shaggy, needle-edged granite peaks would not be summited until the 1880s, readers too might recoil from the image of Le Cointe beginning heedlessly to scramble up the Aiguille, ignoring the passionate pleas of his party, then clutching onto a loose boulder and falling together, rock and man, to an instant death.[6]

As usual, Bourrit told the story upside-down. Hill's diary explains that they approached the Charmoz from the heights of Montenvers—not the Mer de Glace in its valley—and he, the guide, and Le Cointe began a descent toward the glacier. Realizing that the path chosen was "too direct" and thus dangerous, Hill and the guide pulled back. Le Cointe refused, kept going, and disappeared from sight, not to be found until the next day, dead in a gully. Obviously he had slipped, though perhaps the rock was spared.[7]

And there was the seductive kiss of celebrity that contact with the massif offered. Simply visiting the peaks elevated one's status. John Moore, a doctor shepherding the 8th Duke of Hamilton on his Grand Tour, said that they had gone to Chamonix in 1773 prompted "by the air of superiority assumed by some" who had already done so. "One could hardly mention anything curious or singular, without being told by some of those travelers, with an air of cool contempt—'Dear Sir, that is pretty well; but, take my word for it, it is nothing to the glaciers of Savoy.'"[8] What would climbing Mont Blanc not do? How could one not be touched by its glamour?

The snows of the summit were climbed first by Paccard and Balmat in August 1786. This is the event against which so much of the history of the Alps is measured. The path chosen by the first ascenders was new, unexpected, and as it happened, one of the most dangerous of any possible routes, and not used today except for its final section. The northwest ridge of the mountain—the Arête des Bosses—had been previously the objective of attempts on the Aiguille and Dôme du Goûter, including Saussure's in 1785. Paccard and Balmat instead headed straight up from the Montagne de la Côte through the Jonction, onto the Grand Plateau and then up and up on a slope between the Rochers Rouges, to the *northeast* ridge and the summit. These last landmarks—the Rochers Rouges and the Grand Plateau—though famous now in Alpine history, were named only after the ascents made them culturally visible. The northeast ridge itself is climbed today on the Three Monts Route, which takes one from Mont Blanc du Tacul to Mont Maudit to the summit, but no one had reached it before the two Chamoniards.

The slope to the northeast ridge, with its ribs of red rocks, can be seen from the summit of the Brévent, across the valley. It was from there that Paccard discovered the way forward, in one telling of the story. Paccard's route-finding ability is undeniable, sharpened as it was from explorations of the massif he had made since childhood, botanizing and searching for routes up Mont Blanc from the northeast as well as the northwest. He was only eighteen years old when he guided Thomas Blaikie in 1775 on his botanizing trip, when they walked and climbed together above the Mer de

Glace and its tributaries, in the Aiguilles Rouges, and via the Montagne de la Côte to the Aiguille du Goûter. Though they did not summit the peak, "they undoubtedly reached a higher altitude than any visitor had previously attained in the range of Mont Blanc."[9] Paccard, even more intimately than Saussure, was attuned to the massif as a body by his medical expertise, as well as his advantages in living in the valley. Trained in Turin, he had spent three years in Paris on a residency, returning to Chamonix in 1782.[10] He then began to use his imported telescope to observe Mont Blanc from the vantage point offered earlier in figure 5.5.[11]

He could see that the slopes to the northeast ridge were climbable, in terms of its being physically possible to scale them. However, they seemed constantly to be bombarded by avalanches. From the Dôme du Goûter looking face on, however, the presenting flank to the ridge had looked, to those who were on the Goûter in 1784 and 1786, even too steep to climb.[12] In climbers' terms, they might be inaccessible. "Climbable" in this parlance "is a quality of the way up, and it obviously means that any physical difficulties on the route can be surmounted by foot and hand." "Accessible," however, "is a property of the end-point . . . an imaginary summit might be obviously climbable, but yet so constantly bombarded by stone-falls that no climber could hope to reach the top alive. In such a case the mountain is climbable but not accessible."[13]

So Paccard spent hours, whenever possible, watching the slopes from the Brévent. He was looking for patterns that would indicate an accessible route. Could there be an association of weather with avalanche behavior? Could the times between avalanches be predicted? Was any section of that snow-spread run from the summit to the plateau less subject to these rapid and accelerating slabs of rocklike snow? Paccard chose the steeper-looking slope between the two ribs of rock probably because its avalanches are formed only by the funneling of its own snows. The less steep passage to the west of the upper line of rocks—the path later taken by Saussure—could sweep up the snows of the summit's skirt above most of the Grand Plateau and become larger and even more deadly.[14]

The case for Balmat's discovery of the route that would take him and Paccard up through the Grand Plateau to the summit ridge is supported by Saussure in the *Voyages*. Having earlier that summer of 1786 tagged along with a party of guides who were hoping to find a good path from the Montagne de la Côte to the Dôme du Goûter, and on to the summit, Balmat lost track of them in the descent. They did not want him along—he was highly unpopular—and he was forced to bivouac in the snow.[15] The next morning, knowing that "he had all day to make his descent, he decided to devote some time to these vast and unknown solitudes, searching for a route by which one could get to the summit of Mont Blanc." "That is how he discovered the one that they followed," Saussure recounts, adding that it was the only feasible way.[16] That is, Saussure meant, as opposed to that via the Aiguille du Goûter to the Dôme du Goûter to the Arête des Bosses, which was tried by Saussure in 1785 and by several parties of guides, and which will not be climbed until 1861. Balmat's adventure most clearly proved that it was possible to survive a night above the snowline.[17] This enabled the later ascents and Saussure's laboratory on the Col du Géant in 1788, since it reassured guides and porters that doing so did not mean death.

It might be, however, that what Balmat discovered was the relative ease of crossing onto the plateau, whose expanse had been avoided through fear of heat and suffocation. It was a snow-covered plain, hemmed in by peaks, where one could overheat in the blazing sun or sicken in the stagnant air, the guides had worried.[18] Balmat would have wandered onto and over enough of that snow-space to become convinced that it could be tolerated and its summit slopes tried, perhaps, but not far onto it, if at all. For when Saussure had reached 3800 meters on the Grand Plateau (the larger second shelf) on his way to the summit in 1787, he spoke of Paccard and Balmat as being the first to have been there, and together, on their first ascent. He reflected on their courage being there, "without shelter, without support, without even the certitude that humans could survive in the places that they hoped to go."[19]

While the weight of historical sympathy supports Paccard against Balmat, mystery still attends their adventure. It is no surprise that Sherlock Holmes has been brought in to detangle it in the inventions of Pierre Charmoz (pseudonym of Pierre Laurendeau) and Jean-Louis Lejonc in *Sherlock Holmes à Chamonix: Enquêtes sur la mort de Whymper et sur la première ascension du mont Blanc*. The authors also enlist the interesting Mrs. Hudson ("Miss Hudson" to them), also on site in Chamonix.[20] Readers can find a polemic in favor of Dr. Paccard in Graham Brown and De-Beer's *The First Ascent of Mont Blanc* and a contextualization of the controversy in terms of nationalism in Hansen's *Summits of Modern Man*, as well as other references in the notes here, should they wish to find their own way across these historical crevasses.

In any case, on 7 August, with Paccard saying afterward that Balmat was hired as his porter and some claiming afterward that Balmat was his guide,[21] the two met in the late afternoon to set off for the peak.[22] They slept on the Montagne de la Côte, at a height of 2329 meters,[23] left at dawn, and reached the Jonction at 5 a.m. They then spent hours wending their way through the dangerous maze of crevasses and seracs that the crashing together of the two glaciers, the Bossons and the Taconnaz, had created, "like the meeting of two angry seas at a submerged reef."[24] (To visualize the still-dangerous crevasses of the Jonction today, readers can choose from a number of postings on YouTube by climbers who have filmed their reconstruction of the route taken in 1786.) Following Paccard's later suggestion, Saussure will have ladders made for the crossing of these dangerous cracks in the massive ice, which he and Balmat had had to negotiate around. Onto the Taconnaz Glacier itself they veered, then, at approximately 12:30 p.m., up the snowy slopes to the Petit Plateau. At around 2 p.m. and at approximately 3825 meters, they encountered another crevasse to skirt and then went up the slopes to the Grand Plateau, reaching it at mid-afternoon; Saussure later mused on their courage there. Around 3:30 they crossed this polar space and were at the bottom of the steep slope that ran up to the northeast ridge of the peak, its steepness "broken into small ice walls which ... run across it from side to side at various levels."[25] At 6:23 p.m.—the time noted by observers below—they were on the summit, presumably together, with Balmat claiming later that he had had to pull the doctor, who was fainting with fatigue, up to the top. With no place to bivouac, a dangerous nighttime descent back to the Montagne de la Côte and sleep ensued; both men were frostbitten, and Paccard was snow-blind. For athletic ability, physical courage, and route finding, Alpinists say, theirs was one of the "greatest feats" of mountain climbing.[26]

The news of their ascent that reached Saussure in Geneva was electrifying, triggering a flow of that desire to stand on the highest peak of the Alps that had been born of his climbs in the Jura in the 1750s. It would be a different type of climb, however, than that of the pioneers. Climbing as a test of manhood had never been Saussure's goal, in contrast to Balmat, who almost immediately portrayed his summiting as a demonstration of his virility and power, echoing assertions of the Bourrits in 1785. The strength of the robust crystal hunter had carried the doctor-savant to the top (he claimed falsely, and despite Paccard's own youth and demonstrable ability in the peaks; Paccard was twenty-nine and Balmat, twenty-four). Saussure would have skipped the climb itself, given his awareness of his ailing and aging body, if he could have otherwise found his way to the highest peak. If Saussure could have flown a hydrogen or hot-air balloon to the summit, he would have, he explained to a correspondent, the Prince de Ligne, in 1785, after the challenging and abortive effort with the Bourrits, though he knew well its impossibility.[27] This was a technology he was becoming expert in. He had been in Lyon in early 1784, meeting with the Montgolfier brothers and discussing and observing their experiments with the hot-air balloon. Later that year he made his own balloons, launching one from the Bonnets' terrace at Genthod and failing to get one aloft at the farm in Conches, his irritation memorably noted by Rosalie Constant. He was sharp with his sons and stony-faced in response to questions from the collected savants of Geneva.[28] He was working out the various merits of hydrogen -filled balloons versus hot-air balloons. For meteorological experiments perhaps hydrogen would work better, and for transport, the hot-air ones. Gas balloons sent aloft could aid in "ascertaining the constitution of the upper layers of the atmosphere."[29] Balloons could not work to solve the problem of Mont Blanc, however, "since on high mountains one is subject to violent and irregular gusts of wind that might break the machine by driving it against the cliffs, and it would further be needful to have very perfect means of control, in order to reach points so precisely determined."[30]

Saussure recognized that summiting the mountain would be difficult for him at his age and in his physical condition. He was a walker more than a climber, despite the advantages he had in being comfortable at altitudes that triggered altitude sickness to others. He was fine on the summit of the Buet and sleeping on the Col des Rognes. He felt great on the Col du Géant in 1788 and "never better" than when he camped there for sixteen days.[31] He kept in shape during the winter by climbing up and down the steps of the town house in Geneva. Still, Paccard and Balmat were in their twenties and were practiced climbers when they summited Mont Blanc in one long day, while this was beyond Saussure's means. He turned forty-six in 1786 and was forty-seven when he managed the climb. And, though he kept his illness hidden as much as possible, whatever was wrong with his digestive system was a continuing problem. While waiting for the weather to break in Chamonix for the successful climb the next year, his stomach was in distress. He felt nauseated, his food would not "settle," and he had to purge (make himself vomit).[32]

Thus, on 19 August 1786, when news of the first ascent reached him in Geneva by way of special messenger, he wrote back to his contact, Jean-Pierre Tairraz, with instructions to help him prepare for an entirely different type of climb.[33] Tairraz, the proprietor of the Hôtel de Londres, was a former guide and thus in the position of being able to commandeer help for Saussure. He was trusted to pay very generously for this and confident of being reimbursed. He was "mon cher Jean-Pierre," and Saussure, "Votre Bien affectionné, De Saussure." He was to hire a team of five or six men to build two shelters on the mountain in anticipation of Saussure's attempt. One shelter would be as high up as possible on the Montagne de la Côte. This the guides could use while they were working to establish as safe a route as possible for Saussure through the Jonction Glacier.

Saussure thought they could tamp down some of the rough bits for him and use ladders to cross the crevasses. Tairraz should have made for Saussure a fifteen-foot ladder with flat lengths and rungs for this purpose; the guides could begin with an ordinary one. The ladders could also be used for "surmounting rough rocks" (as they are today in a fixed position on the Aiguille du Dru and elsewhere). They were also to build a second *cabane*—or rough shelter—above the snow line (*au milieu des neiges*) "in some rocks," on what will be called afterward the Grands Mulets. It would be "too hard for me to go from the Montagne de la Côte up to the heights in one day," wrote Saussure; "I might sleep there or take refuge there in case of bad weather." He "was not deluding himself," he said to Tairraz. He wanted to follow Paccard's route, but he "ha[d] neither the youth nor the agility of the doctor." So although he might not have been able to go the whole way (*jusqu'au bout*), he might have been able at least to climb high enough to be able to "make the observations and experiments that are so very important to me."[34]

That first attempt at establishing a laboratory on the high pitches on Mont Blanc came to nothing. When Saussure and his party of guides reached the Montagne de la Côte, bad weather drove them back to Chamonix. It was not until the next summer that Saussure's famous ascent of Mont Blanc was achieved, with great fanfare and an attending audience of family and "visitors of distinction" such as William Hodges, Cook's illustrator on his second circumnavigation of the globe (1772–75),[35] and with *le monde* of Paris, eager for news. Geneva sent Jean-Jacques de Tournes, one of the four syndics of Geneva, who arrived as early as 11 July, two days after the Saussures.[36] Mme. Necker told Saussure that she and her husband, the once and future finance minister of France, read the account of his climb, "trembl[ing] while following you among the precipices and perils . . . we have fancied ourselves enjoying with you the magnificent spectacle with which you were greeted when, a modern Enceladus [a Titan, born of Earth and Sky],[37] you scaled Mont Blanc." She mourned, she claimed, "the weakness that hinders me from following in your footsteps."[38] Representatives of the Savoy state were there as well: Hansen tells how "the intendant of Faucigny watched the ascent through a telescope from Chamonix" and reported on the good news: "It is to be hoped that his discoveries encourage foreigners to visit this valley. There is no doubt of the number who have come in the last few years nor the amount of money they bring to this province."[39]

The Saussure family party that summer of his successful ascent included his wife, Albertine; their sons, Théo (age twenty) and Alphonse (age seventeen); and Albertine's sisters, Jeanne-Françoise, who had married a Turrettini at the same time Albertine became a Saussure, and Anne-Caroline, known as Minette. Both sisters were widows, Minette's husband, Jean-Louis Tronchin, having been one of the notable suicides of Geneva, as we have seen. Missing were their daughter Albertine-Adrienne, who was expecting a child with her husband, Jacques Necker, and Saussure's sister Judith, still self-exiling in Montpellier. It is unknown whether Judith was invited, though it would have been logistically very challenging for her to join them, with a very short lead time to get from Montpellier to Geneva and then an open-ended stay *en famille* to face. And perhaps emotionally the visit would be fraught.

Married since 1765, it was only the second time that Albertine had traveled to the place that had so dominated her husband's thoughts and around which so much of their life together had revolved. The first was fifteen years after their union, in 1780. Albertine climbed to Montenvers, and Saussure guided thirteen-year-old Théo down and onto the Mer de Glace. Juxtaposed against Isaac Bourrit's posturing and Balmat's similar claim to have triumphed in the Alps through his undiluted virility—no studying for him!—Albertine's earlier reluctance to join Horace-Bénédict appears as strongly gendered. Yet, this is again to read the Enlightenment Alps in nineteenth-century terms, a history that is itself in need of revision. Undeniably, the large footprint of the British Alpine Club on Chamonix–Mont Blanc in the succeeding century was very male. Women were excluded from membership, and a Ladies Alpine Club was not established until 1907. Though women undoubtedly climbed in the Alps, the question of masculinities is shot through much of the history of alpinism, with the peaks understood by its historians as a stage for a performance of Victorian, bourgeois, imperial, and, later, fascist "maleness."

Hints that the peaks could have offered space for women to explore new identities are just beginning to appear in the literature.[40] Henriette d'Angeville climbed Mont Blanc in 1838, the second woman to summit, though the first, Marie Paradis, in 1808 was part of a publicity stunt led by that inveterate self-promoter Jacques Balmat. She was pushed and pulled up to the top by Balmat and two other guides. D'Angeville, like the elite men who summited in this period, was helped by her Chamonix guides and porters, though she was a tough climber, wore almost-appropriate clothes (knickerbockers), and is credited with the peak. She urged other women to climb in her *Mon excursion au Mont Blanc*.[41] Emmeline Lewis Lloyd, who was the eighth woman to summit Mont Blanc, often climbed with her sister and with Isabella Charlet-Straton, who in 1876 was the first woman to make a winter ascent of the peak. Charlet-Straton further broke norms by marrying her guide, Jean Charlet, of the Compagnie des Guides de Chamonix.[42]

Mary Mummery and her husband climbed together, with Fred (Albert Frederick) Mummery "upend[ing] the status quo, [by] climbing difficult routes with women, to the annoyance of more conservative elements in the Alpine Club."[43] Mary explained that women were "in actual fact, better suited to the really difficult climbs than to the monotonous snow grinds usually considered more fitting." She would know, having completed a first ascent in winter of the Teufelsgrat, the southwestern ridge of the Täschhorn, a peak of 4491 meters. It is "a ridge of exceptional enormity,"[44] "legendary," as it is described today on the Zermatt Matterhorn website.[45] Elizabeth le Blond, an heiress from Wicklow, Ireland (it is she who founded the Ladies Alpine Club), explained that she "owe[d] a supreme debt to the mountains for knocking from me the shackles of conventionality."[46] Also interesting are Lily Bristow, who climbed with Mummery several times and was the first woman to summit the Aiguille du Grépon in 1895, one of the most staggeringly challenging Aiguilles de Chamonix, and beautiful in orange granite. The authors of the blog about these "Legends" from which much of this detail is taken also tell us about Miriam O'Brien Underhill, who introduced the practice of "'manless climbing.'" Not only would she climb without a guide, guideless climbing having been the norm since the Mummery days, but the team of climbers would be exclusively female.[47] Adapting Leslie Stephen's famous phrase, the Alps might also have been a "playground" for women's desires as well as for men's.[48] Its dangers, paradoxically, may have opened up a safe place in which the meaning of being a woman could be pushed beyond the norms of Victorian femininity.

When a feminist history of the age of mountaineering is written, our look back at Chamonix in the 1780s might be less surprising, with Albertine and her sisters, wealthy Genevan women, recognizably "in place," there, not out of place, despite Albertine's personal hesitations. Chamonix's development as a tourist site was firmly woman-friendly from its earliest moments. The first hotel was Mme. Coutterand's, as noted earlier. This is where the Saussure family stayed in the summer of 1787, for the three weeks from 9 July until after Saussure's successful ascent of Mont Blanc. Coutterand's establishment catered to women, one of her employees being Jacques Balmat *dit* des Dames, who specialized in guiding families to the glaciers and into the peaks. These groups hiked up to Montenvers and down to the Mer de Glace. The Le Cointe family was there in 1784, the mother and sisters witnessing the death of the brother, Ami, on the Aiguille des Grands Charmoz from one of these spaces, depending on the account. In another example, we see the Bérenger family from Geneva walking the Col de Balme about the same time.[49] This pass is, at 2204 meters, below the snowline, and scenic, though a five-hour walk from Chamonix via Argentière and Le Tours. It is a serious stage on the *tour du Mont Blanc*. Most dramatically, two sisters and their cousin from Devonshire summited the Buet in 1786, where we saw Saussure in 1776 sketching his panorama. Still called Mont Blanc des Dames, this was the first high peak in the Alps—that is, a mountain over 3000 meters—to be climbed by a woman, and the first "high altitude" peak there ever to be summited (in 1770, by the DeLucs.)[50]

Nothing prevented Albertine and her sisters from embracing Chamonix, and her sisters did so with enthusiasm, despite the three weeks of almost constant rain that followed their arrival. Saussure rode with his sisters-in-law to the Bossons Glacier, where it began to rain heavily as soon as they began the climb on foot. Nonetheless, says he, they managed to reach almost to the edge of the glacier, where he took a reading on the barometer, before turning back in "a horrible rain," the three of them soaked to the skin.[51] They also went together to Montenvers, Jeanne-Françoise, Minette, Horace-Bénédict, and the younger son, Alphonse, but not Albertine. They took mules from the Hôtel Coutterand, at the lower edge of the village, to the beginning of the footpath up to the Montenvers plateau. (The mule path, which will be supplanted by the cog railway, was cut through only in 1802.) With Pierre Balmat and Coutet for guides, the approximately five kilometers took a reasonable two hours to walk, while in the very hot afternoon it meant a strenuous doubling of this time on the way down.[52] Albertine was satisfied with local scenery (once was enough for Montenvers), and she joined in festivities with the family and others. They attended a dance on the town square on a Sunday after a walk along the Arve near the hamlet of Tines.[53] Albertine and her husband paid social visits together to other visitors, though there were tensions. He worried about why, during an excursion on the grounds above the church, she had left their new acquaintances to go walking by herself.[54]

Folding his family into his Chamonix life would seem to be a matter of satisfaction to Saussure. We saw how bringing the Alps into his homes in Geneva and Genthod, where he spent most of every year, distinguished those spaces. His laboratory, cabinet, and library were where the mountains came alive in his writings, and these attracted curious visitors to the *maison Saussure*. The summer estate on the lake offered a vista of the high peaks. Mont Blanc shone in, like the moon, through its windows. Letters between husband and wife remained very loving, though hopes and promises that Albertine would join him the next time alternate with promises to never leave her again after just this one more trip to the Alps.[55] These suggest all sorts of tensions between Saussure and Albertine over his dedication to the Alps, but not an effort to exclude her from that life.

More adventurous, intellectual women interested him, though maybe as a sign again that Albertine's lack of interest in the Alps marks less an ideal of womankind for her husband than simply a cross-current of their lives. Minette, to judge from letters home, was the sister-in-law with whom he talked politics. He referred to himself as her "'best friend.'"[56] It was his daughter, Albertine-Adrienne, with whom he discussed Locke and education reform. More interestingly, his private journal from August 1768 while the couple were in London on their Grand Tour mentions Harriet Blosset a number of times. This person presents as a small footnote in the life of Joseph Banks, famous for his travel to the South Seas with Captain Cook, and highly influential as the president of the Royal Society of Science for forty-one years and director of Kew Gardens. Like Judith de Saussure, however, Blosset may deserve more from history. She was a botanist also, the ward and student of James Lee (1715–1795), a celebrated horticulturalist who owned a nursery of exotic and other plants that catered to gardens throughout Britain and in France. It was at Lee's Vineyard Nursery in Hammersmith that she and Banks met, their interest in plants joined to their interest in each other. Richard Holmes, in his chapter on Banks in *The Age of Wonder*, suggests that she would have joined the voyage of the Endeavour herself ("eagerly") if this could have been allowed.[57]

The Saussures and Blosset met at the opera and had supper together afterward with Harriet's supposed fiancé, Banks, on the eve of his sailing with Cook to Tahiti. She was "desperately in love with Mr. Banks," Saussure thought.[58] During the following few days, the Saussures and the Blossets—Harriet, her mother, and her two sisters—shared breakfasts, visits, and promenades at Ranelagh. Saussure loved all the social life of London (he would happily live there, he told his mother), but Harriet's interests zeroed in on his own. "Afterwards [on the afternoon of 19 August, as he noted in his private journal] took Miss Harriet Blosset in my carriage to see the garden and the rosaries of Lyse, a gardener patronized by Mr. Banks, on the road to Richmond, walked about with her, collected many plants.... Thence, still with Miss Blosset, to see the insects of Mr. Banks, a superb collection beautifully arranged, insects pinned with the name underneath each, English and foreign in drawers covered with glass and framed in cedar wood." At tea later, on that last day before the Saussures left for York, while his wife was at the opera with Harriet's older sister, he worked to console her: "I had a serious conversation with Miss Harriet.

Her deep melancholy, her persuasion she should die, her firm resolve to live in the country to show her true love, make her very interesting."[59]

Like Judith, Blosset is remembered for the contemporary mockery of her relationship with a "great man." (And at about the same time: Judith met Voltaire in 1768, the scandalous dinner occurred in December 1772, and rumors followed thereafter.) After Banks returned from the South Seas in 1771, he broke off the relationship, which in Blosset's eyes was an engagement, though in his, not quite. Social London laughed at "all the worked waistcoats she made for him during the time he was sailing round the world." Part of the joke was that he would supposedly pay her for the cost of the materials used. Another "joke" was that the vests were embroidered in wildflower designs.[60] Lots of laughs.

The main tension of the three weeks in Chamonix with family in 1787 was the incessant rain. Every day was spent waiting for a change in the weather so the summit attempt could begin. This it did on the night of 31 July–1 August, with barometer and visual readings promising fair days ahead.[61] "It finally arrived, the moment so long desired,"[62] thought Saussure as he left Chamonix in the early morning of 1 August and headed to the Montagne de la Côte. Left behind were three people closely connected to Saussure, the reasons for their exclusion revealing something more about his expectations for the climb than this delight.

First of all, Théo. As the oldest son and at twenty years of age, he ardently wanted to join the climbing party. The father refused, believing that he lacked the experience and fitness for the climb.[63] What Théo could and would do was record measurements and other observations parallel to those Saussure would manage on Mont Blanc and that Senebier would effect in Geneva. A vital contribution to the ascent of Mont Blanc, but hardly heroic, yet it does broadcast Saussure's intentions, loudly and clearly. Mont Blanc will make sense in a context inclusive of Chamonix and Geneva, that is, of the valley below and the outlet of the Arve, the river cutting that valley and flowing into the Rhône. As neither the *Voyages* nor Saussure's *Journals* report on Théo's climbing in the Alps to date (unless one counts Montenvers), allowing him to try to summit Mont Blanc, then, would seem like criminal lunacy. But it would be hard for Théo to see this point. He had been spending the three rainy weeks in Chamonix socializing with the Bourrits, who had followed the Saussures to Chamonix.[64] All talk would have been about Mont Blanc, including plans for Charles Bourrit, just fifteen years old, to summit Mont Blanc with his father on the heels of Saussure. This was a wild plan that failed, of course, and on repeated tries as well, but that was still to be seen. Théo would also have remembered that Charles's older brother Isaac, just a year older than Théo was now, had gone with both their fathers in 1785 to try for an ascent via the Aiguille de Goûter. Saussure certainly did, and it was a nightmarish thought.

Bourrit, then, was the second important person to be disappointed in the makeup of Saussure's party, though the refusal could hardly have been a surprise. Bourrit could climb Mont Blanc, of course he could, just not with Saussure, and not until Saussure was well on the way. "The moment so long desired" was not to be sunk in the enthusiasm of Bourrit. Paccard also intensely desired to make the ascent with Saussure. His ascent of the peak in 1786 was motivated by his interest in determining its height, which was why he carried a barometer with him. Saussure's instruments were far superior and many, and it would have been a learning experience for him to work alongside Saussure. His interest in science was real and recognized: he had been elected to the Royal Academy of Sciences of Turin as a corresponding member in 1785.[65] Saussure had already shared with him methods for extrapolating height from the barometer readings so that Paccard's account of his summit could be certain to be accurate.[66] Paccard in turn had reported to Saussure the details of his first ascent (recorded by Saussure afterward in his journal).[67] That Saussure should have welcomed Paccard's interest in climbing Mont Blanc with him, first in the attempt of 1786 and finally in 1787, has been a refrain of some observers.[68] He should have been collegial, he should have invited Paccard along. Maybe he should have. All Saussure offered Paccard was the role played by Théo and Senebier. For the attempted ascent in 1786, Saussure formally asked this of Paccard, but Paccard was obviously reluctant. For the ascent the next year, Paccard absented himself to Courmayeur.

Saussure and Paccard, the journals of each make clear, found each other difficult to like. Each seems to have been prickly, perhaps misunderstanding the other's overtures. (When Saussure invited Paccard to dinner in 1784 when they first met in Chamonix, Saussure's journal says Paccard seemed to take offense, thinking he, Paccard, should have been the one to ask Saussure first, and faux pas such as this.)[69] That Saussure had sworn never again to climb with colleagues, even close friends such as François Jallabert, Jean Trembley, and the Pictets, Jean-Louis and Marc-Auguste, and of which the disastrous attempt at an ascent with Bourrit had very recently reminded him, makes some sense of this. As Albert Carozzi has explained with respect to Saussure's approach to his explorations in general, "going alone was his guiding principle."[70] He needed to maintain his focus, to store his impressions for later analysis.

Certainly, both Balmat and Paccard could not go. A fight on the streets of Chamonix on the day of Saussure's arrival over whose account of their ascent was true had made this very clear. It may have begun at the bar of Coutterand's hotel between Balmat's supporters and Paccard's. Paccard was met on the street by Balmat and his crowd as they were on their way to Paccard's house to force him to retract statements describing his role in the ascent. Paccard hit Balmat with his umbrella when he was accused of having forced Balmat to sign an affidavit saying that the doctor *had* reached the summit just before or at the same time as Balmat, and that Balmat had not dragged Paccard to the top.[71] This is the controversy—who was first?—that will rage through mountaineering history into today, and that this new history of Saussure quickly skirts.

No to his inexperienced son; no to the unfit Bourrit; no to the local savant, Dr. Paccard, who wished to summit again, and with him. The third ascent of Mont Blanc, Saussure's one and only, would be simply his, simply Saussure and his experience of Mont Blanc, assisted by his eighteen guides and porters, along with his personal servant, François Têtu,[72] who would get him and his instruments to the top.[73] Saussure ordinarily traveled with only a few guides, and typically with just one. He and Jean-Laurent Jordanay of Courmayeur had climbed on the Miage Glacier, Pierre Balmat guided him on the Aiguilles de Chamonix, and Pierre Simon worked with him as his travels began in the 1760s, taking him across the Mer de Glace and up the Brévent. The summit attempt with the Bourrits in 1785 was the exception, and as here, Chamoniard guides were needed to help carry and keep safe the instruments for a mobile laboratory. Such an extraordinary undertaking demanded such a team. The laboratory was to be established at 4808 meters on top of Mont Blanc, the first of this size on a high peak. Paccard had taken readings on his barometer on Mont Blanc, and the DeLucs had done the same on Buet along with temperature experiments, as had Saussure. However, nothing on this scale had been attempted before. All the guides who helped him with this were named by Saussure. The Alps were never empty spaces to this Genevan: they were always peopled, his associates always individualized and set within a working—not romanticized—environment. Saussure wanted his readers to know their names, as always giving Chamoniards their credit and ensuring that they as well as he figured into his *Voyages*. Their sobriquets were included, as honorifics that offered prestige and enhanced their reputation, and that would help them with future employment. Still, no climber paid as much as did Saussure, ordinarily, and extraordinarily for Mont Blanc.[74]

Jean-Baptiste Lombard *dit* Jorasse was of the party. He had climbed with Paccard and the doctor's brother two weeks after the first ascent in an attempt to replicate it. That effort failed, so Lombard knew well what challenges Saussure would face. Jacques Balmat *dit* Mont Blanc—along with

Jean-Michel Cachat *dit* le Géant and Alexis Tournier—had made the second ascent of Mont Blanc (on 5 July 1787), having been hired by Saussure to confirm the route to be taken by himself as soon as possible afterward. It is they who decided to shift the line up to the northeast ridge slightly to the west of Paccard's, to a slope with an easier incline though even more avalanche-prone.[75] Also ready were his "usual guides," Pierre Balmat and Marie Coutet, along with Jacques Balmat *dit* des Dames, whom we met before at Coutterand's hotel; Alexis Balmat; Jean-Louis Dévouassou and four other Dévouassous, the brothers Jean-Michel, Michel, François and Pierre Dévouassou; and finally, François Coutet, François Ravanet, Pierre-François Favret, and Jean-Pierre Cachat.[76] All their names are reproduced here, first and last and sobriquets, to honor Saussure's intentions to ground his ascent in Chamoniard life with their associations with hotels and explorations of the massif. The only illustrations of Saussure *in* the Alps show him in the midst of these guides, crossing over and along crevasses, distinctly not on the summit and thus deliberately not as the supreme conqueror of a peak (see figs. 6.1 and 6.2). These were made to illustrate a short "Account of the Ascent of Mont Blanc," and though they depict the party

FIGURE 6.1 The Ascent. Marquard Wocher, *Voyage de Mr. Saussure à la cime du Mont-Blanc au mois d'Août MDCCLXXXVII*, plate 1 (1790). Photo credit: © Fitzwilliam Museum, Cambridge. Reproduction by permission of the Syndics of The Fitzwilliam Museum, Cambridge. Accession number: P.10921-R.

FIGURE 6.2 The Descent. Marquard Wocher, *Voyage de Mr. Saussure à la cime du Mont-Blanc au mois d'Août MDCCLXXXVII*, plate 2 (1790). Photo credit: © Fitzwilliam Museum, Cambridge. Reproduction by permission of the Syndics of The Fitzwilliam Museum, Cambridge. Accession number: P.13130-R.

working its way through the junction of the Bossons and Taconnaz Glaciers, they are based on sketches made of largely the same group the next year—1788—on the equally dangerous Talcul Glacier below the Col du Géant.[77] One visual clue to the site is the inclusion of Théo, so unhappily left behind in 1787. Guides, yes, Théo, no on Mont Blanc.

The instruments carried to the summit of Mont Blanc (as can be seen in figs. 6.1 and 6.2) included two barometers and two hygrometers with glass fronts, and just these were a challenge to preserve. Paccard broke two barometers on his climbs, and the one he carried to the summit of Mont Blanc had been damaged probably by a slip, an indication of the fragility of these tools. Paccard's barometer was meant to get a confirmed measure of the height of Mont Blanc. Saussure's two will work alongside many other sensitive instruments intended for examining the atmosphere, a more technical project than Paccard's. In a close call for Saussure's instruments, and thus his project overall, the pedestal used for his barometer, compass, telescope, "and several other instruments" slipped into a crevasse on the ascent, just below the Grands Mulets—a fissure so deep "one could not see its bottom." With incredible luck, it shot into the wall of the opposite side, like an arrow, so, with incredible pluck, a roped guide lowered down and across the gap could retrieve it.[78]

Of course, that Saussure's bed was also carried up high, at least to the Montagne de la Côte, seems excessive but in the absence of sleeping bags and with only one known overnight above the snow line recorded—Balmat's in 1786—and Saussure's recognition of his limits, this makes some sense. And it was a type of portable bed, not a four-poster! These were typically used for "all the major scientific expeditions of the era," whose reports Saussure read, as the catalog of his library shows.[79] It was this type of expedition, not simply a climb, that he was on.

That first night Saussure, Têtu, and several guides slept in a tent at the very top of the Montagne de la Côte while others climbed down to the *cabane* constructed below.[80] A late departure at 6:30 a.m., then the crevasses and seracs of the Jonction were faced. They passed a crevasse that Marie Coutet had nearly fallen into the day before while on a reconnaissance of the glaciers. Roped to two companions, he was on an ice bridge when it collapsed under his feet. After some moments of dangling, he was pulled to safety, but the sight of the crevasse "augmented the fear" they all were feeling as they "crossed over these vaults thinly suspended above the abysses."[81] Three hours in the Jonction, then on to the plateau and the lower part of the Grands Mulets. That ridge of rock was reached shortly before 11 a.m. More climbing until they reach the second-highest rock of this ridge, at around 3500 meters. Saussure will name it the "Rocher de l'Heureux Retour," it being the first space of relative safety they will touch on their descent, and where they will camp for the night after summiting. The guides wanted Saussure to stay there now, on the ascent, with hopes, he thought, that he would jettison the attempt the next day. The fear was of having to sleep in the snows of the plateau, where only Balmat had survived before. And here is where Saussure mused on the courage of Paccard and Balmat, adding his reflections on this otherworldly space. Hemmed in by Mont Blanc to the south, the aiguilles jaggedly high in the east, and the Dôme du Goûter to the west, "practically all one sees is snow. It is a pure white snow, a dazzling white snow." Saussure paints it high on the summits of the peaks in stunning contrast to the sky, which is such a deep blue as to appear almost black. It is a starkly visual space, yet also one of "cold and silence": "One sees no other living being, no sight of vegetation."[82]

It being only 1:30 p.m., Saussure prevailed, and the team set off again, walking through the snowy slopes west and south, and up, with the Dome du Goûter on their right. At 4 p.m. the tent was erected in the snow of the Grand Plateau. They spent an uncomfortable night at approximately 4000 meters, with twenty people in one tent, all gasping for breath.[83] A feeling of nausea and suffocation, Saussure reported.[84] Around midnight,[85] all were alarmed by the sound of a large avalanche crashing over the path they were to follow the next day.[86] At around 2 a.m., beauty nonetheless: "superb view of this magnificent basin resplendent in the light of the moon shining brilliantly in the black sky, with Jupiter risen behind the Aiguille du Midi."[87]

Early morning came, and they made their way through the path of the avalanche. Pierre Balmat, Saussure's longtime guide and friend, advised that they climb quickly through it without stopping for breath. Saussure gently dismissed this suggestion: it would be impossible for him to manage. And would not the safest route be wherever the unstable snows had already fallen? They would head up the slope leading to the summit ridge—a very dangerous crossing. He negotiated "a crevasse at the corner of a serac that barred the passage,"[88] with Pierre Balmat and Marie Coutet steadying him with a pole held between them.[89] Nausea and shortness of breath overtook him. Toward the end, on the easier ridge to the summit, he rested more than he walked. If he made "the least movement, such as pushing the snow from the top of my shoes," he came close to collapsing (*défaillance*).[90] The last hours of the ascent "were the most fatiguing ... as one can imagine." Finally, at 11:05 a.m., he reached the summit, "that goal so long desired."[91]

It was no *coup de théâtre*, the view from the roof of Europe.[92] On the climb up he had had "under his eyes" almost everything already that could be seen from the top.[93] What difference did a few hundred meters make? Moreover, his goal was never simply the summit itself, as he made absolutely clear in the *Voyages*. The imperative was "above all to make his observations and perform his experiments"—work in his laboratory, in short—"which alone would give some value" to what he had done.[94] As he stepped onto the cone formed by the curved ridges of the northeast and northwest approaches,[95] he felt irritated and disappointed. How much it all had cost him and his family in anxiety, in time, and in money, adding: "I tramped the snows that crown the summit with something like anger rather than with a feeling of pleasure," and footnoted Lucretius: "Thus is ... trampled underfoot."[96] The goal was a chimera, a fantasy like superstition or religion, which is what the ellipsis in the quotation stood for. It was clear by the time he summited that a successful set of experiments at 4808 meters was beyond his reach. Experiments on the Grand Plateau the day before had been almost impossible. Under these conditions, every test and observation cost as much in fatigue and breathlessness as did a steep climb.[97]

Still, he set to work. First, the mountains below and on every side had to be surveyed. It was vital to seize the moment for this, since clouds could form at any time and obstruct his view.[98] He found, after all, "a keen satisfaction" in confirming earlier views.[99] Notes taken on the spot that were summarized in his *Relation abrégée* exude a feeling of optimism. In one sweeping look were swept away the doubts about mountain formation that years of work below had not been able to resolve.[100] Not only was the relationship between primary and secondary mountains now clear, with the secondaries leaning toward the granite primaries, but what he saw supported the theory he hoped to present (though he died before he was able to do so) on the origin of mountains. The patterns he saw in the ranges beyond supported a general theory of strata shifting. Beds of rock that had originally been laid down horizontally had been pushed up vertically or turned backward above themselves. High peaks such as Mont Blanc would seem to have been formed by general causes and were not the result of separate eruptions from the crust of the Earth.

Then to his experiments and observations of the atmosphere. First the barometers and hygrometers were set up to do their measurements and the thermometers were plunged into the snow and set up in the sun and the shade. Next came experiments on the composition of air at that altitude.[101] Using a solution of calcium hydroxide (*eau de chaux*) and confirmed with a caustic potash (*alkali caustique*), he tested for carbon dioxide, finding a detectable quantity.[102] This result was a significant contribution to the new science of chemistry, following Lavoisier's discoveries of the makeup of air and water.[103] Other chemistry experiments were abandoned because the mental concentration needed to perform them was too draining.[104] Using his diaphometer, intended to measure the transparency of air, was also beyond his abilities. He had pasted black circles of diminishing sizes on sheets of cardboard. In something like an optometry exam, the plan was to record "the distance at which the discs could no longer be seen,"[105] but this was "impossible à mes forces."[106] The purpose of the experiment was to find the relative transparency of the air at different altitudes by comparing the distance at which something could be seen on Mont Blanc to the distance at which it was visible at Chamonix and Geneva.

Measuring the color of the sky, toward a similar goal, was more successful. His assumption was that "the intensity of blue in the sky varied according to 'opaque vapors' in the sky,"[107] and for this he had invented his cyanometer. This was a sheet of cardboard to which were affixed sixteen numbered squares of blue paint and ink, ranging from very dark to very light. The blue squares alternated with cutout squares that one looked through to find a color match. He recorded a hue of 1–2, on the deep end of his scale, while a 5–6 was noted in Chamonix and a 7 in Geneva.[108] The imprecision—1–2, 5–6, and so on—would be corrected for on the Col du Géant, where he would bring an improved cyanometer, a circular arrangement of fifty-one shades, a type Alexander von Humboldt would borrow on Chimborazo in 1802.[109] (Saussure's cyanometer—sometimes credited to the later Humboldt—may have been inspired by Abraham Gottlob Werner's *On the External Characteristics of Fossils* [1774], which served as a guide whereby minerals could be identified by color and other visible signs. This found new life after the transformation in mineralogy by crystallography in Patrick Syme's *Werner's Nomenclature of Colours adapted to Zoology, Botany, Chemistry, Mineralogy, Anatomy, and the Arts* [1st ed. 1814]. This work was used by Charles Darwin on the *Beagle* voyage of 1831–36, as the book's recent publisher explains, "to craft his descriptions of what he saw, such as the changing colour of cuttlefish, noting the 'clouds, varying in tint between hyacinth red and chestnut brown'... and the 'beryl blue' colour of the glaciers he saw in South America."[110])

Some of the air from the summit and a sample of its snow were boxed up for later study. Saussure also tested for sound and smell in these conditions, shooting off a pistol and recording his impressions. It sounded like a firecracker, and there was no odor. Furthermore, just before leaving, carefully so as to capture the body at rest, not climbing, the pulse of each man was measured. Saussure's was 100, Têtu's 112, and Balmat's 98.[111] After four and a half hours, clouds began to threaten Mont Blanc, and with a "heavy heart" he began the descent at 3:30 p.m. He "counted for little" the work he had managed to do, compared to what he had hoped to accomplish.[112] He had been surprised by how much his difficulty breathing had affected his ability to think (so different from his experience on the Buet).[113] He felt like "a gourmet invited to a superb feast" who then found a sudden disgust for food preventing him from taking part in it.[114]

If this book were a history of Mont Blanc, the map that illustrated chapter 5, "High Peaks" would be festooned with reports of subsequent ascents. These began almost immediately. The Bourrits tried and failed on 4 August and then again on 6 August (and again, incredibly, with another attempt the next year.)[115] The first British ascent, beginning a long series of these that will temper into the "golden age of mountaineering," was achieved on 9 August by twenty-three-year-old Mark Beaufoy, who took with him nine guides, one valet, a sextant, a thermometer, and a burning glass.[116] Saussure's story takes us physically and intellectually elsewhere, onto the Col du Géant and into his culminating vision of his project, and that is what this study of his life and his *Voyages* is all about. So we turn the page on Mont Blanc, as Saussure did when traveling "happily" back to Geneva. He would no longer be troubled by Mont Blanc. He could see it "with unalloyed pleasure," from the heights of the town or the shores of the lake. It could no longer "trigger that agitation, excitement and distress" that the mixed reality of summiting had relieved.[117]

Unlike Mont Blanc, though part of the massif, the Col du Géant (3466 m) is a high-altitude pass.[118] Lying between Chamonix and Courmayeur, it is accessed from the Chamonix side via the Mer de Glace, then the Talcul Glacier. The Chamoniards' Jean-Michel Cachat *dit* le Géant and Alexis Tournier *dit* l'Oiseau were first to discover the way across these glaciers to Courmayeur on 26–27 June 1787, followed on 28 June by Jean-Michel Tournier, Jean-Marie Couttet, and the Savoyard administrator Charles Exchaquet, the inspector of mines. Exchaquet recommended the space to Saussure when he sought advice on where to set up a laboratory to continue the work begun on Mont Blanc "that the shortness of time, and the malaise" from the climb truncated.[119]

It needed to be high—3600 meters would be desirable—and open, "where the winds and all the forces of the atmosphere" could play out around him.[120] And he needed to be able to camp for a significant amount of time. Not just four hours, nor for four days; rather, more than fourteen days and nights would be good. Observations of the weather at high altitudes—if only from barometers, hygrometers, and thermometers—had only been taken at midday or so when on peaks such as the Buet, or when he was on Mont Blanc. He had thought for some time that "to fill this lacuna" of information on the atmosphere, serial observations were needed. He wanted to observe closely (*épier*) the different forces of the atmosphere—the rains, the winds, the storms—as they were formed and as they raged.[121] He wanted to be with them where they began.

The plan for a laboratory of the Col du Géant was settled on for the summer of 1788, with Saussure and his son Théo in Chamonix from early June waiting for the summer weather. On 2 July they began the dangerous climb from the Mer de Glace onto the Talcul Glacier, then along the base of the Noire Mountain to the Géant Glacier, where they were to stay. This last stage, along the Noire, was "réellement dangereuse."[122] One of the team, Alexis Balmat, fell into a sixty-foot-deep crevasse; he landed on a small ledge about halfway down, and his best friend swooped him back up with him on his rope.[123]

At first there was disappointment. The space chosen by the guides was lower than Saussure had wanted, at 3350 meters (1763 toises). However, a storm that began on the night of the 4th and lasted until midday of the 5th—the most terrible he had ever witnessed, he said, with thunder sounding like cannon and snow filling their *cabane*—and then the succeeding cold, especially, mitigated their regret. Every afternoon starting around 5 p.m., the wind would flow down from the peaks, often with snow or hail, and always brought with it a cold "from which even the warmest furs were no protection."[124]

However, the regularity of work offered space for deep, peaceful concentration. "Toward 10 o'clock in the evening, when the wind calmed down," Saussure would leave the sleeping Théo in the *cabane* and go off to one of the two tents that held his instruments. There, wrapped in furs, his feet warming on a hot stone, he would update his journal, "taking notes on what I had done that day." At regular intervals he would go off to the other tent for instrument readings and to look at the sky, which "almost always at that time of night was perfectly clear."[125] As on the Miage Glacier and at the base of the Aiguille du Goûter, it was also a world of color. On their last night, the 16th, the wind was still, while the peaks and the snows of the slopes were drenched in hues of rose and rich, deep carmine. A purple band filled the horizon looking southward toward Italy. The full moon rose above it in red-gold vermilion.[126] In the fullness of night, the royal colors of red and purple then shifted to white. "How to paint that beautiful evening?" The moon was alone in the sky. Its light was silvering a world that in the daytime was too bright to bear, the glaring expanse now softened into somber granite rocks looking sharply cut and distinct among the moon-bright snows. "What a magnificent contrast" of color and shape and texture the night had revealed![127]

Saussure's empiricism, his noticing of colors, shapes, and sounds, becomes poetic in a way defined by Seamus Heaney in his essay "The Government of the Tongue." Poetry works by "open[ing] unexpected and unedited communications between our nature and the nature of the reality we inhabit."[128] In Heaney's case this inhabited reality was the Irish landscape, political and natural; in Saussure's it was the mountain sensorium. In this final vision, the last of the *Voyages*, he articulates what that relationship can be for a Genevan on the Mont Blanc massif, standing in for any human there: "in the midst of this majestic silence, one believes one hears the voice of Nature and that one has become the confidant of its most secret operations."[129] This is what it means to touch the natural world, Saussure is saying. It means remaining fully human, while being fully aware of the "other." In this communication between one's self and the mountain, one's own humanity is shaped, as a "confidant," not a master, not as one exercising "dominion ... over all the earth, and over every creeping thing that creepeth upon the earth." It is the voice of Nature that one listens to, not the voice of God, as Saussure's early mentors Bonnet and Haller had believed. It is not "that Adorable Being" that Saussure felt on Mont Blanc when he quoted Lucretius on the summit and whose voice could be heard on the Col du Géant. This Nature is not God, and yet it is not reducible to one's own self either, as in the popularized romanticism of Bourrit, where the mountains are the backdrop for human emotions. In its transcendence of a world otherwise simply about ourselves, Saussure's aesthetic empiricism beautifully articulates an ecological awareness that ascribes value to the planet independent of its use in sustaining human life. This is an aspect of the Enlightenment experience of nature that gets lost in the telling by reducing him to his Genevan milieu, or by squeezing Saussure's *Voyages* forward into the golden age of mountaineering.

❋ 7 ❋
The Legacy

Ten days after French troops flooded into the city ending Genevan independence, a *traité de réunion* was signed formalizing the absorption of the former city-state into the territory of France. On 26 April 1798 (7 Floréal An VI of the French Revolutionary calendar) Geneva became the prefecture, or administrative center, of the new department of Léman. This department stretched to the Mont Blanc massif, the southern part of which became, also through annexation by France, the department of Mont-Blanc. The line delineating the two departments crossed the summit of the peak. Geneva and Chamonix were now connected politically, not only with Geneva as prefecture of the department, but also with Geneva as head of a sub-unit containing ten cantons stretching along the Arve and enclosing Chamonix.[1] These units of France created with the Revolution (from 1790) were named for prominent spaces of nature, in a break from the names of provinces that spoke to the history of the kingdom and to noble and monarchial control such as Berry, Orléanais, Anjou, Provence, Burgundy, and Normandy. However, the guiding hand in shaping the Léman and Mont-Blanc departments was that of an expansionist state, and not the imperatives of the landscape (fig. 7.1).

So, too, was Napoleon's crossing of the Alps in May 1800 through the Great St. Bernard Pass an exercise in conquest and a representation of human dominance over nature, as fictionalized by Jacques-Louis David in one of his great paintings. After a short stay in Geneva, pontificating to its "men of science," appraising their wives, and then paying his respects to the widowed Albertine de Saussure at the mansion on the rue de la Cité, Napoleon met his gathering troops for the invasion of Italy.[2] His feint was a visit to the spas for his health. The secret plan was an early-season crossing of the pass to surprise the Austrian army and drive it out of Italy in what was to be the Battle of Marengo in June 1800. This success enabled Napoleon's concentration of power, which culminated in 1804 with the

FIGURE 7.1 *Atlas National de France* (1800–14). "Département du Mont Blanc. Département du Léman." Cartographer: Pierre-Grégoire Chanlaire (1758–1817). Engraver: François d'Houdan (1748–1828). Collection musée alpin, Chamonix-Mont-Blanc, Carte Géographique AG.544.

Empire. Even today the road through the pass is closed until early June, so the risks were real, though much more hazardous, for the soldiers pushing and pulling cannon, and for the horses themselves, than for the First Consul, led carefully along while bundled up on a steady mule, both translated by David into a rearing horse and its expert rider. This was "the most famous image ever" of Napoleon, in the words of David A. Bell, writing about "the power of charisma in the Age of Revolution."[3] Napoleon is riding into glory on the forces of nature: the twelve-hundred-pound horse, the gale-force winds, and the steep path of 8100 feet (2469 meters) up and down as the snows of winter still threatened.[4] It is a masterly performance of masculine dominance of the Alps. The painting represents the invincible military forces of France and their general as they sweep through the Alps into northern Italy.

How different from the vision of Geneva and Chamonix that emerges from the *Voyages* was their absorption into the territory and imagery of revolutionary France. From Saussure's first steps along the Arve valley, he recognized and described the geological links between the city on the lake and the villages at the high end of the Arve, nestled below the high peaks. The great boulders scattered along the lakefront and along the path of the river must have come from the mountains of granite beyond and above. The raging torrent of the Arve and its feeder streams were colored by the minerals that rocks from the upper Arve, ground down by the raging water, were bringing to the confluence of the Rhône as it exited Geneva. Saussure saw that the high peaks to be seen from Geneva—and, by extension, mountains overall—were the result of general causes. Mont Blanc was not a specific outburst from the surface of the Earth. The granite of the high peaks—the primaries—had to have been shifted up from below, leaving limestone layers to define the Prealps, including the layered beauty of the Salève, which defines the vista south of Geneva. Along the Arve he saw the famous folding of rock layers turned upward and backward suggesting this movement, which Albert Carozzi insisted was the first step toward understanding plate tectonics, thus answering a basic question of how the Earth evolves and connects. Saussure's explorations of the Bernese Oberland (as readers will also recall) and the Grisons in 1777 and 1783 were to confirm the general disposition of rock layering, as were his climbs on and around Monte Rosa and the summiting of the Rothorn in 1789, along with his final climbs on the Klein Matterhorn in 1792. Saussure's travels trace the arc of the Alps—if only its western slice—and their regional connections, with Geneva, his Geneva, as a point of reference.

Saussure's conception of the Alps as a region with an integrity based on its natural characteristics rather than on political boundaries anticipates the Alpine Convention of the late twentieth century. Signed in 1995 by eight states with alpine regions along with the European Union, the Convention was "the world's first international treaty considering a transnational mountain area in its geographical entirety."[5] It promised "transnational and cooperative" decision-making that would work toward preserving the Alps as a network of ecosystems and cultural traditions, and it offered a "common vision for the Alps as a pioneer region for sustainable living in the heart of Europe" based on "mutual respect and understanding."[6] Such are the guiding principles of the Convention, and one hopes the agreement succeeds in its goal of reconciling "economic interests . . . with ecological requirements."[7] These are formulations complementary to the 1992 United Nations Framework Convention on Climate Change and subsequent Protocols and Conferences of the Parties, meant to further compliance with the Paris Agreement of 2015. Though climate change triggered by human behaviors—and especially, in what we label now the Little Ice Age, global warming—was beyond Saussure's ken, that the Alps could be imagined as a region, not a set of political states, and that the Alps are "the people and the land," are constructions embedded in the *Voyages* of Saussure. "We are the Alps," says the Convention, echoing Saussure's references to "our Alps," as he draws Genevans in to a common interest in the peaks.

Saussure's vision of integration—Geneva and the peaks—precluded lines of thought being worked out by other minds of the century. Montesquieu notably, in *The Spirit of the Laws* (1748), associated climate and forms of society. Haller's pastoral poem *The Alps*, celebrating the virtues of the alpine folk as shaped by the adversities of the peaks, has already been discussed. Both Haller and Montesquieu drew on classical ideas about "the stimulus of a harsh environment" in developing a culture of industrious, freedom-loving, luxury-eschewing people.[8] Mountain people are different. That Genevans and Chamoniards lived in different cultural universes was belied, however, by Saussure's experience, and this he shared in the *Voyages*. Only a very few times do we hear him contrasting city mores with those of the countryside. The first was an anecdote about picking pears from along the path of the Arve. It was the summer of 1761, and he was walking to Chamonix for the second time. His friends were with him. They were hot and thirsty, and after resting in the shade of an orchard, they found the ripe pears hanging above their heads irresistible. When they saw the owner of the trees walking toward them, they hastened to offer payment for the fruit that they had picked. The woman declined. No, no—simply enjoy them, she said. He who made them, made them for all of us, and not for the enjoyment of only a one. "What a contrast," Saussure exclaimed, "between that way of thinking and the egoism of people who live in great cities!"[9] However, not only did this encounter take place in the village of Contamines-sur-Arve, "three short leagues" away from Geneva, out of the eighteen short leagues to Chamonix, but the geology of the area was the same as that of the environs of Geneva: "All the country until the village of Contamine at three leagues from Geneva rests, like the environs of the city, on a base of sand, clay, and rounded stones."[10] We are still far from the high peaks and the mountain landscape. It is a country people he is lauding, not the alpine world.[11]

This is the register—the "city" and the "country"—in which he describes Chamoniards as losing "a little" of their "antique simplicity" in the face of the influx of tourists and the considerable sums of money they brought. In their eagerness to serve as guides, occasionally one of them would pretend to be the person requested by the visitor, or would offer himself in another's stead, claiming that his colleague is sick or away. Someone even posed as Pierre Simon, about whom Saussure spoke so highly in the first volume of his travels, "despite the fact that that excellent man had been dead for some four or five years."[12] The later Compagnie des Guides de Chamonix was established not only to provide for families of guides in need but to rectify this, by establishing a fair order of turns by which guides were assigned to climbers. (This was a practice that came to irk members of the British Alpine Club such as Leslie Stephen, who wanted to be able to climb with guides of his own choosing.)[13]

Saussure's tone in describing the people he meets in the Alps is never condescending, despite divides of education and religion. The *Voyages* present Catholic priests, hotelkeepers, mountain guides, and other villagers with respect (not occasions for amusement, as later guidebooks might in sketching scenes of "local color"). For instance, his account of women from the village of Le Tour scattering dirt on the deep snows of March is placed in the context of his own—not more empirical—experiments on the nature of heat.[14] In his correspondence, Chamoniards appear as friends. Jean-Pierre Tairraz, former guide and then proprietor of the Hôtel de Londres, was addressed, as we saw in chapter 6, as "mon cher Jean-Pierre," while referring to himself as "votre bien affectionné, de Saussure."[15] The correspondence with Mme. Coutterand lasted nearly twenty years, from 1767 to 1786, as did their avowed friendship.[16] The "earliest known letter by a Chamonix guide" was written to Saussure. Pierre Simon, who appears so vividly in the *Voyages*, sent a note in July 1775.[17] Saussure, who understood and could speak the patois of the guides, sought this closeness.[18] He tells the readers of the *Voyages* that to be a naturalist in the Alps was "in some respects" to be like a chamois hunter—which his guides also were. They faced the same dangers and the same "alternations of hope and fear."[19]

When he had himself depicted on the slopes of the Mont Blanc massif for an "Account of an Expedition to the Summit of Mont Blanc," it was with his guides, and almost as if he himself were a guide. In "The Descent"—which was reproduced earlier as figure 6.2—he is shown glissading, that is, about to slide downward on the ice with the help of a long, pointed stick. This is exactly the maneuver that Simon had begun teaching him to do in 1760 on the Mer de Glace. Saussure was explicit in his instructions to the artist. He wanted to be represented "in a standing glissade on the snow in the attitude of a guide that we see in the vignette in the first volume of the *Voyages*,"[20] shown earlier as figure 3.6. It was Simon who had taught him how to use his body on ice and snow and on the heights, such that it was reshaped in the manner that so perplexed the savants at his autopsy in 1799. (The climbing muscles that must have forced his intestines upward, the appetite that must have impacted his city digestion.) Like the guides, his muscles seemed to have been formed by climbing, his arms and legs coordinating with the glissade as he balances on the ice above a crevasse. Saussure is Genevan, his clothes and hat say, but he is also Chamoniard, at home on the ice. It's an idealized image of a younger Saussure. It is also a homage to the guides and to his years in the Alps.[21]

And though the revolutionary Republic of Geneva in 1794 will exclude Catholics from citizenship—indeed, reserving civic freedoms for Calvinists—religion was never a divide for Saussure.[22] Italian elites were part of his circle.[23] So too were regional clerics such as Laurent-Joseph Murith (1742–1816), the abbot of the Great St. Bernard Hospice, with whom he explored the peaks and glaciers surrounding the Great St. Bernard Pass. A man who "loves and cultivates with much success the study of natural history," as he was described in the *Voyages*, he corresponded with Saussure for over ten years.[24] Murith was typical of the type of person who filled Saussure's correspondence. By European standards of secondary importance to Franklin, Condorcet, La Place, and others with whom he also communicated, and well out of the range of the La Rochefoucaulds and the Prince de Ligne, with whom Saussure was close, Murith represented the regional tilt of Saussure's interests. What was distinctive about Saussure's network of associates was its "relative disconnection with respect to the classic scientific networks centered on the Parisian Academy of Sciences, London's Royal Society, the University of Leiden and others."[25] Instead, Saussure formed connections with "tout l'arc alpin," as Jean-Daniel Candaux's analysis of his correspondence has shown.[26] He broke out of the walls that encircled his Genevan mentors.

Eric Golay, in his study of Saussure's role in the Genevan Revolution, suggests that it was because of his training as a natural historian that Saussure was able to see the patrician world he was a part of—*la microsociété aristodémocratique*—for what it was: as no longer tenable in modern times, "even before it was destroyed by the Revolution in December 1792."[27] This empiricism also allowed him to see the people of Chamonix and other, smaller, villages as the rational humans they were, and on their own terms, rather than through a romanticist lens, representing mountain virtue to urban vice. It was through an Enlightenment frame that he viewed all his associates. In Geneva, his insistence on the principle of equality and the value of a system of equal opportunity prompted his proposed education reforms. These would have recast Genevan society as a meritocracy, shifting power away from the small set of patrician families and their inherited system of privilege. He articulated these thoughts during the Genevan Revolution: "It is a horrible disease, Aristocracy: it spreads everywhere, it infects everything, it degrades everything. Take a society of the most brave, the most proud democrats and give to them some power, the demon of Aristocracy will spread in their hearts, forcing them to augment these powers and while working simply to satisfy their own desires [*passions*] they pretend to safeguard the cause of the people."[28]

This is a draft of a speech never given, presumably, that Carozzi found in the Saussure family archives. The handwriting, Carozzi explains, is almost impossible to read, and he only transcribed for readers the first paragraph, here translated. The draft documents ("a series of rough drafts") were written between 21 October 1792 and June 1793. Golay interprets Saussure's meaning narrowly in the context of the shift in meaning of the term *aristocracy* during the course of the French Revolution, away from the meaning of inherited privilege and toward the sense of a group of persons acting in their own interests, especially deceptively, and not in the interests of the people. Golay suggests that Saussure was reacting to the proposed expulsion from the Genevan National Constituent Assembly in June 1793 of all members who refused to take the oath to liberty, equality, and fraternity, with Saussure's speech targeting the group driving the Revolution forward.[29]

Yet Saussure's views are consistently in favor of meritocracy and dialogue. The "Projet de réforme pour le Collège de Genève" proposed to the government in 1774 would have radically changed the objectives of schooling in Geneva, a system set in place by Calvin to train students to enter the ministry and the administration of the city. Boys entered the Collège at age five or six. They were taught reading, writing, and arithmetic, then later Latin and Greek. Only children of the professional classes attended. It was not for artisans, whose apprenticeships began at an early age. And the children of the very wealthy were schooled at home. Saussure's new Collège would have opened the doors to all children in Geneva, girls as well as boys in the early years, boys in the upper grades. History and especially science would be privileged at the expense of classical languages. Talented students from whatever background would continue their education at the Academy, breaking the hold the patrician class had on the administration of the city-state in both its clerical and its secular arms. Moreover, children from different economic and social backgrounds would get to know one another. Education would break apart the narrow circles that ghettoized Genevan life.[30]

After the government rejected the proposed reforms, Saussure published a response, titled "Eclaircissements sur le project de réforme pour le Collège de Genève," which pointedly countered the conservative counterproposal for separate technical schools for the children of artisans.[31] Thwarted anew, he then moved in a different direction to achieve somewhat similar aims. The Société pour l'Encouragement des Arts et de l'Agriculture was initiated in 1776 by Saussure and, less predictably, a master watchmaker, Louis Faizan. Like other societies throughout Enlightenment Europe, the Société des Arts was established as a place to share ideas about improving and reforming the practices of industry and farming. As its historians note, given the importance of watchmaking in Geneva, it should not be a surprise that the challenges of this profession were a focus of the Society, and that its leaders played an active role within it.[32] Yet this was its "particularity: one finds nothing like it in the French provincial academies, from which workers were excluded, nor even in the English societies where their role remained minor."[33] And finally, a doomed attempt to integrate all classes of Genevans in a Cercle républicain or Cercle de la République was proposed by Saussure in January 1790.[34] This was to have been modeled on the social circles that grounded Genevan life, but on a grand scale, meeting not in a host's apartment but in a hall across from the Hôtel de Ville. Refreshments would be served to facilitate the discussion of political opinions held by all classes of society.[35] These ideas too were rejected by the government, and a few weeks afterward, de facto by the emerging leaders of the Genevan Revolution who formed for themselves a Cercle de l'Égalité.[36] Saussure's vision of community may already have been out of date, and only his proposed reforms of the Genevan school system will have a life after the Revolution, beginning with changes to the Collège in the 1830s.[37]

It is not in Geneva, however, where the legacy of Saussure's life's work is most alive, but in Chamonix. When Saussure walked out of his walled Calvinist state up the Arve valley and into Chamonix, it was a personal revolution. It was also a plunge into a series of revelations about humans' place in the greater natural world, insights that we share today and that can be recognized directly by taking that same journey into the high peaks, physically or by proxy, from Chamonix.

Today some 100,000 visitors from around the globe cram Chamonix's streets in July and August, at the height of the summer season. They cram the rue Michel Croz (named for the Chamonix guide who fell to his death on the Matterhorn in 1865, his rope cut or snapped) and crowd into the

Savoyard specialty stores along the rue du docteur Paccard,[38] named for the Dr. Paccard who made the first ascent of Mont Blanc in 1786, in tandem with Jacques Balmat, that other Chamoniard, the year before Saussure's success. The homage of the street name goes some way toward correcting the impression offered by the prominent statues of Balmat and Saussure that stand together at the top of that street, depicting the sturdy Balmat pointing, almost lunging, toward the real Mont Blanc, as if it were only he who could show our Genevan the way. These were erected in 1887 to commemorate the centennial of Saussure's ascent and to celebrate Balmat. A statue of Paccard is placed a little further along the Arve, depicting him sitting alone, contemplating Mont Blanc, and, some say, placed to be looking over and beyond Balmat. This memorial appeared in 1986 and stands in recognition of Paccard's achievement, and for tourists, as a hint at the drama associated with the mountain that has drawn them to the town.

On the Place Balmat, in the din of the Arve rushing under the nearby pedestrian bridge, well-to-do couples from Japan and families from the Middle East mix with the European bourgeoisie and with hikers from New Zealand and other points south, trailed by happy if dusty dogs. Talk is often of the pleasures of the *tour du Mont Blanc*, which begins and ends in the Chamonix valley, as it did when Saussure inaugurated that walk around the massif in 1767.[39] American accents are heard less often than British, reflecting the durable love of the English for the region and the success the more exclusive St. Moritz and Zermatt have had in selling luxury to rich Americans.[40] By mid-afternoon climbers returned from the Mont Blanc massif—some of them expert, some not—begin to cut through the crowds. Their equipment alone sets them apart from ordinary hikers, who might be leaning on alpenstocks and wearing sensible boots. Regulations now dictate that anyone climbing the *voie normale*—the most popular route up the summit that takes one from the Tête-Rousse Glacier (above the Nid d'Aigle), to the Aiguille du Goûter, the Dôme du Goûter, and finally the Arête (ridge) des Bosses and which was first achieved by Leslie Stephen in 1861[41]—must have basic climbing equipment. Minimal, sensible requirements are a helmet; a headlamp; two pairs of gloves, one light and one warm; gaiters; a warm jacket; socks; waterproof trousers; mountain boots; crampons; a harness; crevasse rescue equipment; a rope; an ice axe; walking poles; a GPS or altimeter; a hat; glacier sunglasses; sunscreen; and a ski mask.[42]

The rules about how to dress for Mont Blanc were issued in 2017 by the mayor of St. Gervais and councillor for the Mont Blanc region in an attempt to keep inexperienced people off the mountain, though the Compagnie des Guides de Chamonix continued afterward to find novices trying on crampons for the first time at 3500 meters. In covering this story, the television station France 3 showed an image of a young woman beginning the deadly *couloir du Goûter* in shorts, light hiking shoes, baseball cap, poles, and day pack.[43] The death of a "lightly dressed" twenty-eight-year-old Frenchman from Brittany who slipped off the Arête des Bosses ridge was also widely covered. He was in athletic shoes, which fell off in the fall, and he lacked both helmet and harness. A week before that accident, a forty-six-year-old man from Lyon had died on the Bosses; he was inadequately dressed for hiking, let alone climbing.[44]

The Chamoniarde, the valley's official "mountain rescue and awareness organization," is housed in the center of Chamonix at the Place d'Église in the house of the former curé (now the Maison de la Montagne). It works to counter misunderstandings about Mont Blanc.[45] "Non, le Mont-Blanc ce n'est pas facile!" and "L'Ascension du Mont Blanc, une affaire d'alpiniste" are the warnings in its information brochures. Summiting is not hiking, it is mountaineering: "Climbing Mont Blanc is not easy!" The classic routes are dangerous in themselves. "Tons of rocks can come down from hundreds of meters above" in the Couloir du Goûter. Ice slopes and crevasses are further risks on the Goûter route. On the Trois Monts route, which crosses Mont Blanc du Tacul (4248 m) and Mont Maudit (4465 m), one faces avalanches and serac falls. "The steepness (. . . slopes up to 45 degrees) and the eventual issues to cross bergschrund should also be taken into account." With respect to the Grand Mulets route, "Risks are the same [as those] encountered on the Trois Monts route (serac falls, avalanches) with a higher risk to fall down in a crevasse."[46] (Their translations for each quote, preserving the urgency of their message to English-language-reading climbers.)

Myths about the ease of climbing Mont Blanc began with the golden age of mountaineering, when the pattern of targeting first ascents of peaks, then aiguilles, then north faces was set in place by British, then by other climbers. In 1866 in a famous essay titled "Alpine Dangers" in the *Alpine Journal*, Leslie Stephen explained the stages that a summit might pass through, in the eyes of the (male) climbing community. First, it was "inaccessible." Then, "the most difficult point in the Alps." Next, "a good hard climb, but nothing out of the way." Subsequently, "a perfectly straightforward bit of work." And finally, "an easy day for a lady."[47] A sturdy sexist trope, it was heard in the response to the first ascent of the Aiguille du Grépon, those two needle points 3482 meters high above Chamonix, by two women climbing without male guides or companions in 1929: "'The Grépon has disappeared,' it was said. 'Now that it has been done by two women alone, no self-respecting man can undertake it. A pity, too, because it used to be a very good climb.'"[48] In 1920 Freshfield, in his biography of Saussure, offered the image of mountaineers nonchalantly running along the narrow ridge leading to the summit of Mont Blanc, with its the dangerously steep slope to the south running into Italy, and its north slope, to France: "The ridge of the Bosses, given calm weather and ordinary conditions, affords a comfortable footpath. Mountaineers today walk up and run down it with their hands in their pockets." The climber, he added, "the youth who on a fine day walks up the mountain by a trodden track, is apt to wonder how the climb can ever be thought perilous. He may even dare to describe it as 'a dull grind.'"[49]

The Chamoniarde organization blames consumerism for distorting Mont Blanc. Capitalism has captured its appeal, amplifying it in the age of the Internet. Summiting is a status symbol, to be noted on one's résumé, or as a post on social media. It is an "object of consumption" and emulation.[50] The champion trail runner Kilian Jornet's (b. 1978) video posting on Facebook of himself at the summit on 21 June 2017 in shorts, T-shirt, and sneakers has been viewed more than a half a million times.[51] The "Kilian effect" has been blamed by local authorities for the reckless behavior of some climbers.[52] Though mountaineers recommend climbing six high peaks (those with summits above 3000 m) before attempting Mont Blanc, for the "philistine" it is only the highest peak that counts: "The Alpinist never begins with Mont Blanc! One learns to climb in stages, on slopes that in themselves may be just as impressive. The ascent of Mont Blanc then becomes an act of consecration, rather than an exploit marked by disrespect."[53] The Compagnie des Guides de Chamonix, the Chamoniarde, elected officials of the valley and of the department of Haute-Savoie all concur: "It is imperative to return the ascent of Mont Blanc to its true value by recognizing the physical and moral testing that the risks taken presume, and the magic and the grandeur of place suppose."[54]

What saves Chamonix from Disneyfication is the pressing reality of the landscape. "Montblanc" may be a company that makes pens, and Mont Blanc may stand for France in the way of the Eiffel Tower, as one of "the two major symbols that represent France to foreign tourists," in the words of one of its historians.[55] However, Mont Blanc is never a simulacrum. Its physicality is always present, irreducible, and potentially deadly. Even global warming has not mitigated its dangers. To the contrary, the subsequent melting of the permafrost has led to instabilities throughout the massif. Rockslides are increasingly common, and the glaciers are shifting.[56]

The beauties of the massif also have a keener edge. Though the Mer de Glace directly below the Montenvers is newly rocky and slopes above the valley look green where formerly they were brown, in the heat of newly broiling summers the high glaciers of the massif reflect down on the streets of Chamonix with an even more dazzling beauty, as if generating their white light from within. It is light with the power of lightning. Our recognition of this independence, so to speak, of the Mont Blanc massif and by implication of nature overall, is the gift Chamonix offers to us today. One finds it a stronger testament to Saussure's eighteenth-century experience than his rigid statue standing along the still ice-cold Arve.

Was Saussure an environmentalist? The *Voyages* laid various tracks for historians to follow, in part a consequence of their shifting focus, for they appeared in print in staggered succession from 1779 to 1786 to 1796.[57] Volume 1 begins with a description of the neighborhood of Geneva: the lake, the hills that surround the lake, the rocks that are to be found "scattered throughout the environs," as Saussure put it. Then we are taken to the Salève and the Jura Mountains, and to Saussure's discovery in the 1750s of his vocation to become the "historian of the Alps," and his declaration to study the mountains in situ by traveling to the Mont Blanc massif. The volume abandons its readers, however, after taking us up the Arve River into Chamonix and onto a side excursion to the Buet. It was not until 1786 that volume 2 was published, with apologies for the delay. He had had doubts, he says, about his observations, and they needed to be resolved. He had had to battle illness, though "except for that of 1782, he had not let a summer go by without making at least one excursion into the Alps." And there was new work on minerology published, though it had convinced him of the inadequacy of the field. There was work for him to do in understanding rocks.[58] The volume of 1786 promised that another two books would appear in short order. Though volume 2 would complete his description of the Mont Blanc massif, he explained, he had traveled elsewhere in the meantime. His report on these other regions would follow in volume 3, and then volume 4 would be a general analysis and summation of his findings. Or so he thought.

For then came the summiting of Mont Blanc in 1787 and the brilliant two-week experience on the Col du Géant in 1788, neither of which was anticipated in April 1786, when he finished volume 2.[59] And then came the French and Genevan Revolutions and the collapse of his fortune and his health. The final two volumes were only published in 1796 with the help of his son Théo, and in very limited editions.[60] In 1789 and 1792 he had traveled—with Théo—up and around Monte Rosa and the Matterhorn, though no new discoveries were made. (The timing suggests they were escaping political tensions.) But these travels too had had to be gathered into the *Voyages*, as they are in the last half of volume 4. In lieu of a completed theory of the Earth, the *Voyages* end with a three-page survey (*coup d'œil*) of his findings and a long "Agenda" of unanswered questions. What he tells us in the foreword to volume 2 about its having become "impossible to enclose in one single volume" everything he wanted to say is true in more general terms about the *Voyages* overall.[61] It is open-ended; it escapes itself.

On one level, the book was meant to introduce Genevan readers—Saussure addresses them directly—to the mountain world that lay beyond their walls. This is a prominent theme in the first two volumes, where explicit directions for traveling to the Jura Mountains, to the Chamonix valley, and around the massif are given. It can read like a guidebook, which is why nineteenth-century guides to the region often plagiarized the material. At the same time, the *Voyages* were meant to establish his position as a leading savant, not just in Geneva but in Europe overall. The Alps would be his laboratory, where the sciences of the Earth would be established. Natural processes would be studied on a scale never before realized in the cabinet of objects that antiquarians had focused upon, or through the microscopes of his Genevan mentors. These would be established empirically, avoiding the speculations of Buffon writing from his country home in France.

He set concrete goals for himself. He would determine the position and composition of the rocks that lay in the valleys, the Prealps, and the peaks themselves. Establishing that, universally, granite formed the high peaks and that limestone lay below would suggest general causes for mountain formation, rather than that peaks—Mont Blanc, for example—were expressions of specific eruptions. Finding summits from which to view the arrangement of the Alps and the Jura as mountain ranges would help answer questions about general versus specific causes. He might confirm that alpine valleys were formed by some natural force—he supposed it was water—cutting through the center of a range. The evidence of parallel, matching heights—the highest peaks of the Jura, say, matching the Mont Blanc massif, with their sibling peaks declining on each side—would support this explanation.

Several things happen to Saussure as he encourages Genevans to travel in the Alps and as he introduces himself to the world as a historian of the Alps. His functional research plan for the Earth sciences, for what he will be one of the first to call geology, becomes in practice an intensely physical, sensual attraction to the mountains. His senses are electrified when they come into connection with the Earth. What had been a framing device for his project, made visible to him from the summit of the Dôle when he saw the Alps, the Prealps, and the lakes as one body, becomes a living metaphor. As he builds descriptions of what he sees, tastes, smells, and hears, a portrait of a living Earth develops. These are the bits of Saussure's science that escaped even the assiduous undertaking of the geologist and historian of science Albert Carozzi. After a career as a working geologist in the postwar United States, Carozzi began to follow Saussure's paths into the Alps, Saussure's field notebooks in hand, seeing what Saussure saw, touching the same rocks. It was as if he were one geologist in conversation with another and therefore able to establish Saussure's importance in anticipating the theory of plate tectonics. Saussure's conversation, however, was not only about science, and not only with his readers. The *Voyages* depict an intimacy with nature, close to but just beyond the reach of science, that he reached with all his senses and that could not be bagged up in a collection of rocks. This conversation with the natural world is what the *Voyages* invite us to emulate. It is what the Compagnie des Guides de Chamonix and the Chamoniarde today perform in their insistence on respecting the physicality of Mont Blanc, and it is what our own developing respect for a nature outside ourselves charges us to do.

Acknowledgments

I walked to high meadows and hiked above the clouds in the Vanois National Park with the Morlot family and am grateful for the opportunity to thank them for introducing me to the Alps and for their many acts of kindness in Paris. If a place could be thanked as if it were a person, however, it would be Chamonix–Mont Blanc to which these acknowledgments would be addressed. I thank its representatives in La Chamoniarde and their Office de Haute Montagne, which provides vital information to climbers on mountain conditions and itineraries and also to researchers like me, asking out-of-the-way questions such as what might have been Thomas Blaikie's route from the Mer de Glace to Argentière, and having the answers sketched on their giant relief map of the Mont Blanc massif, scaled at 1:10,000. The Bibliothèque de Genève is another welcoming space. I want to thank Paule Hochuli Dubois for her help in identifying sources in the Archives de Saussure and in the Constant family archives.

My travel and research have been supported by the Borden W. Painter, Jr., '58/H'95 Chair, and I thank the donors and Trinity College, Connecticut, for enabling this project. My home institution has been central to its success in other ways also. The Watkinson Library holds first editions of the four volumes of Saussure's *Voyages dans les Alpes*, which made establishing the relationship of images to text possible, since the illustrations in the digital editions are missing or distorted. I thank Erik Johnson-DeBaufre, Special Collections Librarian, and Amanda M. Matava, Digital Archivist, for their help with the *Voyages*. And I am fortunate in having colleagues with a common interest in the history of nature. I thank Sean Cocco and Tom Wickman, with whom I have team-taught for almost as long as I have been writing this book, for their openness to debating methods and meanings in environmental history. I am also very grateful to Zayde Antrim, who read early drafts of the manuscript and has helped me with it in a myriad of ways.

I thank Peter Hansen for presenting his work with me at a French Historical Studies Conference in Cambridge, Massachusetts, a long time ago and whose work has helped me think through my own ideas about Saussure. I especially owe a debt to the Boston French History Group, which read an early version of the introduction. I thank Jeffrey Ravel for inviting me. I benefited immensely from the comments offered by Marie-Hélène Huet and Thomas Dodman and also from the group's encouragement to continue with the book. I thank Ann Blair, another member, for sharing sources on Conrad Gesner and early alpinism.

Darrin McMahon generously introduced my manuscript to the University of Chicago Press, and I am honored that it will be published in his innovative series, The Life of Ideas. I am grateful to the two anonymous readers for the press whose comments forced me to streamline and strengthen the arguments of the book, and it has found its perfect editor in Dylan J. Montanari. I am fortunate also in the assistance of Fabiola Enríquez Flores. My debt to Patrice and Margaret Higonnet continues to grow. Patrice offered suggestions for revision as he read and reread early drafts, and Margaret edited a penultimate version of the manuscript. My sister, Mary Lou, helped with solutions to some knotty intellectual problems, and I also thank my brother, Phil, for his careful reading of chapter 1. Most of all I thank my husband, Dan, and daughter, Julia, for sharing the adventure of this book with me in Geneva and in Chamonix, and in lively and loving conversation. To these two brilliant companions I dedicate this book.

Notes

Abbreviations

ARCH. DE SAUSSURE: Archives de la famille de Saussure. Bibliothèque de Genève, Geneva, Switzerland.

CORRESPONDENCE H/B: *The Correspondence between Albrecht von Haller and Charles Bonnet*. Edited by Otto Sonntag. Bern: Hans Huber, 1983.

CORRESPONDENCE H/S: *The Correspondence between Albrecht von Haller and Horace Bénédict de Saussure*. Edited by Otto Sonntag. Bern: Hans Huber, 1990.

VOYAGES: Horace-Bénédict de Saussure, *Voyages dans les Alpes précédés d'un essai sur l'histoire naturelle des environs de Genève*, 4 vols. Vol. 1, Neuchâtel: Samuel Fauche, 1779; vol. 2, Geneva: Barde, Manget, 1786; vol. 3, Neuchâtel: Fauche-Borel, 1796; vol. 4, Neuchâtel: Fauche-Borel, 1796.

UN REGARD SUR LA TERRE: *H.-B. de Saussure (1740–1799): Un regard sur la terre*. Edited by René Sigrist and Jean-Daniel Candaux. Vol. 4 of *Bibliothèque d'histoire des sciences*. Geneva: Georg, 2001.

Introduction

1. Excerpts of the autopsy report are given in G. de Morsier and R. de Saussure, "Description clinique et autopsie d'Horace-Bénédict de Saussure par le Docteur Louis Odier," in *Gesnerus: Swiss Journal of the History of Medicine and Sciences* 27, nos. 3–4 (1970): pp. 127–37, at p. 127.

2. On Tronchin's suicide, see Jeffrey R. Watt, *Choosing Death: Suicide and Calvinism in Early Modern Geneva* (Kirksville, MO: Truman State University Press, 2001), pp. 266–67, quotes at p. 266. Douglas W. Freshfield, with the collaboration of Henry F. Montagnier, *The Life of Horace Benedict de Saussure* (London: Edward Arnold, 1920), pp. 135–36.

3. "Conclusions du Procureur Général Jean Robert Tronchin sur le *Contrat Social* et l'*Émile* de Rousseau, [17 June 17, 1762]." In Jean-Jacques Rousseau, *Lettres écrites de la Montagne*, with a preface by Alfred Dufour (Lausanne: Éditions L'Age d'Homme, 2007), Annexe III, pp. 319–23. Tronchin's defense of his decision, published as *Lettres écrites de la Campagne* (1763), prompted Rousseau's *Lettres écrites de la Montagne*. Rousseau's first letter in particular addresses the question of how to live a Christian life.

4. A "multiplicity of instances," as reported by John Moore; see Freshfield, *Saussure*, p. 136. (Letter 32 from Geneva in John Moore, *A View of Society and Manners in*

France, Switzerland, and Germany, vol. 1 [London, 1779], p. 301, *Eighteenth Century Collections Online*, accessed 10 December 2023, https://link-gale-com.ezproxy.trincoll.edu/apps/doc/CW0101367812/ECCO?u=a21tc&sid=primo&xid=2167f26c&pg=319.) Watt shows that the rate of suicide rose after 1750, and "contemporaries certainly perceived that suicide was becoming more common after 1750"; see Watt, *Choosing Death*, pp. 27 and 26. Watt cites Voltaire and Pierre-Michel Hennin, the French Résident in Geneva, for this view.

5. Jean-Pierre Ferrier, "Le XVIIIème siècle — Politique intérieure et extérieure," in Société d'histoire et d'archéologie de Genève, *Histoire de Genève des origines à 1798* (Geneva: A. Jullien, 1951), pp. 401–82, at p. 420. This volume is hereafter cited as SHAG, *Histoire de Genève*.

6. On the incomes of nobles in Paris, see Peter McPhee, *Liberty or Death: The French Revolution* (New Haven, CT: Yale University Press, 2016), p. 16. John E. Joseph, in *Saussure* (Oxford and New York: Oxford University Press, 2012), p. 655 n. 67, estimated Saussure's income as approximately 400,000 euros in 2001 terms. Joseph's work is a biography of Ferdinand de Saussure. Saussure's finances are discussed in Barbara Roth-Lochner, "Comment Saussure perdit sa fortune," in *Un regard sur la terre*, pp. 471–85.

7. Letter to his mother dated 20 April 1768; Arch. de Saussure 223-6; p. 15 of "typed copies of the letters."

8. Still amusing for some biographers of Voltaire. The exception to this careless treatment of Judith is Jacques Proust, "Une 'victime' de Voltaire en exil à Montpellier à la fin du xviiième siècle: Judith de Saussure," *Studies on Voltaire and the Eighteenth Century* 296 (1992): pp. 17–32.

9. *Correspondance littéraire, philosophique et critique par Grimm, Diderot, Raynal, Meister, etc.*, ed. Maurice Tourneux, vol. 10 (Paris: Garnier Frères, 1879), pp. 135–36. Judith was named—"Mlle de Saussure"—though she was described as being eighteen years old, not twenty-seven.

10. Pierre Milza, *Voltaire* (Paris: Perrin, 2007). On Mme. Denis's intentions, see p. 746. On Richelieu and Louis XV, see Milza, *Voltaire*, pp. 746–47. On Richelieu, see Pierre Trousson, *Voltaire* (Paris: Tallandier, 2008), p. 639.

11. C. Monday, 31 December 1770 (Gregorian). Electronic Enlightenment. Letter no. D16929 in *Digital Correspondence of Voltaire*, general ed. N. Cronk, letter ed. T. D. N. Besterman (2008), accessed 12 December 2023, https://www.e-enlightenment.com/item/voltfrVF1210188b1c/. There is a postscript: "regards to Mme Denis."

12. Judith's letter of July 1778 to her sister-in-law: Arch. de Saussure 223-3, p. 70.

13. The height of the Col du Géant is as given by Michel Grenon (of the Observatoire de Genève) in "Observations météorologiques et climatiques," in *Un regard sur la terre*, pp. 141–58, at p. 144. Sources vary.

14. Freshfield, *Saussure*, p. 395, "brief references in his mother's letters."

15. René Sigrist, *Les Origines de la Société de physique et d'histoire naturelle (1790–1822): La Science genevoise face au modèle français* (Geneva: Société de Physique et d'histoire naturelle de Genève 1990), p. 156 and his n. 78.

16. Jean-Michel Pictet, "Nicolas-Théodore de Saussure (1767–1845)," in *Les Savants genevois dans l'Europe intellectuelle du XVIIème au milieu du XIXème siècle*, ed. Jacques Trembley (Geneva: Éditions du Journal de Genève, 1987), p. 433.

17. *L'Éducation progressive; ou, étude du cours de la vie* (Paris: A. Sautelat, 1828–38), 3 vols. What Necker de Saussure meant by "progressive" was an education that

"progresses" or developed over the course of one's life. Clarissa Campbell Orr, "Albertine Necker de Saussure, the Mature Woman Author, and the Scientific Education of Women," *Women's Writing* 2, no. 2 (1995): pp. 141–53, makes a good start toward a modern biography of Albertine yet gets some facts wrong. Orr says that Albertine's father, Horace-Bénédict de Saussure, "was the first conqueror of Mont Blanc "(p. 144), though he was not. And she says that Théodore "followed [their] father into geology" (p. 145), when in fact he became a celebrated botanist. And saying that her mother "took an interest in science" (p. 144.) is quite a stretch! Nothing in the journal that her mother wrote in Paris or in letters written to H. B. suggests that interest.

18. Jacques Naef, "La Botanique," in *Les Savants genevois*, pp. 329–76, at p. 341.

19. Naef, "La Botanique," p. 341,"l'auto-impression." On "nature self impression" or *autophytotypie*, see H. Walter Lack, *A Garden of Eden : Masterpieces of Botanical Illustration = Ein Garten Eden : Meisterwerke der botanischen Illustration = Un Jardin d' Eden : Chefs-d'œuvre de l'illustration botanique*, rev. ed. (Cologne: Taschen, 2016), pp. 14–17, 31, and 206.

20. William Monter, "Women in Calvinist Geneva (1550–1800)," *Signs: Women in Culture and Society* 6, no. 2 (Winter 1980): pp. 189–209, at p. 207, makes reference to the "cultural marginality of women in Geneva.".

21. Albertine Necker de Saussure, "Notice sur le caractère et les écrits de Mme de Staël," in *Œuvres complètes de Mme la baronne de Staël publiées par son fils, précédées d'une notice sur le caractère et les écrits de Mme de Staël par Madame Necker de Saussure* (Paris: Treuttel & Würtz, 1820). Installation piece, Brooklyn Museum, Sackler Center for Feminist Art.

22. Charles Magnin and Marco Marcacci, "Le Projet de réforme du Collège (1774): Entre instruction publique, politique et économie," in *Un regard sur la terre*, pp. 409–30.

23. Freshfield, referencing a letter of Necker de Saussure to her husband, says Saussure died in the arms of Théodore. Freshfield, *Saussure*, p. 393.

24. Pictet, "Nicolas-Théodore de Saussure (1767–1845)," p. 433. He would like "'to deliver my friends and then burn the town. Let it be no more mentioned,'" he wrote to his sister. Quoted by Freshfield in *Saussure*, p. 379.

25. On the Genevan Terror, July 1794, see Eric Golay, "Un paratonnerre pour l'arbre de la liberté," in *Les Plis du temps: Mythe, science et Horace-Bénédict de Saussure*, ed. Albert Carozzi, Bernard Crattez, and David Ripoll (Geneva: Musée d'ethnographie, and Annecy: Conservatoire d'art et d'histoire de Haute-Savoie, 1998), pp. 155–99; and Golay, *Quand le peuple devint roi: Mouvement populaire, politique et révolution à Genève de 1789 à 1794* (Geneva: Éditions Slatkine, 2001), pp. 525–86.

26. Freshfield, *Saussure*, p. 373. Morsier and Saussure, "Description clinique et autopsie d'Horace-Bénédict de Saussure," quoting Odier, say this happened at the end of 1793: p. 128. Sigrist and Candaux give 1794 for the "first attack of paralysis" in "Horace-Bénédict de Saussure: Une vie en quelques dates," in *Un regard sur la terre*, p. 527.

27. Morsier and Saussure, "Description clinique et autopsie d'Horace-Bénédict de Saussure," quoting Odier, p. 129. Philip Rieder and Vincent Barras, "Santé et maladie chez Saussure," in *Un regard sur la terre*, pp. 501–24, at p. 504.

28. Christine Chicoteau, *Chère Rose: A Biography of Rosalie de Constant (1758–1834)* (Bern: Peter Lang, 1980), p. 178.

29. Morsier and Saussure, "Description clinique et autopsie d'Horace-Bénédict de Saussure," p. 130. Rieder and Barras, "Santé et maladie chez Saussure," p. 504.

30. Morsier and Saussure, "Description clinique et autopsie d'Horace-Bénédict de Saussure," p. 129.

31. See Freshfield, "Addenda and Corrigenda," p. 461, for the title of her book. Freshfield, *Saussure*, p. 389, quoting a letter of Rosalie to her brother about the reading of the novel. Now at the Bibliothèque de Genève, Archives de la famille de Constant.

32. Recent work: Meghan K. Roberts, *Sentimental Savants: Philosophical Families in Enlightenment France* (Chicago: University of Chicago Press, 2016); and Jessica Riskin, *Science in the Age of Sensibility: The Sentimental Empiricists of the French Enlightenment* (Chicago: University of Chicago Press, 2002). Saussure's relationship to his family will be shown here in its particular—and in some ways peculiar—Genevan context, distinct from that of the French.

33. The list of works on Victorian mountain climbing is growing. Begin with Caroline Schaumann, *Peak Pursuits: The Emergence of Mountaineering in the Nineteenth Century* (New Haven, CT: Yale University Press, 2020); Alan McNee, *The New Mountaineer in Late Victorian Britain: Materiality, Modernity, and the Haptic Sublime* (Cham: Palgrave Macmillan, 2016); and Peter H. Hansen, *The Summits of Modern Man: Mountaineering after the Enlightenment* (Cambridge, MA: Harvard University Press, 2013). For mountains as culture more generally, see Simon Schama, *Landscape and Memory* (New York: Alfred A. Knopf, 1995), and Robert Macfarlane, *Mountains of the Mind: Adventures in Reaching the Summit* (London: Granta Books, 2003). Each addresses Victorian mountain climbing.

34. Though Stephen did climb again, including a summiting of Mont Blanc in 1873. In "The Regrets of a Mountaineer"—one of his beautiful essays, published in 1871—he explained that "the fate which has cut me off . . . in the flower of my youth, and doomed me to be a non-climbing animal in future, is one [marriage] which ought to exclude grumbling." In Leslie Stephen, *The Playground of Europe*, introd. G. Winthrop Young (Oxford: B. Blackwell, 1946), p. 243.

35. "But I would so much rather have known my father than to have grown up in the shadow of a legend, a hero." John Mallory, foreword to David Breashears and Audrey Salkeld, *Last Climb: The Legendary Everest Expeditions of George Mallory* (Washington, DC: National Geographic Society, 1999), p. 17.

36. Freshfield, *Saussure*, p. 382. On hot springs visited by Saussure, see Albert Carozzi, *Horace-Bénédict de Saussure (1740–1799): Un pionnier des sciences de la terre* (Geneva: Slatkine, 2005), p. 313.

37. Rieder and Barras note a section on sulfur springs in the *Voyages* (secs. 255–72, vol. 1, pp. 202–14); "Santé et maladie chez Saussure," p. 516.

38. Rieder and Barras, "Santé et maladie chez Saussure," pp. 518 and 517.

39. Jean-Antoine Giobert, *Des Eaux sulphureuses et thermales de Vaudier*, is called "un classique de genre" in Rieder and Barras, "Santé et maladie chez Saussure," p. 516.

40. Rieder and Barras, "Santé et maladie chez Saussure," p. 516. Saussure's "Mémoire sur les eaux minérales et leurs différentes espèces" addresses the problem of the imbalance of humors specifically in the section on alkalis. This unpublished manuscript is dated by Carozzi to 1796 and printed in full in his *Horace-Bénédict de Saussure (1740–1799)*, pp. 315–19; see p. 316 for alkalis.

41. Views that reach back to antiquity. See Paolo Rossi, *The Dark Abyss of Time: The History of the Earth and the History of Nations from Hooke to Vico*, trans. Lydia G. Cochrane (Chicago: University of Chicago Press, 1984), on seventeenth-century views of the body of the Earth being like the body of animals, p. 7.

42. Haller's *Elementa physiologiae corporis humani* (Elements of human physiology) was published in eight volumes between 1757 and 1766.
43. Sigrist, *Les Origines de la Société de physique et d'histoire naturelle*, pp. 40–41.
44. Odier says that Saussure was his patient for over twenty years.
45. As was Théodore Tronchin, notably.
46. Sigrist, *Les Origines de la Société de physique et d'histoire naturelle*, pp. 40–41.
47. Morsier and Saussure, "Description cinique et autopsie," p. 505.
48. Rieder and Barras, "Santé et maladie chez Saussure," pp. 505–6.
49. Quoted by Rieder and Barras, "Santé et maladie chez Saussure," p. 506.
50. Quoted by Rieder and Barras, "Santé et maladie chez Saussure, " p. 505 and p. 506.
51. Rieder and Barras, "Santé et maladie chez Saussure," p. 506.
52. Rieder and Barras, "Santé et maladie chez Saussure," p. 506.
53. Morsier and Saussure, "Description clinique et autopsie," p. 137.
54. Morsier and Saussure, "Description clinique et autopsie," p. 136.
55. Rieder and Barras, "Santé et maladie chez Saussure," p. 502. Lester S. King and Marjorie C. Meehan, "A History of the Autopsy," *American Journal of Pathology* 73, no. 2 (November 1973): pp. 514–44, at pp. 523–24.
56. For Odier's views on autopsies as consolation to the living, see Rieder and Barras, "Santé et maladie chez Saussure," p. 502.
57. Rieder and Barras, "Santé et maladie chez Saussure," p. 510.
58. Rieder and Barras,"Santé et maladie chez Saussure," p. 502. On meetings, see Sigrist, "Annexe 2: Règlement de 1791," in *Les Origines de la Société de physique et d'histoire naturelle*, pp 195–96. Odier's manuscript report is housed at Geneva's Museum of the History of Science.
59. Annexed in 1798 by France, with Geneva forming part of the department of Léman.
60. Rieder and Barras,"Santé et maladie chez Saussure," p. 506.
61. Barbara Roth, "Comment Saussure perdit sa fortune," in *Un regard sur la terre*, pp. 471–86.
62. In 1795. Freshfield, *Saussure*, p. 385.
63. In 1795. Quoted in Freshfield, *Saussure*, p. 384.
64. Freshfield, *Saussure*, p. 383.
65. Freshfield references (Déodat Gratet de) Dolomieu (1750–1801) a friend of the Saussure family and fellow geologist, after whom the Dolomites are named, when he says that the post in Paris came without pay. Freshfield, *Saussure*, p. 386. Actually, records in Paris show that a salary of 3000 livres was offered in 1796. Roger Hahn, *The Anatomy of a Scientific Institution: The Paris Academy of Sciences, 1666–1803* (Berkeley and Los Angeles: University of California Press, 1971), corrects historians on this. Hahn, review of Albert V. Carozzi and Gerda Bouvier, *The Scientific Library of Horace-Bénédict de Saussure (1797): Annotated Catalog of an Eighteenth-Century Bibliographic and Historic Treasure*, *Isis* 86, no. 4 (December 1995): pp. 655–56, at p. 656. Dolomieu was one of the scientists Napoleon took along with him to Egypt.
66. Freshfield, *Saussure*, p. 369. Neither did most of his peers: Golay, "Un paratonnerre pour l'arbre de la liberté," p. 198.
67. Golay, *Quand le people devint roi*, p. 529.
68. Golay, "Un paratonnerre pour l'arbre de la liberté," p. 198.
69. Quoted in Rieder and Barras, "Santé et maladie chez Saussure," p. 506.

70. That December he had a major stroke.
71. Quoted in Freshfield, *Saussure*, p. 389.
72. Rieder and Barras, "Santé et maladie chez Saussure," p. 511.
73. Rieder and Barras, "Santé et maladie chez Saussure," p. 513.
74. Augustin-Pyramus de Candolle, *Mémoires et Souvenirs (1778–1841)*, ed. Jean-Daniel Candaux and Jean-Marc Drouin (Geneva: Georg, 2004), p. 83.
75. "Éloges historiques de Bonnet et de Saussure, lu le 3 janvier 1810," in Georges Cuvier, *Recueil des éloges historiques lus dans les séances publiques de l'Institut de France*, 3 vols. (Paris: Firmin Didot frères, 1861), vol. 1, pp. 261–95; section on Saussure, pp. 280–95.
76. Claude Reichler, *La Découverte des Alpes et la question du paysage* (Geneva: Georg, 2002), p. 69. Yasmine Marcil, "Saussure savant, ou voyageur? Les *Voyages dans les Alpes* dans les périodiques des années 1780," in *Un regard sur la terre*, pp. 351–66, at p. 352.
77. Immanuel Kant, *Critique of Judgement*, trans. James Creed Meredith, ed. and introd. Nicholas Walker (Oxford and New York: Oxford University Press, 2007), p. 95: "On the sublime in nature." Hansen notes this too, as does Reichler. Hansen, *The Summits of Modern Man*, p. 112. Reichler, *La Découverte des Alpes*, p. 69.
78. *Voyages*, "Discours préliminaire," vol. 1, pp. x–xi.
79. Freshfield underestimates the length of these trips. Freshfield, *Saussure*, p. 281.
80. Saussure's private means permitted this. And though Thomas Blaikie's (whom we will meet later in this book) boldness in searching for plants is amazing, he is never on the peaks for any length of time. On Blaikie's climbing, see Henry F. Montagnier, "Thomas Blaikie and Michel-Gabriel Paccard," *Alpine Journal* 45, no. 246 (May 1933): pp. 1–34. Blaikie crossed over to Argentière from the Mer de glace, for instance, through a route that remains challenging for climbers today.
81. Quoted in Rieder and Barras, "Santé et maladie chez Saussure," p. 506.
82. Jean et Renée Nicolas, *La Vie quotidienne en Savoie au XVIIème et XVIII ème siècles*, 2nd ed., rev. and enl. (Montmélian: La Fontaine de Siloé, 2005), p. 198.
83. Steven Kaplan describes an urban bias toward wheat bread, especially pronounced in Paris. Steven Laurence Kaplan, *The Bakers of Paris and the Bread Question, 1700–1775* (Durham, NC: Duke University Press, 1996), pp. 24–51.
84. Piero Camporesi, *The Magic Harvest: Food, Folklore and Society*, trans. Joan Krakover Hall (Cambridge: Polity Press, 1993), p. 21, from Anon., *Istruzioni mediche per le genti di campagna* (N.p.: 1785).
85. Quoted in Rieder and Barras, "Santé et maladie chez Saussure," p. 507.
86. Rieder and Barras mention his reassurances in "Santé et maladie chez Saussure," p. 515. Saussure tells his readers how well he feels in the mountains in the *Voyages* when describing his experiences on the Brévent, the Buet, on the slopes of the Aiguille du Goûter, and on the Col du Géant. His summiting of Mont Blanc is an exception.
87. *The Correspondence between Albrecht von Haller and Horace-Bénédict de Saussure*, ed. Otto Sonntag (Bern: H. Huber, 1990). Saussure to Haller, letter 365, 15 January 1772, p. 459. See editor's n. 3 for the explanation of *huile de tartre par défaillance*. Rieder and Barras, "Santé et maladie chez Saussure," p. 513.
88. See above, bismuth.
89. See Claude Reichler's website of images: *Viaticalpes*, University of Lausanne, accessed 9 December 2023, https://www.unil.ch/viaticalpes/home.html. Blaikie notes, for instance, how the glacier "runs down almost to a little town called the

Hameau de Bois," and he describes the "great arch of ice" under which the Aveyron issues. Thomas Blaikie, *Diary of a Scotch Gardener at the French Court at the end of the Eighteenth Century*, ed. and with an introduction by Francis Birrell (London: Routledge, 1931), p. 76.

90. John Edward Huth, *The Lost Art of Finding Our Way* (Cambridge, MA: Harvard University Press, 2013). Less sophisticated, while also offering a way to recover the "art of natural navigation," is Tristan Gooley, *The Natural Navigator: The Art of Reading Nature's Own Signposts* (London: Virgin Books, 2010).

91. We are losing our cognitive maps. See Greg Milner, *Pinpoint: How GPS Is Changing Technology, Culture, and Our Minds* (New York: Norton, 2016).

92. Kim Tingley, "The Secrets of the Wave Pilots," *New York Times Magazine: The Voyages Issue* (17 March 2016), accessed 12 October 2018, https://www.nytimes.com/2016/03/20/magazine/the-secrets-of-the-wave-pilots.html?searchResultPosition=49.

93. Quoted in Chicoteau, *Chère Rose: A Biography of Rosalie de Constant*, p. 169.

94. The Swiss were the first to copy these Indian textiles successfully. See René Guerdan, *Histoire de Genève* (Paris: Mazarine, 1981), p. 198. He explains the advantages of the Genevan locale in terms of the ample space and water needed for the making of this complicated fabric.

95. Blaikie, *Diary of a Scotch Gardener*, pp. 85–87, at p. 87.

96. As Alexandra Walsham explains for the British Isles in *The Reformation of the Landscape: Religion, Identity and Memory in Early Modern Britain and Ireland* (Oxford and New York: Oxford University Press, 2011).

97. Jean Picot, *Histoire de Genève depuis les temps les plus anciens jusqu'à nos jours*, vol. 3 (Geneva: Manget & Cherbuliez, 1811), p. 298.

98. Hansen cites Marc-Théodore Bourrit—who will be introduced later in this book—for this report. Hansen, *The Summits of Modern Man*, p. 39.

99. *Voyages*, sec. 743, vol. 2, pp. 161–62.

100. On the popularity of Haller's poem. see Reichler, *La Découverte des Alpes*, p. 9. The translation is Edward Hamley's from 1795: "Translation from *The Alps* of Haller in *Poems of Various Kinds* in the online collection *Spencer and the Tradition: English Poetry, 1579–1830*, a Gathering of Texts, Biography and Criticism compiled by David Hill Radcliffe," accessed 14 February 2019, http://spenserians.cath.vt.edu/Welcome.php.

101. *La Nouvelle Héloïse*, vol. 2, ed. Henri Coulet (Paris: Gallimard, 1993), part 4, letter 17, p. 141. Translated into English as *Julie, or The New Eloise: Letters of Two Lovers, Inhabitants of a Small Town at the Foot of the Alps*, trans. and abridged Judith H. McDowell (University Park: Pennsylvania State University Press, 1968), p. 335.

102. Gavin Rylands De Beer, "Haller's *Historia Stirpium*," *Annals of Science* 9, no. 1 (28 March 1953): pp. 1–46, at pp. 1–2.

103. *The Confessions of Jean-Jacques Rousseau*, trans. and with an introd. by J. M. Cohen (London: Penguin, 1953), p. 64. That Rousseau thinks while walking is stressed in Antoine de Baecque, *La Traversée des Alpes: Essai d'histoire marchée* (Paris: Gallimard, 2014). He cites *Les Confessions*, book 4: "'Je ne puis méditer qu'en marchant. . . . Sitôt que je m'arrête je ne pense plus et ma tête ne va qu'avec mes pieds'"; his p. 55.

104. The country house rented by Mme. de Warens; quoted in Freshfield, *Saussure*, p. 24.

105. Rousseau, *Les Rêveries du promeneur solitaire*, ed. Erik Leborgne (Paris: Flammarion, 1997), p. 135. Daniel Mornet cites a different passage from Rousseau in *La*

Sentiment de la nature en France (Paris: Hachette, 1907), p. 273. All translations from *Les Rêveries* are mine unless otherwise noted.

106. It's 1600 meters. Rousseau describes botanizing on La Chasseron in *Les Rêveries* in the "Septième promenade," p. 146.

107. In the 1790s he developed an anemometer. On the Col du Géant he estimated the speed of the wind by observing clouds: see *Voyages*, and Anne Fauche and Stéphane Fischer, "The Skies of Mont Blanc: Following the Traces of Horace-Bénédict de Saussure (1740–1799), Pioneer of Alpine Meteorology," trans. Liz Hopkins (Geneva: Musée d'histoire des sciences, 2011), p. 6.

108. Rousseau explains in the "Seconde promenade" that his imagination—exhausted, wrung dry—could no longer do what he was wont to do in his *solitude*, and, as the editor of the Flammarion edition explains, what he had done when writing *La Nouvelle Héloïse*. *La Nouvelle Héloïse*, ed. Erik Leborgne (Paris: Flammarion, 1997), pp. 66–67, p. 67 n. 1. See *The Confessions*, p. 48, on how his imagination worked. He becomes the characters he imagines.

109. In letter 23, *Julie, or The New Eloise*, p. 66. Saussure echoes this scene in a letter to his wife. See chap. 4, "Bodies of Desire."

110. Rousseau, *Les Rêveries*, "Seconde promenade," p. 66.

111. Rousseau, *Les Rêveries*, "Cinquième promenade," p. 114. Saussure de scribes his own visit to the Lac de Bienne and the Île de Saint Pierre in 1779. *Voyages*, secs. 398–99, vol. 1, pp. 321–23. Rousseau was there in 1765.

112. *Géologie*, Saussure explains, is concerned with a "Théorie de la Terre" as distinct from the "description de notre Globe." *Voyages*, "Discours préliminaire," vol. 1, vol. 1, p. ii.

113. Yi-Fu Tuan, *Topophilia: A Study of Environmental Perception, Attitudes, and Values* (Englewood Cliffs, NJ: Prentice Hall, 1974).

114. The excellent essays in Anne C. Vila, ed., *A Cultural History of the Senses in the Age of Enlightenment* (London: Bloomsbury, 2014), establish the importance of taste, touch, hearing, and smell in the real and conceptual worlds of the eighteenth century.

115. Reichler, *La Découverte des Alpes*, p. 77.

116. "Odeur," in Marco Troussier, *Pourquoi nous aimons gravir les montagnes: Abécédaire (non exhaustif) de l'alpinisme* (Les Houches: Les Éditions du Mont-Blanc, 2017), pp. 133–34.

117. See the chapter below on the Arve.

118. Reichler, *La Découverte des Alpes*, p. 77.

119. Interest in "exploration narratives" from the 1770s on is discussed in Carl Thompson, *The Suffering Traveller and the Romantic Imagination* (Oxford: Clarendon Press, 2007), pp. 150–51.

120. Thus missing that key clue about glaciation. *Voyages*, secs. 68–219, vol. 1, pp. 45–162. On Alpine origin, see sec. 211, pp. 152–53.

121. *Voyages*, "Discours préliminaire," vol. 1, p. ii. On earlier uses of term to describe the new field, see René Sigrist, "La Géographie de Saussure," in *Un regard sur la terre*, pp. 215–48, at p. 227 n. 46; and Martin J. S. Rudwick, *Bursting the Limits of Time: The Reconstruction of Geohistory in the Age of Revolution* (Chicago: University of Chicago Press, 2005), pp. 134 ff.

122. Some scholars, however, credit Saussure for asking the questions that lead to the correct answers about glaciers. See Amédée Zryd, "Saussure, 'Glaciologue,'" in *Un regard sur la terre*, pp. 159–73.

123. Albert Carozzi, "Avant-propos," in Horace-Bénédict de Saussure, *Voyages dans les Alpes, augmentés des voyages en Valais, au Mont Cervin et autour du Mont Rose: Partie pittoresque* (Geneva: Slatkine, 2004), pp. 1 and 1–14. Editions include the first of 1834, the second of 1852, the third of 1855, and a reprint of the second in 1880.

124. Freshfield, preface to *Saussure*, p. v.

125. Freshfield, preface to *Saussure*, p. v. On Freshfield and Montagnier, see Hansen, *Summits of Modern Man*, pp. 217 and 219–26, at pp. 223–25.

126. Wade Davis, *Into the Silence: The Great War, Mallory, and the Conquest of Everest* (New York: Knopf, 2012), pp. 437 and 560.

127. On Freshfield, see Davis, *Into the Silence*, p. 69. Freshfield's importance is woven throughout Maurice Isserman and Stewart Weaver, *Fallen Giants: A History of Himalayan Mountaineering from the Age of Empire to the Age of Extremes* (New Haven, CT: Yale University Press, 2010). Tom George Longstaff, who was part of the British Everest Expedition in 1922, credits Freshfield's influence for enabling the British expeditions: Longstaff, "Douglas Freshfield, 1845–1934," *Geographical Journal* 84, no. 4 (April 1934): pp. 257–62, at p. 259.

128. Yves Ballu, preface, *Voyages dans les Alpes* (Geneva: Slatkine, 1978.)

129. Michel Gabriel Paccard and Jacques Balmat on 8 August 1786; Jacques Balmat on 5 July 1787; Saussure and guides on 3 August 1787.

130. From the colloquium held in conjunction with the bicentennial of Saussure's death, *Un regard sur la terre*. Also Albert V. Carozzi, Bernard Crettaz, and David Ripoll, eds., *Les Plis du temps: Mythe, science et H.-B. de Saussure* (Geneva: Musée d'ethnographie, and Annecy: Conservatoire d'art et d'histoire de Haute-Savoie, 1998). and Jean-Claude Pont and Jan Lacki, eds., *Une cordée originale: Histoire des relations entre science et montagne* (Geneva: Georg, 2000). On Saussure's library, see Carozzi and Bouvier, eds., *The Scientific Library of Horace-Bénédict de Saussure*. A thematic study of Saussure's life in science is Carozzi, *Horace-Bénédict de Saussure (1740–1799): Un pionnier des sciences de la terre*.

131. Rudwick, *Bursting the Limits of Time*, p. 639.

132. Albert Carozzi, "Découverte d'une grande découverte: H.-B. de Saussure et les refoulements horizontaux en sens contraire dans la formation des Alpes," in *Les Plis du temps*, pp. 308–63.

133. Cuvier, "Éloges historiques de Bonnet et de Saussure," pp. 284–85.

134. The classic works on the history of ideas about nature in the eighteenth century are Daniel Mornet, *Le Sentiment de la nature en France de J. J. Rousseau à Bernardin de Saint-Pierre* (Paris: Hachette, 1907), and Jean Ehrard, *L'Idée de nature en France à l'aube des Lumières* (Paris: Flammarion, 1970). On shifting ideas about nature from antiquity through the eighteenth century, see Marjorie Hope Nicolson, *Mountain Gloom and Mountain Glory: The Development of the Aesthetics of the Infinite* (Ithaca, NY: Cornell University Press, 1959), and Clarence J. Glacken, *Traces on the Rhodian Shore: Nature and Culture in Western Thought from Ancient Times to the End of the Eighteenth Century* (Berkeley and Los Angeles: University of California Press, 1967). In another realm entirely is Philippe Descola, *Par-delà nature et culture* (Paris: Gallimard, 2005), published in English as *Beyond Nature and Culture*, trans. Janet Lloyd (Chicago: University of Chicago Press, 2013).

135. James J. Gibson, *The Ecological Approach to Visual Perception* (Boston: Houghton Mifflin, 1979), and Gibson, "The Theory of Affordances," in *Perceiving, Acting, Knowing: Toward an Ecological Psychology*, ed. Robert Shaw and James Bransford

(Hillsdale, NJ: Erlbaum, 1977), pp. 67–82. John Huth, "Conclusions: A Cross-Disciplinary Journey through Spatial Orientation," *Structure and Dynamics e journal* vol. 9, no. 1 (2016): pp. 154–78, at p. 156.

136. 3350 meters. 4–5 June1773. Cuvier quotes Saussure on this, as do others after him.

137. *Voyages*, "Discours préliminaire," vol. 1, pp. xiv–xv.

138. *Voyages*, "Discours préliminaire," vol. 1, pp. xiv–xv. Carozzi, *Horace-Bénédict de Saussure*, gives the reference to Lucretius, *De rerum natura*, book 2, on p. 108. Lucretius, according to Carozzi, was Saussure's "auteur préferé." Carozzi, "Essai sur la personnalité de Horace-Bénédict de Saussure d'après ses manuscrits," in *Les Plis du temps*, pp. 289–307, atp. 306.

139. *Voyages*, sec. 1991, vol. 4, p. 175, Saussure's n. 1: "*Pedibus submissa vicissim Opteritur*. Lucret. [Saussure has *submissa* for *subiecta*]" (By this victory [superstition or religion] is trampled underfoot).

140. Stephen Greenblatt, *The Swerve: How the World Became Modern* (New York and London: Norton, 2011), pp. 10–11ff.

141. *Voyages*, sec. 1111, vol. 2, p. 562.

142. On visualizing the Earth, see Denis Cosgrove, *Apollo's Eye: A Cartographic Genealogy of the Earth in the Western Imagination* (Baltimore, MD: Johns Hopkins University Press, 2001).

143. *Voyages*, sec. 2033, vol. 4, p. 225.

Chapter One

1. Presumably, that gate though other historians have suggested he left by the Porte de Rive or the Porte de Neuve, which opened up the city to Savoy. However, the Cornavin was the gate most convenient to the denizens of Saint-Gervais, and Daniel Jütte, "Entering a City: On a Lost Early Modern Practice," *Urban History* 41, no. 2 (May 2014): pp. 204–27, at p. 216, explains that "most citizens used the same gate every time—the one intended for their part of the city. That Rousseau took off for Savoy does not indicate much. The *Confessions* tell us that Rousseau wandered for several days around the city after his night beyond the walls before taking off for Savoy: Rousseau, *Les Confessions*, preface by J.-B. Pontalis, ed. Bernard Gagnebin and Marcel Raymond, notes by Catherine Koenig (Paris: Gallimard, Folio Classique, 1973), p. 80.

2. Jütte, "Entering a City," p. 221.

3. Blaikie, *Diary of a Scotch Gardener*, p. 30.

4. Rousseau, *The Confessions*, trans. Cohen, p. 49; *Les Confessions*, ed. Gagnebin and Raymond, p. 76. Jütte refers to "the term '*Torschluspanik*' (literally 'panic of gate closure') now used in German in a figurative sense [which] still resounds with the anxiety of pre-modern people faced with the prospect of not being allowed to enter the city." Jütte's essay also suggests that the soldiers would have recognized Rousseau, since gatekeepers in early modern cities typically knew the residents who entered and left by their gates. Jütte, "Entering a City," p. 221.

5. Rousseau, *The Confessions*, trans. Cohen, p. 51; *Les Confessions*, ed. Gagnebin and Raymond, p. 78.

6. Rousseau, *The Confessions*, trans. Cohen, p. 52; *Les Confessions*, ed. Gagnebin and Raymond, p. 79.

7. Guerdan, *Histoire de Genève*, 75.

8. In Caesar's *The Gallic Wars*. Guerdan, *Histoire de Genève*, p. 17.
9. Louis Blondel, "Genève Ville Episcopale," in Société d'histoire et d'archéologie de Genève [hereafter cited as SHAG], *Histoire de Genève*, p. 68.
10. Blondel, "Genève République protestante," in SHAG, *Histoire de Genève*, p. 222.
11. Blondel, "Genève République protestante," in SHAG, *Histoire de Genève*, p. 222: "Une forte diminution . . . unique dans les annales d'une ville."
12. Guerdan, *Histoire de Genève*, p. 75.
13. Guerdan, *Histoire de Genève*, 75. Freshfield, *Saussure*, p. 33.
14. Jütte, "Entering a City," p. 209, quoting Shakespeare's *King John*, act 2, scene 1: "the 'city's eyes.'" Calvin returned to power in 1541. See Herbert Lüthy, *La Banque protestante en France de la révocation de l'Édit de Nantes à la Révolution*, vol. 1, *Dispersion et regroupement, 1685–1730* (Paris: S.E.V.P.E.N, 1959), p. 37, on the welcoming of coreligionists and absorbing them into the civic life of the city.
15. See Freshfield, *Saussure*, pp. 47–48, for the history of the Saussure family; quote at p. 48.
16. Freshfield, *Saussure*, p. 34: "In the four months following the massacre of St. Bartholomew (1572) over sixteen hundred refugees, in the five weeks after the Revocation of the Edict of Nantes (1685) eight thousand, entered the town."
17. Richard Whatmore, *Against War and Empire: Geneva, Britain, and France in the Eighteenth Century* (New Haven, CT: Yale University Press, 2012), p. 30. William E. Monter, "De l'Évêché à la Rome protestante," in *Histoire de Genève*, ed. Paul Guichonnet (Toulouse: Privat, and Lausanne: Payot, 1974), pp. 129–84, at p. 156.
18. Lüthy, *La Banque protestante en France*, vol. 1, p. 40.
19. Lüthy, *La Banque protestante en France*, vol. 1, p. 39.
20. Even after the ban on French manufacture of *indiennes* was lifted in 1759, French production lagged behind that of Geneva. See Guerdon, *Histoire de Genève*, p. 198.
21. Lüthy, *La Banque protestante en France*, vol. 1, p. 189.
22. Lüthy, *La Banque protestante en France*, vol. 1, p. 216.
23. Leïla el-Wakil, "Aspects of Genevois Architecture from the Reformation to the Nineteenth Century," trans. Mavis Guinard, in *1000 Years of Swiss Art*, ed. Heinz Horat (New York: Hudson Hills Press, 1992), 220–41, at p. 222.
24. Freshfield, *Saussure*, p. 77.
25. Guerdan, *Histoire de Genève*, p. 84.
26. Guerdon, *Histoire de Genève*, p. 120.
27. Guerdon, *Histoire de Genève*, p. 121.
28. Whatmore, *Against War and Empire*, p. 26.
29. For example, the pamphlet, "Le Vray Discours de la miraculeuse délivrance," cited in Monter, "De l'Évêché à la Rome protestante," p. 165. Also, Guerdon, *Histoire de Genève*, p. 122.
30. Guerdon, *Histoire de Genève*, p. 182.
31. The first to bring the Genevan revolutions into the broader study of the eighteenth century was R. R. Palmer, *The Age of the Democratic Revolution: A Political History of Europe and America, 1760–1800*, 2 vols. (Princeton, NJ: Princeton University Press, 1959, 1964). Whatmore's *Against War and Empire* shows renewed interest in the political history of Geneva, as does Janet Polasky, *Revolutions without Borders: The Call to Liberty in the Atlantic World* (New Haven, CT: Yale University Press, 2015).
32. Whatmore, *Against War and Empire*, p. 38. On "how the history of antiquity became the object of contention in Geneva," see Helena Rosenblatt, *Rousseau and*

Geneva: From the First Discourse to the Social Contract, 1749–1762 (Cambridge: Cambridge University Press, 1997), p. 111.

33. Whatmore, *Against War and Empire*, p. 38.
34. Whatmore, *Against War and Empire*, p. 32.
35. Whatmore, *Against War and Empire*, p. 33. The reference to Colley is mine: Linda Colley, *Britons: Forging the Nation, 1707–1837* (New Haven, CT: Yale University Press, 1992).
36. Rosenblatt, *Rousseau and Geneva*, p. 110.
37. In 1735.
38. Quoted by Whatmore, *Against War and Empire*, p. 41.
39. Frédéric Barbey, "De la Révolution à l'annexion," in SHAG, *Histoire de Genève*, pp. 525–39, at p. 536.
40. Whatmore, *Against War and Empire*, p. 41.
41. A "desire" that Rousseau claimed was "utterly futile": Whatmore, *Against War and Empire*, p. 78.
42. Whatmore, *Against War and Empire*, p. 42.
43. As the *Requêtes, avertissement, plaçet et mémoire du Sieur Micheli du Cres*.
44. When working in the survey office in Chambéry while living with Mme. de Warens. *The Confessions*, trans. Cohen, pp. 208–9. *Les Confessions*, ed. Gagnebin and Raymond, pp. 278–80, at pp. 279–80. Whatmore, *Against War and Empire*, p. 58.
45. Text in Jean-Jacques Rousseau, *Lettres écrites de la Montagne*, preface, Alfred Dufour (Lausanne: Éditions l'Age d'homme, 2007), Annexe II, pp. 303–18.
46. Guerdon, *Histoire de Genève*, p. 196. Rousseau, *Lettres écrites de la Montagne*, Annexe II, p. 307. Article XII says membership will be increased by twenty-five. With the 225 with which it is already composed, membership will now total 250. Age of admission changed to thirty in Article XI.
47. Whatmore, *Against War and Empire*, p. 47.
48. Whatmore, *Against War and Empire*, p. 31.
49. Guerdon, *Histoire de Genève*, p. 196. (Burlamaqui quoted.)
50. Ferrier, "Le XVIIIème siècle: Politique intérieure et extérieure," in SHAG, *Histoire de Genève*, p. 420.
51. Guerdon, *Histoire de Genève*, p. 195.
52. Rousseau, *The Confessions*, trans. Cohen, p. 202; *Les Confessions*, ed. Gagnebin and Raymond, p. 271.
53. Paul Chaponnière, "Les Sciences, les lettres et les arts au XVIIIème siècle," in SHAG, *Histoire de Genève*, p. 490, and other accounts.
54. Rosenblatt, *Rousseau and Geneva*, pp. 220 and 221.
55. On France being understood as a "constant corrupting influence," see Rosenblatt, *Rousseau and Geneva*, p. 23.
56. D'Alembert's essay on Geneva in the *Encyclopédie* criticizing the ban on theater prompted Rousseau's *Lettre à d'Alembert sur les spectacles* (Letter to d'Alembert on the theater). Voltaire's plays were put on in Geneva when possible and otherwise at Ferney to Genevan audiences, and in estates outside the city.
57. Chaponnière, "Les Sciences, les lettres et les arts au XVIIIème siècle," p. 489.
58. *The Confessions*, trans. Cohen, p. 327. *Les Confessions*, ed. Gagnebin and Raymond, p. 430.
59. Haller, *The Alps*, trans. Hamley.

60. See Linda Kirk, "'Going Soft': Genevan Decadence in the Eighteenth Century," in *The Identity of Geneva: The Christian Commonwealth, 1564–1864*, ed. John B. Roney and Martin Klauber (Westport, CT: Greenwood Press, 1998).

61. On the Rhône River in modern France, see Sara Pritchard, *Confluence: The Nature of Technology and the Remaking of the Rhône* (Cambridge, MA: Harvard University Press, 2011).

62. Freshfield's collaborator, Henry Fairbanks Montagnier, was the major researcher in Geneva; however, Freshfield describes the site as if he were seeing it through his own eyes.

63. Freshfield, *Saussure*, p. 51.

64. Freshfield, *Saussure*, p. 51.

65. Dominique Zumkeller, "Un père agronome: Nicolas de Saussure (1709–1791)," in *Un regard sur la terre*, pp. 395–408, at p. 397. Blaikie was impressed by this manner of growing vines, which was new to him. Blaikie, *Diary of a Scotch Gardener*, pp. 31–32.

66. Saussure, *Voyages*, sec. 355, vol. 1, p. 289.

67. From Mont Aetna, the Crammont, on the slopes of Mont Blanc, and on the Col du Géant.

68. "Walnut oil [was] widely used in Central France until the middle of the nineteenth century. . . . Its flavor is 'delicious'"; Maguelonne Toussaint-Samat, *History of Food*, trans. Anthea Bell (Cambridge, MA: Blackwell, 1994), pp. 220–21.

69. Zumkeller, "Un père agronome," p. 398: agreement from 1753. Some of these apples and pears are mentioned in Thouin's instructions to the gardener accompanying La Pérouse. Roger L. Williams, *French Botany in the Enlightenment: The Ill-Fated Voyages of La Pérouse and His Rescuers* (Dordrecht and Boston, MA: Kluwer Academic, 2003), p. 48, offers translations for the varieties.

70. Zumkeller, "Un père agronome," p. 398.

71. Zumkeller, "Un père agronome," p. 405: agreement from 1789.

72. Zumkeller, "Un père agronome," p. 400.

73. The first being that of approximately 10,000 years ago.

74. Zumkeller, "Un père agronome," p. 400. Joseph, *Saussure*, p. 14 (biography of Ferdinand).

75. On Théodore de Saussure's contribution to understanding plant growth and the contemporary context, see Jane F. Hill, introduction to *Chemical Research on Plant Growth: A Translation of Théodore de Saussure's "Recherches chimiques sur la végétation,"* trans. Jane F. Hill (New York: Springer, 2013).

76. Zumkeller, "Un père agronome," p. 399.

77. On gentlemen farmers and the question of agricultural improvement, see Peter M. Jones, *Agricultural Enlightenment: Knowledge, Technology, and Nature, 1750–1840* (Oxford and New York: Oxford University Press, 2016).

78. Jean-Christian Petitfils, *Louis XVI* (Paris: Perrin, 2005), in his chapter on Turgot, p. 190: "On connaît la phrase de Voltaire dans son *Dictionnaire philosophique*."

79. On the dispute between Galiani and Morellet, see Dena Goodman, *The Republic of Letters: A Cultural History of the French Enlightenment* (Ithaca, NY: Cornell University Press, 1994.) On grain, see Steven Kaplan's books, including *Raisonner sur les blés: Essais sur les Lumières économiques* (Paris: Fayard, 2017.) Turgot was dismissed in May 1776, and Necker was appointed director general of finances in June 1777.

80. *Correspondence H/B*. Their names for each other were clever and affectionate.

Bonnet was sometimes Philorhizotome, for someone who loves rhizomes (plant stems that spread underground.) Haller was occasionally Cosmopolite. The French were *les Allobroges*. Editor's "Key to Nicknames and Periphrases," pp. 29–30.

81. "Appendice: La Chambre des blés," in Guerdon, *Histoire de Genève*, p. 164. Zumkeller, "Un père agronome," p. 401.

82. "Appendice: La Chambre des blés," in Guerdon, *Histoire de Genève*, pp. 164ff.

83. Béla Kapossy, "Genevan Creditors and English Liberty: The Example of Théodore Rilliet de Saussure," in *Genève, lieu d'Angleterre, 1725–1814*, ed. Valérie Cossy, Bela Kapossy, and Richard Whatmore (Geneva: Slatkine, 2009), p. 175.

84. Corinne Walker and Anastazja Winiger-Labuda, "Saussure et l'architecture: Entre goût et nécessité," in *Un regard sur la terre*, pp. 453–70, at p. 454. The house was built by Nicolas's father, also named Théodore.

85. On the French garden at Frontenex, see Walker and Winiger-Labuda, "Saussure et l'Architecture," p. 454.

86. Quoted in Freshfield, *Saussure*, p. 35, n. 1.

87. "Maison Charles Bonnet, Recensement architectural du canton de Genève, Object no. 2011–26120: République et canton de Genève, Office du patrimoine et des sites, date de génération, 2018-09-24, accessed 9 December 2023, http://ge.ch/geodata /SIPATRIMOINE/SI-EVI-OPS/EVI/edition/objets/2011-26120.htm.

88. Freshfield was unaware of the apartment in the city. Information on its location and some detail on Frontenex is from Walker and Winiger-Labuda, "Saussure et l'architecture, " p. 454.

89. René Sigrist, "Science et société à Genève au XVIIIème siècle: L'Exemple de Charles Bonnet," in *Charles Bonnet: Savant et philosophe (1720–1793)*, ed. Marino Buscaglia, René Sigrist, Jacques Trembley, and Jean Wüest (Geneva: Éditions Passé Présent, 1994), pp. 19–39, at p. 22.

90. Rosalie's unpublished memoirs are quoted in Lucie Achard, *Rosalie de Constant: Sa famille et ses amis, 1758–1834*, 2 vols. (Geneva: Ch. Eggimand, 1901–2), vol. 1, p. 3.

91. Achard, *Rosalie de Constant*, vol. 1, p. 16.

92. James Boswell, *The Journal of His German and Swiss Travels*, ed. Marlies K. Danziger (1764; Edinburgh: Edinburgh University Press, and New Haven, CT: Yale University Press, 2008), pp. 309–10.

93. Picot, *Histoire de Genève*, vol. 3, p. 303 n. 1, details this history. Joan DeJean, "Bright Lights, Big City," in *The Essence of Style: How the French Invented High Fashion, Fine Food, Chic Cafés, Style, Sophistication, and Glamour* (New York: Free Press, 2005), pp. 201–16, at p. 208, says, however, that street lighting in Geneva was a resisted French import and was not introduced until 1793.

94. For *auditeurs du droit* and the *lieutenant de police*, see Whatmore, *Against War and Empire*, p. 31. For details of the work of *auditeurs*, see Watt, *Choosing Death*, pp. 15–17.

95. Zumkeller, "Un père agronome," p. 395.

96. As all such inauguration ceremonies were. Sigrist, *Les Origines de la Société de physique et d'histoire naturelle*, p. 156.

97. *Correspondence H/S*, Saussure to Haller, letter 59, dated "second half of December 1762," p. 114.

98. Jean Senebier, *Mémoire historique sur la vie et les écrits de Horace-Bénédict Desaussure* (Geneva: J. J. Paschoud, 1801), p. 11.

NOTES TO PAGES 37-39 211

99. Senebier, *Mémoire historique sur la vie et les écrits de Horace-Bénédict DeSaussure*, pp. 8 and 9.

100. Senebier, *Mémoire historique sur la vie et les écrits de Horace-Bénédict DeSaussure*, pp. 9–10.

101. Senebier, *Mémoire historique sur la vie et les écrits de Horace-Bénédict DeSaussure*, p. 9.

102. Henri-Albert had to work hard for his own success. His family expected him to continue the family's bookselling business in Geneva on the rue de la Cité. He chose instead to study in Paris, taking courses in anatomy and chemistry and enrolling in the École royale de pharmacie. Jean-Michel Pictet, "Henri-Albert Gosse (1753–1816)," in *Les Savants genevois*, p. 407.

103. Sigrist, *Les Origines de la Société de physique et d'histoire naturelle*, p. 156.

104. Sigrist, *Les Origines de la Société de physique et d'histoire naturelle*, p. 156 and n. 77 (for the suicide).

105. Freshfield, *Saussure*, p. 43. The quip is translated in Joseph, *Saussure*, p. 38.

106. Sigrist, *Les Origines de la Société de physique et d'histoire naturelle*, p. 156 and n. 78. The reference is to Isaac Macaire, "Notice sur la vie et les écrits de Théodore de Saussure," in *Bibliothèque universelle de Genève*, n.s. 57 (1845).

107. Carozzi, "Essai sur la personnalité de Horace-Bénédict de Saussure d'après ses manuscrits," in *Les Plis du temps*, p. 303.

108. Necker de Saussure, "Notice sur le caractère et les écrits de Mme de Staël," p. xxxiv. Albertine was the daughter of Horace-Bénédict. On Germaine de Staël's upbringing by her mother, see Kete, *Making Way for Genius: The Aspiring Self in France from the Old Regime to the New* (New Haven, CT: Yale University Press, 2012), pp. 23ff and references there.

109. *Correspondence H/S*, Haller to Saussure, letter 51, 7 September 1762, pp. 105–6. As Leo Damrosch has noted about Boswell, his "consciousness was haunted by the Calvinist ethic that goes back to Saint Augustine, who said in the *Confessions*, "From a perverted act of will, desire had grown, and when desire is given satisfaction, habit is forged; and when habit passes unresisted, a compulsive urge sets in. By these close-knit links I was held.'" Damrosch, *The Club: Johnson, Boswell, and the Friends Who Shaped an Age* (New Haven, CT: Yale University Press, 2019), p. 86.

110. *Correspondence H/S*, Saussure to Haller, letter 67, 7 April 1763, p. 120.

111. *Correspondence H/S*, Saussure to Haller, letter 67, 7 April 1763, p. 122.

112. Freshfield, *Saussure*, p. 58.

113. Sigrist, "Science et société à Genève au XVIIIème siècle: L'Exemple de Charles Bonnet," p. 23.

114. Haller wrote 13,000 letters (that we know of) and had 1200 correspondents: Alexandra Cook, *Jean-Jacques Rousseau and Botany: The Salutary Science* (Oxford: Voltaire Foundation, 2012), p. 81.

115. *Correspondence H/B*, Haller to Bonnet, letter 103 from Roche, 6 May 1760, p. 199.

116. Otto Sonntag, "Introduction," *Correspondence H/B*, p. 19. The grandson of Haller had reported that his grandfather had fathered children on the family's maid when at Roche.

117. *Correspondence H/B*, Bonnet to Haller, letter 104 from Geneva, 10 May 1760, p. 200. The charity hospital of Geneva would take an outsider, though the cost would be high, about double the cost to a Genevan. In any case, the mother of the child

would be brought before a court and would have to say who the father of the child was. Haller's letter back declines this solution: "the situation of his friend" would not allow for public exposure. letter 105 from Roche, 19 May 1760, p. 201.

118. Freshfield, *Saussure*, p. 77: presumably read by Montagnier. See Freshfield's introduction.

119. *Correspondence H/S*, Saussure to Haller, letter 67, 7 April 1763, p. 120.

120. *Correspondence H/S*, Saussure to Haller, letter 67, 7 April 1763, p. 121.

121. Jean Starobinski, "L'Essor de la science genevoise," in *Les Savants genevois*, p. 11. Albert V. Carozzi and John K. Newman, "The Academy, the Student and the Professor: Brief History of the Academy of Geneva between 1559 and 1775," in *Lectures on Physical Geography Given in 1775 by Horace-Bénédict de Saussure at the Academy of Geneva* (Geneva: Editions Zoé, 2003), p. 13.

122. *Correspondence H/S*, Saussure to Haller, letter 67, 7 April 1763, p. 120.

123. *Correspondence H/S*, Saussure to Haller, letter 67, 7 April 1763, p. 121.

124. *Correspondence H/S*, Saussure to Haller, letter 67, 7 April 1763, p. 121.

125. Patrick Singy, "Medicine and the Senses: The Perception of Essences," in *A Cultural History of the Senses in the Age of Enlightenment*, ed. Anne C. Vila (London and New York: Bloomsbury Academic, 2014), chap. 6, pp. 133–53; for "consultation by letter," see pp. 140–45.

126. Philip Rieder and Vincent Barras, "Écrire sa maladie au siècle des Lumières," in *La Médecine des Lumières: Tout autour de Tissot*, ed. Vincent Barras and Micheline Louis-Courvoisier (Chêne-Bourg: Georg, 2001), pp. 201–22, at p. 203. Frédéric Sardet based his essay in the same collection on a sample of one hundred letters from the last quarter of the eighteenth century. Sardet, "Consulter Tissot: Hypothèses de lecture," in *La Médecine des lumières*, pp. 55–66, at p. 55.

127. Tissot's *De la santé des gens de lettres* is at the center of Anne C. Vila, *Suffering Scholars: Pathologies of the Intellectual in Enlightenment Europe* (Philadelphia: University of Pennsylvania Press, 2018).

128. Patrick Singy, "The Popularization of Medicine in the Eighteenth Century: Writing, Reading and Rewriting Samuel Auguste Tissot's *Avis au people sur sa santé*," *Journal of Modern History* 82, no. 4 (December 2010): pp. 769–800, at p. 792.

129. Singy, "The Popularization of Medicine in the Eighteenth Century," p. 776 n. 21.

130. Edinburgh, 1772.

131. Sardet, "Consulter Tissot," p. 57.

132. Sardet, "Consulter Tissot," p. 61.

133. *Correspondence H/S*, Saussure to Haller, letter 67, 7 April 1763, p. 121.

134. Sardet, "Consulter Tissot," p. 63.

135. Sardet, "Consulter Tissot," p. 62.

136. Solange Simon-Mazoyer, "Le Conflit entre les excès de la mode et de la santé au XVIIIème siècle: L''Habillage' du visage," in *La Médecine des Lumières*, pp. 41–53, at p. 50. She quotes from Alexandre Guillaume, Mouslier de Moissy's *Les Jeux de la petite Thalie* (1769). Pierre Choderlos de Laclos's *Les Liaisons dangereuses* was published in 1782.

137. Marie-Elisabeth, 1743–1808. Elisabeth Badinter, *Le Pouvoir au féminin: Marie-Thérèse d'Autriche, 1717–1780, l'impératrice-reine* (Paris: Flammarion, 2016) p. 227 n. 3.

138. Possibly *dartres*. The implication is that *dartres* was an affliction of all the de la Rives, though the sister is not specifically mentioned. *Correspondence H/S*, Saussure to Haller, letter 67, 7 April 1763, p. 121.

139. *Correspondence H/B*, Bonnet to Haller, letter 42, 7 September1757, p. 114.
140. *Correspondence H/S*, Saussure to Haller, letter 388, 11 December 1773, p. 477.
141. As noted above in "Introduction: Saussure and the Alps."
142. *Correspondence H/S*, Saussure to Haller, letter 67, 7 April 1763, p. 121.
143. Rieder and Barras, "Écrire sa maladie au siècle des Lumières," p. 206.
144. Rieder and Barras, "Écrire sa maladie au siècle des Lumières," p. 209.
145. Rieder and Barras, "Écrire sa maladie au siècle des Lumières," p. 210.
146. Rieder and Barras, "Écrire sa maladie au siècle des Lumières," p. 207.
147. *Correspondence H/S*, Saussure to Haller, letter 54, 15 October 1762, p. 108.
148. *Correspondence H/S*, Saussure to Haller, letter 64, 19 March 1763, p. 118.
149. *Correspondence H/S*, Saussure to Haller, letter 67, 7 April 1763, p. 123.
150. Roger L. Williams, *Botanophilia in Eighteenth–Century France: The Spirit of the Enlightenment* (Boston: Kluwer Academic, 2001), p. 86.
151. *Correspondence H/S*, Saussure to Haller, letter 67, 7 April 1763, p. 122 and 123.
152. *Correspondence H/S*, Saussure to Haller, letter 67, 7 April 1763, p. 125.
153. *Correspondence H/S*, Haller to Saussure, letter 76, 12 May 1763, p. 141.
154. *Correspondence H/S*, Saussure to Haller, letter 70, 20 April 1763, p. 133.
155. *Correspondence H/S*, Saussure to Haller, letter 72, c. 25 April 1763, p. 135.
156. *Correspondence H/S*, Saussure to Haller, letter 72, c. 25 April 1763, p. 135.
157. *Correspondence H/S*, Haller to Saussure, letter 71, 21 April 1763, p. 134 ("ces sucs de plante, en les lavant avec de l'eau minerale de selter").
158. Quoted in Freshfield, *Saussure*, p. 79.
159. *Correspondence H/S*, Saussure to Haller, letter 44, 12 January 1762, p. 100.
160. *Correspondence H/S*, Saussure to Haller, letter 106, 28 February 1764, p. 178.
161. René Sigrist, "Horace-Bénédict de Saussure en quelques dates," in *Un regard sur la terre*, p. 525.
162. Candolle established botany as a science for the nineteenth century, working alongside Cuvier in Paris. He established a taxonomy of plants (his coinage) that overcame the weaknesses of the Linnaean system.
163. Candolle, *Mémoires et souvenirs (1778–1841)*, p. 83.
164. Andrea Wulf's biography of Humboldt: *The Invention of Nature: Alexander von Humboldt's New World* (New York: Knopf, 2015) argues that Humboldt "invented the web of life, the concept of nature as we know it today," p. 5. He certainly did "c[o]me up with the idea of vegetation and climate zones that snake across the globe," p. 5.
165. In letters to Saussure, for instance, in August 1760 and October 1761. *Correspondence H/S*, letter 4, p. 60; letter 34, p. 91.
166. Cook suggests this in *Jean-Jacques Rousseau and Botany*, p. 78. Haller's work "provided the bio-geographical contours of a greater Switzerland."
167. Cook, *Jean-Jacques Rousseau and Botany*, p. 81.
168. Gavin De Beer, "Haller's *Historia stirpium*," in *Annals of Science* 9, no. 1 (1953): pp. 1–46, at p. 3. Quoted in Cook, *Jean-Jacques Rousseau and Botany*, p. 81.
169. *Correspondence H/S*, Saussure to Haller, letter 1, 11 July 1760, p. 55.
170. *Correspondence H/S*, Saussure to Haller, letter 1, 11 July 1760, p. 56.
171. *Correspondence H/S*, Saussure to Haller, letter 3, late July 1760, p. 57.
172. *Correspondence H/S*, Saussure to Haller, letter 3, late July 1760, p. 58.
173. *Correspondence H/S*, Haller to Saussure, letter 4, 2 August 1760, p. 60.
174. *Correspondence H/S*, p. 61 n. 3, quoting Bonnet in a letter to Haller dated 12 August 1760.

175. *Correspondence H/S*, Haller to Saussure, letter 6, 3 August 1760, p. 61.
176. *Correspondence H/S*, Saussure to Haller, letter 7, 29 September 1760, p. 61.
177. *Correspondence H/S*, Saussure to Haller, letter 7, 29 September 1760, p. 62.
178. *Correspondence H/S*, Haller to Saussure, letter 8, 5 October 1760, p. 64.
179. *Correspondence H/S*, Haller to Saussure, letter 10, 26 October 1760, p. 66. By contrast, in 1775 Blaikie found a great many interesting plants in the Chamonix region including (at the source of the Aveyron) and along the Mer de Glace, where Saussure went early in his explorations. Blaikie, *Diary of a Scotch Gardener*, pp. 76 and 80.
180. *Correspondence H/S*, Saussure to Haller, letter 14, 17 March 1761, p. 70.
181. *Correspondence H/S*, Haller to Saussure, letter 15, 10 April 1761, p. 71.
182. See the collection of essays edited by David Philip Miller and Peter Hanns Reill based on a conference held in 1991 at the William Andrews Clark Memorial Library, UCLA: Miller and Reill, *Visions of Empire: Voyages, Botany, and Representations of Nature* (Cambridge and New York: Cambridge University Press, 1996).
183. Adanson quoted in preface to Michel Adanson, *Voyage au Sénégal*, edited and annotated by Denis Reynaud and Jean Schmidt (Saint-Étienne: Publications of the University of Saint-Étienne, 1996), p. 16. The quote is from Adanson, *Famille des plantes* (1763).
184. *The Scientific Library of Horace-Bénédict de Saussure*, no. 85, p. 82 (1757).
185. See Reynaud and Schmidt for 1769 being the turning point: "Vie de Michel Adanson," in *Voyage au Sénégal*, p. 17. On Adanson's failure to maintain a position in the Parisian scientific establishment, see Kete, *Making Way for Genius*, pp. 132–34.
186. On Banks, see Richard Holmes, *The Age of Wonder: How the Romantic Generation Discovered the Beauty and Terror of Science* (New York: Vintage Books, 2010).
187. Yvonne Letouzey, *Le Jardin des Plantes à la croisée des chemins avec André Thouin* (Paris: Éditions du Muséum National d'Histoire Naturelle, 1989), pp. 675–78. Hydrangeas are from Japan, dahlias from Mexico.
188. On the estate of Paul Gaussen. Blaikie had a letter of recommendation to Gaussen, and the two become friends. On the ginkgo, see de Candolle, *Histoire de la botanique genevoise* (Geneva, 1830), pp. 44–45, cited in Blaikie, *Diary of a Scotch Gardener*, p. 240 editor's n. 1. On Blaikie and Gaussen, see *Diary of a Scotch Gardener*, pp. 30–32 and 37.
189. On the Jardin des Plantes in Paris, see E. C. Spary, *Utopia's Garden: French Natural History from the Old Regime to Revolution* (Chicago: University of Chicago Press, 2002), and Letouzey, *Le Jardin des Plantes*.
190. *Mémoire par l'Académie des Sciences, pour server aux Savans embarquées sous les ordres de M. de La Pérouse*, sec. 4, "On Materia Medica," point 10, extracted and translated in Williams, *French Botany in the Enlightenment*, pp. 27–28.
191. Jean-Louis Moret, "L'entourage scientifique de Rosalie de Constant," pp. 33–34, at p. 33 n. 1. Luc Breton, Anne Hofmann, Joëlle Magnin-Gonze, Jean-Louis Moret, and Gino Müller, *L'Herbier peint de Rosalie de Constant: Le Dessin de fleurs à la fin du XVIIIème siècle* (Lausanne: La Bibliothèque des Arts, 2008).
192. On the revision of "greening measures" budgeted by the European Common Agricultural Policy and a model of integrated farming in Ireland, see Ella McSweeney, "'Life Attracts Life': The Irish Farmers Filling Their Fields with Bees and Butterflies," *Guardian*, 6 June 2020. For outside Europe, see Ramachandra Guha, *Environmentalism: A Global History* (New York: Longman, 2000).
193. Published posthumously in the 1780s. "Lettres sur la botanique," in *Œuvres*

complètes de Jean-Jacques Rousseau, vol. 4, *Émile, éducation, morale, botanique*, ed. Charles Wirz and Pierre Burgelin (Paris: Gallimard, Bibliothèque de la Pléiade, 1969), p. 1151. Cook, *Jean-Jacques Rousseau and Botany*, pp. 189–99.

194. The "Herbier peint de Rosalie Constant" is held at the Musée et Jardin botaniques de Lausanne. A selection of her paintings and notes has been published by the Jardin botanique as *L'Herbier peint de Rosalie de Constant: Le Dessin de fleurs à la fin du XVIIIème siècle*, cited in n. 191 above. The essays in this volume are illuminating.

195. *Mrs Delany and Her Circle*, Yale Center for British Art, exhibition, 24 September 2009–3 January 2010. Ruth Hayden, *Mrs. Delany: Her Life and Flowers* (London: British Museum Press, 1980). Clarissa Campbell Orr, *Mrs Delany: A Life* (New Haven, CT: Yale University Press, 2019).

196. Rousseau, *Les Rêveries du promeneur solitaire*, ed. Erik Leborgne (Paris: Flammarion, 1997), pp. 138, 142, and 143.

197. *Correspondence H/S*, Saussure to Haller, letter 56, 23 October 1762, p. 111.

198. Bonnet and Haller represented the two directions botany was taking in the eighteenth century, as Candolle saw it. One—Bonnet's—had to do with the physiology of plants, while the other—Linnaeus's—concerned taxonomy. Patrick Bungener, "Les Rapports de Saussure avec la botanique," in *Un regard sur la terre*, pp. 33–49, at p. 47.

199. Rousseau, *Les Rêveries du promeneur solitaire*, p. 135.

Chapter Two

1. The word *alpinism* entered the French language in 1876. Paul Guichonnet, "Le Mont Blanc ou la fascination des 'neiges éblouies,'" in Marie-Christine Vellozzi, Marie-Thérèse Vercken, Paul Guichonnet, Philippe Joutard, and Hugues Lebailly, *Mont Blanc: Conquête de l'imaginaire* (Montmélian: Fontaine de Siloé, 2002), p. 15. Hereafter the volume is cited as *Mont Blanc: Conquête de l'imaginaire*.

2. Senebier, *Mémoire historique sur la vie et les écrits de Horace-Bénédict Desaussure*, p. 11.

3. *Voyages*, sec. 284, vol. 1, p. 226.

4. See chap. 3 of this volume.

5. *Voyages*, sec. 356, vol. 1, pp. 290 and 291. Edelweiss is *Leontopodium (alpinum)*; ragwort, also known as "le *Senecio alpinus*," is *Senecio jacobaea*.

6. *Voyages*, sec. 364, vol. 1, p. 297. Blaikie, *Diary of a Scotch Gardener*, p. 39.

7. *Voyages*, sec. 364, vol. 1, p. 298. Blue-sow-thistle: "Sonchus alpinus" or *Cicerbita alpine*.

8. *Voyages*, sec. 365, vol. 1, p. 298.

9. Bungener, "Les Rapports de Saussure avec la botanique," p. 34 n. 5.

10. *Correspondence H/S*, letter 35, 10 November 1761, pp. 94–95 and 96.

11. As in a letter from Haller to Saussure of October 1761. *Correspondence H/S*, letter 34, 6 October 1761, p. 91.

12. *Correspondence H/S*, Haller to Saussure, letter 25, 29 June 1761, p. 82 n. 2.

13. Quoted by Bungener in "Les Rapports de Saussure avec la botanique," p. 34 n. 5.

14. Joan DeJean, "The Senses in the Marketplace: Coffee, Chintz, and Sofas," in *A Cultural History of the Senses in the Age of Enlightenment*, ed. Anne C. Vila, vol. 4 of *A Cultural History of the Senses* (London: Bloomsbury, 2014), pp. 65–84, at p. 76.

15. DeJean, "The Senses in the Marketplace," p. 74.

16. DeJean, "The Senses in the Marketplace," p. 75, discusses the "high profile appearance" of this decoration at Versailles. If one visits Versailles in the summer, one may see how some of the royal apartments with their summer chintz décor echo the gardens. They did so in 2017.

17. *Voyages*, "Discours préliminaire," vol. 1, p. x.

18. *Observations sur l'écorce des feuilles et des pétales* was published in1762. His last work was published posthumously as "Opinion de DeSaussure sur les mouvements de la sève," in Senebier, *Physiologie végétale*, vol. 4 (Geneva, an VIII), pp. 127–37.

19. "Jalabert," in *Correspondence H/B*, letters and notes, and in the *Voyages*; "Jallabert" in *Un regard sur la terre* and in Carozzi, *Horace-Bénédict de Saussure (1740–1799)*.

20. *Voyages*, sec. 648, vol. 2, p. 54.

21. For the numbers of hikers, see Kev Reynolds, *The Tour of Mont Blanc: Complete Two-Way Hiking Guidebook and Map Booklet*, 5th ed. (Kendal: Cicerone Press, 2020), p. 16.

22. In the sense that it could not be replicated.

23. Paola Bertucci, "Therapeutic Attractions: Early Applications of Electricity to the Art of Healing," in *Brain, Mind and Medicine: Essays in Eighteenth-Century Neuroscience*, ed. H. A. Whitaker, C. U. M. Smith, and S. Finger ((Boston: Springer, 2007), p. 277. Report of 1748 to Jean Antoine Nollet and the French Academy of Science.

24. *Voyages*, sec. 648, vol. 2, p. 55.

25. *Correspondence H/B*, Bonnet to Haller, letter 478, 19 August 1767, p. 641.

26. "Biographe," in "Dossier" to Rousseau, *Les Confessions*, p. 780.

27. Guichonnet, "Mont Blanc ou la fascination des 'neiges éblouies,'" in Vellozzi, Vercken, Guichonnet, Joutard, and Lebailly, *Mont Blanc: Conquête de l'imaginaire*, p. 15.

28. Philippe Joutard, "De la montagne maudite à la montagne sublime ou les métamorphoses de la representation," in Vellozzi, Vercken, Guichonnet, Joutard, and Lebailly, *Mont Blanc: Conquête de l'imaginaire*, p. 26.

29. Rousseau, *Les Rêveries du promeneur solitaire*, "Septième promenade," p. 135.

30. Jean-Daniel Candaux, "Jacques-André Mallet, Jean-Louis Pictet: Deux vocations pour un même voyage," in *Deux astronomes genevois dans la Russie de Catherine II: Journaux de voyage en Laponie russe de Jean-Louis Pictet et Jacques-André Mallet pour observer le passage de Vénus devant le disque solaire, 1768–1769*, based on the original manuscripts with introductions and notes by Jean-Daniel Candaux, Sophie Capdeville, Michel Grenon, René Sigrist, and Vladimir Somov (Ferney-Voltaire: Centre International d'Étude du XVIIIème siècle, 2005), p. 4.

31. Candaux, "Jacques-André Mallet, Jean-Louis Pictet: Deux vocations," p. 4.

32. Dava Sobel, *The Glass Universe: How the Ladies of the Harvard Observatory Took the Measure of the Stars* (New York: Viking, 2016), p. 83.

33. François-Charles Pictet suggests this in the preface: "Avant-propos," in *Deux astronomes genevois dans la Russie de Catherine II*, p. v.

34. Jean-Louis Pictet, "Journal d'un voyage en Russie et en Laponie fait pendant les annees [sic] 1768 et 1769 à l'occasion du passage de Venus sur le disque du Soleil" (dated January 1772, notes for 3 July and 5 July 1768), in *Deux astronomes genevois dans la Russie de Catherine II*, p. 100.

35. François-Charles Pictet, "Avant-propos," in *Deux astronomes genevois dans la Russie de Catherine II*, p. v. Swedish Lapland was better known.

36. Candaux, "Jacques-André Mallet, Jean-Louis Pictet: Deux vocations," p. 7.

37. For the phrase "un Nord mystérieux," see François-Charles Pictet, "Avant-propos," in *Deux astronomes genevois dans la Russie de Catherine II*, p. v.

38. John Dunmore, *French Explorers in the Pacific*, vol. 1, *The Eighteenth Century* (Oxford: Clarendon Press, 1965), pp. 281–82, at p. 282.

39. On the voyage of La Pérouse, primary and other secondary sources exist. Two more recent books are by Catherine Gaziello, *L'Expédition de Lapérouse, 1785–1788: Réplique française aux voyages de Cook* (Paris: Comité des Travaux Historiques et Scientifiques, 1984), and Naomi J. Williams, *Landfalls* (New York: Picador—Farrar, Straus & Giroux, 2015.) The latter is an interesting historical novel.

40. Lissa Roberts, "The Senses in Philosophy and Science: Blindness and Insight," in *A Cultural History of the Senses*, pp. 109–32, at p. 121, referencing Kapil Raj.

41. Sophie Capdeville, "La Laponie," in *Deux astronomes genevois dans la Russie de Catherine II*, p. 45. La Condamine's expedition was led by the astronomer Louis Godin (1704–1760).

42. Werner Herzog's 1972 film *Aguirre, der Zorn Gottes (Aguirre, the Wrath of God)*, with Klaus Kinski in the title role, is in this tradition, though imagined as a story of *conquistadores*.

43. Hansen, *The Summits of Modern Man*, p. 102. "Widely reprinted in journals throughout Europe" and published separately as Saussure, *Relation abrégée d'un voyage à la cime du Mont Blanc en août 1787* (Geneva, 1787).

44. René Sigrist, "La Géographie de Saussure à l'horizon des savoirs du XVIIIème siècle," in *Un regard sur la terre*, pp. 215–248, at p. 246 n. 128. BGE [Bibliothèque de Genève], Papiers Rilliet, dossier E1, letter to Pictet, 19 October 1795.

45. Sigrist, "La Géographie de Saussure," in *Un regard sur la terre*, p. 246. His n. 127 cites: "(BGE, Papiers Rilliet, dossier E1/Lettre á Marc-Auguste Pictet, 22 juin 1798)."

46. Martin J. S. Rudwick, *Bursting the Limits of Time: The Reconstruction of Geohistory in the Age of Revolution* (Chicago: University of Chicago Press, 2005), pp. 133ff.

47. On the "Chimborazo Map (of 1807) and biogeography," see Karl S. Zimmerer, "Mapping Mountains," in *Mapping Latin America: A Cartographic Reader*, ed. Jordana Dym and Karl Offen (Chicago: University of Chicago Press, 2011), pp. 125–30, at p. 127.

48. Maren Meinhardt, *A Longing for Wide and Unknown Things: The Life of Alexander von Humboldt* (London: Hurst, 2018), p. 48.

49. Rudwick, *Bursting the Limits of Time*, p. 54.

50. Philippe Joutard offers a short summary of early maps of the Alps in *L'Invention du Mont Blanc* (Paris: Gallimard, 1986), p. 63.

51. *Correspondence H/S*, Saussure to Haller, letter 106, 28 February 1764, p. 178.

52. Carozzi, "Essai sur la personnalité de Horace-Bénédict de Saussure," p. 290. On Cassini's mapping progress by 1760, see Josef W. Konvitz, *Cartography in France, 1660–1848: Science, Engineering, and Statecraft* (Chicago: University of Chicago Press, 1987) p. 25.

53. *Voyages*, sec. 329, vol. 2, p. 267.

54. *Voyages*, sec. 327, vol. 2, p. 265.

55. Read the plagiarism of Saussure's directions to the Dôle in Charles Louis Richard, *Le Nouvel Ebel: Manuel du Voyageur en Suisse . . . Avec l'itinéraire complet de la vallée de Chamouni . . . rev., coordonnée, mis en ordre et augmenté* (Paris: Maison, n.d). p. 34 (published 1845 or earlier; a personal copy is dated). Thank you to Margaret Higonnet for this source. On guidebooks plagiarizing Saussure, see Guichonnet, "Le

Mont Blanc ou la fascination des 'neiges éblouies,'" in Vellozzi, Vercken, Guichonnet, Joutard, and Lebailly, *Mont Blanc: Conquête de l'imaginaire*, p. 18.

56. *Voyages*, sec. 363, vol. 1, pp. 296–97.

57. *Manuel du Voyageur en Suisse*, p. 34.

58. *Voyages*, sec. 355, vol. 1, p. 288.

59. Blaikie, *Diary of a Scotch Gardener*, p. 73.

60. She is identified in Claire Eliane, *A History of Mountaineering in the Alps*, foreword by F. S. Smythe (London: George Allen, 1950), p. 31. Burney was "co-Keeper of the Robes" at court from 1786 to 1790.

61. Jean André de Luc, *Lettres sur quelques parties de la Suisse et sur le climat d'hiéres: Adressées à la reine de la Grande Bretagne* (La Haye [The Hague]: Gosse, 1778), letter 13, Montpellier, 3 April 1775, p. 191, accessed 10 December 2023, https://www.e-rara.ch/zut/content/zoom/2361074.

62. Reichler, "Les Larmes d'une ingénue," in *La Découverte des Alpes et la Question du Paysage*, pp. 55–57, at p. 55. Reichler quotes only some of letter 13.

63. de Luc, *Lettres sur quelques parties de la Suisse*, letter 13, p. 193.

64. *Voyages*, sec. 330, vol. 1, p. 267.

65. *Voyages*, sec. 343, vol. 1, p. 279.

66. For a description of the ideas of Philippe Buache and Athanasius Kircher, see Gabriel Gohau, *Les Sciences de la terre aux XVIIème et XXVIIIème siècles: Naissance de la géologie* (Paris: Albin Michel, 1990), p. 142. In vol. 1 of the *Voyages* (in the introduction to his section "Voyage autour du Mont-Blanc," pp. 355–56), Saussure noted that Mont Blanc was the highest of peaks that have been measured "with any exactness not only in Europe but also in Asia and Africa. The Cordillera in South America are the only known mountains that surpass Mont Blanc in height."

67. Alain Corbin, *Terra Incognita: A History of Ignorance in the Eighteenth and Nineteenth Centuries*, trans. Susan Pickford (Cambridge: Polity Press, 2021).

68. *Voyages*, sec. 355, vol. 1, p. 289.

69. *Voyages*, secs. 2304–27, vol. 4, pp. 467–528: "Agenda, ou Tableau général des observations and des recherches dont les résultats doivent server de base à la théorie de la terre."

70. George Sarton, review of Douglas W. Freshfield, *The Life of Horace Benedict de Saussure*, *Isis* 6, no. 1 (1924): pp. 64–71, at p. 70.

71. Sarton, review of *The Life of Horace Benedict de Saussure*, p. 70.

72. *Voyages*, sec. 2313, points 1–3, vol. 4, p. 485.

73. *Voyages*, sec. 329, vol. 1, p. 267.

74. Jon Mathieu, *History of the Alps, 1500–1900: Environment, Development, and Society*, trans. Matthew Vester (Morgantown: University of West Virginia Press, 2009), p. 9.

75. *Voyages*, sec. 2313, points 1, 4, 5, 6, 7, and 10, vol. 4, pp. 485–86: "Sur les montagnes en général."

76. "Qu'une ville qui comptait alors de 20,000 à 30,000 habitants ait pu être, de 1750 à 1850, un des pôles de l'Europe savante constitue pour l'histoire sociale des sciences une source féconde de réflexion," as Jean-Marc Drouin notes in his review of Sigrist's *Les Origines de la Société de physique et d'histoire naturelle de Genève*, *Revue d'histoire des sciences* 45, no. 1 (1992): p. 157.

77. Guichonnet, "De la Genève des Lumières aux clartés des glaces éternelles,"

in Vellozzi, Vercken, Guichonnet, Joutard, and Lebailly, *Mont Blanc: Conquête de l'imaginaire*, p. 78.

78. Carozzi and Newman, "The Academy, the Student and the Professor," in Saussure, *Lectures on Physical Geography*, p. 13.

79. Carozzi and Newman, in "The Academy, the Student and the Professor," p. 14. The essay about the Academy draws heavily on Starobinski's in Trembley, *Les Savants genevois*.

80. See Thomas Laqueur, *Making Sex: Body and Gender from the Greeks to Freud* (Cambridge, MA: Harvard University Press, 1990).

81. *Correspondence H/S*, Haller to Saussure, letter 76, 12 May 1763, p. 141.

82. Bonnet wrote to Haller about it on 7 September. *Correspondence H/B*, Bonnet to Haller, letter 42, 7 September 1757, p. 114.

83. *Correspondence H/B*, Bonnet to Haller, letter 63, 10 April 1758, pp. 138 and 140; Haller to Bonnet, letter 64, 8 May 1758.

84. Saussure, *Lectures on Physical Geography*, pp. 82–83. See Joyce Chaplin, *Round About the Earth: Circumnavigation from Magellan to Orbit* (New York: Simon & Schuster, 2012), for a history of circumnavigation and for her argument about its importance to the development of a "planetary consciousness."

85. Saussure, *Lectures on Physical Geography*, p. 85. Roberts, "The Senses in Philosophy and Science: Blindness and Insight," p. 124, explains that "a researcher's sensuous engagement remained as much a practical requisite for the field of experimental physics as for other experimental sciences such as chemistry (into the nineteenth century)." The context is her discussion of John Gough (1757–1825).

86. Burnet is quoted in Simon Schama, *Landscape and Memory* (New York: Knopf, 1995), p. 452. Nicolson discusses Burnet as a stylist in *Mountain Gloom and Mountain Glory*, pp. 192–93. For Burnet, Whiston, and Woodward, see Rhoda Rappaport, "The Earth Sciences," in *The Cambridge History of Science*, vol. 4, *Eighteenth-Century Science*, ed. Roy Porter (Cambridge: Cambridge University Press, 2003), pp. 417–35.

87. Georges Louis Leclerc Buffon, "Histoire et théorie de la terre," in *Œuvres complètes de Buffon: Mises en ordre et précédées d'une notice historique...*, ed. Georges Cuvier, Achille Richard, and R. P. Lesson (Paris: Baudouin frères, 1827), vol. 1, pp. 121–22. Buffon published the "Théorie de la terre" in 1749.

88. Buffon, "Histoire et théorie de la terre," p. 122.

89. Gohau, *Les Sciences de la terre*, p. 86.

90. Buffon, "Histoire et théorie de la terre," p. 123.

91. *Voyages*, sec. 355, vol. 1, p. 289.

92. At the Kunsthalle, Hamburg.

93. Perhaps implied too in the painting. The painting is about how one sees. The "swathes of mist ... suggest that we are seeing the most fleeting of moments, and that the view could in an instant be replaced be another." Johannes Grave, *Caspar David Friedrich* (Munich and New York: Prestel, 2012), pp. 203–6, at p. 205.

94. *Voyages*, sec. 355, vol. 1, p. 289.

95. Twenty-nine volumes and seven supplements published between 1749 and 1804, with Louis Jean-Marie Daubenton (1716–1800) working alongside him: *Histoire naturelle, générale et particulière*, 15 vols. (Paris: Imprimerie royale, 1749–67); *Histoire naturelle des oiseaux*, 9 vols. (Paris: Imprimerie royale, 1770–83); *Histoire naturelle, générale et particulière... Supplément*, 7 vols. (Paris: Imprimerie royale, 1774–89); and

Histoire naturelle des minéraux, 5 vols. (Paris: Imprimerie royale, 1783–88). On Buffon's work having been "not based on much fieldwork of his own," see, among others, Rudwick, *Bursting the Limits of Time*, p. 142.

96. Title of Gavin De Beer, *Early Travellers in the Alps* (1930; New York: October House, 1967).

97. "Lettre de Conrad Gesner à Jacques Vogel," in W. A. B. Coolidge, *Josias Simler et les origines de l'alpinisme jusqu'en 1600* (Grenoble: Allier Frères, 1904), p. iii. With thanks to Ann Blair for a download of this source. Haller's letter to Johann Gesner (1709–1790), who was a descendant of Conrad, is dated 16 October, 1754: "While I have strength I must make a journey to the Alps every year, and this year it will be to the valley of Gadmen." G. R. De Beer, "Haller's *Historia Stirpium*," *Annals of Science* 9, no. 1 (1953): pp. 1–46, at p. 25. Haller's letter was translated from the Latin by De Beer.

98. On Grataroli, see Joutard, *L'Invention du mont Blanc*, pp. 60–62. Dominque Lejeune, in his review of Joutard's book, corrects his reading, explaining that Grataroli meant the iron attachments to the soles of one's boots were to be used on rock, not ice, so technically they were not the first crampons. Lejeune, review of *L'Invention du mont Blanc*, *Annales, Histoire, Sciences Sociales* 41, no. 6 (November–December 1986): pp. 1429–31, at p. 1430.

99. On the snowshoes, see Joutard, *L'Invention du mont Blanc*, p. 63. On Simler's section title, see Coolidge, *Josias Simler et les origines de l'alpinisme*, p. 211.

100. Quoted and translated by Freshfield, *Saussure*, p. 26. Achard, *Rosalie de Constant, sa famille et ses amies*, vol. 2, p. 28.

101. Roger L. Williams, *Botanophilia in Eighteenth-Century France*, International Archives of the History of Ideas 179 (Dordrecht: Kluwer Academic Publishers, 2000), p. 1. He cites Donald Charlton following Daniel Mornet. Of course, what people read as opposed to what was in their library is harder to ascertain.

102. Pierre Serna, *Comme des bêtes: Histoire politique de l'animal en Révolution (1740–1840)* (Paris: Fayard, 2017), p. 17.

103. Rudwick, *Bursting the Limits of Time*, p. 139. Rudwick draws on Jacques Roger's *Buffon: A Life in Natural History*, trans. Sarah Lucille Bonnefoi (Ithaca, NY: Cornell University Press, 1997); French ed.: *Buffon, un philosophe au Jardin du Roi* (1989). Also on Buffon, see Spary, *Utopia's Garden*.

104. Entry 811, p. 154, under the heading "Geology (Authors of Theories of the Earth)." In Carozzi and Bouvier, *The Scientific Library of Horace-Bénédict de Saussure*.

105. On the date, see Carozzi and Bouvier, *The Scientific Library of Horace-Bénédict de Saussure*, p. 52. Joseph, in his biography of Ferdinand de Saussure, claims Nicolas wrote for the *Encyclopédie*, but this has not been verified. Joseph, *Saussure*, p. 654 n. 38 and p. 14.

106. *Correspondence H/B*, Haller to Bonnet, letter 641 [from Bern], 4 June 1769, p. 822.

107. *Correspondence H/B*, Bonnet to Haller, letter 638, 12 May 1769, pp. 818–19.

108. *Correspondence H/B*, Haller to Bonnet, letter 639 [from Bern], 14 May 1769, p. 820: "Tout ce qui se passe par ces plumes prend la teinte du métal dont elles sont composées."

109. *Correspondence H/B*, Haller to Bonnet, letter 639 [from Bern], 14 May 1769, p. 819.

110. Gohau, *Les Sciences de la terre*, p. 142.

111. *Correspondence H/B*, Haller to Bonnet, letter 639, 14 May 1769, p. 820.

112. *Correspondence H/B*, Bonnet to Haller, letter 640, 25 May, 1769, p. 821.
113. *Correspondence H/B*, Bonnet to Haller, letter 642, 10 June 1769, p. 823.
114. A given for us today. Gohau, *Les Sciences de la terre*, p. 142.
115. *Correspondence H/B*, Haller to Bonnet, letter 644, 18 June 1769, p. 826.
116. Rudwick, *Bursting the Limits of Time*, p. 459. Though Cuvier would also insist on the frivolity of scientific expeditions, the age of fieldwork being over. The scientist should work with collected specimens.
117. *Correspondence H/S*, Saussure to Haller, letter 309 [from Paris], 24 April 1768, p. 405.
118. Buffon, "Des époques de la nature," in *Œuvres complètes de Buffon*, vol. 5, p. 418. He calls it Mont Saint-Gothard.
119. Rudwick, *Bursting the Limits of Time*, pp. 62–63. See Rappaport on the "so-called basalt controversy" in "The Earth Sciences," in *The Cambridge History of Science*, vol. 4, pp. 426–31.
120. Rappaport, "The Earth Sciences," in *The Cambridge History of Science*, vol. 4, pp. 423–24.
121. Rudwick, *Bursting the Limits of Time*, pp. 86 and 87.
122. Rudwick, *Bursting the Limits of Time*, p. 84.
123. Rudwick, *Bursting the Limits of Time*, p. 87.
124. Robert Fox, "Science and Government," in *Cambridge History of Science*, vol. 4, *Eighteenth-Century Science*, ed. Roy Porter (Cambridge and New York: Cambridge University Press, 2003), pp. 107–28, at p. 119.
125. Fox, "Science and Government," p. 119. Rachel Lauden, *From Mineralogy to Geology: The Foundations of a Science, 1650–1830* (Chicago: University of Chicago Press, 1987), pp. 87–112.
126. On Stenon's having visited these mines, see Gohau, *Les Sciences de la terre*, p. 106.
127. Gohau, *Les Sciences de la terre*, p. 107.
128. Gohau, *Les Sciences de la terre*, p. 107.
129. Rudwick, *Bursting the Limits of Time*, p. 92.
130. Rudwick, *Bursting the Limits of Time*, pp. 90–91, at p. 91 n. 43.
131. Roger, *Buffon: A Life in Natural History*, p. 66.
132. Roger, *Buffon: A Life in Natural History*, pp. 17ff, 21–22, and 34ff.
133. Roger, *Buffon: A Life in Natural History*, p. 44.
134. Quoted in Elisabeth Badinter, *Les Passions intellectuelles*, vol. 2, *Exigence de dignité (1751–1762)* (Paris: Fayard, 2002), p. 304. Badinter says Diderot had already expressed this view in his *Interprétation de la nature* (1753).
135. Andrew S. Curran, *Diderot and the Art of Thinking Freely* (New York: Other Press, 2019), examines Diderot's relationship with d'Alembert, with d'Alembert's break with the *Encyclopédie* described pp. 164–166.
136. Roger, *Buffon: A Life in Natural History*, p. 82.
137. Roger, *Buffon: A Life in Natural History*, p. 82.
138. Roger, *Buffon: A Life in Natural History*, p. 82 (this theme is explored throughout the essays in Vila, *A Cultural History of the Senses in the Age of Enlightenment*).
139. Begin with Samuel S. B. Taylor, "The Enlightenment in Switzerland," in *The Enlightenment in National Context*, ed. Roy Porter and Mikulás Teich (Cambridge and New York: Cambridge University Press, 1981), pp. 72–89.
140. *Correspondence H/B*. For example, Bonnet to Haller, letter 113, 1760, p. 212:

"le DIEU de verité paroit étendre sa main pour soutenir le Protestantisme." Ten years later Bonnet again, lambasting d'Holbach, that "nouveau Lucrèce" (*Système de la Nature*): "Je prie du fond de mon Cœur cet ETRE ADORABLE dont l'Insencé combat l'existence, de susciter dans son Eglise des Hommes capable de deffendre" (original spelling). letter 677, 1770,p. 878.

141. Saussure makes only one reference to God in his letters to Haller, that in reference to the consolations offered by religion to his wife and her sisters after the suicide of their father: *Correspondence H/S*, Saussure to Haller, letter 214 from Geneva, 25 November 1766, p. 302. Carozzi notes the absence of God in Saussure's lectures on physical geography and in his oeuvre overall in "La Géologie," chap. 6 of *Les Savants genevois*, pp. 203–65, at p. 206. Carozzi discusses the "anti-religious statements" Saussure makes in these lectures in "The Academy, the Student and the Professor," p. 30. Only once in the *Voyages* is the "Creator" noted, Carozzi emphasizes, and that in the "texte lyrique" of the preface to the *Voyages*: Carozzi, "Essai sur la personnalité de Horace-Bénédict de Saussure," in *Les Plis du temps*, p. 306. Reichler makes similar points in *La Découverte des Alpes*, pp. 64–65.

142. *Correspondence H/B*, Haller to Bonnet, letter 99 [from Roche], 4 March 1760, p. 193.

143. Buffon, "Histoire et théorie de la terre," pp. 120–21.

144. Bungener quoting Saussure in "Les Rapports de Saussure avec la botanique," p. 35, referencing Saussure, Archives de Saussure 254/7, p. 2. This document is a set of Saussure's own notes for his "Leçons de physique du 13e aoust aux 12 sept(em)bre 1770. Histoire de la phys (ique). Elé(ments) en general. Terre." "Sensualist philosophy" is Bungener's phrase.

145. Patrick Singy, "Medicine and the Senses: The Perception of Essences," in *A Cultural History of the Senses in the Age of Enlightenment*, pp. 133–54, at p. 145.

146. Gohau, *Les Sciences de la terre*, p. 40.

147. *Voyages*, sec. 916, vol. 2, p. 337.

148. From an essay on *Tremella* published in 1790, with reference to the "entire vegetable world," explains Bungener in "Les Rapports de Saussure avec la botanique," p. 38.

149. Jan Synowiecki, "Plant conversation in the Jardin du Roi (1715–1789)," *H-France Salon* 12, no. 7 (2020) accessed 10 December 2023, https://www.youtube.com/watch?v=NwKf0FEiLNA; and "Ces plantes qui sentent et qui pensent: Une autre histoire de la nature au XVIIIe siècle," *Revue historique* 694, no. 2 (April 2020): pp. 73–104. Along these lines, see Stefano Mancuso, *The Nation of Plants*, trans. Gregory Conti (New York: Other Press, 2023).

150. See "Our Living Planet from Space," NASA/Goddard Media Studios, released 13 November 2017, accessed 26 April 2018, http://svs.gsfc.nasa.gov/12777. Ferris Jabr, "The Earth Is Just as Alive as You Are: Scientists Once Ridiculed the Idea of a Living Planet; Not Anymore," *New York Times*, Sunday Review, 20 April 2019.

Chapter Three

1. Michael Kwass, *Contraband: Louis Mandrin and the Making of a Global Underground* (Cambridge, MA: Harvard University Press, 2014), p. 84.

2. Described by Saussure in a draft letter to Haller: *Correspondence H/S*, Saussure to Haller, letter 30, 25 July 1761, p. 88. Freshfield suggests the link to the Seven Years' War.

3. Freshfield, *Saussure*, p. 223.

4. Description of the Nant Nailliant or "Nallien or Naglian" with respect to this incident is in Saussure, *Journal d'un Voyage à Chamouni et à la Cime du Mont Blanc en juillet et aoust 1787*, ed. E. Gaillard and H. F. Montagnier (Lyon: Maudin, 1926), p. 40 n. 39. On Paccard's mission, see Saussure, *Journal de l'ascension du Mont Blanc*, ed. Anne Fauche and Samuel Cordier (Chamonix: Éditions Guérin, 2007), p. 93 n. 29.

5. *Voyages*, sec. 484, vol. 1, p. 408.

6. *Correspondence H/S*, Saussure to Haller, letter 3, late July 1760, p. 58.

7. Freshfield, *Saussure*, p. 60.

8. *Voyages*, sec. 740, vol. 2, pp. 158–59.

9. David Bodanis, *Passionate Minds* (New York: Crown, 2006), chaps. 12 and 13. Bodanis, *Passionate Minds*, p. 321. Robyn Arianrhod, *Seduced by Logic: Émilie du Châtelet, Mary Somerville and the Newtonian Revolution* (Oxford and New York: Oxford University Press, 2012), pp. 80–96. Châtelet showed that heat and color are related.

10. Bodanis, *Passionate Minds*, 155.

11. *Correspondence H/B*, Bonnet to Haller, letter 108, Geneva, 27 June 1760, p. 204.

12. *Correspondence H/B*, Bonnet to Haller, letter 113, Geneva, 30 July 1760, p. 212.

13. *Correspondence H/B*, Bonnet to Haller, letter 136, Genthod, 25 July 1761, p. 241.

14. Marcel Golay, "Pictet, Jean-Louis," in the *Dictionnaire historique de la Suisse*; the article is dated 18 January 2011. Accessed 10 December 2023, https://hls-dhs-dss.ch/fr/search/?text=jean-louis%20pictet&r=1.

15. Percy Bysshe Shelley, *Mont Blanc: Lines Written in the Vale of Chamouni* (1816), part 2, first two lines.

16. "Un grand chien Braque": a large pointer, useful for chasing away wolves. *Voyages*, sec. 291, vol. 1, p. 233.

17. *Voyages*, vol. 1, "Introduction to the Voyage autour du Mont-Blanc," pp. 357–58. Up the Arve valley in "1760, 61, 64, 67, 70, [1774, turning to the massif before Chamonix at St. Gervais] twice in 76, and the last in 78." He had made a circuit around the Mont Blanc massif three times, in 1767, 1774, and 1778. He had intended the tour of 1774 to be definitive; however, he returned with "missing answers and second thoughts," and the tour of 1778 was organized to settle these. This checking and rechecking is a basic part of Saussure's methodology.

18. Charles Vallot, *Saussure aux Alpes*, vol. 1 (Paris: Fischbacher, 1938), p. 69.

19. *Voyages*, sec. 434, vol. 1, p. 360.

20. *Voyages*, vol. 1, "Introduction to the Voyage autour du Mont-Blanc," p. 357.

21. *Voyages*, sec. 435, vol. 1, p. 360.

22. *Voyages*, sec. 435, vol. 1, pp. 360–61, sec. 436, p. 361.

23. *Voyages*, sec. 436, vol. 1, p. 361.

24. *Voyages*, sec. 437, vol. 1, p. 361.

25. *Voyages*, sec. 437, vol. 1, p. 361.

26. *Voyages*, sec. 437, vol. 1, p. 362.

27. *Voyages*, sec. 441, vol. 1, p. 365. It is thirty-three kilometers from Geneva to Bonneville.

28. *Voyages*, sec. 440, vol. 1, p. 364.

29. *Voyages*, sec. 440, vol. 1, p. 365.

30. *Voyages*, sec. 441, vol. 1, p. 365.

31. *Voyages*, sec. 279, vol. 1, p. 221.

32. A full bibliography for maps begins with Matthew H. Edney and Mary Sponberg Padley, *Cartography in the European Enlightenment*, vol. 4 of *The History of Cartography* (Chicago: University of Chicago Press, 2020). On maps of Mont Blanc, Laura and Giorgio Aliprandi's *La Découverte du Mont-Blanc par les cartographes, 1515–1925* (Ivreal [Turin]: Priuli & Verlecca, 2000) is an exhibition catalog with important visuals. Macfarlane explains that "contour lines were an invention of the sixteenth century, but they could not properly be used until advances in survey techniques provided the detail required for them. *Mountains of the Mind*, p. 183.

33. Lydie Touret, "Charles-François Exchaquet (1746–1792) et les plans en relief du Mont-Blanc," *Annals of Science* 46 (1989): pp. 1–20, at pp. 7 and 8. Touret has Saussure's map resting in a private collection still in 1989. I examined it in Geneva in the summer of 2018 in the Saussure rooms at the Museum of the History of Science.

34. "The soul as an active force": Fernando Vidal, *The Sciences of the Soul: The Early Modern Origins of Psychology* (Chicago: University of Chicago Press, 2011), p. 154.

35. Carole Huta, "Jean Senebier (1742–1809): Un dialogue entre l'ombre et la lumière; L'art d'observer à la fin du XVIIIème siècle," *Revue d'histoire des sciences* 51, no, 1 (January–March 1998): pp. 93–105, at p. 95.

36. Vidal, *The Sciences of the Soul*, pp. 143 and 144; see p. 143, n. 148 for silver medal. Senebier, *Essaie sur l'art d'observer et de faire des expériences*, 2nd ed. (Geneva: Paschoud, an. X [1802]), BnF/Gallica.

37. Huta, "Jean Senebier," p. 95, and Vidal, *Sciences of the Soul*, p. 143 n. 148. Patrick Singy, "Huber's Eyes: The Art of Scientific Observation before the Emergence of Positivism," *Representations* 95, no. 1 (Summer 2006): pp. 54–75, p. 54 on Senebier and *L'Art d' observer*. Lorraine Daston, "Attention and the Values of Nature in the Enlightenment," in *The Moral Authority of Nature*, ed. Lorraine Daston and Fernando Vidal (Chicago: University of Chicago Press, 2004.)

38. *Encyclopédie*, quoted in Vidal, *Sciences of the Soul*, p. 152. See *Encyclopédie, ou dictionnaire raisonné des sciences, des arts et des métiers, etc.*, ed. Denis Diderot and Jean le Rond d'Alembert, University of Chicago: ARTFL Encyclopédie Project (Autumn 2017 ed.), ed. Robert Morrissey and Glenn Roe, accessed December 10, 2023, http://encyclopedie.uchicago.edu/, vol. 11 (1765), "Observation [Physique/ Grammaire/ Médecine]," accessed 10 December 2023, https://artflsrv04.uchicago.edu/philologic4.7/encyclopedie0922/navigate/11/1731, p. 313.

39. Vidal, *Sciences of the Soul*, 152.

40. Jean-Louis Pictet accompanied Saussure on his first tour of Mont Blanc in 1767. Marc-Auguste Pictet on the third TMB in 1778.

41. Vidal, *Sciences of the Soul*, p. 145.

42. Vidal, *Sciences of the Soul*, p. 145.

43. Virginia P. Dawson, "Foundations of Natural Philosophy in Eighteenth-Century Geneva," in *Reconceptualizing Nature, Science, and Aesthetics: Contribution à une nouvelle approche des Lumières helvétiques*, ed. Patrick Colemen, Anne Hofman, and Simone Zurbuchen, vol. 1 of *Travaux sur la Suisse des Lumières* (Geneva: Slatkine, 1998), p. 42: "Members of the Bonnet Circle (Dawson names Saussure as one of these) confidently studied nature, convinced that the visible world provided proof of God's perfection and evidence for the rationality of the universe He had created." Hansen, *Summits of Modern Man*, p. 45: "The order of nature . . . did not necessarily entail a shift away from a natural theology toward a rationalization of natural history. . . . On the contrary, mid-eighteenth-century naturalists in the Alps such as Haller, Charles

Bonnet, Jean-André Deluc, and Horace-Bénédict de Saussure all embedded their natural histories in natural theologies."

44. Vidal, *The Sciences of the Soul*, p. 150. Dawson, "Foundations of Natural Philosophy," p. 42. Huta, "Jean Senebier," pp. 100–102.

45. Vidal, "Remarks on the Role of the Enlightenment in Switzerland in the Emergence of the 'Science of Man,'" in Patrick Coleman, Anne Hofmann, Simon Zurbuchen, ed., *Reconceptualizing Nature, Science, and Aesthetics: Contributions à une nouvelle approche des lumières Helvétiques* (Geneva: Slatkine, 1998), p. 85.

46. David Hume, *A Treatise of Human Nature*, ed. David Fate Norton and Mary J. Norton (Oxford and New York: Oxford University Press, 2000), book 1, part 4, sec. 6, "Of Personal Identity," pp. 164–71, at p. 165.

47. *Voyages*, sec. 472, vol. 1, p. 397.

48. Described in Paul Mougin, *Les Torrents de la Savoie* (1914; Montmélian: La Fontaine de Siloé, 2001), pp. 499–500.

49. *Voyages*, sec. 500, vol. 1, p. 423.

50. Macfarlane, introduction to Nan Shepherd, *The Living Mountain* (Edinburgh: Canongate Books, 2011), p. xxix. Macfarlane quotes Shepherd, p. xxix. Shepherd wrote *The Living Mountain* in Aberdeen toward the end of the Second World War, though it was not published until 1977.

51. Shepherd, *The Living Mountain*, p. 8.

52. *Voyages*, sec. 233, vol. 1, p. 178.

53. *Voyages*, sec. 288, vol. 1, p. 231.

54. On the body as technology as part of the climbing experience of the twentieth century, Kerwin Lee Klein, "A Vertical World: The Eastern Alps and Modern Mountaineering," *Journal of Historical Sociology* 24 (2011): 519–548.

55. *Correspondence H/S*, Haller to Saussure, letter 323, 31 July 1769, p. 428. Erich Hintzsche, "Haller, (Victor) Albrecht von," in *Dictionary of Scientific Biography*, ed. Charles Coulston Gillispie (New York: Charles Scribner's Sons, 1970–80), vol. 6, pp. 61–67, at p. 62: "In his old age his weight—238 pounds—hindered his taking even easy mountain strolls."

56. *Voyages*, sec. 442, vol. 1, p. 366.

57. *Voyages*, sec. 282, vol. 1, p. 230.

58. *Voyages*, sec. 442, vol. 1, p. 366.

59. *Voyages*, sec. 675, vol. 2, p. 85. One toise is equal to 1.949 meters.

60. *Voyages*, sec. 464, vol. 1, p. 383.

61. *Voyages*, sec. 451, vol. 1, p. 372.

62. *Voyages*, sec. 464, vol. 1, p. 383.

63. *Voyages*, sec. 480, vol. 1, p. 403.

64. *Voyages*, sec. 472, vol. 1, p. 396.

65. *Voyages*, sec. 481, vol. 1, p. 405.

66. *Voyages*, sec. 485, vol. 1, p. 409.

67. *Voyages*, sec. 492, vol. 1, p. 413.

68. *Voyages*, sec. 508, vol. 1, p. 427.

69. *Voyages*, sec. 508, vol. 1, p. 428.

70. *Voyages*, sec. 509, vol. 1, p. 428.

71. *Voyages*, sec. 510, vol. 1, p. 429.

72. *Voyages*, sec. 510, vol. 1, p. 429.

73. *Voyages*, sec. 510, vol. 1, p. 430.

74. On specificity, Robert Macfarlane, *Landmarks* (London: Hamish Hamilton, 2015), esp. "The Word-Hoard," pp. 1–14. On not being the "focal point" in a landscape, see Shepherd, *The Living Mountain*, p. 11. On "requir[ing] things to have their own lives if they are to enrich ours," see Macfarlane, *Landmarks*, p. 25.

75. Huth, "Conclusions: A Cross-Disciplinary Journey through Spatial Orientation," p. 156, accessed 10 December 2023, https://escholarship.org/uc/item/64r1r4qg.

76. Voltaire, quoted in John Leigh, "Voltaire and the Myth of England," in *The Cambridge Companion to Voltaire*, ed. Nicolas Cronk (Cambridge and New York: Cambridge University Press, 2009), p. 86: "On y parle français, on y pense à l'anglaise.'" Jean Charles Léonard Simon de Sismondi, quoted similarly by Guichonnet, "L'Invitation au voyage," in Vellozzi, Vercken, Guichonnet, Joutard, and Lebailly, *Mont-Blanc: Conquête de l'imaginaire*, p. 77.

77. Eric W. Nye, "Pounds Sterling to Dollars: Historical Conversion of Currency," accessed 24 July 24 2023, https://www.uwyo.edu/numimage/currency.htm. For the jilting, see John Shipley Rowlinson, "'Our Common Room in Geneva' and the Early Exploration of the Alps of Savoy," *Notes and Records of the Royal Society of London* 52, no. 2 (July 1998): pp. 221–35, at p. 226. Herbert Lüthy, *La Banque protestante en France, de la révocation de l'Édit de Nantes à la Révolution*, vol. 2 (Paris: S.E.V.P.E.N., 1961), p. 97 on the Chapeaurouges.

78. Rowlinson, "'Our Common Room in Geneva,'" p. 222.

79. The date given by the Musée d'art et d'histoire de Genève is 1740; other sources give it as 1738.

80. On Pococke and the Sphinx: Maya Jasanoff, *Edge of Empire: Lives, Culture, and Conquest in the East, 1750–1850* (New York: Knopf, 2005), pp. 220–21.

81. Aileen Ribeiro, "The Beauty of the Particular: Dress in Liotard's Images of Women," in Christopher Baker, William Hauptman, and Mary Anne Stevens, *Jean-Étienne Liotard, 1702–1789* (London: Royal Academy of Arts, 2015), pp. 35–41.

82. "Letter 35 of his Eastern correspondence sent from Ephesus on 15/26 December 1739," accessed 10 December 2023, http://pocockepress.com/portrait.php. On the red cap and Liotard's self-portraits, see Duncall Ball, "Self-Portraits and the Artist's Family," pp. 42–51, and Marc Fehlmann, "Orientalism," pp. 65–71, in Baker, Hauptman, and Stevens, *Jean-Étienne Liotard, 1702–1789*, pp. 65–71.

83. Title of chap. 8 of De Beer, *Early Travellers in the Alps*.

84. In 1669 and 1673–74. De Beer, *Early Travellers in the Alps*, p. 73.

85. De Beer, *Early Travellers in the Alps*, pp. 76 and 73.

86. Rowlinson, "'Our Common Room in Geneva,'" p. 226.

87. Rowlinson, "'Our Common Room in Geneva,'" p. 226.

88. Quoted in Rowlinson, "'Our Common Room in Geneva,'" p. 222.

89. Rowlinson, "'Our Common Room in Geneva,'" p. 226.

90. On Windham's election being based on the "Account," see Rowlinson, "'Our Common Room in Geneva,'" p. 227.

91. Hansen, *Summits of Modern Man*, p. 32. Quoting from Pococke's journal, June 1741.

92. "An Account of the Glacières or Ice Alps in Savoy," pamphlet reproduced in in De Beer, *Early Travellers in the Alps*, pp. 99–114, at p. 102. On the history of Windham's account and for a reproduction of the pamphlet in its original French and in a modern annotated translation, see Albert V. Carozzi and John K. Newman, *Horace-Bénédict de Saussure: Forerunner in Glaciology; New Manuscript Evidence on the Earliest*

Explorations of the Glaciers of Chamonix and the Fundamental Contribution of Horace-Bénédict de Saussure to the Study of Glaciers between 1760 and 1792 (Geneva: Éditions Passé Présent, 1995), pp. 5–28.

93. Windham, "An Account of the Glacières or Ice Alps in Savoy," in De Beer, *Early Travellers in the Alps*, pp. 102 and 103.

94. Windham, "An Account of the Glacières or Ice Alps in Savoy," in De Beer, *Early Travellers in the Alps*, p. 103.

95. Quoted in Hansen, *Summits of Modern Man*, p. 32, from "An Account of the Glacières or Ice Alps in Savoy" (London, 1744).

96. *Voyages*, sec. 732, vol. 2, p. 145.

97. Hansen, *Summits of Modern Man*, p. 32. Quoting from Pococke's journal, June 1741.

98. Nineteenth-century account interposed by De Beer in "Account of the Glacières or Ice Alps in Savoy," *Early Travellers in the Alps*, p. 103.

99. Nineteenth-century account interposed by De Beer in "Account of the Glacières or Ice Alps in Savoy," *Early Travellers in the Alps*, p. 103.

100. Hansen, *Summits of Modern Man*, p. 32. Quoting from Pococke's journal, June 1741.

101. Ardbraccam is popularly understood as the site of Bile Torthain or Tortan, one of the supposed five protector trees of Ireland cut down by Christian elites in the seventh century. On how the English changed the landscape of Ireland, see William J. Smyth, *Map-Making, Landscapes and Memory: A Geography of Colonial and Early Modern Ireland, c. 1530–1750* (Notre Dame, IN: Notre Dame University Press, 2006). On how the Reformation changed the landscape of Britain and Ireland, see Alexandra Walsham, *The Reformation of the Landscape: Religion, Identity and Memory in Early Modern Britain and Ireland* (Oxford and New York: Oxford University Press, 2011): on holy wells in Ireland, see pp. 171–74; on woods and trees, see pp. 26–29.

102. Windham, "An Account of the Glacières or Ice Alps in Savoy," in De Beer, *Early Travellers in the Alps*, p. 105.

103. Windham, "An Account of the Glacières or Ice Alps in Savoy," in De Beer, *Early Travellers in the Alps*, p. 107.

104. In Mary Wollstonecraft Shelley with Percy Bysshe Shelley, *Frankenstein; or, The Modern Prometheus*, ed. Charles E. Robinson (Oxford: Bodleian Library, 2008), book 1, chap. 15, pp. 119–25.

105. Windham, "An Account of the Glacières or Ice Alps in Savoy," in De Beer, *Early Travellers in the Alps*, p. 109.

106. Windham, "An Account of the Glacières or Ice Alps in Savoy," in De Beer, *Early Travellers in the Alps*, pp. 110–11. Edward Vernon (1684–1757) captured Porto Bello (Panama) in 1739 but lost the battle for Cartagena de Indias (Colombia) in 1741. The toast was premature. David A. Bell, *Men on Horseback: The Power of Charisma in the Age of Revolution* (New York: Farrar, Straus & Giroux, 2020), p. 46, explains that Vernon was a "political celebrity," one of the first in Britain.

107. John Tyndall (1820–1893) resigned from the Alpine Club in response to Stephen's speech, taking his comments as a personal insult. The quote is from Stephen's "The Rothhorn," in *The Playground of Europe* (London: Longmans, Green, 1904) pp. 108–9.

108. Isserman and Weaver, *Fallen Giants*, p. 35.

109. Albert Frederick Mummery, *My Climbs in the Alps and Caucasus*, introd.

M.[ary] Mummery (Oxford: Basil Blackwell, Blackwell's Mountaineering Library, 1895), p. 5. The disaster is discussed in *Fallen Giants* on pp. 45-50.

110. Rowlinson, "'Our Common Room in Geneva,'" p. 226.

111. Windham, "Account of the Glacières or Ice Alps in Savoy," in De Beer, *Early Travellers in the Alps*, p. 101.

112. This is a continuing theme in alpinism. George Mallory forgot his compass at Camp V when pressing on to his Camp VI and his and Irvine's fatal attempt on Everest in 1924. At something like 26,000 feet, the conditions are some excuse, though Mallory was known for absentmindedness. Davis, *Into the Silence*, pp. 541-43. Joe Simpson and Simon Yates simply did not think of taking a compass on their near-fatal climb of the West Face of Siula Grande in the Andes in 1985. "Wish we had a compass," Simpson thought while lost in a white-out on their descent. Joe Simpson, *Touching the Void* (New York: Harper Collins Perennial, 1988), p. 64.

113. Windham, "Account of the Glacières or Ice Alps in Savoy," in De Beer, *Early Travellers in the Alps*, p. 108.

114. Windham, "Account of the Glacières or Ice Alps in Savoy," in De Beer, *Early Travellers in the Alps*, p. 108.

115. Saussure *Voyages*, sec. 614, vol. 2, p. 9; sec. 612, vol. 2, p. 8.

116. Saussure, translated in Macfarlane, *Mountains of the Mind*, pp. 115-16. Windham is quoted with admiration.

117. *Voyages*, sec. 611, vol. 2, p. 7.

118. *Voyages*, sec. 615, vol. 2, p. 10.

119. *Voyages*, sec. 615, vol. 2, pp. 10-11.

120. *Voyages*, "Discours préliminaire," vol. 1, p. vi.

121. Freshfield, *Saussure*, p. 71, notes the approximate date of Simon's death. Saussure, *Voyages*, sec. 733, vol. 2, p. 146, says Simon "had been dead for four or five years."

122. *Voyages*, sec. 616, vol. 2, p. 11.

123. *Voyages*, sec. 616, vol. 2, p. 11.

124. *Voyages*, sec. 616, vol. 2, p. 12.

125. Daniela Vaj and Martin Bernard, "La Conquête du Mont-Blanc: Horace-Bénedict de Saussure et se guides," VIATICALPES Productions, 2017, video multimedia, color, accessed 24 July 2023, https://www.unil.ch/viaticalpes/fr/home/menuguid/recits-animation.html. The vignette appears on p. 355 of vol. 1, heading Saussure's introduction to "Voyage autour du Mont-Blanc," and Saussure directs the reader's attention to this illustration of "a man who is gliding in this manner on the snow" in *Voyages*, sec. 616, vol. 2, p. 12.

126. *Voyages*, sec. 639, vol. 2, p. 39.

127. *Voyages*, sec. 648, vol. 2, pp. 53-54.

128. Last three lines of Shelley's *Mont Blanc: Lines Written in the Vale of Chamouni.*

Chapter Four

1. Twenty-eight houses: Paul Guichonnet, "De l'Hospitalité à l'hôtellerie," in Vellozzi, Vercken, Guichonnet, Joutard, and Lebailly, *Mont-Blanc: Conquête d'imaginaire*, pp. 230-40, at p. 232.

2. Twelve feet of snow: *Voyages*, sec. 740, vol. 2, pp. 158-59 and 91. "The highest and coldest": *Voyages*, sec. 680, vol. 2, pp. 158-59 and 91.

3. Roger Couvert du Crest, *Une vallée insolite*, p. 35. His sources: remarkable events

noted by inhabitants and on hotel registers. On alpine glaciers including those touching the Chamonix Valley, Emmanuel Le Roy Ladurie, *Times of Feast, Times of Famine: A History of Climate since the Year 1000*, trans. Barbara Bray (Garden City, NY: Doubleday, 1971.)

4. Couvert du Crest, *Une vallée insolite*, p. 39. The reference is to "L'État des récoltes à Chamonix (1782)," Archives, département de la Haute-Savoie (série H-H-7).

5. *Voyages*, sec. 742, vol. 2, p. 161.

6. Mathieu, *History of the Alps*, pp. 51–52.

7. Nicolas, *La Vie quotidienne en Savoie*, p. 23.

8. "The average size of holdings in the Chamonix valley": 1–2 hectares (2.5–5 acres) of arable land, approximately 2.5 acres of meadow and orchards, and some pasturage, along with common rights in woods, and to the alps. Couvert du Crest, *Une vallée insolite*, p. 39. The most favored lands were in Chamonix and Les Houches, the less preferred at Argentière and Vallorcine. Couvert du Crest, *Une vallée insolite*, p. 39. One hectare equals 2.47 acres.

9. Some copper, some silver mines. Couvert du Crest, *Une vallée insolite*, p. 40: "It appears they were abandoned after 1792, due to poor returns." Balmat would die looking for gold in the peaks. Hansen discusses mining, making the point that the valley was neither "isolated" nor "discovered" in the eighteenth century. There were lead and coal mines at Servoz. Hansen, *Summits of Modern Man*, p. 35.

10. Guichonnet, "De l'hospitalité à l'hôtellerie," p. 228.

11. Hansen, *Summits of Modern Man*, p. 85, notes this.

12. On rock crystal for faux diamonds, see DeJean, "King of Diamonds," in *The Essence of Style*, pp. 161–76, at p. 175.

13. *Voyages*, sec. 666, vol. 2, p. 73.

14. *Voyages*, sec. 737, vol. 2, p. 153. Saussure predicted that in less than a century, the chamois and marmots would share the fate of the bouquetins (ibex), already hunted out of their Alps.

15. *Voyages*, sec. 1102, vol. 2, p. 550.

16. *Voyages*, sec. 1102, vol. 2, p. 550. Clarified by Edward Whymper, *Chamonix and the Range of Mont Blanc: A Guide* (London: John Murray, 1896), p. 14.

17. Hansen further identifies them in *Summits of Modern Man*, p. 62. Victor Tissay was the fourth climber in 1775. The three guides who climbed in 1783 were Jean-Marie Coutett, Lombard Meunier *dit* Jorasse and Joseph Carrier. *Voyages*, sec. 1104, vol. 2, p. 551. Coutterand is spelled variously as Coutteran and Couteran. Unless in a quote, I have spelled the name Coutterand.

18. Hansen, *Summits of Modern Man*, p. 84 and note 92 on p. 325.

19. Moore, *A View of Society and Manners in France*, p. 234.

20. Guichonnet, "Le Mont Blanc ou la fascination des 'neiges éblouies,'" in Vellozzi, Vercken, Guichonnet, Joutard, and Lebailly, *Mont-Blanc: Conquête d'imaginaire*, p. 16. Couvert du Crest, *Une vallée insolite*, p. 39.

21. Hansen, *Summits of Modern Man*, p. 96, cites official statistics from the intendant of Faucigny on the number of notable visitors. A publication of the town of Chamonix-Mont-Blanc reports 1500 visitors in 1783: *Les Journées du patrimoine, Chamonix-Mont-Blanc: 900 ans d'histoire; Les Hôtels du Bourg de Chamonix* (Service imprimerie de la Mairie, 1998), p. 4.

22. Couvert du Crest, *Une vallée insolite*, p. 32.

23. *Voyages*, sec. 732, vol. 2, p. 145.

24. *Les Hôtels du Bourg de Chamonix*, p. 4 and p. 3.

25. On the name, see Guichonnet, "De l'hospitalité à l'hôtellerie," p. 232.

26. Guichonnet, "De l'hospitalité à l'hôtellerie," p. 232.

27. *Vue de l'extrémité du village de Chamouni* by Jean-François Albanis Beaumont (1739–1810) is dated c. 1787. It is reproduced and identified in Jean-Pierre Spilmont, *Jacques Balmat, héros du Mont Blanc* (Chamonix: Guérin, 2014/1986), pp. 290, 35. The work is described in *Les Hôtels du Bourg de Chamonix* as representing the "auberge de Madame Coutterand" as the most important in Chamonix, p. 3,

28. Guichonnet, "De L'Hospitalité à l'hôtellerie," p. 232. *Les Hôtels du Bourg de Chamonix*, pp. 4–5. *Voyages*, sec. 732, vol. 2, p. 145.

29. Guichonnet, "Le Mont Blanc ou la Fascination des 'neiges éblouies,'" p. 16.

30. *Les Hôtels du Bourg de Chamonix*, p. 6 and 8.

31. Shelley, line 1, "Mont Blanc: Lines Written in the Vale of Chamouni."

32. Philippe Joutard, "De la montagne maudite à la montagne sublime ou les métamorphoses de la representation," in Vellozzi, Vercken, Guichonnet, Joutard, and Lebailly, *Mont-Blanc: Conquête de l'imaginaire*, pp. 19–72, at p. 24.

33. Susan Barton, *Healthy Living in the Alps: The Origins of Winter Tourism in Switzerland, 1860–1914* (Manchester and New York: Manchester University Press, 2008), p. 89.

34. Barton, *Healthy Living in the Alps*, p. 89.

35. Mathieu, *History of the Alps*, p. 49.

36. Marc-Théodore Bourrit (1739–1819), *Relation of a Journey to the Glaciers in the Duchy of Savoy*, trans. Cha. and Fred. Davy, 3rd ed. (Dublin, 1776), p. 64. Bourrit is cited in Freshfield, *Saussure*, with a different translation, p. 71.

37. Joutard, "De la montagne maudite à la montagne sublime," p. 24. Philippe Joutard (b. 1935) is a historian of the Camisard Revolts. His work has helped to legitimize the subject of Mont Blanc from the cultural history point of view. He published *L'Invention de Mont Blanc* with Gallimard in 1986 (in conjunction with the bicentennial of the first ascent) and contributed to the lavish *Mont-Blanc: Conquête de l'imaginaire*, 2002, which is based on the Collections Payot et images de montagne, Archives département de Haute-Savoie.

38. Walker and Winiger-Labuda, "Saussure et l'architecture," p. 469.

39. *Correspondence H/S*, Saussure to Haller, letter 276. 4 July 1767, p. 370.

40. *Correspondence H/S*, Saussure to Haller, letter 279 from Geneva, 10 July 1767, p. 375. Marc J. Ratcliff, "Saussure et la découverte de la division des animalcules," in *Un regard sur la terre*, pp. 51–82.

41. *Correspondence H/S*, Saussure to Haller, letter 279 from Geneva, 10 July 1767, p. 375. René Sigrist, "Saussure en quelque dates," in *Un regard sur la terre*, p. 525.

42. Freshfield, *Saussure*, p. 90.

43. Reproduced in *Les Plis du temps*, fig. 2, p. 279. The document is in Arch. de Saussure, MS 14, 1774, 1/1, 1.

44. *Voyages*, vol. 1, "Introduction to Voyage autour du Mont-Blanc," p. 357.

45. *Lettres de H.-B. de Saussure à sa femme*, ed. E. Gaillard and H. F. Montagnier (Chambéry: Imprimeries réunies, 1937), letter 17, "25 july (1777) from Meiringen," p. 36.

46. *Lettres de H.-B. de Saussure à sa femme*, letter 17, "25 july (1777) from Meiringen," p. 36.

47. Albert Carozzi, "Saussure et la controverse sur le basalte (1772–1798)," in *Un regard sur la terre*, pp. 175–96.

48. Albertine-Adrienne was born on 9 April 1766, Nicolas-Théodore in October 1767. Recall that the father of Albertine-Amélie Boissier, the wife of Saussure, killed himself in October 1766. Marie-Charlotte, Albertine-Amélie's mother, died when her daughter was a young child.

49. Letter to his mother from Amsterdam, 1 July 1768, Arch. de Saussure 223-6: typed copies of letters from Paris, London, and Calais (typed by Henry F. Montagnier), p. 28.

50. Quoted in Freshfield, *Saussure*, p. 116. Letter to the Rector of the Academy of Geneva from Leeds, 3 September 1769; his translation.

51. "Voyage aux volcans d'Auvergne, 1776. Retour de l'Auvergne par le Languedoc, le Dauphiné et la Bourgogne. Dépenses de voyage (en livres de France) pour le parcours Lyon-Beaune-Dijon-Semur-enAuxois-Dole-Besançon-Pontarlier-Morges-Nyon-Genève." Saussure's notes reproduced in *Les Plis du temps*, fig. 6 in "Essai sur la personnalité de Horace-Bénédict de Saussure d'après ses manuscrits," p. 85.

52. Bourrit, *Relation of a Journey to the Glaciers in the Duchy of Savoy*, p. 72 (translation, 1776), in *Description des glaciers, glaciers et amas de glace du duché de Savoie* (Geneva, 1773).

53. *Voyages*, sec. 648, vol. 2, pp. 54–56.

54. Bourrit, *Relation of a Journey to the Glaciers in the Duchy of Savoy*, pp. 60–61.

55. He is quoted describing Bourrit's writing as "unmixed bombast." Freshfield, *Saussure*, p. 187.

56. Bourrit, *Relation of a Journey to the Glaciers in the Duchy of Savoy*, pp. 62–63.

57. Bourrit, *Relation of a Journey to the Glaciers in the Duchy of Savoy*, p. 9.

58. Freshfield, *Saussure*, pp. 184–185.

59. Bourrit, *Relation of a Journey to the Glaciers in the Duchy of Savoy*, p. 80. My slightly improved translation.

60. Bourrit, *Relation of a Journey to the Glaciers in the Duchy of Savoy*, p. 81.

61. *Voyages*, sec. 655, vol. 2, p. 62.

62. *Voyages*, sec. 667, vol. 2, p. 74.

63. While in Cluses. Saussure, "Notice d'un nouveau magnétomètre," in *Voyages*, secs. 455–61, vol. 1, pp. 375–81.

64. Arianrhod, *Seduced by Logic*, p. 87.

65. Margarida Archinard, *Collection de Saussure: Images du musée d'art et d'histoire de Genève* (Geneva: Musée d'art et d'histoire, 1979), pp. 28–29.

66. Archinard, *Collection de Saussure*, p. 28. On instruments: Anita McConnell, "Instruments and Instrument Makers, 1700–1850," in *The Oxford Handbook of the History of Physics*, ed. Jed Buchwald and Robert Fox (Oxford and New York: Oxford University Press, 2013), pp. 326–57, at pp. 349–50; and G. L. E. Turner, "Eighteenth-Century Scientific Instruments and Their Makers," in *The Cambridge History of Science*, vol. 4, pp. 511–35.

67. Presumably the establishment begun by Michael Butterfield (c. 1635–1724). Marc J. Ratcliff, *The Quest for the Invisible: Microscopy in the Enlightenment* (Farnham, England and Burlington, VT: Ashgate, 2009), p. 295 and pp. 19 and 47 for Butterfield, Paris instrument maker.

68. Archinard, *Collection de Saussure*, p. 32, object 16. On the history of micrometers, especially for use with microscopes, though telescopes are mentioned see Ratcliffe, *The Quest for the Invisible*, 168, 169.

69. Archinard, *Collection de Saussure*, p. 32, object 17.

70. Archinard, *Collection de Saussure*, p. 31, object 14.

71. Archinard, *Collection de Saussure*, p. 31, object 15.

72. *Correspondence H/S*, Saussure to Haller, letter 168, 4 March 1766, p. 251.

73. "Abstract," in Carozzi and Bouvier, *The Scientific Library of Horace-Bénédict de Saussure*, p. vii.

74. Carozzi and Bouvier, *The Scientific Library of Horace-Bénédict de Saussure*, p. 18. Comments on *Archives de Saussure*, Ms 104-10: "Saussure's price list of valuable books for sale, ca. 1795."

75. Carozzi, "Introduction," in Carozzi and Bouvier, *The Scientific Library of Horace-Bénédict de Saussure*, p. 1.

76. "Preface," in Carozzi and Bouvier, *The Scientific Library of Horace-Bénédict de Saussure*, p. viii, and Carozzi, "Introduction," in same, p. 1.

77. *Correspondence H/S*, Haller to Saussure, letter 242, 15 March 1767, p. 337. Also quoted in Carozzi and Bouvier, *The Scientific Library of Horace-Bénédict de Saussure*. I slightly amended their translation.

78. "Preface," in Carozzi and Bouvier, *The Scientific Library of Horace-Bénédict de Saussure*, p. viii.

79. On Saussure's book orders, see the transcribed documents in Carozzi and Bouvier, *The Scientific Library of Horace-Bénédict de Saussure*, pp. 18–43. They reference Arch. de Saussure 104-6: "List of books *à demander* (wish list) and lists of books *demandés* (ordered) from booksellers, 1769–1770"; 104-8: "Lists of books ordered between 1772 and 1788"; 104-9: "Lists of books ordered between 1791 and 1792."

80. *Correspondence H/S*, Saussure to Haller, letter 311 from London, 16 August 1768, p. 411. He gives his address to Haller as "Chez Mrs Boissier et Comp, Banquiers à Londres."

81. *Correspondence H/S*, Saussure to Haller, letter 313 from London, 15 November 1768, p. 414.

82. Saussure's memorandum is quoted on p. 28 of Carozzi and Bouvier, *The Scientific Library of Horace-Bénédict de Saussure*.

83. *Correspondence H/S*, Haller to Saussure, letter 97 from Roche, 23 September 1763, p. 167. On *Rathausammann*, see p. 167 n. 2.

84. *Correspondence H/S*, Saussure to Haller, letter 98 from Geneva, 3 October 1763, p. 167.

85. *Correspondence H/S*, Haller to Saussure, letter 84 from Roche, 25 July 1763, p. 152.

86. *Correspondence H/S*, Saussure to Haller, letter 85, c. 30 July 1763, p. 154.

87. *Correspondence H/S*, Haller to Saussure, letter 86, 2 August 1763, p. 155.

88. *Correspondence H/S*, Haller to Saussure, letter 88 from Roche, 11 August 1763, p. 157. He adds that he found the Hume elsewhere. On what works by Mallet and Voltaire Haller requested: p. 157 n. 2 and p. 159 n. 4.

89. Patrick F. O'Mara, "Geneva in the Eighteenth Century: A Socio-Economic Study of the Bourgeois City-State during its Golden Age" (Ph.D. dis., University of Chicago, 1954), p. 56. Conversion rates given on p. xiii: "3.5 florins = one livre (Geneves); 1 livre tournois equals 2.12 florins." Most of this wealth was in letters of exchange.

90. O'Mara, "Geneva in the Eighteenth Century," p. 56 n. 29. Lüthy, *La Banque protestante en France*, vol. 1, p. 216 n. 56.

91. Jean-Étienne Liotard, *Marie Charlotte Boissier*, 1746. In a private collection.

92. O'Mara, "Geneva in the Eighteenth Century," p. 63.
93. Mara, "Geneva in the Eighteenth Century," p. 46.
94. Freshfield, *Saussure*, p. 121.
95. O'Mara, "Geneva in the Eighteenth Century," p. 61. Roth, "Comment Saussure perdit sa fortune," in *Un regard sur la terre*, pp. 471–86. Rebecca Spang, *Stuff and Money in the Time of the French Revolution* (Cambridge, MA: Harvard University Press, 2017).
96. Corinne Walker and Anastazja Winiger-Labuda, "Saussure et l'architecture: Entre goût et nécessité," in *Un regard sur la terre*, pp. 453–70, at p. 454.
97. El-Wakil, "Aspects of Genevois Architecture from the Reformation to the Nineteenth Century," p. 222. The reference is for both quotes.
98. Walker and Winiger-Labuda, "Saussure et l'architecture," pp. 461–62. For photographs of the *boiseries*, see Helen Barnes, "*La Maison de Saussure*: Restoring the Elegance of a Sumptuous Past in Geneva," *Architectural Digest*, July–August 1978, pp. 37–43 (2019 Architectural Digest Archive). Thank you to Taylor Antrim for this article.
99. Walker and Winiger-Labuda, "Saussure et l'architecture," p. 457.
100. Watt, *Choosing Death*, p. 304.
101. Quoted by Freshfield, *Saussure*, p. 78.
102. Freshfield, *Saussure*, p. 79.
103. Freshfield, *Saussure*, p. 78.
104. *Correspondence H/S*, p. 201 ed.'s n. 1.
105. His soul was "orageuse et inquiète." He was "distrait." He feared the happiness he had in sight would escape him. Senebier, *Mémoire historique sur la vie et les écrits de Horace-Bénédict DeSaussure*, p. 30.
106. Cited in Freshfield, *Saussure*, p. 79.
107. *Correspondence H/S*, Saussure to Haller, letter 127, late January or early February 1765, p. 201.
108. *Correspondence H/S*, Saussure to Haller, letter 127, late January or early February 1765, p. 201.
109. *Correspondence H/S*, Saussure to Haller, letter 127, late January or early February 1765, p. 201.
110. *Correspondence H/S*, Saussure to Haller, letter 127, late January or early February 1765, p. 201.
111. *Correspondence H/S*, Saussure to Haller, letter 127, late January or early February 1765, p. 202.
112. *Correspondence H/S*, Saussure to Haller, letter 127, late January or early February 1765, p. 202.
113. *Correspondence H/S*, Saussure to Haller, letter 127, late January or early February 1765, p. 202.
114. *Correspondence H/S*, Saussure to Haller, letter 122, 8 September 1764, p. 196. A variant: Saussure to Haller, letter 125, 13 November 1764, p. 199: "Je suis avec la plus profonde respect et le plus entier dévouëment, Monsieur, Votre très humble et très obéissant serviteur H. B. De Saussure."
115. Bonnet to Haller, letter dated 14 May 1765, quoted in *Correspondence H/S*, p. 204 n. 2.
116. *Correspondence H/S*, Saussure to Haller, letter 127, late January or early February 1765, p. 201.
117. *Correspondence H/S*, Haller to Saussure, letter 323, 31 July 1769, p. 428.

118. Hintzsche, "Haller," *DSB*, p. 62: insomnia, probably from his consumption of "inordinate amounts" of tea, was treated with opium, and he became addicted.

119. Tronchin's work as a doctor left little time for exercise. After suffering a severe attack of gout, he had resolved to become more active—to be sure to go out every day and not spend all his time in his office working and receiving patients. He would go riding and to the country. *Correspondence H/S*, Saussure to Haller, letter 89, c. 16 August 1763, p. 158.

120. Carozzi, *Horace-Bénédict de Saussure (1740–1799)*, pp. 307–9, at p. 309. In 1794–95.

121. Walker and Winiger-Labuda, "Saussure et l'architecture," p. 459. They refer to the description given by Saussure's grandson. Carozzi, *Horace-Bénédict de Saussure (1740–1799)*, pp. 167–70, summarizes the account of the collection offered by Jean III Bernoulli in a letter from Geneva of 24 November 1774: *Lettres sur différens sujets . . . 1774 et 1775*, vol. 2, letter 4, pp. 1–7, accessed 10 December 2023, https://gallica.bnf.fr/ark:/12148/bpt6k1074837/f1.double#.

122. On new ways of preserving birds and other animals, see Mary Terrall, *Catching Nature in the Act: Réaumur and the Practice of Natural History in the Eighteenth Century* (Chicago: University of Chicago Press, 2014), pp. 144–53, pp. 146 and 148 for the details given here. On early ways to preserve animals for exhibition and study, see Dániel Margócsy, *Commercial Visions: Science, Trade, and Visual Culture in the Dutch Golden Age* (Chicago: University of Chicago Press, 2014), pp. 112–14.

123. On Pictet and birds, see chap. 2, "The Jura Mountains." On Saussure's bird collecting, see *Voyages*, sec. 284, vol. 1, p. 226.

124. An offshoot of the Société du physique et du d'histoire naturelle.

125. *Lettres de H.-B. de Saussure á sa femme*, letter 8, "From Courmayeur, le vendredi matin 15 juillet 1774," p. 17.

126. Carozzi, "La Méthode de recherché," in *Horace-Bénédict de Saussure (1740–1799)*, p. 18.

127. *Voyages*, sec. 675, vol. 2, pp. 85–86. The reference is to descending the Aiguilles de Chamonix with Pierre Balmat in 1784.

128. Publisher Fauche at Neuchâtel.

129. Explains Vidal, *Sciences of the Soul*, fig. 9.1, p. 335.

130. Paula Radisich, review of the exhibition, *Hvis engle kunne male . . . Jens Juels portraetkunst* (If angels were to paint . . . Jens Juels, portraitist) (6 August–20 October 1996), Det National historiske Museum, Frederiksborg, Denmark, *Eighteenth-Century Studies* 31, no. 1 (Fall 1997): pp. 135–37, at p. 136.

131. Reproduced in Freshfield, *Saussure*, before p. 79.

132. For the two plantings, see Walker and Winiger-Labuda, "Saussure et l'architecture," p. 467. For the impression made by Castle Howard, see Freshfield, *Saussure*, p. 110.

133. "À cette image de la nature domestiquée correspond celle du lac et des montagnes lointaines, que les visiteurs pouvaient apercevoir depuis la galerie." Walker and Winiger-Labuda, "Saussure et l'architecture," p. 466, fig. 8.

134. *Lettres de H.-B. de Saussure á sa femme*, letter 7, 10 July 1774, p. 14.

135. Carozzi suggests these thoughts arise at Genthod. *Horace-Bénðict de Sausure (1740–1799)*, p. 61. For Saussure's comments, see *Voyages*, sec. 2023, vol. 4, p. 215.

136. "Lettres de Madame de Saussure à son mari," "Madame de Saussure à son mari, alors aux glaciers en Savoie, Mercredi à 11 h. du matin," no year or month given, Archives de Saussure 223-3, p. 98.

137. *Lettres de H.-B. de Saussure á sa femme*, letter 1, "Au chalet de Pliampra, á trois mille cinquante pieds au-dessus de Chamouni, le mardi 21 juillet 1767 á 8 h. du matin," p. 2.

138. *Lettres de H.-B. de Saussure á sa femme*, letter 6, "Mortara [in Lombardy], le 6 juillet [1771]," p. 13.

139. *Lettres de H.-B. de Saussure á sa femme*, letter 7, "á Sallanches, ce dimanche 10 juillet (1774), allant au Saint-Bernard seul. . . . ," p. 14.

140. Carozzi, *Horace-Bénédict de Saussure (1740–1799)*, p. 195.

141. *Lettres de H.-B. de Saussure á sa femme*, letter 4, "De Sion le samedi 28 juillet 1770," p. 6.

142. *Lettres de H.-B. de Saussure á sa femme*, letter 19, "A Domodossola ce samedi 30 juillet à 11 h. du soir (1777)," p. 39.

143. *Lettres de H.-B. de Saussure á sa femme*, letter 10, "Tourtemagne ce dimanche après-midi 16 juillet 1775," p. 25.

144. For the description of the hair used, see "L'Invention de l'hygromètre á chevee," in Carozzi, *Horace-Bénédict de Saussure (1740–1799)*, p. 134.

Chapter Five

1. For description of the Buet, see *Voyages*, vol. 1, sec. 549, p. 470; for getting there, see secs. 542–49.

2. "Une ballade touristique et romantique" with his closest friends. Carozzi, *Horace-Bénédict de Saussure*, p. 184.

3. "Hiking—Aiguilles Rouges and Mont Buet," website of the Compagnie des Guides, accessed 17 August 2023, https://www.chamonix-guides.com/en/activities/details/hiking-aiguilles-rouges-and-mont-buet.

4. Grenon, "Les Observations météorologiques et climatiques de Saussure," p. 144. René Sigrist, "Scientific Standards in the 1780s: A Controversy over Hygrometers," in J. L. Heilbron and René Sigrist, *Jean-André Deluc, Historian of Earth and Man* (Geneva: Slatkine, 2011), pp. 148–83.

5. Published in "The Rothorn," in *The Playground of Europe*, pp. 108–9.

6. Recounted in Freshfield, *Saussure*, p. 177; published in 1772.

7. *Voyages*, sec. 551, vol. 1, p. 473.

8. Jean-Michel Pictet, "Jean-André Deluc (1727–1817): Météorologie, géologie, philosophie." In *Les Savants genevois*, p. 398. Rudwick, *Bursting the Limits of Time*, pp. 326–33. Deluc would leave Geneva for England in 1773.

9. Saussure published his *Essais sur l'hygrométrie* in 1783. Discussed in Sigrist, "Scientific Standards in the 1780s," pp. 148–83.

10. Pierre Bouguer, *La Figure de la terre, déterminée par les observations de Messieurs Bouguer et de La Condamine . . . envoyés par ordre du Roy au Pérou, pour observer aux environs de l'équateur. Avec une relation abrégée de ce voyage qui contient la description du pays dans lequel les opérations ont été faites* (Paris, 1749), p. xxxvii, accessed 10 December 2023, https://gallica.bnf.fr/ark:/12148/bpt6k1051288w.

11. On "mountaineers" insisting that "mountain sickness" was "due to a combination of fatigue, cold, bad feeding," see Joseph Barcroft, (1872–1947), "Mountain Sickness," *Nature* 114 (1924): pp. 90–92, https://doi.org/10.1038/114090a0. On Everest and oxygen, see sections of Davis, *Into the Silence*, especially pp. 76–80 on Alexander Kellas (who died on the approach to Everest in 1921) and his research on the body

and altitude. On some of controversy that ensued about using supplemental oxygen in the attempt on Everest, see also pp. 384–91.

12. Carozzi and Bouvier, *The Scientific Library of Horace-Bénédict de Saussure*, p. 159, cat. No. 887. *Voyages*, sec. 559, vol. 1, p. 482, is where Saussure discusses Bouguer in this context.

13. *Voyages*, sec. 559, vol. 1, p. 484.

14. *Voyages*, sec. 559, vol. 1, pp. 482–83.

15. *Voyages*, sec. 559, vol. 1, p. 484.

16. *Voyages*, sec. 561, vol. 1, p. 486.

17. "Astonishingly," as Davis explains, "it was not until 1878 that the actual culprit was identified: a lack of oxygen due to reduced atmospheric pressure at altitude." He continues, "Despite this discovery, wild theories continued to gain notice." Davis, *Into the Silence*, p. 77.

18. *Voyages*, sec. 559, vol. 1, p. 484.

19. *Voyages*, sec. 559, vol. 1, p. 485.

20. *Voyages*, sec. 573, vol. 1, p. 507.

21. *Voyages*, sec. 916, vol. 2, p. 337.

22. *Voyages*, sec. 919, vol. 2, p. 339.

23. *Voyages*, sec. 919, vol. 2, pp. 339–40.

24. *Voyages*, sec. 919. vol. 2, p. 340, and as discussed in earlier chapters.

25. Nicolson, *Mountain Gloom and Mountain Glory*, p. 289. "Shaftesbury's Mountain Rhapsody" was published in *The Moralist*.

26. Étienne Geoffroy Saint-Hilaire, *Études progressives d'un naturaliste pendant les années 1834 et 1835* (Paris: Roret, 1835), quoted in Kete, *Making Way for Genius*, p. 156.

27. *Voyages*, "Discours préliminaire," vol. 1, n.p.

28. *Voyages*, "Discours préliminaire," vol. 1, n.p. "The 'Naturalist' will often doubt whether his spent forces will be enough to take him to the top of a mountain, something he so desires to do, or if the precipices which protect it can be passed. However once climbing, the fresh and bracing air acts as a balm while thoughts of the spectacle which he will enjoy and the new truths that will come from those views, revive his strength and his courage."

29. *Voyages*, "Discours préliminaire," vol. 1, n.p.

30. Rudwick, *Bursting the Limits of Time*. Saussure's "Lectures on Physical Geography" address the planet as a whole.

31. *Le Petit Larousse illustré* (2008), s. v. "dominer," p. 332. The fourth definition reads, "Être en position surélevée par rapport à autre chose."

32. Hansen, *Summits of Modern Man*, p. 62. On imperialism and fascism in contests to summit 8000-meter peaks in the Himalaya, see Isserman and Weaver, *Fallen Giants*. On Everest itself in the 1920s, see Davis, *Into the Silence*.

33. Hansen, *Summits of Modern Man*, pp. 87 and 86.

34. *Voyages*, sec. 569, vol. 1, p. 503.

35. *Voyages*, sec. 578, vol. 1, p. 512.

36. David Ripoll, "L'Iconographie des *Voyages dans les Alpes*," in *Un regard sur la terre*, pp. 315–36; see p. 326 for a similar point, and see pp. 325–31 on Saussure's directing vision of the panorama. On how strictly Saussure guided Bourrit's illustrations, see Carozzi, "Essai sur la personnalité de Horace-Bénédict de Saussure," p. 293.

37. *Voyages*, sec. 565, vol. 1, pp. 497–98.

38. *Voyages*, sec. 565, vol. 1, p. 498.

39. *Voyages*, sec. 565, vol. 1, p. 497.

40. Brian E. Vick, *The Congress of Vienna: Power and Politics after Napoleon* (Cambridge, MA: Harvard University Press, 2014), p. 67.

41. Vick, *The Congress of Vienna*, p. 67.

42. Vick, *The Congress of Vienna*, pp. 73–74 and 69–70.

43. See Michael Brune, "Pulling Down Our Monuments," by executive director of the Sierra Club, published online on 22 July 2020. Brune was executive director of the Sierra Club; the controversy his comments triggered led to his resignation. The "wilderness" Muir worked to protect could be considered empty of humans only if one airbrushed out of history the Native Americans who had been forcibly removed from that land.

44. Quoted in and commented on in Schaumann, *Peak Pursuits*, p. 286.

45. John Muir, *My First Summer in the Sierra* (1911), cited in Schaumann, *Peak Pursuits*, p. 285. Schaumann references John O'Grady (*Pilgrims to the West*, p. 59) for Muir's "'para-human love affair'" with the mountains. Schaumann, *Peak Pursuits*, p. 286.

46. *Voyages*, secs. 885–96, vol. 2, pp. 311–21. Unusually for the *Voyages*, Saussure gives us only the nickname of this guide: he was called "Patience." Graham Brown and De Beer refer to Jean-Laurent Jordanay dit Patience when reporting an attempted ascent of Mont Blanc by Thomas Ford Hill and other guides via the Col du Géant from Courmayeur in September 1786. T. Graham Brown and Gavin De Beer, *First Ascent of Mont Blanc* (London and New York: Oxford University Press, 1957), p. 435.

47. *Voyages*, sec. 895, vol. 2, p. 319.

48. On the Miage Glacier and its history, see Patrizia Imhof, "Glacier Fluctuations in the Italian Mont Blanc Massif from the Little Ice Age until the Present: Historical Reconstructions for the Miage, Brenva, and Pré-de-Bard Glaciers" (master's thesis, Geographisches Institut der Universität Bern, 2010), p. 17.

49. *Voyages*, sec. 889, vol. 2, p. 314.

50. *Voyages*, sec. 890, vol. 2, p. 314.

51. *Voyages*, sec. 892, vol. 2, p. 316.

52. Based on the map on p. 19: "Figure 2: Map showing the outline of the Miage Glacier," in Imhof, "Glacier Fluctuations."

53. *Voyages*, sec. 895, vol. 2, p. 320.

54. Saussure took notes in wax pencil as he observed. He then recopied these rough notes into a journal at night.

55. Gaillard and Montagnier, introduction, *Journal d'un voyage à Chamouni*, p. ii.

56. *Voyages*, sec. 1975, vol. 4, p. 158. Saussure also introduces the term *moraine*. "The peasants of Chamouni call these piles of debris (at the edge of glaciers) *la moraine* of the glacier." *Voyages*, sec. 536, vol. 1, p. 455.

57. *Voyages*, sec. 1102, vol. 2, p. 550. Mont Blanc could not be climbed, Simon concluded.

58. Graham Brown and De Beer, *The First Ascent of Mont Blanc*, p. 64.

59. Graham Brown and De Beer, *The First Ascent of Mont Blanc*, pp. 228–29.

60. Gaillard and Montagnier, introduction, *Journal d'un voyage à Chamouni*, p. ii.

61. *Voyages*, sec. 667, vol. 2, p. 74. The event is described in the previous chapter.

62. Jacques Balmat (of the first ascent with Paccard) would prove that sleeping above the snow line did not lead to death when he had to do so in 1786 during an attempted ascent of Mont Blanc.

63. Also killed were his fellow guides Auguste Tairraz and Pierre Carrier. The Compagnie des Guides also established the Tour de Rôle, which established a sequence of who would guide climbers and when. The establishment of the Company of Guides was a major landmark in the history of Chamonix. It allowed a more equitable relationship of power between climber and guide and reduced the possibility of exploitation.

64. Graham Brown and De Beer, *The First Ascent of Mont Blanc*, p. 32.

65. Graham Brown and De Beer's claim, based on the description offered by the guides in the context of their own experience of climbing Mont Blanc. *The First Ascent of Mont Blanc*, p. 76.

66. Graham Brown and De Beer, *The First Ascent of Mont Blanc*, pp. 79–81. *Voyages*, sec. 1103, vol. 2, p. 551.

67. Graham Brown and De Beer, *The First Ascent of Mont Blanc*, pp. 91–93. *Voyages*, sec. 1103, vol. 2, p. 551.

68. *Voyages*, sec. 1103, vol. 2, p. 552.

69. "Born in Chamonix in 1734 and, when he was 20, he acted as a guide to the well-known highwayman Mandrin." Claire Eliane Engel, "François Paccard and Bourrit," *Alpine Journal* 57, no. 279 (November 1949): pp. 167–71, at p. 167. Freshfield, *Saussure*, p. 200 n. 1. On Mandrin, see Kwass, *Contraband*.

70. Gaillard and Montagnier, introduction, *Journal d'un voyage à Chamouni*, p. xiv.

71. It was the chalet Simon[d]. Gaillard and Montagnier, introduction, *Journal d'un voyage à Chamouni*, p. xiv. For visits in Geneva, see Graham Brown and De Beer, *The First Ascent of Mont Blanc*, p. 65. Freshfield, *Saussure*, p. 221. Samuel Cordier, "Un regard depuis les sommets," in Saussure, *Journal de l'ascension du Mont-Blanc*, p. 65. Saussure in Geneva was asked for advice about visiting the Alps by British and other elite visitors, whom he only occasionally had time to accommodate. The *Voyages* were addressed to an audience presumed to want to follow him to the Alps, though not to the summit of Mont Blanc, an experience of the massif that he made clear was accessible to the very expert few.

72. Gaillard and Montagnier, introduction, *Journal d'un voyage à Chamouni*, p. xii n. 1.

73. *Voyages*, sec. 1104, vol. 2, p. 553.

74. The other group was made up of the guides Joseph Carrier, Jean-Marie Couttet, and Jean-Baptiste Lombard, *dit* Jorasse. For a list of early attempts to summit Mont Blanc, see Graham Brown and De Beer, *The First Ascent of Mont Blanc*, p. 433, and noted elsewhere also.

75. Gaillard and Montagnier, introduction, *Journal d'un voyage à Chamouni*, p. iii.

76. Graham Brown and De Beer describe the "St. Gervais route" in *The First Ascent of Mont Blanc*, pp. 433 and 434. Completed only in 1861, this route's high section goes from Tête Rousse (above the Nid d'Aigle) to the Aiguille du Goûter to the Dôme du Goûter along the Arête des Bosses to the summit. Alas for the fatigue of Saussure's summitting, it was not the route of the first ascents.

77. Saussure's letter to the Prince de Ligne, 26 September 1785, reproduced in Freshfield, *Saussure*, p. 206.

78. Carozzi completes the names of Saussure's group of friends who accompanied him on the third *tour du Mont Blanc* in 1778 (11 July–5 August): "Marc-Auguste Pictet, Jean Trembley, Albert Turrettini et Isaac Budé de Boisy, along with two servants (Gédéon et François)." Carozzi, *Horace-Benedict de Saussure (1740–1799)*, p. 178.

79. *Voyages*, sec. 1112, vol. 2, p. 563.

80. *Voyages*, sec. 1112, vol. 2, p. 562.
81. On the son being sick in the night and the father's fur-lined boots being inadequate for the climb, see *Voyages*, sec. 1119, vol. 2, p. 573.
82. Saussure's letter to the Prince de Ligne, 26 September 1785, in Freshfield, *Saussure*, p. 207.
83. "The common use of the rope on all climbing expeditions above the snow-line spread from its origin at Chamonix, and not from the Oberland; and the birth of that technique at this attempt in 1785 was the only valuable outcome of the expedition." Graham Brown and De Beer, *The First Ascent of Mont Blanc*, p. 125:
84. *Voyages*, sec. 1119, vol. 2, p. 572; Saussure's footnote.
85. Freshfield, *Saussure*, p. 204.
86. *Voyages*, sec. 1108, vol. 2, p. 559.
87. *Voyages*, sec. 1109, vol. 2, p. 559. The exact elevation was 2701 meters (recorded as 1422 toises) above sea level, approximately 1710 meters (recorded as 900 toises) above the valley of Chamonix.
88. The rushed thermometer was the work of the Genevan instrument maker Jacques Paul.
89. *Voyages*, sec. 1111, vol. 2, p. 561.
90. *Voyages*, sec. 1111, vol. 2, p. 561.
91. *Voyages*, sec. 1111, vol. 2, p. 562: "et que je voyois son cadavre étendu sous mes pieds." That the phrase "sous mes pieds" means the space spread below him under the heights he looking down from is clear from the context and as used in earlier paragraphs. Hansen, for instance, translates this as "at my feet" and understands the expression as meaning that Saussure was positing himself as "master of the universe." Hansen, *Summits of Modern Man*, p. 80.
92. Quoted in Glacken, *Traces on the Rhodian Shore*, p. 7.
93. *Voyages*, sec. 355, vol. 1, p. 289, chap. 15, "La Dôle."

Chapter Six

1. 1790. Kant, *Critique of Judgment*, 95. I have modified the translation, substituting "had" for "got" and making other changes. On mountains and the sublime, begin with Nicolson, *Mountain Gloom and Mountain Glory*.
2. Cordier, "Saussure, un regard depuis les sommets," in Saussure, *Journal de l'ascension du Mont-Blanc*, ed. Fauche and Cordier, p. 25.
3. *Voyages*, sec. 673, vol. 2, p. 80.
4. *Voyages*, sec. 685, vol. 2, pp. 82–84.
5. Gaillard and Montagnier, introduction, *Journal d'un voyage à Chamouni*, p. xiii n. 1, continued from p. xii. This is the first published edition of Saussure's *Journal* covering the ascent and its immediate preparation. The second is Fauche and Cordier's, referenced in n. 2. Both versions are used here for their excellent introductions, notes, and other essays.
6. Gaillard and Montagnier, introduction, *Journal d'un voyage à Chamouni*, pp. xii–xiii n. 1. Bourrit told the story to Antoinette Bérenger, the wife of the historian and democrat Jean-Pierre Bérenger, who wrote about it to a Mme. Roget (possibly the mother of Peter Mark Roget, of *Thesaurus* fame).
7. Jerry Lovatt, "Thomas Ford Hill: An Alpine Footnote," *Alpine Journal* 99, no. 343 (1994): pp. 38–40. Based on Hill's manuscript diary, in private hands. The guide is not

named in either this or the *Journal*. For Hill's exploration of a route to the summit of Mont Blanc in September 1786, see Graham Brown and De Beer, *The First Ascent of Mont Blanc*, p. 435. Described as "Mr. Hill" by Bourrit.

8. Moore, *A View of Society and Manners*, vol. 1, p. 201.

9. Montagnier, "Thomas Blaikie and Michel-Gabriel Paccard," p. 23. Graham Brown and De Beer, *The First Ascent of Mont Blanc*, appendixes, "Mont Blanc: Attempts and Ascents, 1762–1854," p. 433. Blaikie, *Diary of a Scotch Gardener*, p. 78.

10. Hansen, *Summits of Modern Man*, pp. 70–71.

11. Graham Brown and De Beer, *The First Ascent of Mont Blanc*, p. 28. Gaillard and Montagnier, introduction, in *Journal d'un voyage à Chamouni*, p. vii: "very probable" that he had discovered the route independently of Balmat.

12. Graham Brown and De Beer, *The First Ascent of Mont Blanc*, p. 28.

13. Graham Brown and De Beer, *The First Ascent of Mont Blanc*, p. 73.

14. Graham Brown and De Beer, *The First Ascent of Mont Blanc*, p. 28.

15. On 8 June 1786 Joseph Carrier, François Paccard, and Jean-Michel Tournier met up with Pierre Balmat and J.-M. Couttet, who had left from St. Gervais, trying the route from there. Balmat's unpopularity is noted in Graham Brown and De Beer, *The First Ascent of Mont Blanc*, p. 122.

16. *Voyages*, sec. 1964, vol. 4, p. 139.

17. *Voyages*, sec. 1965, vol. 4, p. 140.

18. *Voyages*, sec. 1965, vol. 4, p. 140.

19. Saussure, "Relation abrégée d'un voyage à la cime du Mont-Blanc, en août 1787" (first published soon after the ascent), in *Voyages*, vol. 4, pp. 141–49, at p. 145.

20. Pierre Charmoz (pseudonym for Pierre Laurendeau) and Jean-Louis Lejonc, *Sherlock Holmes à Chamonix: Enquêtes sur la mort de Whymper et sur la première ascension du mont Blanc* (Paris: Ginkgo noir, 2008).

21. Jacques Balmat was not considered a guide, at least until after the ascent. He had not worked as one and was not welcomed by the Chamoniards.

22. Details of timing and the basic narrative of the ascent are taken from the reconstruction in Graham Brown and De Beer, *The First Ascent of Mont Blanc*, pp. 29–42. Other specifics are referenced below.

23. Graham Brown and De Beer, *The First Ascent of Mont Blanc*, p. 31.

24. Graham Brown and De Beer, *The First Ascent of Mont Blanc*, p. 25.

25. Graham Brown and De Beer, *The First Ascent of Mont Blanc*, p. 38.

26. Graham Brown and De Beer, *The First Ascent of Mont Blanc*, p. 46.

27. Letter to the Prince de Ligne dated 26 September 1785, quoted in Freshfield, *Saussure*, p. 208. Philip Mansel, *Prince of Europe: The Life of Charles-Joseph de Ligne, 1735–1814* (London: Weidenfeld & Nicolson, 2003), does not mention Saussure, even though their paths might have crossed in Lyons in 1784 or in Geneva or at Ferney.

28. On Bonnet and Conches, see Freshfield, *Saussure*, 341. On Rosalie Constant, see Constant, "Journal de l'enfance de M. le baron de Constant de Rebecque General au service de Hollande par sa sœur Mademoiselle Rosalie de Constant," book 5, p. 68. *Archives de la famille de Constant*, Ms suppl. 1494.

29. Letter to Faujas de Saint-Fond, quoted in Freshfield, *Saussure*, p. 341. On the letter and on his interest in balloons, see Carozzi, *Horace-Bénédict de Saussure (1744–1799)*, pp. 221–22.

30. Letter to the Prince de Ligne, 26 September 1785, quoted in Freshfield, *Saussure*, p. 208.

31. *Lettres de H.-B. de Saussure à sa femme*, p. 83, letter 55 from the Col du Géant, 17 July 1788: "Ce n'est pas ma santé qui m'en empêche, car jamais je ne me suis mieux porté."

32. Saussure, *Journal de l'ascension du Mont-Blanc*, ed. Fauche and Cordier, p. 99: Saussure's entry of Sunday, 29 July. Saussure had been purging for more than ten years.

33. The letter is reproduced in Saussure, *Journal d'un voyage à Chamouni et à la cime du Mont Blanc*, ed. Gaillard and Montagnier, pp. vii–ix.

34. Letter reproduced in Saussure, *Journal d'un voyage à Chamouni et à la cime du Mont Blanc*, ed. Gaillard and Montagnier, introduction, quotations p. viii.

35. Cook's Second Voyage. Saussure notes that "M. Hugues le dessinateur Anglais qui a fait le tour du monde avec le capitaine Cook" came by to see him on the evening of 26 July. This must have been William Hodges (1744–1797). Saussure, *Journal de l'ascension du Mont-Blanc*, ed. Fauche and Cordier, p. 95, Saussure's entry for 26 July.

36. Saussure, *Journal de l'ascension du Mont-Blanc*, ed. Fauche and Cordier, p. 81 eds. note 13, Saussure's entry for 11 July.

37. Also, one of Saturn's moons. William Herschel will see this in his telescope two years later, in 1789. It will not be named until 1847.

38. Quoted in Freshfield, *Saussure*, p. 235. Hansen, *Summits of Modern Man*, pp. 102–3, quotes longer passages from *Mélanges: Extraits des manuscrits de Mme. Necker* (Paris, 1798), vol. 2, pp. 180–81.

39. Hansen, *Summits of Modern Man*, p. 102.

40. Clare Roche, "Women Climbers, 1850–1900: A Challenge to Male Hegemony?," *Sport in History* 33, no. 3 (September 2013): pp. 236–59, DOI: 10.1080/17460263.2013 .826437. The title of Roche, "Enabling Women: The Influence of the Alpine Environment," paper presented to the 2013 Rural History Conference, Bern, suggests this welcome theme. Ann C. Colley, "Ladies on High," in *Victorians in the Mountains: Sinking the Sublime* (Burlington, VT: Ashgate, 2010), is another possible source. Online references are given below.

41. "Lady Legends of the Alps"/"Mon excursion au Mont Blanc," online posting by professional women guides, members of the Compagnie des Guides de Chamonix, 28 March 2019, accessed 6 February 2020, https://chamonixallyear.com/lady-legends -women-in-mountaineering.

42. "Lady Legends of the Alps." Claude Gardien, 6 June 2015, "Jean-Esteril Charlet and Mary Isabella Straton: A Fairy Tale," *Alpinist* 50 (Summer 2015), posted 6 June 2015, accessed 27 July 2023, http://www.alpinist.com/doc/ALP50/77-mountain -profile-the-aguille-du-drus-1871-1925.

43. Ed Douglas, *Himalaya: A Human History* (New York: Norton, 2021), p. 362.

44. Mary Mummery, "The Teufelsgrat," in Albert Mummery, *My Climbs in the Alps and Caucasus*, pp. 45–65, at p. 46.

45. Zermatt/Matterhorn: The Täschhorn, accessed 10 December 2023, https:// www.zermatt.ch/en/Media/Attractions/Taeschhorn.

46. Quoted by Rosemary Raughter in "Elizabeth (Lizzie) Le Blond: Alpinist, Photographer and Author," entry in the online/virtual Women's Museum of Ireland, accessed 27 July 2023, https://www.womensmuseumofireland.ie/exhibits/lizzie-le -blond.

47. "Lady Legends of the Alps."

48. Leslie Stephen, *The Playground of Europe*, is a book of essays on his climbs in the Alps, first published in 1871.

49. Mentioned in a letter from Antoinette Bérenger to a friend, cited in n. 6. Gaillard and Montagnier, introduction to Saussure, *Journal d'un voyage à Chamouni*, pp. xii–xiii n. 1.

50. "Hiking—Aiguilles Rouges and Mont Buet," website of the Compagnie des Guides de Chamonix, accessed 6 February 2020, https://www.chamonix-guides.com/en/activities/details/hiking-aiguilles-rouges-and-mont-buet.

51. Saussure, *Journal de l'ascension du Mont-Blanc*, ed. Fauche and Cordier, p. 87: Saussure's entry for 18 July.

52. Saussure, *Journal de l'ascension du Mont-Blanc*, ed. Fauche and Cordier, pp. 96–97: Saussure's entry for Saturday, 28 July.

53. Saussure, *Journal de l'ascension du Mont-Blanc*, ed. Fauche and Cordier, p. 84: Saussure's entry for 15 July.

54. Saussure, *Journal de l'ascension du Mont-Blanc*, ed. Fauche and Cordier, p. 84: Saussure's entry for 17 July.

55. *Lettres de H.-B. de Saussure à sa femme*. For instance: promises "to return to her for always": letter 9, 24 July 1774, p. 23; promises to "never make such long trips without her": letter 15, 2 August 1775, p. 32.

56. Freshfield, *Saussure*, p. 100.

57. On Blosset, James Lee, and Banks, see Holmes, *The Age of Wonder*, p. 11.

58. Quoted in Freshfield, *Saussure*, p. 105. In Arch. de Saussure 26: "Journal du 'Grand Tour' à Paris, en Hollande et en Angleterre de février à septembre 1768."

59. Freshfield, *Saussure*, p. 108.

60. Lady Mary Coke's *Journals*, 11 August 1771 quoted in Freshfield, *Saussure*, p. 108, and summarized in Holmes, *The Age of Wonder*, p. 12. Holmes says they were "patterned with wildflowers." They were presumably very nice.

61. Saussure, *Journal de l'ascension du Mont-Blanc*, ed. Fauche and Cordier, p. 101: Saussure's entry for 31 July.

62. Saussure, "Relation abrégéé d'un voyage à la cime du Mont-Blanc, en août 1787," in *Voyages*, vol. 4, p. 142.

63. Saussure, "Relation abrégéé d'un voyage à la cime du Mont-Blanc, en août 1787," in *Voyages*, vol. 4, p. 142.

64. Gaillard and Montagnier, introduction, in *Journal d'un voyage à Chamouni*, pp. xiv–xv. They reference Charles Bourrit's "Journal."

65. Graham Brown and De Beer, *The First Ascent of Mont Blanc*, p. 129. On Paccard's impressive accomplishments in medicine, botany, and natural history, see Hansen, *Summits of Modern Man*, pp. 68–72.

66. Graham Brown and De Beer, *The First Ascent of Mont Blanc*, p. 175.

67. Saussure's entry for 22 March 1786. Translated in Graham Brown and De Beer, *The First Ascent of Mont Blanc*, pp. 175–78. The French text is given on pp. 388–90.

68. Graham Brown and De Beer, *The First Ascent of Mont Blanc*, pp. 173–74.

69. Freshfield, *Saussure*, pp. 201 and 223. Saussure's *Journal* entries for 20 August and 22 August 1786 are reproduced in *The First Ascent of Mont Blanc*, pp. 387–88.

70. For a discussion of Saussure's trip to the St. Gotthard pass in 1783, see Carozzi, *Horace-Bénédict de Saussure*, p. 218.

71. Sources for this are slight, though accepted. Hansen, *Summits of Modern Man*, p. 99. Graham Brown and De Beer, *The First Ascent of Mont Blanc*, pp. 230–35. Saussure, *Journal d'un voyage à Chamouni*, ed. Gaillard and Montagnier, p. 36 eds. n. 14.

72. His first name is identified in Graham Brown and De Beer, *The First Ascent of Mont Blanc*, p. 7.

73. Each edition of Saussure's journal—*Journal d'un voyage à Chamouni et à la cime du Mont Blanc* and *Journal de l'ascension du Mont-Blanc*—includes a list of the items taken along by Saussure on the ascent.

74. Hansen, *Summits of Modern Man*, pp. 101–2: Each guide received "5 louis (120 livres) as payment" upon his return from Mont Blanc. Hansen cites the report of the intendant of Faucigny on this welcome infusion of cash into the economy of Chamonix.

75. They summited on 5 July 1787. It was the second ascent of Mont Blanc (after that the rains began). Saussure and his family left Geneva for Chamonix on 7 July.

76. Saussure, "Relation abrégéé d'un voyage à la cime du Mont-Blanc, en août 1787," in *Voyages*, vol. 4, p. 142. The list of guides is given by Saussure in a footnote.

77. Drawn by a Genevan artist for an edition of Saussure's *Relation abrégée d'un voyage à la cime du Mont-Blanc, en août 1787*. The *Relation abrégée* appears in vol. 4 of the *Voyages* without the illustrations. Hansen, *Summits of Modern Man*, p. 110 n. 56.

78. *Voyages*, sec. 1978, vol. 4, p. 161.

79. For the quote about the bed, see Saussure, *Journal de l'ascension du Mont-Blanc*, ed. Fauche and Cordier, p. 80 eds. n. 9. On the books owned by Saussure, see Carozzi and Bouvier, *The Scientific Library of Horace-Bénédict de Saussure*: sec. 2, items 185–333, "Natural History Travels," pp. 82–96, and sec. 5, items 459–561, "Travels—Geography," pp. 112–22.

80. Saussure, *Journal de l'ascension du Mont-Blanc*, ed. Fauche and Cordier, p. 109.

81. *Voyages*, sec. 1973, vol. 4, p. 157.

82. Saussure, "Relation abrégéé d'un voyage à la cime du Mont-Blanc, en août 1787," in *Voyages*, vol. 4, p. 145: "c'est le séjour du froid et du silence."

83. Saussure, *Journal de l'ascension du Mont-Blanc*, ed. Fauche and Cordier, sec. 29, p. 119. Once the ascent began on 1 August, Saussure labeled his entries by section number.

84. Saussure, *Journal de l'ascension du Mont-Blanc*, ed. Fauche and Cordier, sec. 25, p. 117.

85. Saussure, *Journal de l'ascension du Mont-Blanc*, ed. Fauche and Cordier, sec. 25, p. 118: "Avalanche et grand bruit entre minuit et une heure."

86. Saussure, "Relation abrégéé d'un voyage à la cime du Mont-Blanc, en août 1787," in *Voyages*, vol. 4, pp. 145–46.

87. Saussure, *Journal de l'ascension du Mont-Blanc*, ed. Fauche and Cordier, sec. 25, p. 118: "je me lève 'a 2h. 15. Je sors de la tente, coup d'œil superbe. . . ." The "Relation abrégée d'un voyage à la cime du Mont-Blanc" reports the avalanche as happening after Saussure's view of the snowfield in the moonlight. Saussure, *Voyages*, vol. 4, p. 145.

88. Freshfield's translation. In Freshfield, *Saussure*, p. 230.

89. Saussure, *Journal de l'ascension du Mont-Blanc*, ed. Fauche and Cordier, sec. 29, p. 119.

90. Saussure, *Journal de l'ascension du Mont-Blanc*, ed. Fauche and Cordier, sec. 32, pp. 121–22.

91. *Voyages*, sec. 1991, vol. 4, p. 175.

92. *Voyages*, sec. 1991, vol. 4, p. 175.

93. *Voyages*, sec. 1991. vol. 4, p. 175.

94. *Voyages*, sec. 1991, vol. 4, p. 175: "à ce voyage."

95. Saussure, *Journal de l'ascension du Mont-Blanc*, ed. Fauche and Cordier, p. 131: "Forme de la cime," no. 6 in his section labeled "Geology."

96. *Voyages*, sec. 1991, vol. 4, p. 175 n. 1: "*Pedibus submissa vicissim Opteritur*. Lucret." Saussure closes the quote and omits the ending—"and makes us equal to the heavens"—which in any case does not suit the mood of exhaustion and disappointment he describes for that moment.

97. *Voyages*, sec. 1991, vol. 4, p. 175.

98. *Voyages*, sec. 2002, vol. 4, p. 186.

99. *Voyages*, sec. 1991, vol. 4, p. 176.

100. Saussure, "Relation abrégéé d'un voyage à la cime du Mont-Blanc, en août 1787," in *Voyages*, vol. 4, p. 147.

101. Saussure, *Journal de l'ascension du Mont-Blanc*, ed. Fauche and Cordier, pp. 133–41: Agenda, His section labeled "Observations et expériences mêlées."

102. Saussure, *Journal de l'ascension du Mont-Blanc*, ed. Fauche and Cordier, pp. 133–34: Agenda, "Observations et expériences mêlées," no. 3. Grenon, "Les Observations météorologiques et climatiques de Saussure," in *Un regard sur la terre*, pp. 141–57, at p. 150. Anne Fauche, "Un éclairage sur les observations et mesures citée dans le *Journal*," in Saussure, *Journal de l'ascension du Mont-Blanc*, ed. Fauche and Cordier, pp. 157–88, at p. 180.

103. Grenon, "Les Observations météorologiques et climatiques de Saussure," p. 150. Fauche, "Un éclairage sur les observations et mesures citée dans le *Journal*," p. 180.

104. Saussure, *Journal de l'ascension du Mont-Blanc*, ed. Fauche and Cordier, p. 134: Agenda, "Observations et expériences mêlées," nos. 4, 5, and 7.

105. Fauche and Fischer, "The Skies of Mont Blanc," p. 6.

106. Saussure, *Journal de l'ascension du Mont-Blanc*, ed. Fauche and Cordier, p. 136: Agenda, "Observations et expériences mêlées," no. 23.

107. Fauche and Fischer, "The Skies of Mont Blanc," p. 5.

108. Fauche and Fischer, "The Skies of Mont Blanc," p. 5. Grenon, "Les Observations météorologiques et climatiques de Saussure," p. 147.

109. Fauche, "Un éclairage sur les observations et mesures citée dans le *Journal*," p. 174.

110. "Publisher's Note to Patrick Syme's *Werner's Nomenclature of Colours, with additions, arranged so as to render it highly useful to the arts and sciences particularly zoology, botany, chemistry, mineralogy, and morbid anatomy*, 2nd ed. (Edinburgh, 1821; London: Natural History Museum, 2018), n.p.

111. Saussure, *Journal de l'ascension du Mont-Blanc*, ed. Fauche and Cordier, p. 135: Agenda, "Observations et expériences mêlées," no. 21.

112. Saussure, *Journal de l'ascension du Mont-Blanc*, ed. Fauche and Cordier, p. 137: Agenda, "Observations et expériences mêlées," no. 34.

113. Saussure, *Journal de l'ascension du Mont-Blanc*, ed. Fauche and Cordier, p. 136: Agenda, "Observations et expériences mêlées," no. 34.

114. Saussure, *Journal de l'ascension du Mont-Blanc*, ed. Fauche and Cordier, p. 136: Agenda, "Observations et expériences mêlées," no. 34: "J'étais comme un gourmet invité à un superbe festin et qu'un dégoût extrême empêche d'en profiter."

115. Graham Brown and De Beer, appendixes, "Mont Blanc: Attempts and Ascents, 1762–1854," in *The First Ascent of Mont Blanc*, p. 435.

116. For Beaufoy's summiting, see Graham Brown and De Beer, *The First Ascent*

of Mont Blanc, pp. 7–8. Beaufoy became "a prominent astronomer": Rudwick, *Bursting the Limits of Time*, p. 21. In an appendix, Graham Brown and De Beer list some eighty-eight attempts and ascents of Mont Blanc between Saussure's on 3 August 1787 and 1855, when the so-called golden age of alpinism begins, and British dominance is marked by the establishment of the Alpine Club in 1857. *The First Ascent of Mont Blanc*, pp. 435–42.

117. *Voyages*, sec. 2024, vol. 4, p. 216.

118. Measurement given by Compagnie des Guides de Chamonix, accessed 28 July 2023, https://www.chamonix-seminaires.com/customized-activities/high-mountain-discovery/randonnee-col-du-geant-3-466m.

119. *Voyages*, sec. 2025, vol. 4, p. 218.

120. *Voyages*, sec. 2025, vol. 4, p. 218.

121. *Voyages*, sec. 2025, vol. 4, p. 217.

122. *Voyages*, sec. 2028, vol. 4, p. 219.

123. *Voyages*, sec. 2028, vol. 4, p. 220.

124. For the storm: *Voyages*, sec. 2031, vol. 4, p. 222. For the cold: *Voyages*, sec. 2032, vol. 4, p. 224.

125. *Voyages*, sec. 2032, vol. 4, p. 224.

126. *Voyages*, sec. 2033, vol. 4, p. 225.

127. *Voyages*, sec. 2033, vol. 4, p. 225.

128. Seamus Heaney, "The Government of the Tongue," in *The Government of the Tongue: Selected Prose, 1978–1987* (New York: Farrar, Straus & Giroux, 1988), pp. 91–108, at p. 93.

129. *Voyages*, sec. 2033, vol. 4, p. 225.

Chapter Seven

1. Paul Guichonnet, Dominique Perrotta, and Jean de Senarclens, eds., *Encyclopédie de Genève*, vol. 1, *Le Pays de Genève* (Geneva: Société genevoise d'utilité publique, 1982), pp. 102–3. Includes a "Carte du Département du Léman," p. 102.

2. On Napoleon's three-day stay in Geneva, see Freshfield, *Saussure*, p. 394.

3. David A. Bell, *Men on Horseback: The Power of Charisma in the Age of Revolution* (New York: Farrar, Straus & Giroux, 2020), p. 15.

4. Bell, *Men on Horseback*, p. 15, says that a "warhorse . . . could weigh as much as twelve hundred pounds." As he explains (p. 126), Napoleon "seems to blend into the sublime natural landscape that the painting depicts and to command the very wind."

5. The Alpine Convention, "Who We Are." The eight countries are Austria, France, Germany, Italy, Switzerland, Liechtenstein, Slovenia, and Monaco, accessed 10 December 2023, https://www.alpconv.org/en/home/organisation/contracting-parties/.

6. The Alpine Convention, "Guiding Principles for Sustainable Life in the Alps."

7. The Alpine Convention, "Preamble."

8. Glacken, *Traces on the Rhodian Shore*, p. 576. Glacken discusses the influence of classical ideas on Montesquieu's climate theory, pp. 576 ff.

9. *Voyages*, sec. 439, vol. 1, pp. 363–64.

10. *Voyages*, sec. 436, vol. 1, p. 361.

11. Julie Boch, who cites this anecdote, sees Saussure through the prism of Rousseau. Boch, "L'Anecdote dans les *Voyages dans les Alpes*," in *Un regard sur la terre*, pp. 337–50.

12. *Voyages*, sec. 733, vol. 2, pp. 144–45.

13. The Compagnie des Guides de Chamonix (established in 1821) became a model for corporations of guides elsewhere in the Alps, and later in the century.

14. Discussed earlier in chapter 3 on the Arve.

15. The letter is reproduced in Saussure, *Journal d'un voyage à Chamouni et à la cime du Mont Blanc*, ed. Gaillard and Montagnier, p. viii.

16. Jean-Daniel Candaux, "Les Réseaux d'un enquêteur: Saussure et ses correspondants," in *Un regard sur la terre*, pp. 249–58, at p. 253.

17. Candaux, "Les Réseaux d'un enquêteur," p. 253. The letter is dated 6 July 1775.

18. Freshfield, *Saussure*, p. 71. On Saussure and patois, Freshfield quotes from Marc-Théodore Bourrit, *Description des aspects du Mont-Blanc (1776)* (Whitefish, MT: Kessinger, 2010).

19. *Voyages*, sec. 736, vol. 2, p. 152.

20. Quoted in Hansen, *Summits of Modern Man*, page111.

21. In a first draft of "The Descent," Saussure is shown being lowered down the slope by two guides, each holding the end of a rope wrapped around Saussure's plumper middle. This is the technique signaled by Graham Brown and De Beer as evidence that the "use of the rope" in alpinism was first developed by Savoy guides. We also see Saussure's nailed boots, since he is sliding in the snow with his legs up, in a cartoonish manner, which must partly explain his rejection of that memorial of his climb.

22. The Constitution of 1794, "une Constitution protestante," in the words of Etienne Salomon Reybaz (1737–1804), who deplored the decision. Reybaz was one of the Genevan exiles from the democratic upheavals of 1782 who formed themselves around Mirabeau and who in 1794 was the Genevan Republic's representative in Paris. Guichonnet and Paul Waeber, "Revolutions et Restauration," in Guichonnet, *Histoire de Genève*, pp. 255–98, quote at pp. 260–61. On the Genevan exiles forming the "atelier de Mirabeau," see Whatmore, *Against War and Empire*, p. 14. On debates on freedom of religion and the Protestant identity of the state leading up to the Constitution, see Golay, *Quand le people devint roi*, pp. 411–13.

23. Candaux, "Les Réseaux d'un enquêteur," p. 250. He traveled to Italy in 1771, in 1772–73 (with his wife, when he climbed Mt. Etna), in 1780, and in passing.

24. In the *Voyages*, Murith is described as someone who "loves and cultivates with much success the study of natural history." *Voyages*, sec. 990, vol. 2, p. 448. On the correspondence, see Candaux, "Les Réseaux d'un enquêteur," p. 254.

25. Candaux, "Les Réseaux d'un enquêteur," p. 257.

26. Candaux, "Les Réseaux d'un enquêteur," p. 257.

27. Golay, "Un paratonnerre pour l'arbre de la liberté," in Carozzi, Crettaz, and Ripoll, *Les Plis du temps*, pp. 155–200, at p. 157.

28. Quoted in Carozzi, *Horace-Bénédict de Saussure (1740–1799)*, p. 295.

29. Golay, "Un paratonnerre pour l'arbre de la liberté," 187.

30. On this, see Charles Magnin and Marco Marcacci, "Le Projet de réforme du Collège (1774): Entre instruction publique, politique et économie," in *Un regard sur la terre*, pp. 409–30.

31. Saussure quoted and summarized Magnin and Marcacci, "Le Projet de réforme du Collège," pp. 420–21.

32. "Some hundreds of thousands of watches were produced each year in workshops of some 800 masters and 4000 workers, constituting the *Fabrique* [of Geneva]."

Jean-Daniel Candaux and René Sigrist, "Saussure et la Société des Arts," in *Un regard sur la terre*, pp. 431–52, at p. 431.

33. Candaux and Sigrist, "Saussure et la Société des Arts," p. 431.

34. Golay, "Un paratonnerre pour l'arbre de la liberté," p. 161.

35. Golay, "Un paratonnerre pour l'arbre de la liberté," p. 162.

36. In February 1790. Golay, "Un paratonnerre pour l'arbre de la liberté," p. 163.

37. Magnin and Marcacci, "Le Projet de réforme du Collège," p. 428.

38. Bringing the summer population up to about 130,000, including about 10,000 year-round residents and 20,000 seasonal workers. Paige McClanahan notes that "the narrow Chamonix Valley attracts 4.3 million visitors a year" ("Overcrowded and More Dangerous, Mont-Blanc Faces a Crisis," *New York Times*, 26 July 2019).

39. The creation of the *tour du Mont Blanc* as a *grande randonnée* dates to 1955. Source: *La Compagnie des Guides de Chamonix Mont Blanc*, booklet *(livret)* (n.d. [2018]).

40. On the exclusivity of St. Moritz and how the developers advertise it as such, see Barton, "St Moritz," in *Healthy Living in the Alps*, pp. 37–65. On Zermatt, Coolidge notes that Saussure "was the first genuine traveler to visit" it, and that that was in 1789. Coolidge, *The Alps in Nature and History*, p. 212. Freshfield does note that a collector for Haller had been to Zermatt at some point. Freshfield, *Saussure*, p. 280.

41. On the ascent of 1861, see Graham Brown and De Beer, *The First Ascent of Mont Blanc*, p. 135.

42. Information from chamonet.com: Ellie Mahoney, "Mont-Blanc Route Kit Requirements Enforced: New By-Law Lists Minimum Equipment List with Immediate Effect," 17 August 2017, updated 21 August 2017.

43. "Une randonneuse dans le fameux 'couloir de Goûter, sur la 'la voie Royale' pour gravir le Mont Blanc, en août 2017," photograph © Philippe Desmazes/AFP. France INFO/France 3 Regions: Auvergne-Rhône-Alps/Haute-Savoie/Chamonix-Mont-Blanc. Cecilia Sanchez, "Permis pour gravir le Mont-Blanc: que sait-on des 'brigades blanches' qui seront chargées du contrôle?," 5 September 2018, updated 12 June 2020, accessed 7 September 2023, https://france3-regions.francetvinfo.fr/auvergne-rhone-alpes/haute-savoie/chamonix/permis-gravir-mont-blanc-que-sait-on-brigades-blanches-qui-seront-chargees-du-controle-1535796.html.

44. Chamonet.com reporting from regional newspapers.

45. "*La Chamoniarde* is the Chamonix-based mountain rescue and awareness organization. Its mission is to provide daily information about conditions in the alpine, and promote safety and reduce accidents in the mountains." Their translation is from their brochure, "Caution, High MOUNTAIN!/Attention Haute MONTAGNE!" (n.d. [2018])

46. La Chamoniarde, "Climbing Mont Blanc, a Mountaineer's Concern/L'Ascension du Mont Blanc, une affaire d'alpiniste" (n.d. [2018]).

47. Leslie Stephen, "Alpine Dangers," *Alpine Journal* 2 (1865–66): pp. 273–85, at p. 274, quoted in McNee, *The New Mountaineer*, p. 39. Albert Mummery notes how commonplace this phrase was; see "The Grépon," in *My Climbs in the Alps and Caucasus*, p. 113. A. Mummery is credited with the first ascent of the Aiguille du Grépon in 1881: he climbed it with Lily Bristow in 1893. This was the first ascent of the peak by a woman.

48. Étienne Bruhl, quoted in "Lady Legends of the Alps."

49. Freshfield, *Saussure*, p. 210. He is wondering why Chamoniards (in June 1786) stop at the Arête des Bosses. Why did they think it too dangerous—too narrow and steep—to attempt?

50. "Le Mont Blanc, objet de consommation?," subsection of La Chamoniarde, "Climbing Mont Blanc, a Mountaineer's Concern/L'Ascension du Mont Blanc, une affaire d'alpiniste," n.p.

51. As of 9 July 2019, he had had 573,000 views, accessed 9 July 2019, https://www.facebook.com/kilianjornet/videos/live-from-mont-blanc-summitsalomon-running-suunto/10154485452705178/.

52. The mayor of St. Gervais referred to the Kilian effect in arguing for regulating access to Mont Blanc. Beginning in 2019 a quasi–quota system was set in place. Pre-registration to sleep in the refuges along the "normal way" was required, and, more controversially, a prison sentence time of two years and a fine of 300,000 euros were established for those camping or bivouacking on the slopes. Arrêté préfectoral du 31 mai 2019 and "communiqué de presse du 31 mai 2019." Links on the site Refuge du Goûter, Fédération Française des clubs alpins et de montagne (FFCAM), accessed June 2019, https://montblanc.ffcam.fr/index.php?_lang=GB&alias=home&_lang=FR&_setlang=1.

53. "Le Mont Blanc, une récompense d'alpiniste!," subsection of La Chamoniarde, "Climbing Mont Blanc, A Mountaineer's Concern/L'Ascension du Mont Blanc, une affaire d'alpiniste," n.p.

54. "Le Mont Blanc, objet de consommation?," n.p. The mayor of Chamonix, Eric Fournier, worried that the quota system set in place through the agency of the mayor of St. Gervais would mean more "traffic" on the even riskier routes. However, he agrees about the danger and speaks of maintaining the "nobility" of the mountain.

55. Guichonnet, "Mont-Blanc: Conquête de l'imaginaire," in *Mont-Blanc: Conquête de l'imaginaire*, p. 16.

56. This is happening throughout the alpine region. On the massif, major landslides occurred on the north face of the Aiguille du Midi in 2018 and in August 2023. The Planpincieux Glacier on the Grand Jorasses peak facing Courmayeur seemed on the verge of collapse in 2019 and 2020, forcing evacuations of the hamlet below. The Chamoniards posted warnings in August 2023 to climbers about the collapse of snow bridges and crevasses and the deterioration of the "normal way" up Mont Blanc. The glaciers too "are suffering." Accessed 21 August 2023, https://www.chamoniarde.com/en/mountain-topics/mountain-conditions#GynmBu7JzAxRLaiMN.

57. The *Voyages dans les Alpes, précédés d'un Essai sur l'histoire naturelle des environs de Genève* was published in four volumes; see chap. 1, n. 78. Why the printing shifts from Neuchâtel to Geneva and back to Neuchâtel is the subject of Michel Schlup, "Les *Voyages dans les Alpes* (1779–1796): Une édition disputée entre libraires neuchâtelois et genevois," in *Un regard sur la terre*, pp. 367–83. The *Voyages* were issued by the same publishers in a smaller and cheaper format in eight volumes. One can also find the Genevan vol. 2 published under the imprint of Neuchâtel (p. 376).

58. Saussure, "Avertissement," in *Voyages*, vol. 2, p. i.

59. The previous summer—1785—he and the Bourrits had hoped to summit.

60. Saussure, "Avertissement," in *Voyages*, vol. 3, p. viii.

61. Saussure, "Avertissement," in *Voyages*, vol. 2, p. i.

Note on Sources

The Voyages dans les Alpes

The *Voyages dans les Alpes, précédés d'un Essai sur l'histoire naturelle des environs de Genève* was published in four volumes: vol. 1, Neuchâtel: Samuel Fauche, 1779; vol. 2, Geneva: Barde, Manget, 1786; and vols. 3 and 4, Neuchâtel: Louis Fauche-Borel, 1796. Online open-access copies exist, such as Gallica's. For studies of the pull-out maps and illustrations—such as the panorama from the summit of the Buet—the original editions should be consulted. I am fortunate that Trinity College's Watkinson Library contains all four volumes, all in excellent condition, and I am grateful to the librarians there for facilitating my research.

Why the printing shifts from Neuchâtel to Geneva and back to Neuchâtel is the subject of Michel Schlup, "Les *Voyages dans les Alpes* (1779–1796): Une édition disputée entre libraires neuchâtelois et genevois," in *H.-B. de Saussure (1740–1799): Un regard sur la terre*, edited by René Sigrist with Jean-Daniel Candaux (Geneva: Georg, 2001), pp. 367–83. The *Voyages* were issued by the same publishers in a smaller and cheaper format in eight volumes. One can also find the Genevan volume 2 published under the imprint of Neuchâtel.

The conventional way of citing the *Voyages* is by section number, not page number, for clarity across reprints and excerpts. Saussure's spelling and punctuation are followed in the quotes when not translated.

A reprint of the original four volumes was published in 1978 by Slatkine. Senebier's biography of Saussure precedes volume 1 of this reprint. Saussure, *Voyages dans les Alpes, précédés de Mémoire historique sur la vie et les écrits de Horace-Bénédict de Saussure par Jean Senebier*, with a preface by Yves Ballu (Geneva: Slatkine, 1978).

A reprint of the first edition of excerpts of the *Voyages* published in 1834 as the *partie pittoresque des ouvrages* was issued in 2002 with a preface by Carozzi: *Voyages dans les Alpes, augmentés des voyages en Valais, au Mont Cervin et autour du Mont Rose: Partie pittoresque* (Geneva: Slatkine, 2004).

On summiting Mont Blanc: Saussure published an account in the *Journal de Genève* immediately afterward. It appears intact in volume 4 of the *Voyages* between sections 1965 and 1966. Saussure, *Relation abrégée d'un voyage à la cime du Mont-Blanc, en Août 1787* (Geneva, 1787).

Saussure's journal from the ascent is held in the Archives de Saussure (see below) and has been published with commentary as *Journal de l'ascension du Mont-Blanc*, edited by Anne Fauche and Samuel Cordier (Chamonix: Guérin, 2007), and as *Journal d'un voyage à Chamouni et à la cime du Mont-Blanc, en juillet et aoust 1787*, edited by Émile Gaillard and Henry F. Montagnier (Lyon: M. Maudin, 1926). The introduction and notes to both these editions have been used in this book.

Saussure's journal from his attempted ascent of August 1786 is printed in part in T. [Thomas] Graham Brown and Gavin De Beer, *The First Ascent of Mont Blanc*, with a foreword by Sir John Hunt, "published on the occasion of the Centenary of the Alpine Club" (London: Oxford University Press, 1957), pp. 383–91. The authors transcribed the sections having to do with Saussure's travel from Geneva to Chamonix and in Chamonix with his discussions with Dr. Paccard (that is, Michel-Gabriel) and his family. Paccard had made the first ascent of Mont Blanc with Jacques Balmat earlier that month on 8 August. Paccard's *Notebook* of the ascent is printed in *The First Ascent of Mont Blanc*, based on the manuscript held by the (British) Alpine Club in London.

Also important and relevant to the discussion of Saussure's use of instruments to understand the Alps as described in the *Voyages* is his "Essais sur l'hygrométrie" (Neufchatel: Samuel Fauche, 1783), reproduced by Gallica.bnf.fr, http://catalogue.dnf.fr/ark:/12148/cb372775068.

Saussure's "Lectures on Physical Geography," given to the Academy in 1775, have been published, annotated, and translated in Albert Carozzi and John K. Newman, *Lectures on Physical Geography Given in 1775 by Horace-Bénédict de Saussure at the Academy of Geneva* (Geneva: Éditions Zoé, 2003). The edition is based on the notes taken in Latin by a student in his class, Jacques-Louis Peschier, and on Saussure's rough draft of his lectures, which were written in French.

The catalog of Saussure's working library has been annotated and published in Albert Carozzi and Gerda Bouvier, *The Scientific Library of Horace-Bénédict de Saussure (1797): Annotated Catalog of an 18th-Century Bibliographic and Historic Treasure* (Geneva: Société de Physique et d'Histoire naturelle, 1994). As their abstract explains: "The total holdings were at least 1202 items, that is, 1143 books and 59 periodicals and related histories of the leading European academies and learned societies, which covered extensively the field of mineralogy, geology (theories of the Earth), natural history travels, natural history, geographic travels, botany-agriculture, chemistry, medicine, physics, engineering, astronomy, mathematics, and philosophy.... Saussure's collection [is] an example of one of the most diversified and important scientific libraries of the 18th century. An analysis of the holdings gives a rare insight into one of the intellectual treasures of the 18th century, showing what was being written, in what country, and why Saussure ordered these books" (p. vii).

The Archives de la famille de Saussure

These are held in the Bibliothèque de Genève, manuscripts department.

Letters from Albertine-Amélie to her husband are found at Arch. de Saussure 223-3. The letters from Horace-Bénédict to his wife have been published as *Lettres de H.-B. de Saussure à sa femme*, edited by Emile Gaillard and Henry F. Montagnier (Chambéry: Imprimeries Réunies, Librairie Dardel, 1937).

The journal of Albertine-Amélie de Saussure is found at MS Saussure 255: "Copies des 32 premières pages du voyages [sic] de Mme. H.-B. de Saussure à Paris en 1768. Ce voyage comprend 165 pages."

Letters to, from, and about Judith de Saussure can be found at Arch. de Saussure 223-3, 223-6, and 239 along with MS Saussure 2 (former Archives de Saussure E21) and 13. Albertine-Amélie's's letters to her sister-in-law Judith are at Arch. de Saussure 239, fols. 124–141.

MS Saussure 13 also includes a letter from his daughter Albertine, age ten, to Horace-Bénédict, along with copies of letters from Benjamin Franklin, Mme. De Lavoisier, and Mme. Necker (that is, Suzanne Curchod, wife of Jacques Necker), and a letter to Voltaire from Horace-Bénédict.

Arch. de Saussure 223-6 contains letters from Saussure written from Paris, London, and Calais (while on the Grand Tour with his wife) to his mother, father, mother-in-law, and, after their return, his sisters-in-law (especially Minette), as well as his sister, Judith, as noted above. Saussure's journal from the Grand Tour is held in Arch. de Saussure 26: "Journal [détaillé] du voyage de Février à Septembre 1768 à Paris, en Hollande et en Angleterre, avec sa femme." Freshfield has made use of this also, and his translations have been followed for the most part, and to confirm my deciphering of Saussure's handwriting.

Two-thirds of the letters written by Haller to Saussure are held in MS Saussure 9. The correspondence back and forth between them has been published as *The Correspondence between Albrecht von Haller and Horace-Bénédict de Saussure*, edited by Otto Sonntag (Bern: Hans Huber, 1990). Sonntag notes the difficulty of deciphering both the men's handwriting.

He has "followed the authors in most, though not quite all, of their irregularities and inconsistencies" with respect to "spelling, capitalization, punctuation, and related matters" (Sonntag, "Editorial Principles," pp. 50–52, at p. 51). The quotes in this book from the *Correspondence* are exact when not translated. (Haller misspells many words. French is not his first language, and it is obvious that his letters were written very quickly. This reader finds that more care was taken in Haller's letters to Bonnet.)

Saussure's field notes are contained in more than a hundred notebooks. Carozzi has based his interpretation of Saussure's contributions to geology on his reading of these. Carozzi explains that his understanding of what Saussure is saying in the notebooks is based not only on forty years of work reading and transcribing them, but also on following them in his footsteps, one geologist after another, in the Alps. This author has allowed Carozzi's claim to privileged access to the field notes as a geologist to stand. Carozzi, *Horace-Bénédict de Saussure (1740–1799): Un pionnier des sciences de la terre* (Geneva: Slatkine, 2005), pp. xv–xvi, and Carozzi, "Les manuscrits de Horace-Bénédict de Saussure: Clé de sa personnalité et de sa véritable contribution à la géologie moderne," in *Une cordée originale: Histoire des relations entre science et montagne*, edited by Jean-Claude Pont and Jan Lacki (Geneva: Georg, 2000), pp. 27–41.

Important Contemporary Views of Saussure

The Correspondence between Albrecht von Haller and Charles Bonnet, edited by Otto Sonntag (Bern: Hans Huber, 1983). Saussure's mentors were his uncle by marriage, Charles Bonnet, and Haller. Saussure and his family are one of the subjects of their letters. The correspondence is richly valuable in many other ways too, of course, for any cultural history of the eighteenth century, as this book suggests.

Jean Senebier's biography, the *Mémoire historique sur la vie et les écrits de Horace-Bénédict Desaussure* (1801), is the most important and detailed of the éloges published shortly after Saussure's death. Also of interest are Georges Cuvier's *Éloge historique* of Bonnet and Saussure and Augustin-Pyramus de Candolle's appreciation of Saussure, his "Notice sur la vie et les ouvrages de Saussure." Excerpts of the autopsy report appear in G. de Morsier and R. de Saussure, "Description clinique et autopsie d'Horace-Benedict de Saussure par le Docteur Louis Odier," *Gesnerus* 27 (1970): pp. 127–37.

Rosalie Constant's journal and letters offer occasional interesting views of the Saussures. At the Bibliothèque de Genève: Rosalie Constant MS, suppl. 1486–1489, the "Cahiers verts, her journal 1787–1834." Extracts with letters are held in MS.fr. 6849. The "Journal de l'enfance de Victor" is in fols. 61–80, and a copy is in MS suppl. 1494-. She writes about the house at St. Jean, her visit to the Saussures' as he tries to launch a Montgolfier balloon, and her own family's visit to Chamonix, Her book of plant illustrations and more archival material is in Lausanne. She awaits a modern biographer. Christine Chicoteau's *Chère Rose: A Biography of Rosalie de Constant (1758–1834)* (Frankfurt am Main: Peter Lang,1980) is a beginning, drawing nicely on her letters to her cousin Benjamin Constant. Lucie Achard's *Rosalie Constant, sa famille et ses amis*, 2 vols. (Geneva: Eggimann, 1900 and 1903) mines the primary sources and is fascinating to read though is light on the historical context.

Other Travelers to the Alps in the Eighteenth Century

Other travelers introduced in the text include Jean-André Deluc and Marc-Théodore Bourrit. William Windham and Richard Pococke's 1741 expedition to Chamonix is analyzed in chapter 3, "The Arve." Just a note here to emphasize the appeal of Thomas Blaikie. His diary, published as *Diary of a Scotch Gardener at the French Court at the End of the Eighteenth Century*, edited and with an introduction by Francis Birrel (London: George Routledge & Sons, 1931; facs., Cambridge: Cambridge University Press, 2012), is not to be overlooked on account of its title. Blaikie was sent to the Swiss Alps in 1775 by William Pitcairn (1712–1791) and John Fothergill (1712–1780), doctors and gentlemen botanists, to collect plants for Fothergill's botanical garden in London. The first half of the book describes his journey from England to Switzerland (Geneva, the Jura, the Salève, the Bernese Alps, and Chamonix and the glaciers) and back again, ending with a meeting with Joseph Banks in January 1776 and a few subsequent notes until the departure for France in November. Though he and Saussure apparently never met, the diary is a marvelous source for historians of Geneva and the Alps in the 1770s. (Blaikie's spelling is phonetic and his grammar self-taught, so it also offers to the ear a sense of his actual speech.)

Index

Page numbers in italics refer to illustrations

Abeille, Joseph, 25
Achard, Lucie, 210n90, 253
Adams, George, 119
Adanson, Michel, 48–49, 214n183, 214n185
Addison, Joseph, 157
Aetna/Etna. *See* Mount Etna (Italy)
Against War and Empire (Whatmore), 27, 207n31, 246n22
Agassiz, Louis, 17, 137
Age of Wonder, The (Holmes), 168, 214n186, 242n57
agriculture, 14; and arable land, 229n8; English methods of, 33; and environment, 49; and farming, 188, 209n77, 214n192; and gentlemen farmers, 209n77; and greening measures, 214n192; integrated in Ireland, 214n192; in library, 251; women working in, 106
Aguirre, the Wrath of God (Herzog film), 60, 217n42
Aiguille d'Argentière, 117
Aiguille de Bionnassay, 117
Aiguille des Grands Charmoz, 147, 158, 166–67
Aiguille de Tricot, 117
Aiguille du Dru, 101–2, 164
Aiguille du Goûter, 20, 151–53, 169–70, 179, 202n86; and Dôme, 119, 149, 151, 159–61, 174, 189, 238n76
Aiguille du Grépon, 147, 166, 190, 247n47

Aiguille du Midi, 105–6, 116–17, 140–41, *141*, 145, 158, 175, 248n56
Aiguille du Plan, 117–18, 148
Aiguille du Tour, 117
aiguilles, 86, 94, 117, 136, 140, 145, 174, 190
Aiguilles de Chamonix, 117, 128, 147, 158, 166, 171, 234n127. *See also* Chamonix (France)
Aiguilles Rouges, 13, 105, 117, 141, 159–60
air: and altitude, 176; clearness of, 16; humidity of, 15; lightness of, 118; reading of, 118; thinness of, 136; and water, 118, 176; weight of, 113. *See also* atmospheric pressure
Albanis-Beaumont, Jean-François, 109, 230n27
alpages (alpine or high mountain meadows), 105–6
alpiculture, 110
Alpine Club, 5, 17, 31, 35, 100, 133, 153, 227n107; British, 9, 165, 185, 245n116, 250; Centenary, 250; Ladies, 165–66
Alpine Convention, 82, 183–84, 245nn5–7
Alpine Journal, 190
alpine landscapes, 63
alpinism, 165, 228n112; birth and founding of, 17; British dominance of, 245n116; as climbing for fun, 100; early, 196; first death in history of, 158; and geology, 53; golden age of, 245n116; term, usage, 215n1. *See also* mountaineering

Alps (Europe), *146*; aesthetic response to, 6; appeal of, 14; and architecture of aversion, 12, 35; Bernese, 14, 98, 114, 183, 253; cultural history of, 15–16; disorienting space of inner ranges of, 13; and Geneva, 20, 31, 69–70, 83, 104, 132, 155, 167, 184, 253; history of, 15–16, 57, 193–94, 253; instrumentalist approach to, 101; and Jura, 63–65; literature and images of, 16; natural history of, 111–12; naturalists in, 224–25n43; origins of, 136; as other, 13, 20; as physical other, 20; Pre-, 38, 45, 53, 64, 69, 113, 132, 144, 183, 193–94; Rhône, 14, 247n43; Saussure and, 1–20; Savoy, 10, 13, 85, 114–15, 118, 153; structure of, 54; and sublime, 157; Swiss, 50–51, 253; as system, 45–46; travelers to Alps (18th century), sources, 253; and weather, 15. *See also specific mountain(s)*
altitude: and air, 176; and atmospheric pressure, 113, 133, 236n17; and body, and oxygen, 235–36n11; and body, integrate into, 102; and cold, 16, 105, 228n2; and oxygen, 235–36n11, 236n17; and sky color, 113; and weather, 178
American Revolution, 1
Analytical Essay on the Faculties of the Soul (Bonnet), 87–88
anatomy, 6, 57, 211n102
anemometers, 118–19, 127, 204n107
antiquity, 25, 34, 66, 75, 200n41, 205n134, 207–8n32
Antrim, Taylor, 233n98
Aquinas, Thomas, 88
Arctic, 59, 67, 80, 91, 100, 127, 135
Ardbraccam, 99, 227n101
Arduino, Giovanni, 73
Arête des Bosses (Mont Blanc), 149, 159, 161, 189–91, 238n76, 248n49
aristocracy, 2, 28, 96, 115, 122, 187
artisanship, 28, 34, 61, 187–88
Arve River and valley (Chamonix, France), 11–14, 30–31, 47, 53, 109, 127, 133, 135, 149–50, 157, 167, 169, 181, 183–84, 188–89, 192, 223n17; Aveyron, a feeder stream of, 11–12, 202–3n89, 214n179; and Mont Blanc, 79–104; sources, 253. *See also* Chamonix (France)
Ashley-Cooper, Anthony, 138
astronomy, 58–59, 81, 119, 217n41, 245n116; in library, 251. *See also* cosmology; meteorology; sky; solar system; star maps
atmosphere, experiments and observations of, 176
atmospheric pressure, at altitude, 113, 133, 236n17. *See also* air
Augustine. *See* St. Augustine
autopsies, 7, 201n56
Auvergne (France), 38, 114–15
avalanches, 147–48, 160, 172, 175, 190, 243n87

Bacon, Francis, 74
Badinter, Elisabeth, 212n137, 221n134
balloons. *See* hot-air balloons
Ballu, Yves, 17, 205n128, 249
Balmat, Alexis, 172, 178
Balmat, Jacques, 108, 147, 159–63, 165–67, 170–72, 174, 189, 205n129, 229n9, 237n62, 240n11, 240n21, 250; as hero of Mont Blanc (first summited), 111
Balmat, Pierre, 91, 118, 148, 153, 158, 167, 171–72, 174–75, 177, 234n127, 240n15
Balmat family, 111
Banks, Joseph, 48–49, 59, 91, 112, 168–69, 214n186, 242n57, 253
Barker, Robert, 144
barometers, 118, 133, 167, 169–71, 173, 176, 178
Barras, Vincent, 5, 7, 9, 200n37, 201n56, 202n86
Bartholomew. *See* St. Bartholomew's Day Massacre (1572)
basalt, 38, 72, 114–15, 221n119
Beaufoy, Mark, 177, 244–45n116
Bell, David A., 182
Bell, Vanessa, 5
Bérenger, Antoinette, 150–51, 239n6, 242n49
Bérenger, Jean-Pierre, 239n6
Bérenger family, 150–51, 167

Bernoulli, Daniel, 58
Bernoulli, Johann, III, 58, 234n121
big science, 59
biodiversity, 111
biogeography, 61, 213n166, 217n47
Birrel, Francis, 203n89, 253
Blaikie, Thomas, 13, 46, 49, 54, 62–63, 134, 159–60, 195, 202–3n89, 202n80, 209n65, 214n179, 214n188; in Swiss Alps (1775), sources, 253
Blair, Ann, 196, 220n97
Blanc. *See* Mont Blanc (Alps)
Blosset, Harriet, 168–69, 242n57
Boch, Julie, 245n11
bodies of desire, 105–32
Boerhaave, Hermann, 6
Boissier, Albertine-Amélie. *See* Saussure, Albertine-Amélie Boissier de (wife)
Boissier, Jack (in-law), 120
Boissier, Jean-Jacques-André (father-in-law), 122, 125, 231n48
Boissier, Marie-Charlotte Lullin (mother-in-law), 122, 124, 231n48
Boissier-Lullin family, 25, 42, 121–25, 128–29
Bonnet, Charles (uncle and mentor): and Arduino, 73; and asexual reproduction and infertility, 42; and botany, 50–51, 81, 215n198; on Bourguet, 71; as Calvinist, 20; and Conches, 240n28; country house (Genthod), 12, 35, 38, 54, 112–13, 123, 128–32, 162–63, 167, 234n135; death of, 89; d'Holbach lambasted by, 222n140; and experience, 89; as a first *éloge historique* of luminaries, 9; and Haller, 34, 39–40, 46–47, 50–51, 57, 66, 70–71, 73–75, 81, 116, 121, 125–26, 179–80, 209–10n80, 213n174, 215n198, 252; health of, 42; letters, 39, 213n174, 252; and materialism, exhortations against, 74; as mentor, 39, 46–47, 50, 70–71, 87–88, 149, 179–80, 252; mobility of as privilege and mark of high status, 35; and natural history, 46–47, 88; and natural theologies, 224–25n43; and natural world, 88; and Nicolas, 34; and observation, 87; and parthenogenesis, 39; as Philorhizotome (nickname), 209–10n80; and physiology of plants, 50–51, 81–82; portrait of, 128; reading Buffon / de Buffon, 70–71; and Réaumur, 127; on regeneration of animals and reproduction of plants, 39; as savant, 39; as uncle, 9, 34, 39–40, 81, 179, 252
Bonnet, Jeanne-Marie de la Rive (aunt), 39, 42, 66
Bonneville (France), 83–85, 91, 98, 223n27
Bonpland, Aimé, 61
Bonstetten, Charles Victor de, 45
boots: iron attachments to soles of, 220n98; nailed, 153, 246n21
Boswell, James, 35, 210n92, 211n109
botanical gardens: in Britain, 168; of Europe, 49; in France, 48–49, 70, 168, 214n189, 215n194; in London, 48, 62–63, 253; in Paris, 214n189, 215n194; at Turin, Italy, 56. *See also* horticulture
botany, 9, 74, 81, 115, 199n17, 204n106, 209n69, 215n195, 242n65; in 18th century, 48–51, 56, 61, 215n198; in 19th century, 213n162; and Alps, 46–47, 50–51, 54–55; and collecting, 50–51; histories of, 3; library books and publications, 48, 119–20, 251; and nationalism/patriotism, 46; and physiology of plants, 50–51, 215n198; as science for 19th century, 213n162; and sublime, 50; Swiss, 14; and taxonomy, 50–51, 215n198. *See also* horticulture; plants
Bougainville, Louis-Antoine de, 59
Bouguer, Pierre, 135, 235n10, 236n12
Bourguet, Louis, 71
Bourrit, Charles, 169–70, 242n64
Bourrit, (Pierre Marc) Isaac, 152, 165, 169–70
Bourrit, Marc-Théodore (Theo), 89, 115–18, 134, 140–43, 147, 150–55, 158–59, 169–70, 173, 180, 203n98, 230n36, 231n55, 236n36, 239n6, 240n7, 246n18, 248n59; sources, 253
Bourrit family, 152–55, 162, 169–71, 177, 248n59

Bouvier, Gerda, 119, 250
Braudel, Fernand, 82
Brévent, Le (France), 48, 57, 102–3, 105–8, 116–17, 128, 131, 148–49, 150, 159–60, 171, 202n86
Bristow, Lily, 166, 247n47
Brown, Graham: and De Beer, 149, 153, 161, 237n46, 238n65, 238n71, 238n74, 238n76, 239n83, 240n7, 240n15, 240n22, 242n67, 243n72, 244–45n116, 246n21, 247n41, 250
Brune, Michael, 237n43
Buache, Philippe, 218n66
Budé de Boisy, Isaac, 238n78
Buet. *See* Mont Buet (Alps)
Buffon, Georges-Louis Leclerc, Comte de, 39, 57, 67–75, 88, 115–17, 193, 219–20n95, 219n87, 220n103
Buisson, Léonard, 25
Buisson family, 24, 94
Bungener, Patrick, 215n198, 222n144, 222n148
Burke, Edmund, 157
Burlamaqui, Jean-Jacques, 1, 29, 208n49
Burnet, Thomas, 67–68, 219n86
Burnet, William, 98
Burney, Fanny, 63, 218n60
Bursting the Limits of Time (Rudwick), 18, 139, 221n116
Butterfield, Michael, 119, 231n67
butterflies, 106, 127, 131, 214n192
Byron, Lord, 95

Cachat, Jean-Michel, 148, 172, 178
Cachat, Jean-Pierre, 172
calculus, and probability theory, 74
Calvin, John, 23–24, 26, 187, 207n14
Calvinism, 20, 25, 38, 74, 186, 188, 211n109
Camisard Revolts (France), 230n37
Candaux, Jean-Daniel, 186, 199n26, 246n24, 249
Candolle, Augustin-Pyramus de, Dr., 9, 43, 46, 213n162, 214n188, 215n198, 252
capitalism, 25, 191; environmental, 111, 132, 157
Carozzi, Albert V., 18, 89, 119, 170, 183, 187, 194, 200n36, 200n40, 205n130, 206n138, 220nn104–5, 222n141, 226n92, 232nn73–79, 234n121, 234n135, 236n36, 238n78, 240n29, 242n70, 243n79; sources, 249–50, 252
Carrier, Jorasse, 229n17, 238n74
Carrier, Joseph, 149, 229n17, 238n74, 240n15
Carrier, Pierre, 238n63
Cartesian science, 74
Cassini, Jacques, 61–62, 217n52
Cassini, Jean-Dominique, 58
Castle Howard (England), 129, 234n132
Catherine the Great, 59
Catholicism, 13, 23, 25–26, 30, 186
caves, 13, 23, 67, 102, 114
Chamoniarde, La (mountain rescue and awareness organization), 190–91, 194, 247n45
Chamoniards, 95, 102, 107–8, 111, 119, 135, 148–50, 152, 155, 159, 171–72, 178, 184–86, 189–91, 194, 240n21, 248n49, 248n56
Chamonix (France), 3, 10–11, 45–48, 60, 69, 75–83, 91–95, 98–101, 104, 105–12, 117, 126–27, 131–34, 147–54, 157–71, 176–78, 181–95, 230n27, 238n69, 239n83, 248n54, 253; arable land in, 229n8; economy of, 243n74; expeditions, 98, 253; and Geneva, 132, 169, 176, 181, 183; glaciers, 229n3; history of, 238n63; honey from, 13; hotels of, 111; mountain rescue and awareness, 247n45; plants in, 214n179; population of, residential and seasonal, 247n38; and Saussure, growing importance of, 111; Saussure family in, 243n75, 250, 253; sources, 250, 253; Valley, 13–14, 30, 45–46, 58, 79–82, 86, 91, 94, 101, 105–6, 108, 133, 141, 150–51, 157, 189, 193, 229n3, 229n8, 239n87, 247n38. *See also* Aiguilles de Chamonix; Arve River and valley (Chamonix, France); Compagnie des Guides de Chamonix; Mont Blanc (Alps)
Chamonix-Mont-Blanc (France), *109*, 195, 229n21
Chamouni (Mont Blanc), 103, *109*, 237n56

INDEX 259

Chanlaire, Pierre-Grégoire, 182
Chaplin, Joyce, 219n84
Charles-Emmanuel I, Duke of Savoy, 25
Charlet, Jean, 166
Charlet, Michel, 109
Charlet-Straton, Isabella, 165–66
Charlotte, Queen, 63, 116, 134
Charlton, Donald, 220n101
chasms, 67, 117, 137, 157
Châtelet, Émilie du, 81, 118, 223n9
Chaumont (Neuchâtel), 63
chemistry, 119, 176, 211n102, 219n85; in library, 251
Chicago, Judy, 4
Chicoteau, Christine, 203n93, 253
Chimborazo, 61, 177, 217n47
Christianity, 1, 50, 76, 88, 227n101
circumnavigation, 59, 66, 164, 219n84. *See also* navigation
Clemens, Johan Frederik, 128
cliffs, 14, 47, 63, 72–73, 91, 128, 131, 163
climate: of Alps, 184; and forms of society, 184; and society, 184; theory, 245n8; and vegetation, 213n164. *See also* weather
climate change, 20, 184, 248n56. *See also* global warming
climbing. *See* mountaineering
clouds: color of, 16; electricity in, 57; and wind speed, 204n107
Cluses (France), 83, 89, 92, 98–99, 104, 131, 231n63
cold: and heat, 13, 113; and height, 16, 105, 228n2; and silence, 174
Col du Géant, 3, 10, 15, 19–20, 37, 119, 148, 161, 163, 173, 177–80, 192, 198n13, 202n86, 204n107, 209n67, 237n46, 241n31
Colley, Linda, 27–28, 208n35
color: of clouds, 16; and heat, 223n9; and shapes, 94, 179; and shapes, at night, 179; and shapes, of ice, 102; of sky at altitudes, 113, 176; and sound, 94, 179
Compagnie des Guides de Chamonix, 133, 148, 166, 185, 189–91, 194, 235n3, 238n63, 241n41, 242n50, 245n118, 246n13

compasses, 12, 82, 101, 119, 173, 228n112. *See also* navigation
Conches (France), 4, 30–37, 240n28
conchology, library books, 120
Condillac, Étienne Bonnot de, 87
Constant, Benjamin, 4, 200n31, 253
Constant, Rosalie, 4, 35, 49–50, 54–55, 70, 162–63, 200n31, 210n90, 215n194, 240n28, 252–53
Constant, Samuel, 35
Constant family archives, 195
Constantinople, 96
Cook, Alexandra, 211n114, 213n166
Cook, James, Captain, 48, 59, 91, 112, 164, 168, 217n39, 241n35
Copernicus, 58
Coppet, Château de, 12, 35, 45
Corbin, Alain, 64
Cordillera mountains (South America), 218n66
cosmology, 68. *See also* astronomy; meteorology; solar system
Coutet, François, 172
Coutet, Marie, 167, 172, 174–75
Coutterand, Jean-Nicolas, 108, 111, 150–51
Coutterand, spelling of, 229n17
Coutterand, Thérèse Garny, Mme. (hotelier), 109–11, 166–67, 170–72, 185, 230n27
Coutterand family, 111, 150
Couttet, Jean-Marie, 149–51, 178, 229n17, 238n74, 240n15
Cramer family, 24
Cramont/Crammont. *See* Mont Cramont/Crammont (Alps)
crampons, 70, 153, 189–90, 220n98
crevasses, 13, 91, 101–2, 149, 151, 158, 161–62, 164, 172–75, 178, 186, 189–90, 248n56
Critique of Judgment, The (Kant), 9, 157
crystallography, 13, 73, 98, 107, 128, 137, 148, 177
Cuidet, François, 151
cultural history, 15, 230n37, 252
Curchod, Suzanne. *See* Necker, Mme. (Suzanne Curchod, wife of Jacques Necker)

Cuvier, Georges, 9, 17–18, 72, 206n136, 213n162, 221n116, 252
cyanometers, 176–77

d'Alembert, Jean le Rond, 74, 208n56, 221n135
Damrosch, Leo, 211n109
d'Angeville, Henriette, 165
Daubenton, Louis Jean-Marie, 219n95
Davis, Wade, 17, 205n127, 228n112, 235n11, 236n17, 236n32
Dawson, Virginia P., 88, 224n43
De Beer, Gavin Rylands, 220n97, 226n92, 227nn98–99; and Brown, 149, 153, 161, 237n46, 238n65, 238n71, 238n74, 238n76, 239n83, 240n7, 240n15, 240n22, 242n67, 243n72, 244–45n116, 246n21, 247n41, 250
DeJean, Joan, 56, 229n12
Delany, Mary Granville, 50, 215n195
de la Rive, Horace-Bénédict (father-in-law), 37
de la Rive, Jeanne-Marie Franconis (mother-in-law), 37
de la Rive, Pierre-Louis, 92–93, 96, 99
de la Rive family (in-laws), 24, 37, 42, 138n212, 212n138
de Lavoisier, Mme., 251
Deluc, Guillaume-Antoine, 133–34, 167, 171
Deluc, Jean-André, 63, 115–16, 133–34, 167, 171, 224–25n43, 235n8, 253
Denis, Mme. (Marie-Louise Mignot), 2, 198nn10–11
Descartes, René, 88
"Descent, The," 173, 185, 246n21
desire, bodies of, 105–32
Dévouassou, François, 172
Dévouassou, Jean-Louis, 172
Dévouassou, Jean-Michel, 172
Dévouassou, Michel, 172
Dévouassou, Pierre, 172
de Warens, Mme., 14, 29, 203n104, 208n44
d'Holbach, Baron, 222n140
Diary of a Scotch Gardener at the French Court at the End of the Eighteenth Century (Blaikie and Birrel), 214n188, 253

Diderot, Denis, 14, 30, 74, 221nn134–35
Dinner Party, The (Chicago), 4
Diodati, François, 27
Diodati family, 24
Dôle, La (Jura), 31, 48, 54, 56–57, 62–65, 68–70, 72, 155, 193–94
Dolomie, Déodat Gratet de, 201n65
Dolomites mountain range (Italy), 201n65
domesticity, 31, 128–30
Drouin, Jean-Marc, 202n74, 218n76

Earth: and atmosphere, 45; beauty of, 58; body of, 119, 200n41; circumnavigation of, 59, 66, 164, 219n84; cohesion of, 68; embrace of, 16; exploring, 53; formation of, 139; history of, and mountains, 46, 64, 67–68, 137; and humans, 75–76, 139; internal economy of, 6; knowledge of, 16, 119; living, 51, 53, 75–77, 95, 144–45, 194; physical engagement with, 19; and plants, 51; sciences, 9, 18, 56–57, 68–69, 81, 193; secrets of, 32; as sensorium, 51; structure and development of, 57; study of, 45, 50, 57, 65–68, 73–74; as system of checks and balances, 45; temperature of, 90; theories of, 61, 67, 70–72, 134, 192–93, 250; understanding, 19, 46, 61, 65–67, 132; visualizing, 206n142. *See also* environment; nature
Earthrise, 20
ecotourism, 111. *See also* tourist industry
Edict of Nantes (1685), 24, 207n16
electricity, 57, 113
electrometers, 154
éloges, 9, 17, 252
empiricism, 90, 94–95, 101, 104, 135, 179–80, 186
Encyclopédie ou Dictionnaire raisonné des sciences, des arts et des métiers, 119, 224n38
engineering, in library, 251
Enlightenment, Age of, 16, 19–20, 30, 65–66, 68, 70, 74, 82–83, 87–88, 111–12, 123, 149, 165, 180, 186–88
en plein air painting, 99, 146

entomology, library books and publications, 119–20
environment: and agriculture, 49; harsh, stimulus of, 184; and natural world, 19; and travel through life, 89. *See also* Earth; nature
environmental capitalism, 111, 132, 157
environmentalism, 20, 49, 113, 192
environmental psychology, 19, 95
equipment, 70, 189, 247n42. *See also* scientific instruments; specific equipment
Essay Concerning Human Understanding, An (Locke), 74
Etna/Aetna. *See* Mount Etna (Italy)
Europe. *See* Grand Tour of Europe
European Common Agricultural Policy, 214n192
Everest. *See* Mount Everest (Asia)
Exchaquet, Charles-François, 86, 148, 178
exploration narratives, 204n119
External Characters of Minerals (Werner), 72

Faizan, Louis, 188
farms and farming. *See* agriculture
fascism, 139, 165, 236n32
Fatio, Pierre, 26–28
Faucigny (France), 22, 80, 85, 89, 108, 164, 229n21, 243n74
Favre family, 24
Favret, Pierre-François, 172
Finsteraarhorn (Bernese Alps), 98
fire, nature and propagation of, 81
First Ascent of Mont Blanc, The (Brown and De Beer), 161, 238n65, 238n71, 238n74, 238n76, 239n83, 240n7, 240n15, 240n22, 243n72, 247n41, 250
flowers, 15, 31, 43, 53–54, 56, 65, 93–94, 106, 145. *See also* plants; wildflowers
Forbes, James David, 17, 116
Fothergill, John, botanical garden, London, 253
Fournier, Eric, Mayor, 248n54
France: as constant corrupting influence, 208n55; gardens in, 168; Genevan residents in, 29; and Italy, 23, 37–38, 95, 183; military forces of, 183; and plant sensibilities, 76; Protestantism outlawed in, 24; and Switzerland, 21, 23, 29–30, 53, 110, 183, 201n59; and Zurich, 110
Frankenstein (Shelley), 57, 100, 110, 227n104
Franklin, Benjamin, 57, 186, 251
French Academy of Sciences (Paris), 10, 59, 81, 216n23
French Revolution, 2, 7–9, 42, 96, 119, 144, 181, 187, 192
Freshfield, Douglas W., 9–10, 17, 23, 31, 65, 80, 191, 198n14, 199nn23–24, 201n65, 202n79, 205n125, 205n127, 207nn15–16, 209n62, 210n88, 212n118, 218n70, 222n2, 228n121, 230n36, 231n55, 234nn131–32, 240nn27–30, 245n2, 246n18, 247n40, 248n49, 251
Friedrich, Caspar David, 69, 219n93
Frontenex, Saussure home (France), 34–35, 37–38, 47, 54, 56, 210n85, 210n88

Gadmen valley (Alps), 220n97
Galiani, Ferdinand, 33, 209n79
Gallatin family, 24–25
Gallimard (publisher, Paris), 230n37
Gaussen, Paul, 214n188
Geneva (Switzerland), 21–51, 69, 81–82, 104, 117, 125, 127, 132, 150, 165, 167, 232n89, 243n75; Academy, 36, 40, 45, 50, 57–58, 66, 74–75, 80–81, 88, 92, 96, 115, 125, 152, 158, 187, 212n121, 219n79, 250; and Alps, 20, 31, 69–70, 83, 104, 132, 155, 167, 184, 253; as aristo-democracy, 1, 29–30, 186; and Bonneville, 223n27; and capitalism, early center of, 25; and Chamonix, 132, 169, 176, 181, 183; city-state of, 1, 23, 25, 51, 110, 113, 120, 181, 187, 232n89; clerical culture of, 27; culture of, 1; as democratic state, 8; Escalade invasion (1602), 13, 26–27, 36; history of, 253; and Indian textiles (indiennes), 12–13, 203n94, 207n20; and nepotism, 29; patrician, 1–2, 24, 26–30, 51, 102, 116, 122–23, 186–87; politics

Geneva (Switzerland) (*continued*)
of, 26; Puritan values of, 1; and Reformation, 23–25; Revolution, 4, 7–8, 26, 28, 61, 186–87, 192, 207n31; and science, 65; street lighting in, 210n93; visits in, 238n71; as walled and gated city, 12–13, 19, 21–29, 32, 34–35, 42, 51, 69, 155, 188, 206n1, 206n4; wealth of, 1–2; women in, 96, 199n20. *See also* Lake Geneva

Genevan Terror (July 1794), 4, 8, 199n25

Geneva Society of Physics and Natural History, 3, 7, 36

Geoffroy Saint-Hilaire, Étienne, 138

geography, 61, 222n141; lectures, 250; in library, 251. *See also* biogeography; maps; topography

geologia, 16

geology, 9, 16–18, 50, 71, 82, 84, 102, 104, 132, 146, 155, 183–84, 193–94, 201n65, 204n112, 220n104, 252; and alpinism, 53; history of, 18; library books and publications, 119, 250; origins of, 68; sources, 250–52; and superposition, 73

geometry, 35, 61, 84–85, 92

geophilia, 16

Gesner, Conrad, 69–70, 196, 220n97

Gesner, Johann, 14, 220n97

ginkgo, 214n188; first female tree in Europe, 49

glaciers, 11–13, 17–18, 22, 58, 60, 69, 77, 79–80, 94–110, 113–18, 131, 136–37, 142, 145–52, 154, 158–67, 171–74, 177–79, 186, 189, 191–92, 202–3n89, 204n122, 226–27n92, 229n3, 237n48, 237n52, 237n56, 248n56, 253; and glaciation, 204n120

Glacken, Clarence, 155, 245n8

global warming, 11, 80, 111, 184, 191, 248n56. *See also* climate change

God: and consolations offered by religion, 222n141; and creation, 74; and Earth, 67–68; existence of, 88; and geography, 222n141; is everywhere, 13; and man, 76; and natural order, 19; and nature, 20

Godin, Louis, 217n41
Goethe, Johann Wolfgang von, 109
Gohau, Gabriel, 68, 71, 73, 76, 218n66, 221n126
Golay, Eric, 186–87
Gosse, Henri-Albert, 37, 119, 211n102
Gosse, Louis-André, 37
Gosse family, 37
Gough, John, 219n85
GPS (Global Positioning Systems), 12, 189, 203n91
Grand Tour of Europe, 44, 58, 95, 108, 114–15, 129, 138, 159, 168; letters, 251
graphometers, 116, 119, 143
Grataroli, Guillaume, 70, 220n98
Grave, Johannes, 219n93
gravity, 11, 67
Grenon, Michel, 198n13, 216n30
Grimm, Friedrich Melchior, 2, 14
Grimsel Pass, 114, 131
Grindelwald (Switzerland), 96, 98, 110–11, 114
guides and guiding: and climbers, equitable relationship of power between, 238n63; corporations of, 246n13; homage to, 186; and hotels, 109–11, 150; patois of, 185; payments to, 243n74; and porters, 161, 165, 171; Savoy, 246n21

Haarlem Academy, 87
Haller, Albrecht von, 11; and Alps, 14; and anatomy, 57; and Bern, employment in, 121; and bio-geographical contours of Switzerland, 213n166; and Bonnet, 34, 39–40, 46–47, 50–51, 57, 66, 70–71, 73–75, 81, 116, 121, 125–26, 179–80, 209–10n80, 213n174, 215n198, 252; and botany, 46–51, 54, 79, 81, 215n198; children of, 211n116; and collecting and taxonomy, 50–51; as Cosmopolite (nickname), 209–10n80; health decline of, 126, 225n55; insomnia, 234n118; letters, 9, 36, 39–40, 42–48, 125–26, 211n114, 220n97, 225n55, 232n88, 251–52; as mentor, 6, 9, 39, 46–48, 50, 70–71, 81, 125, 179–80, 252; and natural theologies, 224–

25n43; opium addiction, 234n118; poem, 14, 30, 46, 184, 203n100; as polymath, 58; scientific life without family funds, 121; and Zermatt, 247n40
Haller, Rudolf Emanuel, 38
Halley, Edmond, 58
Hamilton, William, Sir, 114
Hansen, Peter H., 18, 108, 139, 161, 164, 202n77, 203n98, 205n125, 224–25n43, 229n9, 229n21, 229nn17–18, 239n91, 242n65, 243n74
Heaney, Seamus, 179
heat: and cold, 13, 113; and color, 223n9; and light, 80–81; nature of, experiments on, 185
Herbier Necker, 3–4
Herschel, William, 67, 241n37
Herzog, Werner, 60, 217n42
Higonnet, Margaret, 217n55
Hill, Thomas Ford, 158–59, 237n46, 239–40n7
Himalayas mountain range (Asia), 17, 64, 100–101, 111, 139, 236n32. *See also* Mount Everest (Asia)
history of ideas, 76, 205n134, 220n101
History of Science Museum (Geneva), 18
Hodges, William, 164, 241n35
Holmes, Richard, 168, 214n186, 242n57, 242n60
Holmes, Sherlock, 161
holy wells, in Ireland, 99, 227n101
hornblende, 16, 90
horticulture, 168. *See also* botanical gardens; botany; plants
hot-air balloons, experiments with, 162–63, 240n29, 253
hotels, 25, 109–11, 150, 228–29n3
hot springs, 60, 200n36
humanists and humanism, 28, 70
Humboldt, Alexander von, 20, 46, 60–61, 64–65, 177, 213n164, 217n48
Hume, David, 89, 121, 225n46, 232n88
hunters, and naturalists, 139–40
hunting, 36, 53, 98, 107, 229n14
Huth, John Edward, 12
hygrometers, 112, 118–19, 127, 132, 134, 154, 173, 176, 178, 250

ichthyology, library books, 120
ideology, and nature, 13
Île de Saint Pierre, 15, 204n111
immortality, 17, 57
imperialism, 95–96, 99–100, 102, 111, 139, 236n32
Indian textiles (indiennes), 12–13, 25, 56, 203n94, 207n20
instruments. *See* scientific instruments
International Archives of the History of Ideas, 220n101
Into the Silence (Davis), 17, 205n127, 228n112, 235n11, 236n17, 236n32
Ireland: agriculture in, 214n192; holy wells in, 227n101; landscape of, 227n101; natural history of, 8
Irving, Andrew, 228n112
Italy, and France, 23, 37–38, 95, 183

Jallabert/Jalabert, François, 57–60, 82, 94, 113, 116, 152, 170
Jallabert/Jalabert, Jean, 57
Jefferson, Thomas, 8
Joch Pass (Uri), 14
Jordanay, Jean-Laurent, 171, 237n46
Jornet, Kilian, 191, 248n52
Joseph, John E., 198n6, 220n105
Joseph II, Habsburg Emperor, 123
Joutard, Philippe, 111, 217n50, 220nn98–99, 230n37
Juel, Jens, 128–30, 234n130
Jura Mountains (France and Switzerland), 15, 21, 31, 35, 38, 45, 48, 50–51, 53–77, 79, 82, 85, 88, 112–13, 115–17, 127, 140, 151, 155, 162, 192–93, 253; and Alps, 63–65; lakes, 62
Jurine, André, 37
Jurine, Louis, 37
Jussieu, Bernard de, 115

Kant, Immanuel, 9, 157
Kaplan, Steven, 202n83, 209n79
Kellas, Alexander, 235–36n11
Kepler, Johannes, 58
Kew Gardens (London), 48
Kilian effect, 191, 248n52
King John (Shakespeare), 207n14
Kinski, Klaus, 217n42

Kircher, Athanasius, 218n66
Knight, Gowan, 119
Kunsthalle, Hamburg, 219n92
Kwass, Michael, 79–80, 238n69

Lac de Bienne (Switzerland), 15, 23, 204n111
La Condamine, Charles-Marie de, 59–60, 66–67, 135, 217n41
Lake Bourguet, 5, 62
Lake Geneva, 12, 39, 53, 62–63, 79, 83, 112, 117–18, 123, 128–29, 137, 155
Lalande, Joseph-Jérome, 58
landslides, 93, 116, 248n56
La Pérouse, Comte de (Jean-François de Galaup), 49, 59, 209n69, 214n190, 217n39
Lautrec, Comte de (Daniel François de Gélas de Voisins d'Ambres), 24, 29–30
Lavoisier, Antoine, 112, 176
Lavoisier, Mme. de, 251
Le Cointe, Ami, 158–59, 166–67
Le Cointe family, 166–67
"Lectures on Physical Geography" (Saussure), 222n141, 250
Lee, James, 168, 242n57
Lejeune, Dominique, 220n98
Lejonc, Jean-Louis, 161
Leonardo da Vinci, 75
Life of Horace Benedict de Saussure, The (Freshfield), 9, 17, 65, 218nn70–71
light: of glaciers, 191–92; and heat, 80–81
lightning rods, 57
light pollution, 12
Lilti, Antoine, 76
linguistics, 3, 35
Linnaeus, Carl, 49, 72, 120, 213n162, 215n198
Liotard, Jean-Étienne, 96–97, 99, 122, 226nn81–82
lithology, and mountaineering, 46
Little Ice Age, 11, 105, 152, 184, 237n48
Lloyd, Emmeline Lewis, 165
Locke, John, 63, 74, 87–89, 168
Lombard, Jean-Baptiste, 149, 171–72, 238n74
Longstaff, Tom George, 205n127

Louis XIV, 25
Louis XV, 2, 24, 198n10
Louis XVI, 117, 123, 209n78
Louis XVIII, 144
Lucretius, 19–20, 102, 144, 155, 175, 179–80, 206n138
Lullin, Ami, 42, 122
Lullin, Antoine-Louis, 43
Lullin, Jean, 24
Lullin, Jean-Antoine, 42, 121–23
Lullin-Camp, Jean-Antoine, 25
Lullin family, 24–25, 42–43, 121–25, 128–29
Lyell, Charles, 17

Macaire, Isaac, 211n106
Macfarlane, Robert, 90, 200n33, 224n32, 225n50, 226n74
macrocosm (cosmos), and microcosm (human), 76
Magellan, Jean-Hyacinthe de, 119
magnetism, 113, 118
magnetometers, 118–19, 127, 231n63
Malgo, Simon, 128
Mallet, Jacques-André, 58–59, 61, 232n88
Mallet, Paul-Henri, 121
Mallet family, 24
Mallory, George, fatal attempt on Everest, 5, 200n35, 228n112
Mallory, John, 5, 200n35
Mandrin, Louis, 79–80, 150, 222n1, 238n69
maps, 22, 72–73, 113, 117, 249; of Alps, 83, 86, 217n50; bibliography for, 224n32; Cassini, 61–62, 217n52; Chimborazo, 61, 217n47; cognitive, and GPS, 203n91; of Earth, 73; of Europe, 61, 144; of France, 61, 182; of Geneva, 22, 27, 83–84, 84; geographical, 61; of glaciers, 22, 237n52; of Mont Blanc, 22, 85–86, 86, 88, 147–48, 195, 224n32; of mountains, 61–62; relief, 13–14, 86, 148, 195; road, replaced by GPS, 12; Saussure's, 224n33; of Saussure's summit path, 147; of Savoy Alps, 85; star, of night sky, 12, 61; survey, with contour lines,

224n32; topographical, 61, 86–87. *See also* geography; topography
Maraldi, Giovanni, 62
Marx, Karl, 106
masculinity, and mountaineering, 5, 37, 139–40, 165, 182–83
materialism, 20, 71, 74
materiality, 102, 112, 145–46
mathematics: and deductive methods, 74; and geometry, 61; library books and publications, 119, 251; and natural history, 73–74; and philosophy, 66, 73–74. *See also* calculus; geometry; trigonometry
Mattenberg (Bernese Alps), 98
Matterhorn (Alps), 188, 192; Klein, 183; as last great trek and last major alpine excursion (1792), 3, 114; Zermatt, 166
Maupertuis, Pierre Louis Moreau de, 59–60, 66–67, 135
meadows, 14, 31, 47, 63, 69, 94, 98–99, 105–7, 131, 229n8
medicine: and electricity, 57; library books and publications, 5, 119, 251; and plants, 43, 46, 49
meditations, 19, 157
Meinhardt, Maren, 61
Mémoire historique sur la vie et les écrits de Horace-Bénédict Desaussure (Senebier), 9, 36, 233n105, 249, 252
Mercier, Isaac, 25–26
Merleau-Ponty, Maurice, 90
meteorology, 3, 163, 204n107. *See also* astronomy; cosmology; sky; weather
Meunier, Lombard, 229n17
Micheli du Crest, Jacques-Barthélemy, 28–29
microcosm (human), and macrocosm (cosmos), 76
micrometers, 119, 231n68
microscopes and microscopy, 50, 113, 118–19, 131, 193, 231nn67–68
Miller, David Philip, 214n182
minerals and mineralogy: as cabinet science, with samples displayed for observation, 72; and color, 177; identification of, 72; library books and publications, 119–21, 250; in river valley, 79; and rocks, 64, 72, 79, 113. *See also* crystallography; rocks
mineral springs and waters, 5–6, 37, 45, 119. *See also* sulfur springs and waters
mines and mining, 11, 72–73, 86, 98, 106, 115, 178, 221n126, 229n9
Mirabeau, Comte de, 246n22
Môle, Le (Alps), 13, 48, 84–85, 90–91, 128, 133–34
Montagnier, Henry Fairbanks, 17, 202n80, 205n125, 209n62, 250–51
Mont Blanc (Alps), 18–19, 93, 126–32, 141, 146–47, 155, 157–80, 172–73, 195, 209n67; access to, 248n52; and Arve, 79–104; ascents, 3, 9–10, 17–20, 80, 151–52, 157–80, 172, 189–91, 230n37, 237n46, 237n62, 238n65, 238n71, 238n74, 238n76, 238n78, 240n7, 240n22, 243n73, 243n75, 243n83, 245n116, 247n41, 250; attempts to find path to top of, 147–48; charisma of, 157; clothing and dressing for, 189–90; cultural history of, 230n37; descent, 173; des Dames, 111, 166–67, 172; early attempts to summit, 238n74; equipment for climbing, 247n42; first ascent, by Paccard and Balmat, 18, 80, 111, 159–63, 189, 230n37, 237n62, 240n22, 250; first tour of (1767), 57, 152, 224n40; as highest of peaks measured, 218n66; journal from ascent, 250; nobility of, 248n54; plotted first stage of route to summit of (via Montagne de la Côte), 111; quota system for, 248n54; respecting physicality of, 194; summiting of, 3, 15, 18, 48, 60, 108, 119, 128, 132, 192–93, 200n34, 202n86, 238n74, 240n7, 250; timing and basic narrative of ascent, 240n22; tours du, 10, 15, 45–46, 57–58, 60, 82, 87–88, 113, 116, 118, 133, 136, 141, 148, 152, 167, 189. *See also* Chamonix (France)
Mont Buet (Alps), 133–36, 139–40, 142, 144, 153, 163, 167, 171, 177–78, 192, 202n86, 235n1, 249
Mont Cramont/Crammont (Alps), 76, 135–37, 139, 145, 209n67

Monte Rosa (Alps), 3, 15, 114, 183, 192
Montesquieu, 184, 245n8
Montgolfier brothers, 162, 253
Mont Salève (French Prealps), 38, 45, 48, 51, 53, 56, 79–80, 84–85, 90, 183, 192, 253
Moore, John, 108, 159, 197n4
Morellet, André, 33, 209n79
Morgagni, G. B., 6
Mornet, Daniel, 203–4n105, 205n134, 220n101
Morsier, Georges de, 7, 197n1, 252
mountaineering, 100–101, 153; and bodily engagement, 16; and body as technology in climbing, 225n54; British, 17, 100; feminist history of age of, 166–67; golden age of, 100, 177, 180, 190; and heightened consciousness, 20; histories of, 111, 139, 171; and intellectual terrain, 57; and masculinity, 5, 37, 139–40, 165, 182–83; and mountain sickness, 149–50, 235–36n11; and natural history, 46; and philistines, 191; and physics, 46; and social alienation, 69; and summiting, 111, 190; Victorian-era, 5, 200n33. *See also* alpinism; summiting
mountains: communicating with, 179; as corpus of information, 75; as culture, 200n33; and Earth's cohesion, 68; and Earth's history, 46; and expansion of physical self, 22–23; formation of, 20, 137–38, 176, 193; history of, 46, 63, 67–68; and human body, 75; massiveness and physicality of, 138–39; as nature's sensorium, 16; in sensibility and culture of the age, 57–58; as sensorium, 16, 51, 179; and sublime, 157, 239n1; underlying order of, 67. *See also* crevasses; glaciers; specific mountain(s)
Mount Etna (Italy), 19, 114, 209n67, 246n23
Mount Everest (Asia): attempts of 1920s, 10, 236n32; British expeditions, 17, 31, 135, 205n127; fatal attempt on, 5, 228n112; and oxygen use, 235–36n11
Muir, John, 144, 237n43, 237n45

Mummery, Albert Frederick (Fred), 100, 166, 247n47
Mummery, Mary, 166
Murith, Laurent-Joseph, 186, 246n24
Musée alpin de Chamonix, 109
Museum of the History of Science (Geneva), 87, 201n58, 224n33, 226n79
My First Summer in the Sierra (Muir), 144, 237n45

nailed boots, 246n21
Nant d'Arpenaz (Arve Valley, France), 89, 89, 92, 98–99
Nant Nailliant / Nallien or Naglian (France), 80, 223n4
Napoleon Bonaparte, 139, 144, 181–82; in Egypt, 96, 138, 201n65; in Geneva, 245n2; in painting, 245n4
NASA (National Aeronautics and Space Administration), 76
NASA/Goddard Media Studios, 222n150
nationalism, 46, 161
Native Americans, 237n43
natural history, 9; of Alps, 111–12; and astronomy, 81; Bonnet and, 46–47, 88; of Ireland, 8; and letters, 74; library books and publications, 119–21, 250–51; and mathematics, 73–74; and mountaineering, 46; and natural theologies, 224–25n43; and philosophy, 128; and solar system, 61; of Spain, library books, 120–21; study of, 246n24; travels, 250–51
Natural History Museum (Geneva), 127
naturalists, 4, 8, 36, 46, 61, 98, 138–40, 185, 224–25n43, 236n28; and hunters, 139–40
natural theologies, and natural histories, 224–25n43
natural world, 19–20, 32, 34, 49, 56–57, 69–70, 74, 82, 88, 102, 111, 138–39, 179, 188, 194
nature: and alpinism, 53; as barrier, 13; capitalization of, 119; changing attitudes toward, 19; and empiricism, 179; Enlightenment experience of, 180; and environment, 19; epochs of,

19; experienced, 19, 32, 51, 108, 139, 180; and geology, 53; and God, 20; history of, 74; history of ideas about, 205n134; and humans, 95; and ideology, 13; inanimate but knowable, 16; as laboratory, 32; living in, 102; and materialism, 20; as mediated by culture, 12; and mountaineering, 5, 16, 138–39; observation of, 224n37; order of, 224–25n43; physical reality of, 16; and preservation of animals for exhibition and study, 234n122; and reason, 74; respect for, 194; and self, 15–16, 20; self impression, 4, 199n19; as sensorium, 16; shifting ideas about, 205n134; sublime in, 202n77; as totalizing, 138; voice of, 20, 179; as web of life, 213n164. *See also* Earth; environment

navigation, 203n90. *See also* circumnavigation; compasses

Necker, Jacques, Finance Minister of France, 33–34, 164, 209n79

Necker, Jacques, husband of Albertine-Adrienne de Saussure, 3–4

Necker, Louis, 3

Necker, Mme. (Suzanne Curchod, wife of Jacques Necker), 38, 164, 251

Neptunism, 73

Newman, John K., 226n92, 250

Newton, Isaac, 60–61, 67

New York Times, 12

Nicolas: and Bonnet, 34

Nicolson, Marjorie Hope, 205n134, 219n86, 236n25, 239n1

nobles, in Paris, incomes of, 2, 198n6

Nord mystérieux, un, 217n37

Oberland (Switzerland), 114, 239n83; Bernese, 183

Odier, Louis, Dr., 1, 3, 6–11, 40–41, 199n26, 201n44, 201n56, 201n58, 252

O'Grady, John, 237n45

On the External Characteristics of Fossils (Werner), 177

On the Nature of Things (Lucretius), 19

orchards, 31, 106, 184, 229n8

Orientalism, 95–96, 98–99, 226n82

ornithology, books and publications, 119–20

"Our Living Planet from Space" (NASA/Goddard Media Studios), 222n150

oxygen, and altitude, 235–36n11, 236n17

Paccard, François, 108–9, 111, 150, 240n15

Paccard, Joseph-Antoine, 80

Paccard, Michel, 108, 150

Paccard, Michel-Gabriel, Dr., 80, 108, 111, 139, 147, 150–51, 159–64, 170–74, 188–89, 223n4, 237n62, 242n65, 250

Paccard family, 111

painting, en plein air, 99, 146

panorama, 13–14, 35, 140, 143–44, 167, 236n36, 249

Paradis, Marie, 165

Parisian Academy of Science, 9, 65, 74, 186

parthenogenesis, 39

Paul, Jacques, 118–19, 239n88

Paul, Nicolas, 119

Peschier, Jacques-Louis, 250

philosophy: library books and publications, 119, 251; and mathematics, 66, 73–74; and natural history, 128; sensualist, 74–75, 222n144

photosynthesis, 3, 33

physics: experimental, and senses, 219n85; library books and publications, 119, 251; and mountaineering, 46; and observations and experiments, 75; and physiology, 134–35

physiology, 45, 121; and anatomy, 6; human, 7, 201n42; and observations, 74–75; and physics, 134–35; of plants, 33, 50–51, 56, 81–82, 209n75, 215n198

Pictet, Charlotte, 35

Pictet, François-Charles, 216n33, 217n37

Pictet, Jean-Louis, 57–60, 81–82, 113, 116, 127, 152, 170, 224n40, 234n123

Pictet, Jean-Michel, 211n102

Pictet, Marc-Auguste, 60–61, 85–88, 114, 133, 136, 152, 170, 224n40, 238n78

Pictet family, 24

picturesque, 17, 31, 68–69, 94

Pitcairn, William, 253
plagiarism, of Saussure, 193, 217–18n55
planets. *See* Earth; solar system
plants, 55; of Alps, 46–47, 54–55; black orchids, 53–54; blue-sow-thistle, 54, 215n7; buttercups, 54; in Chamonix, 214n179; chrysanthemums from China, 48; classification of, 49; dahlias from Mexico, 214n187; dahlias from Spain, 49; dianthus, 53–54; dogtooth violets, 47, 79; edelweiss, 53, 215n5; and elevation, 63; exotic, 49, 56, 115; ginkgo, 49, 214n188; hydrangeas from Japan, 48–49, 214n187; and medicine, 43, 46, 49; native, 49; physiology of, 33, 50–51, 56, 81–82, 209n75, 215n198; ragwort, 53, 215n5; as regression, 76; rock jasmine, 54; study of, 50; Swiss, 46, 54–55; taxonomy of, 213n162; wildflowers, 151, 169, 242n60. *See also* botany; flowers; horticulture; meadows; orchards; vegetation
plate tectonics, 18, 89, 98–99, 104, 183, 194
Plato, 75
Pococke, Richard, 95–102, 110, 226n80; Chamonix expedition (1741), sources, 253; portrait of, 97
politics, and religion, 1
porters, 101, 152; and guides, 161, 165, 171
Principles of Geology (Lyell), 17
probability theory, and calculus, 74
Protestantism, 1, 13, 16, 23–24, 27–28, 37, 74, 88, 95, 99, 134, 246n22
Puritan values, 1

Radisich, Paula, 128, 234n130
Raj, Kapil, 59, 217n40
Ramsden, James, 119
Rappaport, Rhoda, 219n86, 221nn119–20
Ravanet, François, 172
reason and reasoning, and nature, 74
Réaumur, René Antoine Ferchault de, 127
Réaumur temperature scale, 54
Reculet, Le (Jura), 54, 56–57
Reformation, 13, 23–25, 227n101

Reichler, Claude, 16, 63, 202n77, 202n89, 222n141
Reill, Peter Hanns, 214n182
religion, 1, 185, 206n139, 222n141, 246n22. *See also* Catholicism; Christianity; Protestantism; Reformation
Renaissance, 75–76
repose, and silence, 154
Reybaz, Etienne Salomon, 246n22
Rhône River (France and Switzerland), 1, 12–13, 25, 30–31, 47, 79, 122, 131, 140, 169, 183, 209n61
Richelieu, duc de, 2, 198n10
Rieder, Philip, 5, 7, 9, 200n37, 201n56, 202n86
Rilliet family, 24, 34
Roberts, Lissa, 217n40, 219n85
Roberts, Meghan K., 200n32
rock crystal, for faux diamonds, 229n12
rocks, 6, 16–18, 56, 127, 137; folds of, 18; geometry of, 92; identification of, 72; and minerals, 64, 72, 79, 113; and mountains, 77; shapes of, 92. *See also* minerals and mineralogy
Roger, Jacques, 74, 220n103
Roget, Mme., 239n6
Roget, Peter Mark, 239n6
romanticism, 15–16, 50–51, 58, 61, 70, 95, 108, 110–11, 171, 179–80, 186
rope, use in alpinism, 189, 239n83, 246n21
Rothorn (Alps), 114, 183
Rousseau, Jean-Jacques, 1, 14–15, 21–23, 29–30, 35, 49–51, 57–58, 63, 70, 116, 122, 126, 131, 149, 197n3, 203–4nn105–106, 203n103, 204n108, 204n111, 206n1, 206n4, 208n41, 208n56, 245n11
Rowlinson, John Shipley, 98, 101, 226n77, 226n90
Royal Botanical Garden, 70
Royal Geographical Society, 9, 17, 31
Rudwick, Martin, 18, 72–73, 89, 139, 220n95, 220n103, 221n116, 245n116
Ruskin, John, 17

Sainte-Beuve, Charles Augustin, 14
Salève. *See* Mont Salève (French Prealps)

Sarde, Frédéric, 212n126
Sarton, George, 65, 218nn70–71
Saussure, Albertine-Adrienne Necker de (daughter), 3–4, 8–9, 12, 35, 45, 119, 165, 168, 198–99n17, 199n23, 211n108, 231n48; letter, 251
Saussure, Albertine-Amélie Boissier de (wife), 1, 4, 11, 24–25, 38, 42, 45, 112, 121–32, 164–68, 222n141, 231n48; journal, 251; letters, 251; portrait of, *129*
Saussure, Alphonse Jean-François de (son), 3, 164–65, 167
Saussure, Antoine de, 23–24
Saussure, Ferdinand de (great-grandson), 3, 7, 35, 198n6, 209n74, 220n105
Saussure, Henri Louis Frédéric de (grandson), 3, 35
Saussure, Horace-Bénédict de: and Alps, 1–20, 72, 113, 193–94; and Alps, historian of, 57; autopsy of, 1, 3, 5–9, 11–12, 186, 197n1, 252; bird collecting, 59, 127, 234n123; birth and family, 4, 30–38; birth of, 1; and body as tool of science, and bodily engagement with Alps, 10–12, 16, 19, 102–3, 135–36; as celebrity, 9; and Chamonix, growing importance of, 111; childhood, 36–37; children of, 3–5, 37–38; contemporary views of, sources, 252–53; and cosmopolitan aristocracy, by marriage, 122–23; and country house (Genthod), 12, 35, 38, 54, 112–13, 123, 128–32, 162–63, 167, 234n135; death of, 1, 4–5, 7, 199n23; death of, bicentennial of, 205n130; and education, 4; empirical viewpoint of, 5–6, 90, 94–95, 101, 104, 115, 134–35, 150, 154, 179, 180, 185–86; as environmentalist, 192; and family, 164–70; family archives, 17, 187, 197n, 250–52; and family relationships, 200n32; field notes, in notebooks, 194, 237n54, 252; as a first *éloge historique* of luminaries, 9; first tour of Mont Blanc (1767), 224n40; as focused, 170; as founder of alpinism, 17; Galenic viewpoint of, 5–6; and gliding on snow, 228n125; goals of, 193; going alone as guiding principle, 170; inauguration as professor, 36, 210n96; income, 2, 198n6; instruments used by, 250; last alpine excursion (1792), 3, 114; last work published posthumously, 216n18; legacy of, 181–94; library of, 18, 48, 70, 119–21, 205n130, 232n74, 232n79, 232n88, 243n79, 250–51; life history of, 20; methodology of, 223n17; and Montgolfier balloon launch, 253; and natural theologies, 224–25n43; paralysis, first attack of, 199n26; and patois, 147–48, 185, 246n18; patrician privilege of, 1–2, 51; plagiarism of, 193, 217–18n55; and politics of rapprochement, 8; portrait of, *130*; and privileges of wealth and gender, 112; as professor, 36, 50; and purging, 163, 241n32; and rhythm of escape and return, 38; scientific life of, 2, 37–39, 112, 121–22, 202n80, 205n130; as self-disciplined, 36–37, 53; spa visits for bodily humors, 5; as victim of science, 8–9; vigor of, 126
Saussure, Jean Baptiste de, 24
Saussure, Judith de (sister), 42, 198nn8–9; letters, 251
Saussure, Nicolas de (father), 31–39, 51, 210n84, 220n105
Saussure, Nicolas-Théodore de (son), 3–4, 8, 33, 37–38, 164–65, 169–70, 199n17, 199nn23–24, 209n75, 231n48
Saussure, Raymond de (great-great grandson), 7, 197n1, 252
Saussure, Renée de (mother), 2, 24, 31–32, 36–45, 49, 56, 66, 75, 77
Saussure, Théodore Rilliet de (cousin), 34, 210nn83–85
Saussure family, 35–36, 39, 164–66; archives, 187, 197n, 251–52; history of, 207n15
savants and scientists, 4–5, 9, 37, 39, 48–49, 51, 59, 61, 63, 65, 70, 73, 91, 113, 124, 127, 133, 162–63, 171, 186, 193
Schama, Simon, 200n33
Schaumann, Caroline, 200n33, 237nn44–45

Scheuchzer, Johann Jacob, 98
Schlup, Michel, 248n57, 249
Schwellenberg, Juliane Elisabeth von, 63
Schweppe, Jacob, 37
Schweppe, Johan Jacob, 119
Schweppes mineral waters, 119
scientific instruments, 4, 12, 18, 100, 112, 118–20, 134, 231nn66–67, 250. *See also* equipment; specific instrument(s)
Scientific Revolution, 74, 76
Senebier, Jean, 9, 11, 36–37, 53, 87–88, 91, 124, 149, 169–70, 233n105, 249, 252
senses, sensorium, sentimentality, 4–5, 7, 9, 12, 16, 19, 30, 32, 42–43, 51, 53, 56, 67, 69, 74–76, 82–83, 87, 89–90, 95, 104, 106, 118, 127, 135, 145, 179, 193–94, 204n114, 215nn15–16, 219n85, 222nn144–45
Seven Years' War (1756–63), 80, 222n2
Shaftesbury, Earl of, 138
Shakespeare, William, 207n14
Shelley, Mary Wollstonecraft, 100, 110, 227n104
Shelley, Percy Bysshe, 57, 82, 104, 110, 227n104
Shepherd, Nan, 90, 225n50, 226n74
Sierra Club, 237n43
Sigrist, René, 37, 199n26, 201n58, 204n121, 210n96, 218n76, 235n9, 249
silence: and cold, 174; and repose, 154; and solitude, 104. *See also* sound
Simler, Josias, 70, 220n97, 220n99
Simon, Pierre, 102–3, 107–8, 147–50, 158, 171, 185–86, 228n121, 237n57
Simpson, Joe, 228n112
Siula Grande, West Face (Andes), near-fatal climb of, 228n112
sky: blueness of, 15; color of at altitudes, 113, 176. *See also* astronomy; meteorology
snowshoes, 70, 220n99
Society for the Encouragement of Agriculture and the Arts (Geneva), 34, 188
Society of Physics and Natural History (Geneva), 3, 7, 9, 36–37, 234n124

solar system, 58–59, 61, 67, 241n37. *See also* astronomy; cosmology; Earth; star maps
solitude: and imagination, 204n108; and silence, 104
Sonntag, Otto, 251–52
soul, 39, 63, 87–88, 224n34, 233n105
sound: and color, 94, 179; presages of, 16; and shapes, 179; and smell, 177. *See also* silence
Spallanzani, Lazzaro, 131
spas, 5
Sphinx, 96, 226n80
Spirit of the Laws, The (Montesquieu), 184
springs. *See* mineral springs and waters; sulfur springs and waters
Staël, Germaine, de, 4, 8, 12, 38, 45, 211n108
star maps, 12, 61. *See also* astronomy; solar system
Starobinski, Jean, 212n121, 219n79
St. Augustine, 88, 211n109
St. Bartholomew's Day Massacre (1572), 23, 207n16
St. Bernard Pass (Alps), 47, 181, 186
Sténon, Nicolas, 73, 221n126
Stephen, Leslie, 5, 17, 23, 100, 133, 166, 185, 189–90, 200n34, 227n107, 241n48
St. Gervais (French Alps), 21, 82, 151, 206n1, 223n17, 238n76, 240n15, 248n52, 248n54
St. Gotthard pass, 65, 72, 157, 242n70
St. Gotthard Pass, 65, 157, 242n70
Stillingfleet, Benjamin, 95
St. Moritz (Switzerland), exclusivity of, 189, 247n40
strata and stratigraphy, 71–73, 85, 92, 99, 176
sublime, the: and Alps, 157; and botany, 50; and judgment, 9; and meditation, 157; and mountains, 157, 239n1; in nature, 202n77; in paintings, 94, 245n4; and picturesque, 94; role of judgment on experience of, 9–10; and scenery, feelings and emotions about, 150

suicides, 1, 36, 122–23, 165, 197–98n4, 197n2, 210n94, 211n104, 222n141, 231n48
sulfur springs and waters, 5, 200n37. See also mineral springs and waters
summiting, 80, 131–32, 162–63, 174; Beaufoy's, 244n116; of Cramont, 145; of Etna, 114; mixed reality of, 178; of Mont Blanc, 3, 15, 18, 48, 60, 108, 119, 128, 132, 192–93, 200n34, 202n86, 238n74, 240n7, 250; and mountaineering, 111, 190; of Rothorn, 114, 183; as status symbol, 191; and virility and power, 162
Summits of Modern Man, The: Mountaineering after the Enlightenment (Hansen), 18, 139, 161, 203n98, 205n125, 224–25n43, 229n9, 229n17, 229n21, 239n91, 242n65, 243n74
Switzerland: bio-geographical contours of, 213n166; and France, 21, 23, 29–30, 53, 110, 183, 201n59
Syme, Patrick, 177
Synowiecki, Jan, 76

Tairraz, Auguste, 238n63
Tairraz, Jean-Pierre, 111, 163–64, 185
Tairraz, Michel, 111
Tairraz, Victor, 111
Tairraz family, 109, 111
taxonomy, 50–51, 213n162, 215n198
Taylor, Samuel S. B., 221n139
telescopes, 59, 85, 118–19, 160, 164, 173, 231n68, 241n37
Terra Incognita (Corbin), 64
thermometers, 61, 90, 133, 154, 176–78, 239n88
Thomas Aquinas, 88
Thompson, Carl, 204n119
Thouin, André, 49, 209n69, 214n187
Tissay, Victor, 150, 229n17
Tissot, Samuel-Auguste, Dr., 40–42, 212nn126–28
topography, 61, 72, 86–87, 113. See also geography; maps
topophilia, 16, 204n113
Tour de Rôle, 238n63
tourist industry, 150. See also ecotourism

Tournier, Géant and Alexis, 148, 171–72, 178
Tournier, Jean-Michel, 178, 240n15
travel literature, in library, 119
Trembley, Abraham, 88
Trembley, Jean, 24, 87–88, 114, 118, 133, 136, 152, 170, 219n79, 238n78
Trembley family, 24
Tremella (fungi), 222n148
trigonometry, 59, 86
Tronchin, Anne Caroline (Minette) (sister-in-law), 1, 7, 122, 165, 167–68, 251
Tronchin, Jean-Louis (brother-in-law), 1, 122–23, 165, 197nn2–3
Tronchin, Jean-Robert, 1, 122
Tronchin, Théodore, Dr., 38–40, 42–45, 66, 75, 126, 201n45, 234n119
Turgot, Anne-Robert-Jacques, 33–34, 209nn78–79
Turrettini, Albert, 238n78
Turrettini, Jean Alphonse, 122, 124
Turrettini family, 165
Tyndall, John, 227n107

Underhill, Miriam O'Brien, 166
United States Naval Academy, 12

valleys, 18, 63–65, 71, 85–86, 102, 110, 113–14, 133, 139, 193
Vanois National Park (French Alps), 195
vegetables, 140, 222n148, 226
vegetation, 3, 33, 76, 85, 174, 209n75, 213n164. See also plants
Vernon, Edward, Admiral, 100, 227n106
Versailles (France), 25, 29, 56, 107, 216n16
Vila, Anne C., 204n114, 212n127, 221n138
vineyards, 15, 31–33, 69, 168
Virgil, 14
Voirons, Les (France), 47–48, 84–85, 133–34
volcanoes, 38, 67, 85, 114
Voltaire, 1–2, 30, 33, 35, 42, 74, 81, 95, 118, 121, 124, 126, 169, 198n4, 198n8, 208n56, 226n76, 232n88; letter from Saussure, 251

Voyages dans les Alpes (Saussure), 15–20, *103*, *143*, 197n, 237n46; Agenda of unanswered questions, at ending of, 193; cultural pathways in, 15; and Genevan Enlightenment, 20; as immortal, 17; Lucretian frame of, 19; as magnum opus, 3; and natural world, 20; and nature, physical reality of, 16; online open-access copies, 249; and plants, 53–54; printing and publishing of, 248n57, 249; and Saussure fame, 9; somatic in, 19; sources, 249–51; survey in, at ending of, 193

walnut oil, 209n68
Walsham, Alexandra, 203n96, 227n101
wasps, 3
watches, 188, 246n32
water: and agriculture, 49; and air, 118, 176; local sources of, for agriculture, 49; in mountains, 67. *See also* mineral springs and waters; sulfur springs and waters
waterfalls, 14, 69, 89, 98–99, 102
Watt, Jeffrey R., 197n2, 198n4, 210n94
weather, 151; and avalanches, 160; generalizations about Alps, 15; observations of at high altitudes, 178; onslaughts of, 37. *See also* climate; meteorology
Werner, Abraham Gottlib, 72–73, 177
Whatmore, Richard, 26–28, 207n31, 208n41, 246n22

Whiston, William, 67, 219n86
white-outs, 228n112
Whymper, Edward, 23
wilderness, 70, 237n43
wildflowers, 151, 169, 242n60
Williams, Roger L., 43
Windham, William, 95–102, 110, 226n90, 226n92, 228n116; Chamonix expedition (1741), sources, 253
wind speed and velocity, 15, 204n107
Wocher, Marquard, 172–73
women: in agriculture and working world, 106; and eczema, 41; in Geneva, cultural marginality of, 96, 199n20; as guides, 241n41; health recommendations for, 43–44; in mountaineering, 63, 111, 165–68, 190–91, 241nn40–41, 247n47; in paintings, 226n81
Woodward, John, 67, 219n86
Woolf, Virginia, 5
Wulf, Andrea, 213n164

Yale Center for British Art, 215n195
Yates, Simon, 228n112

Zermatt (Switzerland), 100, 189, 247n40; Matterhorn, 166
Zinalrothorn (Alps), 100
zoology, 138; library publications, 119
Zurich (Switzerland): and Berne, 29; and France, 110